BEAR FLAG REPUBLIC

Prose Poems and Poetics from California

BEAR FLAG REPUBLIC

Prose Poems and Poetics from California

Edited by Christopher Buckley and Gary Young

Greenhouse Review Press /Alcatraz Editions

This book is a joint publication of
Greenhouse Review Press/Alcatraz Editions
3965 Bonny Doon Road
Santa Cruz, CA 95060

Designed by Gary Young
Layout by Stephen Pollard

The cover illustration is an 1890 photograph of the original flag of the Bear Flag Rebellion, first hoisted over Sonoma on June 14, 1846. The flag was made by William Todd, a nephew of Abraham Lincoln. The original flag was destroyed in the 1906 San Francisco earthquake and fire.

ISBN 978-0-9655239-4-3

Manufactured in the United States of America

CONTENTS

Poems

Preface by Robert Bly

The Prose Poem as an Evolving Form

Baudelaire thought that the prose poem would be the major form of the twentieth century. We know several sorts of prose poems, the most ancient of which is the fable; David Ignatow and Russell Edson are contemporary masters of the fable. Traditionally in the fable, the story is more important than the language that carries it. Rimbaud, in *Les Illuminations,* invented a second sort of prose poem, inspired by the new color separations, known as "illuminations," in the printing industry; there, image and fiery language draw attention away from the story. A third sort, the object poem, centers itself not on story or image but on the object, and it holds on to its fur, so to speak. My predecessors in the object poem are Jimenez and Francis Ponge. Francis Ponge, writing about rain, says:

> The rain falling into the courtyard where I watch adopts three manners, each distinct. Toward the center it is a delicate netting (or net) often with holes, a determined fall, though somewhat lethargic, and drops light enough, an eternal drizzle with no animal vigor, an obsessed particle of the pure meteor.
>
> *translation by Robert Bly*

Ponge's diction is precise; he offers language in archaeological layers, drawing some words from science, others from reservoirs of words used in earlier centuries, in order to come close to the object and participate in its complication. In his essay "The Silent World Is Our Only Homeland," Ponge says:

> In these terms one will surely understand what I consider to be the true function of poetry. It is to nourish the spirit of man by giving him the cosmos to suckle. We have only to lower our standard of dominating nature, and to raise our standard of participating in it, in order to make this reconciliation take place.
>
> *translation by Beth Archer*

Among other masters of the "thing" poem, we could name Thoreau in his journals, Tomas Tranströmer, and James Wright in his late poems.

It is easy to start a prose poem, but not easy to make it a work of art. The metered poem, as Yeats remarked, finishes with a click as when a box closes, and the metered poem has two subjects: the thought of the poet and the meter itself. One is personal, the other impersonal. The thing poem written in prose has two subjects but quite different ones; the movement of the writer's mind and the thing itself. One is personal, the other impersonal. While the poet concentrates on the object, the movement of his mind cannot be hidden.

Musicians speak of two possible ways of setting a poem to music. In the first way, the composer—Brahms would be an example—finds a tune, and then uses the same tune for all the stanzas; this might be called unvarying composition. But in a through-composed song, as in Hugo Wolf, the composer makes a melody for the first stanza and then alters the melody and rhythm as the poem deepens or changes its mood. One could say that Hugo Wolf sets the movement of the poet's psyche as well as the words. Thing poems then resemble "through composition" in that the focus is not on an unchanging element—meter, for example, or stanza form—but on the changes the mind goes through as it observes.

The prosodic unit in any prose poem is the sentence rather than the line. Despite the difference in length and technique, the nearest relative of the thing poem is not the essay or the short story but the haiku, which evolved in Buddhist Japan through the determination of Buddhist poets to share the universe with flies, frogs, and moonlight. The good haiku is evidence that the poet has overcome, at least for the moment, the category-making mentality that sees everything in polarities: human and animal, inner and outer, spiritual and material, large and small. Issa, a Pure Land Buddhist, died lying in a corncrib during a light snow. His death poem went this way:

> This snow on the bedquilt—this too
> is from the Pure Land.
>
> translation by H. R. Blyth

The haiku and the object poem are usually written away from the writer's desk, and in the presence of the object. Bashō said, "If you want to know about the bamboo, go to the bamboo; if you want to know about the pine, go to the pine." Emerson drew from Coleridge the idea that "every object rightly seen unlocks a new faculty of the Soul." The Buddhists would like Emerson's "rightly." When the human mind honors a stump, for example, by giving it human attention in the right way, something in the soul is released; and often through the stump we receive information we wouldn't have received by thinking or by fantasy.

Why is the thing poem usually composed in prose and not in lines? Lines in free verse or in meter can reach high levels of excitement and emotion which one feels, for instance, in Yeats; the reader flies or is tossed from the emotions to the ideas to the senses and back. But in the prose poem one can stay close to the senses for half a page. Its mood is calm, more like a quiet lake than a sea. When our language becomes abstract, then the prose poem helps to balance that abstraction, and encourages the speaker to stay close to the body, to touch, hearing, color, texture, moisture, dryness, smell. Its strength lies in intimacy. One could also say that in the object poem in prose, the conscious mind gives up, at least to a degree, the adversary position it usually adopts toward the unconscious, and a certain harmony between the two takes place. The gods of the object poem are not Zeus or Athena, but Aphrodite, Hermes, and Demeter.

What is the prose poem's relation to form? I feel that form in art relies on form in nature for its model, and form in nature amounts to a tension between private spontaneity and the hard impersonal. The snail gives its private substance to its private skin or shell, but the shell's curve is utterly impersonal, and follows the Fibonacci sequence. Form in poetry follows this model.

No one can mistake the impersonal side of the sonnet: the hard impersonal includes fourteen lines of ten syllables each, for a total of one hundred forty syllables; syntactically contained thought units, apportioned among three quatrains and a couplet, or an eight-line group and a six-line group; fourteen rhymed lines, and a beat system based on relative loudness of stress, beginning with a relatively soft syllable. The Japanese recognize requirements that make up the impersonal side of the haiku, among them seventeen syllables, a subtle indication of season, and an interlocking and resonant sound.

The prose poem, whether thing poem, fable, or Rimbaudian fire-prose, has no such great tension; it reaches toward no such impersonal shell, and no such hard agreement with the ancestors. As we write it these days, we notice little tension between an impersonal shape it must have and the personal shape it wants to have.

Of course, the writer of the prose poem cannot, despite the seeming freedom, use any rhythm or any sounds he wants to if he or she aims at a work of art. The first twenty or thirty syllables of a prose poem set up, as do the opening syllables of a lined poem, or any human speech, certain expectations felt in the nervous system. For example, if three "oh" sounds appear in the first sentence, intelligences below rational consciousness register these "oh" sounds, even count them, and will expect the following syllables to continue embodying the sound, or to modulate it, possibly to "ow" or "oo." If the writer, ignoring these expectations, provides instead sounds such as "it," "im," "is," the intelligences lose interest, and the game of art collapses. The cat cannot get the mouse to play any more, and either leaves it or eats it. These intelligences hear not only vowel sounds but rhythmic units, consonant repetitions, tunes set up by pitches, and what we could call word-color and word-fragrance. The poem awakens expectations for each of these separate elements. The poet, as he or she proceeds, has then to satisfy these expectations or recognize they are dissatisfied and outwit them. The expectations don't mind being outwitted. The more the prose poet pays attention to the expectations the more density the prose poem achieves; and a good prose poem, like a wolverine's claw, can please us with its consistent density.

The fact that no critics have yet laid out formal standards for the prose poem is a blessing. Sometimes a fox and a human being play together best when no loud sounds are heard. When relaxed and aware of no rigid patterns, the mind sometimes gracefully allows itself to play with something equally graceful in nature, and the elegance of the prose poem appears in that play.

I expect that as more poets write prose poems, the thoughtful ones will suggest boundaries or hard agreements that will eventually create what we have called the hard or impersonal part of form. The poets, for example, might reach a consensus on how many sounds the poem will be faithful to, or how the choice of sounds, determined in rhyming poems partly by rhyme words, will be made.

But it is not a genre for beginners. Having no obvious ancient models in form, it cannot be excused from achieving form; with few models of completed themes before it, it still requires completion, and though it has no obvious elegant shape, the reader nevertheless asks it to arrive at elegance.

Introduction by Christopher Buckley and Gary Young

> What is it, then, that one loses? That everyone loses? Where I grew up, the specific place meant everything. As a child in California, I still thought of myself, almost, as living in the Bear Flag Republic, not in the United States. When I woke, the Sierras, I knew, were on my right; the Pacific was a two-hour drive to my left, and everything between belonged to me, was me.

Our title is taken from the quote above by one of our poetic heroes, the Fresno poet Larry Levis. These sentences are from his essay "Eden and My Generation," and they focus and reinforce one of our main concerns in poetry, the importance of place. In 1999 we compiled the anthology *The Geography of Home: California's Poetry of Place*, which contained seventy-six poets writing about the varying landscapes and regions of California. For our prose poem project, we have gathered the work of ninety poets. We have also added many essays that amplify the history, process, definition and range of the poem in prose. We hoped to uncover in the capacious prose poem form poems that were infused with a sense of vitality, identity, and soul-making. We invited poets who have significant roots in California, poets born and living here, poets who live elsewhere but have deep roots in the state, and poets who have moved here and made California their home. In every case, these are poets who write about California as a substantial portion of their poetic project. We began by looking for prose poems that either directly or indirectly touched on California or on our lives here. We wanted poets and poems motivated by a vision that issues from an appreciation of our gloriously diverse environment—urban, rural, coastal or pastoral.

The great California writer Lawrence Clark Powell, in the introduction to his anthology *California Classics,* had this to say about writers and the pull of California:

> "If I were exiled from California, I could draw a topographical map from memory, so deeply have its configurations entered my consciousness. Seen from the air or seen from the ground, in all seasons and weathers, California's beauty never palls; and it has been blessed with great writers to praise its beauty."

We came to realize that California's unique place on the edge of the continent provides a jumping-off point, and many of the poets grounded with the values of this place have turned their vision to other lands and other traditions. California was the end of the line for American expansion on this continent, but California's poets have continued the migration, at least aesthetically, with the knowledge that if you follow the admonition to "go west," you'll eventually end up in the east. Californians are justifiably renowned for reinventing themselves, and we should expect no less from their poets.

California cannot lay claim to the prose poem, but this mercurial, subversive form has enjoyed a great flowering here, and while we were able to compile a representative and substantial anthology, we did not come close to exhausting the reserves of talent and accomplishment available. We have included many senior poets whose careers have contributed in no small way to the contemporary history and development of the prose poem in the United States. Poets in mid-career are also well represented, and we are proud that about a third of the work presented here is from young poets carrying on and expanding upon the work of those who wrote previously. In addition to a wealth of prose poems, we also offer twenty-two essays divided into two categories: "History, Definition, Nuts and Bolts," and "Processes, Influences and Reflections." Most poets also contributed brief prose complements in addition to their poems. We believe that these supplemental texts will be useful to readers, writers and critics alike.

Charles Baudelaire predicted that the prose poem would be *the* poetic form for the twentieth century, and our contributors have cast a large net over the literatures of the world to suggest precedents and progenitors of the prose poem. The poets describe a pedigree that reaches back millennia to the Chinese *Fu*; the Bible and Shakespeare join Arthur Rimbaud and Aloysius Bertrand in a long line of practitioners that include Anne Bradstreet, Walt Whitman and Ernest Hemingway. There is, of course, a long tradition of poets writing prose poems in the Americas, especially among Mexican poets. Foremost among that group would be Octavio Paz, Jaime Sabines and José Emilio Pacheco; but also Juan José Arreola, Gilberto Owen and Julio Torri. The great Spanish poet Luis Cernuda wrote prose poems all through the 1940s and 50s, and in

South America the two Nobel laureates from Chile, Gabriela Mistral and Pablo Neruda, were practitioners of the form. In the 1950s the longer volley and echo of the prose poem rhythms surfaced in the writing of Allen Ginsberg and Kenneth Patchen. While we could go on naming names of the progenitors, we should not forget the prose poems of James Wright and David Ignatow who moved the prose poem toward clarity, objectivity and assessable beauty. Robert Bly, whose essay *The Prose Poem as an Evolving Form* graces this anthology, set a high standard with his seminal collection, *What Have I Ever Lost by Dying.*

The point then is that we are not inventing anything new; there is a long and rich tradition of writing the prose poem, one shared enthusiastically by California poets. We wanted to present the history of the prose poem, and the wealth of talented practitioners in our state; that's what you'll find in *Bear Flag Republic.* Because of the prose poem's amplitude and generosity, we felt justified in offering such a hefty anthology dedicated to a discrete focus—the prose poem's form is as expansive as our state.

Essays 1

History, Definition, Nuts and Bolts

MAXINE CHERNOFF

Form and Function

According to Russian psychologist Alexander Luria, "With the help of language [humans] can deal with things they have not perceived even indirectly and with things which were part of the experience of older generations. This ability adds another dimension to the world of humans . . . Animals have only one world, the world of objects and situations which can be perceived by the senses. Humans have a double world." In choosing verse or the prose poem, I am trying to accommodate my register of this double world to the form that best suits it. If I am thinking (or dreaming) of a world of objects that float in proximity to each other and create odd connections, as in the Frank O'Hara poem where two people pass each other and their "surgical implements lock for a day," then the best medium for that accidental conjunction is the prose poem. Many of my earliest prose poems written under the influence of masters such as Michaux and Cortazar work in that mode. It is as if the poem were conditional, "if X happens or should happen, then . . ." The prose poem gives me liberty to explore the accidental meetings, the space in which a fan speaks to an anonymous man who enters a room, or an artist designs a windmill of famous moustaches, or bridges of perishable items are erected to console man about mortality. I wanted a space in which I could explore the image and sustain its intensity with a deadpan speaker reporting on such events.

Later I moved to the prose poem to capture dialogue between speakers in a manner that respected the lengths and patterns of human utterance. These more recent prose poems, which are most often arguments between a man and a woman and have been adapted into a play by Mac Maginnes and staged at Small Press Traffic's Poets' Theater Festival in San Francisco, are terse and tense language duets that need the ragged borders and sentence patterns of prose. Were I to pay attention to line break or overly control rhythm, it would undermine the ebb and flow of the dialogue and truncate the human speech which strives to be realistic. These poems record social moments, often discord or misunderstanding and require an expansive form, which prose poems allow perhaps more easily than verse.

3

My other two more recent efforts have been in verse. The first is a series of poems based on "Gift Theory," which spans disciplines from literature to anthropology to philosophy to religion to economics and includes such important figures as Mauss, Godelier, Derrida, Emerson, and Irigaray, among others. My interest here was to extract a narrow, sinuous, sonically constructed poem from far longer non-poetic essays. It was a process of losing words or erasure that led to narrow poems that tumbled down the page.

My goal in extracting the essay's argument and in some poems providing a counter-argument is to contemplate all aspects of the gift as an economy and a vehicle for ethics.

The uneven vertical columns of words serve to emphasize individual phrases, juxtapose them to others, and maintain sonic connections and segues. Prose would not be adept at achieving the type of visual highlighting needed for words and phrases to be isolated and take on a proper weight, nor would it allow for the quickness with which I feel these arguments moving, almost as if they are a liquid medium being poured through a funnel.

In a few later poems of this sequence, I use several texts within one poem to create an argument of sources with each other. It is as if my former strategy in the dialogue poems has returned to pose a thesis and antithesis in the later poems of the gift texts: Here is a poem based upon an "argument" between John Berger's *About Seeing* and Jean-Paul Sartre's *What is Literature?* These fragments, then, become a long rope of connections and disputes with the line serving to insist on their forward movement.

I am again exploring similar possibilities in a book of poems that uses many diverse sources for sampling and borrowing, from *Hamlet* to the news. One long poem in the collection locates sentences in individual texts and joins them together with anaphora using the female pronouns *she* or *her*. The poem explores "she" sentences in a variety of contexts from literary fiction to commercial fiction to prose essays in areas including economics, philosophy, art, and literary theory. I have found in beginning this project that there is a paucity of "she" sentences in most theoretical writing, so I have also given myself permission to change the arbitrary subject of a sentence from "he" to "she" when I so choose. Since I want the repeated word at the beginning of many sentences (such as the words "I saw," which open

4

most lines of Ginsberg's Howl), I am writing in extremely long lines that seem to break down the borders between poetry and prose.

In my case, then, the purpose, texture, speed, and sound of the writing seem to determine the form I choose, whether prose poem or verse. When I want more constraints, I will most often choose verse. When I want a dreamy exploration of objects and images or the ragged shapes of human speech, prose has served me better. Moreover, each project arrives with its own logic and constraints. I try to honor their inherent logic by choosing the form which best suits it.

JAMES HARMS

"Goodtime Jesus" and Other Sort-of Prose Poems

I suspect the reason I can't remember my first encounter with the prose poem has a great deal to do with when I came of age as a poet, the fact that my teachers didn't think of the prose poem as exotic or strange or even particularly sexy. Interestingly, I *can* remember the first time I read James Tate's "Goodtime Jesus," a prose poem that appears in his book *Riven Doggeries,* published in 1979 when I was nineteen. Like a lot of undergraduates of my generation, being assigned Tate in a poetry workshop was a rite of passage and a wake-up call, a little like hearing "London Calling" for the first time (which was also released in 1979). Tate was funny and strange and maybe even a little dangerous; the fact that he often wrote prose poems seemed incidental. In all honesty it still does. I often can't discern a specific or verifiable difference between Tate's poems in lines and those in prose (this is especially true recently, when his work seems written for the most part in lined blocks). I don't doubt that Tate has very good reasons for writing some poems in lines, some in prose, but I can't imagine they'd matter much to the reader.

This leads me to a scandalous assertion (not really, but let's make believe something is really at stake here): I'm not sure it matters all that much whether some poems are lined or not. This isn't to say that free verse poetry lacks rhythmical integrity and/or music, that its relation to the line is random or convenient; for such tired and tedious arguments, one should consult *The New Criterion* for the company policy on the essential slackness of a free verse line. In fact, I'm arguing the opposite. It seems to me that many, *many* prose poems read like lined verse with the breaks removed. This is true of Baudelaire (in many translations), Rilke, Neruda, Simic, and any number of wonderfully fluent poets who move back and forth from line breaks to margins. Each of these poets has a sensibility that is recognizable from across the room. They have a way of inhabiting language that no amount of density is going to mask. When they banish the line break, the language retains its essential poetry; in other words, the character of the image and the coordination of phrases (the musical interaction of syntactical units) remain in effect regardless of the poem's "look."

To clarify this a bit (at the risk of running the ship right up the cul-de-sac), let's return to Tate. What makes his poetry distinctive has more to do with the way he occupies space and time than it does with prosody. His prose poems enact a postmodern relationship to everyday life (without acceding to the existence of anything remotely or theoretically *postmodern*) in exactly the same way his lined poems do. For poets like Tate, prose seems an opportunity to do something different with the shape and texture of language, with how we as readers encounter phrases, and how our expectations are undermined and exploited by extending the horizontal momentum of the language while suspending the vertical. But that's just Tate. And that's why reading "Goodtime Jesus" for the first time in 1979 didn't register as anything more remarkable than reading another cool James Tate poem, though it was, in all likelihood, the first, or one of the first, prose poems I ever read (which says something about my undergraduate education: Baudelaire who?).

Still, other poets take advantage of the prose poem to radically change their use of language. As Robert Hass has suggested, the tonal qualities of a sentence are very different from those of a line or phrase; and perhaps for the poet, the sentence allows us to remain a bit more outside of or external to the language we're using; we're not constantly being seduced by the complexifying nature of line breaks, the way they create their own meaning, their own elegance and/or ugliness. Hass has said, "I unconsciously started writing prose to avoid the stricter demands of incantation." In other words, there were some things going on in his life that he wanted to avoid in his work; incantation would have led him straight to these things.

And thank goodness he decided to avoid lyric disclosure for a while. After all, most of us *do* remember encountering *Human Wishes*, that godsend of a book that did more for prose poetry than any collection in recent memory. I'm mindful of the many prose poetry aficionados who find *Human Wishes* somewhat blasphemous, since Hass quite assertively rejects a certain model of the prose poem, what he calls "a kind of wacky surrealist work," which was, in fact, the version of the form that had come to dominate American prose poetry in the seventies and eighties (see Russel Edson and his crew, i.e., Michael Benedikt, Tate, Knott, Simic, and the rest, all of them wonderful in their own ways). Hass is one poet who quite clearly uses language differently in prose poems, and has discussed at length the distinctions between story and song, why we need them both and how they require very different things from us as poets; he enacts these differences vividly in his poem "My Mother's Nipples" from *Sun Under Wood*, a poem that moves tensely between psychologically fraught passages of prose recollection (the effort to create distance from the painful memories via prose only serves to underscore the need to limit the emotional toll such memories exact; so much for the less exacting demands of prose) and more descriptive and incantatory stanzas that seem interested primarily in transformation and connection (not so much in recording memory as finding a place for it in the world). In the following passage he addresses and enacts this notion of what "song" provides (and how crucial a role, in the Emersonian sense, the poet—the remembrancer—plays in a culture lacking in this sort of music); he then shifts into a plainspoken voice (in prose) that focuses on recollection:

> What we've never had is a song
> and what we've really had is a song.
> Sweet smell of timothy in the meadow.
> Clouds massing east above the ridge in a sky
> as blue as mountain lakes,
> so there are places on this earth clear all the way up
> and all the way down
> and in between a various blossoming,
> the many seed shapes of the many things
> finding their way into flower or not,
> that the wind scatters.
> There are all kinds of emptiness and fullness
> that sing and do not sing.
> I said: you are her singing.

> I came home from school and she was gone. I don't know what instinct sent me to the park. I suppose it was the only place I could think of where someone might hide: she had passed out under an orange tree, curled up. Her face, flushed, eyelids swollen, was a ruin. Though I needed urgently to know whatever was in it, I could hardly bear to look. When I couldn't wake her, I decided to sit with her until she woke up. I must have been ten

8

years old: I suppose I wanted for us to look like a son and a mother who had been picnicking, like a mother who had fallen asleep in the warm light and scent of orange blossoms and a boy who was sitting beside her daydreaming, not thinking about anything in particular.[11]

But it's not just the sonic and song-like qualities of lyric poetry that are allowed to recede a bit into the background in the prose poems of poets like Hass and James McMichael (and, a generation before, James Wright and Richard Hugo). The character of the image is clearly different; there is far less resonance, less investment in the silence surrounding concrete details. When I read Hass's prose poems I think of the way Tomas Tranströmer made the transition from deep imagery to a more discursive (and powerful) poetic vernacular, how he began, in the early seventies to experiment with prose poems that, at first, retained their gorgeously strange and transforming metaphorical images but allowed for more room to talk, more of his coy conversational idiom. Then, slowly, the poems stretched out and moved toward naturalism, though they never abandoned those interior spaces that the early work seemed intent on finding with a flashlight: reading early Tranströmer is like looking at a photo album of someone's dreams; the later work walks us around the dream pointing out the places in the ceiling where a waking consciousness is leaking in. Here is his poem "The Cuckoo" in its entirety:

> A cuckoo sat hoo-hooing in the birch just north of the house. It was so loud that at first I thought it was an opera singer imitating a cuckoo. I looked at the bird in surprise. Its tail feathers moved up and down to each note like a pump handle. The bird was bouncing on both feet, turning round, and screaming toward every point of the compass. Then it took off, muttering, flew over the house away to the west. . . . Summer is growing old and everything is flowing into a single melancholy murmur. *Cuculus canorus* will return to the tropics. Its time in Sweden is over. Its time here was not long! In fact the cuckoo is a citizen of Zaire. . . . I am no longer so fond of making journeys. But the journey visits me. Now when I am more and more pushed into a corner, when the annual growth rings multiply, when I need reading glasses. Always there is much more happening than we can bear. There is nothing to be surprised at. These thoughts bear me as faithfully as Susi and Chuma bore Livingstone's embalmed body right through Africa.[22]

9

Like Tranströmer (who is, admittedly, far less invested in realism than his generational counterparts in the US), Hass is not exclusively interested in the story per se (of the body or otherwise), but he's conscious of the way story organizes experience (interior or exterior), how it shapes reality into paving stones that resemble the sequential (and fictional) paths we walk in everyday life. This resemblance allows for all sorts of things to take place in language that seem less crucial to the lyric temperament of compressed and lineated poems, not least of which is the psychological acuity of plain speech finding its way toward articulation and sense.

Certainly plainspoken narrative poems work wonderfully in lines, but here's the rub: lined narrative poetry often seems to work in opposition to compression, and the danger of flatness is extreme. The prose poem, on the other hand, is ever mindful of compression: it may look like prose but it's trying like hell to be short, to *not* resemble a story or an essay. I suppose there's an irony here: in attempting to overcome the limitations of line and lyric length, the lined narrative poem often tends to slackness; in risking the relative slackness of expository language, the prose poem tends toward tightness, toward concision.

There's also something in-between all this, a prose poem like Killarney Clary's, or Ales Debaljek's, a poem that seems impossible to categorize, whose textures and rhythms are utterly specific to that misty region between poetry and prose: I can't imagine these poems in lines, but they evoke a consciousness that is not easily framed by the sentence. Clary's work, for instance, is gorgeously atmospheric and meditative, yet it resists incantation through discursiveness: the poems often sound like very ambitious conversations, and they are nearly always spoken to an unidentified other (which also takes the incantatory edge off the language):

On the hot streets of Altadena, black boys shouted, watched. Birds waited. Ages shifted in the air. If the trees seemed unsettled maybe they too wondered how they had come to be in place. "I should've married him," she finally said. The light was exhausted but still warm in the yellow grass. Secret in the hills behind us, all we should have done. And we mistook our separate questions for parts of the turning-quiet, yet hoped that mistakes could be repaired. I am sorry.[33]

I've always felt that line breaks would utterly destroy the drifting and circular intelligence of these poems, the way they move through thought and into silence, from rumination to description and back again: for lack of a better term, they feel horizontal in their rhetorical designs, like waves rushing up the beach, slowly flattening out into foam and a thin sheet of water, then receding back to the depths.

It could be possible that my first encounter with Clary's work (also around 1979, though it might have been a year or two later) was my first true taste of prose poetry. If, for many of us, prose poetry is a way of solving the problem of how to write the poem, how to find its best shape and expression, if we are, in fact, just casting around for the right vessel to pour the poem in (Hass talks about beginning to write prose poems this way, that he couldn't get certain poems to work so he wrote them out in prose and, what do you know? they gelled), then perhaps those early Tate poems weren't all that representative; they might as well have been written in lines. But Clary's work never seemed as though it could exist in any other form. Which is why, when I read prose poetry these days, I find myself returning again and again to my not-so-scandalous notion that so very much of it would work just as well in lines, might in fact be improved by the demands of lineation. Since the Modernists, issues of form seem motivated as much by fashion and politics as aesthetics. This has been good for the prose poem, which is certainly not the maligned and misunderstood stepchild of verse that it seemed to be back in 1989, when Louis Simpson complained (a polite word for it) that Charles Simic's Pulitzer Prize–winning collection, *The World Doesn't End*, was not, in fact, poetry. In all honesty, his argument seemed silly even then. I remember thinking at the time, Sorry, Louis, that ship has sailed.

But maybe the point should have been: is Simic really writing prose poetry, or is he simply removing his line breaks? In Simic's case, it's a tough call, and I'm not sure it matters; I certainly don't think it needed to be anything that the Pulitzer committee considered. They're beautiful poems, and I return to them again and again. In fact, reading his astonishing book about Joseph Cornell (*Dime-Store Alchemy*), ostensibly a collection of nonfiction considerations on Cornell's work, it's clear how gifted Simic is at encapsulating imagistic shards of awareness in linguistic boxes. His poems, in fact, rival Cornell's boxes for narrative brilliance (via juxtaposition) and sheer beauty. Clearly the book is more prose poetry than art criticism, but who cares?

When it comes down to it, the prose poem seems simply to add to our choices, to give us another option when we can't figure out how to make the damn thing work. And we should all probably admit that those choices are often arbitrary, just a way of keeping us engaged and curious. It seems like hokum to believe that there's an inevitability to a particular poem and its particular form. Then again, maybe I really did encounter prose poetry back in 1980 when I read Killarney Clary's *By Me, By Any, Can and Can't Be Done*, which seemed unquestionably correct and true. And which is probably why I'm a skeptical enthusiast of the form to this day. Thankfully, my skepticism doesn't keep me from enjoying it.

References

1. Robert Hass, *Sun Under Wood* (New York: Ecco, 1996), 21–22.

2. Tomas Tranströmer, *The Great Enigma: New Collected Poems* (New York: New Directions, 2006), 205.

3. Killarney Clary, *By Me, By Many, Can and Can't Be Done* (Santa Cruz, California: Greenhouse Review Press, 1980), 16.

CLAUDIA KEELAN

The Limits of Accountability:
Where Authority Ends in "Everybody's Autobiography"

> What is a likeness? When a person dies, they leave behind,
> for those who knew them, emptiness, a space: the space has
> contours and is different for each person mourned. This
> space with its contours is the person's *likeness* and is what the
> artist searches for when making a living portrait. A likeness
> is something left invisibly behind.
> —from *The Shape of a Pocket,* John Berger

John Berger's definition of the missing subject quoted above seems to me a good place to start thinking about prose poetry, as in what constitutes prose and poetry, and how are they different? Death is a good instructor. Most often, people labor under the illusion that they are indeed seeing who is in front of them. The space left behind after the loved one is gone begs the question. The "likeness" Berger speaks of is what we achieve, sometimes, in writing. Without the fact of death, we can often fool ourselves into believing that what we see, and what we write from that seeing, is the whole picture. Yet, in so far that what humans ultimately *are* remains invisible in their passage from life and the body, so too our seeking of them succeeds or fails in so far as we are able to represent the contours of their missing identity. "It's a good likeness," someone says, looking at the photograph. "But who are you saying he was?" my mother asks, throwing down my poem about my dead father.

What is prose poetry? Prose poetry is writing driven by two extremes: one, as driven by the necessities of the sentence, is the desire for accountability. The other, as driven by the necessities of ontology, is where accountability disappears into invisibility, which is the province of poetry. Charles Baudelaire's poetry, particularly the poems in *Paris Spleen,* is a good early example. When he read Edgar Allan Poe for the first time, he wrote that he recognized in Poe "not only subjects I had dreamed of, but *sentences* that I had thought and he had written twenty years earlier." They also shared a deep distrust of people, as well as of themselves, and an emphasis on craftsmanship and perfectly controlled art. Baudelaire both loved and hated the people he walked with in Paris, and he also wanted to know what would save them, and him, from what he saw as the avarice of modern life. While Baudelaire was convinced that every good poet had always been a realist, it is interesting that his poems often question the efficacy of realism:

WINDOWS

Looking from outside into an open window one never sees as much as when one looks through a closed window. There is nothing more profound, more mysterious, more pregnant, more insidious, more dazzling than a window lighted by a single candle. What one can see out in the sunlight is always less interesting than what goes on behind a windowpane. In that black or luminous square life lives, life dreams, life suffers.

Across the ocean of roofs, I can see a middle-aged woman, her face already lined, who is forever bending over something and who never goes out. Out of her face, her dress, and her gestures, out of practically nothing at all, I have made up this woman's story, or rather legend, and sometimes I tell it to myself and weep.

If it had been an old man I could have made up his just as well.

And I go to bed proud to have lived and to have suffered in some one besides myself.

Perhaps you will say "Are you sure that your story is the real one?" But what does it matter what reality is outside myself, so long as it has helped me to live, to feel that I am, and what I am?

I love the way I can touch the seams of this poem, see its making as I read it. Within the definition of prose poetry that I'm proposing here, the prose portion is readily available in the exquisite construction of the poem, in its thesis, which proposes the illumination of the closed window over the conventional shining of the open. The "meaning" of the poem becomes tangible, open to paraphrase, as the reader notices the parallel sentence structure of the last line of the first paragraph, and the last line of the final paragraph. The poet gains access to something he seeks, the "inside" of someone's life where "life lives, life dreams, life suffers . . ." as he gazes into a closed window. In the last line of the final paragraph, so does Baudelaire find the tangible answer to his own redemption: *not* in a "reality . . . outside myself . . ." as one might seek looking out an open window, but in the ways in which his looking through a closed

14

window at a "middle-aged woman" enables him "to live, to feel that I am, and what I am . . ." Self-consciousness, then, is available through examination of interiorities, physical and metaphysical. The poet understands something about his own identity, as he spies on the life of another. And yet, "reality" itself is brought into question; the woman, we're told, may just as well have been a man. Poetry, which is driven by the necessities of ontology, demands an exchange. The poem loosens, or gives up, the authority of its detail. Accountability disappears first into interrogatory over the "facts" of the story, and into the multiplicity of identity the poet has imagined, which he also ultimately releases i.e. lets go into the invisible. The poem ends in a question, in the unanswered, outside the dictates of paraphrase.

Until I wrote "Everybody's Autobiography," I had never before written a prose poem. You might say I've spent my life chasing the invisible. At any rate, my father died at my home in Las Vegas a few months before September 11. I live about twenty miles from the University of Nevada, Las Vegas, where I teach. When we moved here eleven years ago, it took about ten minutes to drive there and I remember my husband Donald lying on the road, "to take a nap until the next car comes . . ." he joked, looking at the stars. It now takes fifty minutes to get to school, and is predicted in the next twenty years to redouble. Like most Westerners, we are trapped by our car. When I was a child in California, I remember my mother talking almost ecstatically about the car and freedom. A girl from Chicago, she'd come to the West when she was eighteen. When I think about my childhood, I often remember the song that goes "We like the free, fresh wind in our hair, life without care . . . We're broke, but it's OK, it's California . . ." I don't even know the name of the song, but I still feel immense possibility when I sing it. Strangely, Manifest Destiny—the ideal, not the law—was a lovely, innocent idea about human desire and capability. Ralph Waldo Emerson's essays are manifestos to the largeness of the human spirit, and the spirit's ability to animate the objects to which it turns its attention. Walt Whitman's radical *demos* is also a vision of ontological manifest destiny. I'd been feeling for some years that the freeways I traveled were ones forged in the ideas of early American romanticism, but it wasn't until I wrote "Everybody's Autobiography" that I found I was right.

In writing "Everybody's Autobiography," I was looking both for the contours of my dead father, and to account for the condition of the reality I inhabit with my family and millions of others in the present moment. The poem is very dependent upon information, upon parallel structures, upon repetitions and transitions, all devices more connected to what one thinks of as prose. It also is committed to telling the story of my own father's life through the details of California history, the Southern Pacific Railroad, and the history of US interest in Middle Eastern oil. And yet... The story as such, with its mélange of facts, its proposing of blame, its desire for contour and accountability, its need to bring my father back to life, is over by page 8. The story gives way to the pursuit of Being, to pursuit of soul, and ends with a transitory image of a heaven which "spirals in a dragonfly's hovering, look, just now, and in its vanishing." Perhaps I've given too narrow a reading of accountability in this brief piece. What is acceptance of the transitory, of the invisibility which is poetry's truth, if not a desire for accountability? Baudelaire finds access to his true identity in "Windows" through his observation of others and the "real" is ultimately the power of the imagination. In "Everybody's Autobiography" I discovered a connection to my lost father and to the others who share the circumstances of our particular place, our present moment through my negotiation with historical circumstance. Story and history give way to poetry, and to a split-second image of paradise, which disappears as the poem ends.

MORTON MARCUS

from "*In Praise of The Prose Poem:*
An Interview with Morton Marcus"
by *Ray Gonzalez* (Bloomsbury Review, *March/April* 2001)

RG: *What has writing prose poems done for your vision as a poet?*

MM: When I first immersed myself in the prose poem in the early 1990s, I discovered freedoms I had been unaware I could attain until then. Another way of putting this is that while writing prose poems I discovered restrictions in lined poetry I hadn't known existed. I had learned early on that the way poets of the past had solved the problems of getting from one line to another determined the way I did. They had shown me the way(s), so to speak, in their poems. But I also found that the line in closed verse determined how I used language and how I conceived of developing the structure of a poem. When I gave up closed verse for free verse, I experienced a latitude, a freedom of choice, and found a more lively, vital voice. When I gave up the line, however, I experienced new ways of seeing and saying. It was a complete turnabout of traditional ways of doing things in poetry for me: I came to realize that the line had inhibited my thinking process, since my choice of words and sense of structure (in terms of word choice, syntax and the overall development of the poem) was determined as much by the line as by the way I conceived of moving from one thought, image, or metaphor to another, and how, in the end, I structured the entire poem. In other words, I found content was as much determined by my using or not using the line as free verse had been in releasing me from the tried and true ways of getting from one line to another in closed verse. Thus, in getting rid of the tyranny of the line, I had also gotten rid of the baggage I had not realized came with it. The scales fell away from my eyes all right, but at the same time—joyous surprise!—the chains fell away from my imagination, and I decided to let that shape-shifting beast guide my words and determine the structure of the poem, because ultimately my greatest discovery in writing the prose poem was its ability to free the imagination, and this freeing has everything to do with my vision as a poet, since I seek the level below consciousness from which to speak. My world is composed of fun-house mirror distortions of reality, dream visions rooted in metaphor and symbol which for me evoke a more resonant picture of the world than everyday realism does.

Looked at another way, my choice to abandon the line has allowed me to pursue an unshackled phrase as my basic unit of rhythm, which at times extends phrases to thirteen and even fifteen beats before a caesura—"a sweep of words," as I wrote in *The Prose Poem: An international Journal*, "that in its unfolding opens unexpected vistas of content by releasing my imagination from conventional modes of thought which the line and other poetic devices, it seems, unconsciously dictate." At the same time, I employ all the techniques of poetry, such as figurative language, assonance, consonance, and even internal as well as end-line rhyme to drive my rhythms and energize my poems.

MORTON MARCUS

from *The* Fu: *China and the Origins of the Prose Poem*

There is a popular notion among prose poets and literati from Europe and the Americas that the prose poem originated in the early nineteenth century with Aloysius Bertrand's *Gaspard de la Nuit*, and that Baudelaire continued its development in *Le Spleen de Paris* (*Paris Spleen*). Then Rimbaud followed with *Les Illuminations*, and a half-dozen other poets, almost all French, brought the form into the twentieth century.

In reality, the prose poem started in China during the Han Dynasty. (206 BC–220 AD), where it was known as the *fu*, or rhymed prose. Essentially the *fu* was a court entertainment written for the emperor or for other nobles' amusement to accompany ceremonies, rituals and informal gatherings. Many times barbed with satiric political innuendoes, the *fu* usually consisted of a flamboyant and lengthy description of an object or natural phenomenon in rhymed verse that was introduced and sometimes intermittently interrupted by prose. The prose provided the necessary exposition for a piece, and the verse its rhapsodic language. Typical titles are "The Wind" and "The Owl," although such titles as "Climbing The Tower," "On Partings," and "On The Desolate City" provide a more accurate sense of the variety of subjects and approaches they encompassed. A representative selection of early *fu*, with an excellent introduction, is Burton Watson's *Chinese Rhymed Prose* (Columbia University Press, 1971). The following excerpt from Watson's translation of "The Wind" conveys the early *fu*'s dominant features:

> King Hsiang of Ch'u was taking his ease in the palace of the Orchid Terrace, with his courtiers Sung Yu and Ching Ch'a attending him, when a sudden gust of wind came sweeping in. The king, opening wide the collar of his robe and facing into it, said, "How delightful this wind is! I and the common people may share it together, may we not?"
>
> But Sung Yu replied, "This wind is for your majesty alone. How could the common people have a share in it?"
>
> "The wind," said the king, "is the breath of heaven and earth. Into every corner it unfolds and reaches; without choosing between high or low, exalted or humble, it touches everywhere. What do you mean when you say that this wind is for me alone?"

The poem goes on to exalt the "noble" aspects of the wind, fully revealing its sociopolitical attitude with striking clarity at the poem's conclusion:

"How well you have described it!" exclaimed the king. "but now may I hear about the wind of the common people?" And Sung Yu replied:
"The wind of the common people
Comes whirling from the lanes and alleys,
Poking in the rubbish, stirring up the dust,
Fretting and worrying its way along.
It creeps into holes and knocks on doors,
Scatters sand, blows ashes about,
Muddles in dirt and tosses up bits of filth.
It sidles through hovel windows
And slips into cottage rooms.
When this wind blows on a man,
At once he feels confused and downcast.
Pounded by heat, smothered in dampness,
His heart grows sick and heavy,
And he falls ill and breaks out in fever.
Where it brushes his lips, sores appear;
It strikes his eyes with blindness.
He stammers and cries out,
Not knowing if he is dead or alive.
This is what is called the lowly wind of the common people."

By the Sung (Song) Dynasty (960–1279 AD), the *fu* had developed into the form Western writers have come to recognize as the prose poem. It was completely written in prose, was far-reaching in subject and approach, and had few formal restrictions. To distinguish it from earlier forms of *fu*, it was called *wen fu*, and its greatest practitioner was also one of China's greatest poets, Su Shih (Su Shi), also known as Su Tung-p'o (Su Dong-po), who lived from 1037 to 1101. Su wrote many *fu*, his most famous the two *wen fu* on Red Cliff, which are available in most anthologies of classical Chinese poetry in translation, as well as in Burton Watson's *The Selected Poetry of Su Tung-p'o* (Copper Canyon, 1994). Here is Watson's rendering of the eerie beginning of the first Red Cliff piece, which, characteristically for Su, suggests entrance into a spirit realm, the world of the immortals—an alternate reality he thought could intersect with ours at any moment, and which bears a striking resemblance to the dream landscapes of modern Western prose poetry:

> In a little while, the moon rose from the eastern hills and wandered across the sky between the Archer and the Goat. White dew settled over the river, and its shining surface reached to the sky. Letting the boat go where it pleased, we drifted over the immeasurable fields of water. I felt a boundless exhilaration, as though I were sailing on the void or riding the wind and didn't know where to stop. I was filled with a lightness, as though I had left the world and were standing alone, or had sprouted wings and were flying up to join the immortals.

Su's teacher, Ou-yang Hsui (Ou-yang Xiu), was also a well-known poet and *fu* writer. A translation by A.C. Graham of his famous "The Sound Of Autumn" can be found in Cyril Birch's *Anthology of Chinese Literature*, Volume I (Grove Press, 1965).

After the Sung, the *fu* declined in use among poets, although its importance can be clearly estimated by the publication in 1706 of the *Li-tai-fu-hui, Collected Fu from the Centuries*, a collection of more than 3500 extant *fu* written from antiquity to 1644 (the end of the MingDynasty). Watson thinks the decline of the *fu*'s popularity was caused by the development of fiction in China, specifically the novel, at a time when, I would add, the vast number of out-of-work scholars sought employment anywhere they could find it, which included writing popular fiction and plays, both considered beneath the literary undertakings and social status of the established literati.

This does not mean that the *fu* disappeared from Chinese literature. As late as 1927, Lu Hsun (Lu Xun), China's most famous twentieth-century writer, published *Wild Grass,* a book or *wen fu* which shows the form's continued vitality. A selection from the book can be found in Howard Goldblatt and Joseph S. M. Lau's important *Columbia Anthology of Modern Chinese Literature* (Columbia University Press, 1995).

In the same collection, the half dozen prose poems by Chu Tzu ch'ing (Zhu Ziqing) and Chou Tso-jen (Zhou Zuoren) prove that the *fu* is as viable as ever in Chinese literature. Once again the thought process is the focus of both men. Here is Chu's complete "Haste," translated by Howard Goldblatt.

> The swallows may go, but they will return another day; the willows may wither, but they will turn green again; the peach blossoms may fade and

fall, but they will bloom again. You who are wiser than I, tell me, then: why is it that they days, once gone, never again return? Are they stolen by someone? Then, by whom? Then, where are they now?

I do not know how many days I've been given, yet slowly but surely my supply is diminishing. Counting silently to myself, I can see that more than 8,000 of them have already slipped through my fingers, each like a drop of water on the head of a pin, falling into the ocean. My days are disappearing into the stream of time, noiselessly and without a trace; uncontrollably, my sweat and tears stream down.

What's gone is gone, and what is coming cannot be halted. From what is gone to what is yet to come, why must time pass so quickly? In the morning when I get up there are two or three rays of sunlight slanting into my small room. The sun, does it have feet? Stealthily it moves along, as I, too, unknowingly follow its progress. Then as I wash up the day passes through my washbasin, and a breakfast through my rice bowl. When I am standing still and quiet my eyes carefully follow its progress past me. I can sense that it is hurrying along, and when I stretch out my hands to cover and hold it, it soon emerges from under my hands and move along. At night, as I lie on my bed, agilely it strides across my body and flies past my feet. And when I open my eyes to greet the sun again, another day has slipped by. I bury my face in my hands and heave a sigh. But the shadow of the new day begins darting by, even in the midst of my sighing.

During these fleeting days what can I, only one among so many, accomplish? Nothing more than to pace irresolutely, nothing more than to hurry along. In these more than 8,000 days of hurrying what have I to show but some irresolute wanderings? The days that are gone are like smoke that has been dissipated by a breeze, like thin mists that have been burned off under the onslaught of the morning sun. What mark will I leave behind? Will the trace I leave behind be so much as a gossamer thread? Naked I came into this world, and in a twinkling still naked I will leave it. But what I cannot accept is: why should I make this journey in vain?

You who are wiser than I, please tell me why it is that once gone, our days never return.

"Haste" is described as an "essay" in The *Columbia Anthology of Modern Chinese Literature*, as are Lu Hsun's pieces from *Wild Grass*. But C. T. Hsia, in *A History Of Modern Chinese Fiction*, identifies *Wild Grass* several times as a book of prose poems. The difference between certain kinds of essays and prose poems is many times not made clear by Chinese scholars working in English. Even Su's two pieces on Red Cliff, though identified as prose poems by Watson, are called "essays" and "prose poems" in the same sentence in Birch and "poetic expositions" by Stephen Owen in his monumental *An Anthology of Chinese Literature: Beginnings to 1911* (Norton, 1996).

This is an all too sketchy introduction, but it should be clear that the Chinese prose poem tradition antedates the Western by almost two millenniums. I think its early rise stems from the concision of the Chinese language, and to the development of the stringently condensed yet highly evocative anecdotes which became a Chinese literary staple early on, and which, to mention two works chosen at random, make up such diverse texts as the historical chronicles of the Tso chuan (Zou zhuan) and the philosophical tales of the Chuang Tzu (Zhuang-zi), both written during the Chou (Zhou) Dynasty (1122–221 BC), and available from Columbia University Press, again in translations by Burton Watson, who must be considered the foremost English language translator-scholar of Chinese literature for the last fifty years.

The irony in all this is that it is of little consequence whether the Western prose poet recognizes the true origin of the prose poem, since the prose poem tradition in the West is informed at every point by the milieu and sensibilities of Bertrand and Baudelaire, and most Western writers have adopted those attitudes and approaches as the prose poem's essential elements. I'm talking about the notions of the Romantic movement, under whose spell both men wrote. Their sense of a palpable supernatural world, a reality comprised of the angelic and demonic, have come into the twentieth century as surrealist imagery and depictions of dream landscapes of highly symbolic, mythic, and/or clinically psychological natures, not to mention the most identifiable aspect of the modern Western prose poem, and one which unites it with its Chinese ancestor—its following of the spontaneous twists and turns of the mind at work. There is very little in Western prose poetry of the realism that is the essence of Western fiction.

So what, then, is this little essay about? It is, I hope, a way to adjust our vision—to see from a broadened perspective where we are coming from, and with the new millennium opening before us, to point toward unexplored avenues down which we can go.

DEREK MCKOWN

A Tractatus for the Prose Poem

Life, John Gardner gamely reminds us, is *one damn thing after another;* art, on the other hand, *the best, most important art,* is all subordination: "guilt *because of* sin *because of* pain." Of course, the appeal of accumulation is just that we don't feel the need to sort the relationships between things beyond their most immediate sense—that they are of the world: this event, this moment. There is a sideways organicity to this notion, and it is easy to feel its tug in our, to use Donald Justice's apt description, superannuated Romantic age. And it perhaps helps to explain the periodic upswings in popularity of the prose poem, the most recent accelerating in the last fifteen or so years.

The chatter over the prose poem's legitimacy as a form is just that, and probably reflexive. Even within the loosened confines of free verse the prose poem poses a challenge to the traditional authority of the line. Eliminating lineation we lose those rhythmic opportunities created by counterpoint, and with that, undeniably, layering and shading of tone, the sculptural tactility and density of emotion, and, to a lesser extent, control of pacing. And the question many ask is what does the prose poem possess that makes up for this loss? Still others cheer their freedom from what noted prose poet Morton Marcus refers to as "the tyranny of the line." The Romantic finds esthetic promise in what is perceived as novel; but it is usually those who come late to the party who wave banners and cry revolution. It has probably always been thus.

In this latest renaissance the prose poem often gets treated as a separate, even if similar, species—and we like it that way, I believe. We like having what appears to be a form without rigorous definition, a blurry bordertown where any manner of tawdry behavior is not only tolerated but encouraged. Historic (or mythic) precedence is cited, its presumptive French origin, Baudelaire's *Petits poèmes en prose,* celebrated. But underneath the romantic obstinacy of this outlook is the very real dissatisfaction that *status quo* free verse cannot adequately express the lyrical yearnings of many contemporary poets. Baudelaire *did* write in the teeth of neo-classicist orthodoxy, and asked: "Which of us, in his ambitious moments, has not dreamed of the miracle of a poetic prose, musical, without rhyme and without rhythm, supple enough to adapt itself to the lyrical impulses of the soul, the undulations of the psyche, the prickings of consciousness?"

Working without the obvious artifice of line break and ending may create the *illusion* of immediacy, for both poet and reader; the prose feels more *real*, bearing the cumulative weight of one image after another. Still, if we are to remake the subjective into the objective, recast the original event in the context of art, there must be subordinating features to the form, felt principles of order.

Ira Sadoff helpfully reminds us that the best poets of any age "use all the vehicles of craft to create a dramatized, inclusive experience." The prose poem's initial, preemptory charm lies in its use of the sentence, creating, however illusory, a sense of openness to the immediate world of the poem and of the poet's perceptions. But drama requires tension; something must be at stake. The source of tension in a good and significant prose poem resides in the rhetoric of its brevity. Whether the prose poem is more deliberately narrative (incorporating elements of story—character, setting, plot) or lyrical (a concentration upon devices of repetitive sound), or, perhaps most esthetically pleasing, a particular balance of both, it is in the brief thrust of a single, clear, and sustained voice that demands our attention.

At this point it is probably best to turn to an exemplary example of this. The following is from Gary Young's book, *Braver Deeds* (now collected in the larger *No Other Life*).

> I saw the carcass of a deer, and turned, and walked toward it. I shuddered at the smell, but went on. I was a boy, my life was still new to me; what could I expect if I should lose it? I leaned toward the body. The deer was moving; bees had made a hive in the open belly. A lulling hum droned from the ribs. Where I thought I'd find blood, and bone, and the pearly organs, there was honey, there was gold.

It is Young's fine and exact phrasing that allows us to not only read this event as memory but as linked parts of a perception. We enter physically, by way of the visual, kinetic, and olfactory; the main clauses iambic, movement deliberate, it is the secondary, dependent clauses—now trochaic—that arrest us, and underline the Speaker-as-boy's hesitation. Within two sentences of the narrative, we are gripped by the emotional tension—curiosity and revulsion, fear and courage. Young undercuts the last with the step back in psychic distance—perhaps not courage, then, the adult speaker allows, but naïveté, even ignorance. The immediacy of the physical event is reestablished by cutting against expectation—the deer is inhabited by another life. The poem closes by opening the death of the body up to transformation and beauty. The original event is transformed by memory, recast by deliberate and meaningful intent. In the precision of imagery, the physical clarity of phrasing, the writer's personality, Young's *character*, manifests in the poem's fusion of style and subject.

Another, very different, though equally elegant, voice is Killarney Clary, this poem from *Potential Stranger*:

> Bright planet, dressed in a veil of violet tulle, gold light from many windows, do I wish otherwise?
>
> When the fine strands freeze and split, and bits of purple scatter then gather in the creases, the grid fractures, adjustments are made without reference—fluid in a bottle of liquid glass. For a moment.
>
> Then you remain behind gestures and posture, inside what is said and the manner of birth. I remake the invitation: if my expression must always be your costume, please, lead the dance that keeps threads tense but unbroken.

Here the imagery is more lushly and densely *other*; we remain more abstractly in the speaker's perception of her world. The narrative ploy of direct address steers our attention outward—we are assured that the speaker is connected to an event, a particular occasion. The logic of the poem is the logic of the speaker's perception, the process of seeing and understanding. While the narrative is not so transparently tied to the physical location of Speaker-in-setting, as it does in Young's poem, the dramatic stakes here involve the speaker's shift from observation to disturbance to dilemma—whether the Other in the poem is metaphysical or personal, the speaker longs for better connection but recognizes what keeps them apart is not wholly in her control. She pleads for the Other's good grace. In Clary's prose poem the juxtapositional energy, the dreamlike logic is sustained and *contained* by the immediacy of the moment; the narrative is a framing of the Speaker's problem: opening with bewilderment, closing without resolution, but perhaps strengthened, better prepared.

26

The prose poem, firmly established in American poetry for eighty or more years (of course introduced by Whitman under biblical and French influence 150 years ago), is by now just as varied as lineated poetry. But its lack of more rigorous definition and history of opposition (it may well be the most romantic form in American poetry) leave it too often a domain subject to sloppy metaphysical meditations, bland sequences of impressions, and self-congratulatory "surrealism." The challenge of the prose poem is its openness and intimacy; by eliminating lineation, it is more conspicuously sustained by a dramatic voice that must draw the reader into the immediate occasion, then, deliberately and powerfully, cut away. It is in this rhetoric of brevity, and all the dramatic possibilities of rendering it, that prose poem comes closest to a complete and coherent form.

FRED MORAMARCO

From Shakespeare to Santa Barbara:
The English Language Prose Poem

That oxymoronic genre, the prose poem, like its paradoxical distant cousin, the non-fiction novel, is as difficult to define as silent music. Let me say of it here what Justice Potter Stewart said of pornography, "I shall not today attempt further to define the kinds of material I understand to be embraced ... [b]ut I know it when I see it." I suspect this is true for most readers of poetry, although there are those (especially here in England where I'm writing this essay) who question its very existence. In a witty debunking of the genre, the British poet George Barker wrote:

> Like the Loch Ness monster the prose poem is a creature of whose existence we have only very uncertain evidence. Sometimes it seems to appear, like a series of undulating coils, out of the dithyrambs of Walt Whitman; several French critics claim to have taken photographs of this extraordinary beast, and a great many American poets possess tape recordings of the rhapsodies it chants up from the depths of the liberated imagination.[1]

Browsing through the tissue-thin 2182 pages of the most recent edition of *The Norton Anthology of Poetry* I can't find a single example of a work I would *unqualifiedly* call a prose poem, although Geoffrey Hill's "Mercian Hymns" has something of a prosy look about it.[2]

The roots of the contemporary prose poem and its antecedents are usually traced to nineteenth-century France where the Symbolist poets pushed the formal limits of the poem to and beyond its edges. This view of it ignores the source that's right in front of our noses: the prose poetry of Shakespeare, which provide English-language models of the form long before the Symbolists were a gleam in

---

[1] Originally published in *The Jubjub Bird or Some Remarks on the Prose Poem and a Little Honouring of Lionel Johnson* (Warwick, UK: Greville Press, 1985.)

[2] N. Santilli, author of *Such Rare Citings: The Prose Poem in English* thinks "Mercian Hymns" is a prose poem. He devotes an entire chapter to it in his book. However, even the editors of the Norton, in their glossary entry on prose poetry, note "Hill's 'Mercian Hymns' may look like prose, but the poet insists that his lines are to be printed exactly as they appear [here]; and the reader's ear will detect musical cadences no less linked and flowing than in good free verse..."

anybody's eye. Because Shakespeare's prose poems belong to his dramas, we don't often view them separately, but his cunning use of prose within the plays is well known and understood by actors and directors who know that Shakespeare purposefully loosened the blank verse line and broke into prose when he was intending to tell us something about a character's state of mind. This doesn't mean that he left poetry behind altogether, because his prose passages are infused with metaphors, personifications, similes, alliteration, repetition, rhythmical variations and other poetic devices that make them a likely predecessor to the modern prose poem.

Consider the famous passage from Othello, when Iago tells Roderigo to get over his unrequited love for Desdemona and "put money in thy purse" instead of wallowing in sorrow. When Roderigo says he is thinking of drowning himself, Iago responds:

> . . . Come, be a man. Drown thyself? Drown cats and blind puppies. I have professed me thy friend, and I confess me knit to thy deserving with cables of perdurable toughness. I could never better stead thee than now. Put money in thy purse. Follow thou these wars; defeat thy favour with an usurped beard. I say, put money in thy purse. It cannot be that Desdemona should long continue her love to the Moor—put money in the purse—nor he his to her. It was a violent commencement, and thou shalt see an answerable sequestration—put but money in thy purse. These Moors are changeable in their wills—fill thy purse with money. The food that to him now is as luscious as locusts shall be to him shortly as acerbe as the coloquintida. She must change for youth: when she is sated with his body she will find the error of her choice. Therefore put money in thy purse . . .

Some will argue this is poetic prose rather than a "prose poem," but such distinctions are academic. Of course Shakespearean prose poems do not sound or read like contemporary prose poems because they are written as dialogue and in Elizabethan English, but they do share some qualities that enable us to make a connection.

Shakespeare gives here the rapid movement of a prose poem from one kind of imagery to another ("blind puppies" to "cables of perdurable toughness"), the kind of "fixed base" repetition ("put money in thy purse") that characterizes much modern prose poetry, as well as the exotic diction and metaphoric resonance that lifts the prose into the realm of poetry: ("luscious as locusts" "acerbe as the coloquintida.")

In his excellent book *Playing Shakespeare*, John Barton makes it clear that Shakespeare's transitions from blank verse to prose are quite purposeful and though it's impossible to establish general rules as to why Shakespeare uses blank verse for some passages and prose for others (just over 28% of Shakespeare's play texts are in prose), there is almost always a specific reason when you examine the context. For example, it's easy to see why he switches from verse to prose to convey Othello's confused and agitated state of mind as he contemplates the possibility that Desdemona may have been unfaithful to him:

> Lie with her? Lie on her? We say lie on her when they belie her. Lie with her! Zounds, that's fulsome! Handkerchief—confession—handkerchief! To confess and be hanged for his labour. First to be hanged and then to confess! I tremble at it. Nature would not invest herself in such shadowing passion without some instruction. It is not words that shakes me thus! Pish! Noses, ears, and lips! Is't possible?—Confess? Handkerchief! O devil!

This is the poetry of Othello's fury, conveyed in a disjointed prose that echoes the chaos of his disjointed mind.

As one last example of a quite different kind of prose poem from Shakespeare, let my cite Shylock's famous "I am a Jew" speech which is logical, reasonable, but also the product of a furious mind:

> He hath disgraced me, and hindered me half a million; laughed at my losses, mocked at my gains, scorned my nation, thwarted my bargains, cooled my friends, heated mine enemies; and what's his reason? I am a Jew. Hath not a Jew eyes? hath not a Jew hands, organs, dimensions, senses, affections, passions? fed with the same food, hurt with the same weapons, subject to the same diseases, healed by the same means, warmed and cooled by the same winter and summer, as a Christian is? If you prick us, do we not bleed? if you tickle us, do we not laugh? if you poison us, do we not die? and if you wrong us, shall we not revenge? If we are like you in the rest, we will resemble you in that. If a Jew wrong a Christian, what is his humility? Revenge. If a Christian wrong a Jew, what should his sufferance be by Christian example? Why, revenge. The villainy you teach me, I will execute, and it shall go hard but I will better the instruction.

Here the gathering rhythms of the prose, the parallel structure, the repetitive rhetorical questions, the antithesis and spondaic stresses (Jew eyes/Jew hands/Jew wrong) create an extraordinary prose poem that is as memorable as it is rhetorically effective.

After Shakespeare, examples of the prose poem in English are difficult to come by. In *Such Rare Citings: The Prose Poem in English Literature*, N. Santilli makes a case for passages from Thomas de Quincey's *Confessions of an Opium Eater*, and various fragments from the Romantic poets. We might add some of John Donne's *Devotions on Emergent Occasions*, especially the famous "no man is an island entire of himself" passage, and certainly some of Dickens's stunning descriptions of Victorian London (like the opening paragraphs of *Bleak House*) qualify. But after these, the pickings are slim until well into the twentieth century. Santilli additionally proposes some prose poems by Blake and Oscar Wilde, but his very title connotes the rarity of the form.

However, the situation in the twentieth century is quite different. The lines between poetry and prose became blurred in the work of many Modernist writers. James Joyce embeds many poems in his prose, notably the famous last lines of "The Dead" which give us a prose poem entire in their marvelous evocation of snow falling gently over all of Ireland. And both *Ulysses* and *Finnegans Wake* are filled with prose poems, albeit of a distinctive linguistically inventive Joycean mode. Many innovative twentieth-century novelists—Woolf, Faulkner, Fitzgerald, and Hemingway, to cite the most obvious examples—link poetry and prose in highly memorable passages. Hemingway's *In Our Time* has stories interspersed with prose poems about war; passages from Faulkner's *Absalom, Absalom!*, *The Sound and the Fury* and "The Bear" are prose poems, as is the unforgettable conclusion of *The Great Gatsby* with its Dutch sailors seeing for the first time "the fresh green breast of the new world."

Inevitably, the English language prose poem broke loose from its fictional and dramatic moorings and became a distinctive genre practiced by poets who created their own signature forms of it. A Gertrude Stein prose poem is quite different formally than one by Kenneth Patchen, for example, but both unquestionably wrote prose poems. Enough writers took up the form as a distinct genre over time so that by 1977, Michael Benedikt could put together a major anthology providing an overview that established the prose poem as a viable literary form. Since Benedikt's anthology, other editors have followed suit and if you browse Amazon.com you can find prose poem anthologies edited by David Lehman (of course!), Stuart Friebert, Robert Alexander, Ray Gonzalez and many others. There is even a journal devoted to the genre which gives us international examples of it. Each of these editors offers his own notion of the genre, and the debate as to what exactly is a prose poem is by no means settled. We do seem to have agreed on those contemporary US poets who have moved the genre into new territory, and they include W. H. Merwin, Mark Strand, Robert Bly, Louis Jenkins, Russell Edson, Lyn Hejinian, and John Ashbery.

Ashbery is the author of perhaps both the shortest and the longest prose poems in the English language. As for the shortest, I've always admired this witty one-line poem from *As We Know*:

THE CATHEDRAL IS

slated for demolition.

What Ashbery has done here is to take a simple declarative prose sentence, break it in half and use the subject and verb as the poem's title and the predicate as the poem itself.

In doing this, the title is no longer the actuality that will exist when the action promised by the predicate is completed. That is, the cathedral *is* until it is demolished, and then it *was*. And surely we can see this little prose poem as a commentary on the future of the unified religious western world views as represented by the collective will that was required to construct cathedrals and make them symbols of a world view that is indeed "slated for demolition." (see Henry Adams, *Mont-Saint-Michel and Chartres,* for example.)

As to the longest prose poems in the language, both *Flow Chart* and *Three Poems* are contenders for that honor. *Flow Chart* is longer, but *Three Poems* is more successful, I think, because it incorporates and enacts the dilemma of writing a prose poem—what to include and what to leave out—from its beginning. Of course this quandary is a dimension of all sorts of writing, but it is magnified when the freedom of writing a prose poem tempts the poet to "put in" more than he or she might include were she writing "ordinary" linear verse. In some sense, a *long* prose poem is even more of a contradiction than the prose poem itself, since keeping a continuous stream of language at a poetic pitch for the length of an entire book is a virtually impossible task, but Ashbery has always been drawn to virtually impossible poetic tasks (like writing a poem in two simultaneous columns, and making complex forms like the pantoum even more complicated).

It's not surprising that American writers have stretched the boundaries of the form even further (since George Barker's skepticism about the very existence of the genre is shared by many British writers) and that we're now further down the road and looking at regional manifestations of the genre. It's also not surprising that the prose poem has flourished in California, America's tomorrow place where the next thing always seems to begin. In one sense, the prose poem *is* the next thing from rhymed verse in traditional forms, through blank verse, through free verse to a uninhibited, unrestricted, nonlinear (literally) spontaneity. The prose poem liberates the poet from the tyranny of the line. It is the state of the art of poetic freedom, and though the country has moved even further west, California has always been America's true frontier.

The prose poems in this volume are as various in style, subject matter and technique as the California landscape, which ranges from the lush scenic beauty of Big Sur to the austere breathtaking vastness of Death Valley, to the busy thoroughfares of Los Angeles and San Francisco. Today's California is a land of intersecting cultures, of transient and temporary connections. Here is some lush scenic beauty from Gary Young:

> The air was damp with last night's rain. The matted leaves cushioned my steps, and persimmons blazed in the branches of the tree like a hundred suns.

And here is some austere breathtaking vastness from Derek McKown:

> They did not have to tell him to climb the mountain above toward the parted curtain of air, toward the invisible cities, toward home.

Juan Delgado gives us something from the thoroughfares of Los Angeles (or almost any California city):

> Under the freeway overpass looming over me like a fairy tale vine, I hesitate and stop, thinking about my off-ramp. The overpass straddles me like a giant spider with gray legs, and I stand captive under its long shadows, staring at the patches of sky while a horn blares past me in a gust of wind.

We find the intersecting and clashing cultures of California life in a single sentence by Marilyn Chin:

Moonie and Mei Ling were fighting over a Barbie Doll.

And this marvelous image from Tony Barnstone's "Parable of Aladdin in Oakland" turns a brief encounter between the narrator and a Persian woman in a lighting store into a "blueberry and custard" solar system:

"Would you mind minding my store?" asks the Persian woman in Piedmont Lighting, and she's out the door in a breath leaving me alone with giant lilies that bend brushed steel necks long and tapered as a swan's over a desk. I duck my head not to catch my hair in the solar system dangling from the ceiling, blueberry and custard planets, the halogen dwarfs and incandescent giants, and soak in the brilliant milk of this paradise of lamps.

California is a place of "magical" transformations and the prose poem, with its rapid flow of images from one sentence to the next, is an ideal genre to convey these remarkable metamorphoses. It favors surrealism, and the kaleidoscopic shifting of imagistic ground beneath us from sentence to sentence mirrors the "makeover" lives that so many dreamers still travel there to construct. It is a place where, as Maxine Chernoff puts it, you just might find "the photo that would make all the difference in [your] life." But the search for that photo, in her poem "Lost and Found," takes her into a bizarre maze of lost connections.

Although it's stereotypical to say so, Californians are inveterate optimists—you have to be if you think you can change your life for the better by moving there. And "native" Californians are even more optimistic because they have always breathed the air of hope and promise that infuses the atmosphere of the "Golden State." What other state would elect a perpetually smiling "can do" body builder movie star as its governor? Maybe that's why Peter Everwine, in a poem that turns the phrase "California Dreaming" into a reality, transforms a dream about aging, infirmity, and forgetfulness into an expression of joy and wonder. I'll quote it entire to conclude this essay, because it epitomizes the transformational possibilities of the prose poem as they occur in so many of the poems in this book:

THE BANJO DREAM

One morning Earl Scruggs sits up in bed, reaches for his famous banjo, and plays nine consecutive wrong notes to a tune he's known all his life. What's happening? he cries, holding up his hands, which he no longer recognizes. Meanwhile, of miles away, I have awakened from a disturbing dream to discover that my hands—they no longer seem mine—have become thick-veined and tremble on my quilt like small horses at the starting gate. I am suddenly overwhelmed by happiness. Everything lies open before me: Limpid days. Blue distances. The song that will unlock the gates of paradise.

London, March 2007

DIANE WAKOSKI

Looking for the New Measure

"Marcel, that soufflé is a *poem!*" reads a sentence, illustrating the colloquial use of the word "poem," in a dictionary I consulted many years ago. In our culture, we have so thoroughly lost the original definition of poems as metrical compositions that we've generalized the word "poem" simply to refer to something as a perfect composition. Translating the prose poems of Max Jacob in my French II class at Berkeley in the late fifties gave me this epiphany: the early French surrealists found a way to turn from metrics so entirely that they seemed to invent a form that we now call the "prose poem." It was the images that flowered associatively through the little paragraph-poems (as I called them in my undergraduate days) that created shape, gave the poem its tropaic form, turned it into a descriptive moment of revelation and surprises. This made sense to me, as I was trying to grasp Pound's Imagist concept, a poem where an image could be exploded or developed, antithetical to narrative and without the precise lyricism of traditional prosody. I could see it in Pound's haiku-like "In a Station at the Metro" ("The appearance of these faces in the crowd,/ petals on a wet black bough."), but I couldn't see it in his famous "Hugh Selwyn Mauberley." I realized that I would undoubtedly be condemned as a writer of Amy-gism, were I writing in his time, as he condemned the poems of Amy Lowell, whom he felt falsely claimed to be an "Imagist".

No less mysterious to me than "Hugh Selwyn Mauberley" was William Carlos Williams's "The Red Wheelbarrow". Yet in this poem, as with the "petals on a wet black bough." I could understand the impact of the visual, the image itself as the prophet of the poem. Why, I wondered, didn't he write it out as a prose poem?

Thus, in both Pound and Williams, I found a connection to the prose poems of my French class, those convoluted moments of description, often seemingly like dream material! But prose poems —why didn't I write any? Seems strange in retrospect, as I was so looking for a way to use my love of the descriptive language of D. H. Lawrence's novels to write poetry. That was the rub; I wanted to write poetry, not prose. Following in the footsteps of most American

36

modernists, I too felt the search was for "a new measure," and that prose was still the antithesis of poetry, even though I/we wrote in prosy free verse. My mentor, Professor Tom Parkinson at Berkeley, taught that poems were written in lines, while prose was written in sentences. That definition highlighted the importance of cadence, rhythm, breath-pauses, caesuras, even incantation and rhetorical phrasing, but it emphasized the line. Prose didn't have lines. Yes, exciting that those experimental French poets could paradoxically make "prose poems," but that also didn't fit into another important aspect of poetry to me—what we have come to call "The Whitman Tradition." By the late fifties the poem had become an oral composition, or at least one that took its shape from line breaks we could hear, and rhythms we could speak naturally, yet musically—the emphasis on "natural". Poems were to be read aloud. There was something silent and unspoken about those French prose poems. They were whispers, dreams, the unvoiced unconscious. I suppose in my mind I associated them with the stream-of-consciousness writing of Joyce's "Ulysses" and "Finnegans Wake". That was prose, not poetry.

My earliest poems, written in high school, were sonnets. Bad sonnets, but I prolifically wrote them. Transforming my sense of poetry from traditional prosody to the twentieth century really happened in one investigative moment. It was reading Gertrude Stein's *Autobiography of Alice B. Toklas,* of course written in prose but begging to be musically, wittily, emphatically and rhetorically read aloud. I heard the cadences of poetry there, and the book gave me my "new measure". I guess I was more influenced by those French prose poems than I thought I had been, for here I was reading prose as poetry. Discovering that my sonnets weren't very good was partly discovering that I was not really a lyric poet. And, ironically, those French prose poems were dense, packed, elegant lyrics. So were Pound's and Williams's imagist poems. I wanted to write poems that were letters to the world, both holding and hinting at my secrets. I wanted to write sonatas, with movements, developments, repeating themes, changes of key. I wanted to sprawl, not formally but gracefully, and those French prose poems were coiled springs, folded bodies, not relaxed, lounging ones.

In the seventies, someone sent out a kind of Dadaist invitation to many poets in New York, instructing us to "write a poem about the sky on a postcard." My response is probably the closest thing to an actual French-style prose poem I've ever written, though as I look at it now, I see too much meander, too much prose!

More successful, I think, is a little prose poem that is Part VIII of a poem called "Fifteen Poems for a Lunar Eclipse None of Us Saw":

VIII. LIGHT

The roses glowed in the room, and she wrote by rose light. Her eyes were candles. her fingers had diamonds in them for none to see. Roses bloom in every place like snails in a rainy season. Listen to me: light from roses is not unusual. Turn out all false lights.

(p. 247, *Emerald Ice,* Black Sparrow Press, 1990)

The great challenge of the prose poem is, like Marcel's soufflé, to make you understand what poem-ness is. The essence of poem: something so well constructed that its many ingredients combine to make a new and perfect entity. The so-called "layers" of a poem, the so-called "condensation," the shaping trope and its revelation —could describe other things. But with a prose poem, we have to go back to the concept of prosody, so that we can realize that if a poem is written in lines, then a prose poem is one very long line, one very long breath. It's the reason prose poems need to be one short paragraph, though the breath of one paragraph is still an extended breath. Recently, the editor of a haiku magazine told me about innovations in American haiku, and he spoke of the "one-breath haiku". Like the concept of a prose poem, which is antithetical to the delineated poem (of many breaths), this implies an antithesis to the defining feature of the haiku: its movement from two lines of exposition to the final line of transformation (two breaths). To create the haiku without the break, the surprise revelation, would seem to eliminate its power and reduce it to a sentence, perhaps even an explanatory one. And of course, the same thing would be true of the prose poem. What happens to revelation, the new breath of surprise we have come to expect at the ending of a good poem?

I think one answer to that question is that in a prose poem, each sentence is a small surprise. But it's not enough of a surprise to be a revelation, the kind that completes a poem. In one sense, a prose poem is a post-Newtonian construct with no beginning, middle or ending, just one long breath around which we've arbitrarily put a frame. I've always resisted such post-Modern structures for poems, so despite my inclusion in this anthology, I don't really write prose poems. But my poems have always been filled with prose passages, passages I have written out as prose, not prose poems (because they do not fulfill my definition of the one-breath passage). Here is one example, from a poem called "The Pepper Plant":

> I think you wanted children for the same reason you say you want to write poetry. A good reason: to transform your life. And yet it is action, not object, which transforms a life. I could have a Rembrandt painting hanging in my living room, and it could not transform me; thus my life. But if I were painting a picture because I loved the process of making that object, surely I would then have a very different life? The process itself provides much of the joy. So your children, as objects, are no particular joy to you alone —only when you can show them off (your Rembrandt?) and to whom do you show off a constantly crying baby? And your poetry? It gives you little, joy, for no one reads or publishes it. As an object, it is like your crying baby. Not much to show off.
>
> (p. 66, *Waiting for the King of Spain,* Black Sparrow Press, 1976)

To me, this is prose, not prose poetry. In contrast, here is a prose passage in my poem "Father of My Country," which I believe reads like a prose poem:

> This scene: the trunk yielding treasures of a green fountain pen, heart-shaped mirror, amber beads, old letters with brown ink, and the gopher snake stretched across the palm tree in the front yard with woody trunk like monkey skins, and a sunset through the skinny persimmon trees. You came walking, not even a telegram or post card from Tahiti. Love, love, through my heart like ink in the thickest nibbed pen, black and flowing into words You came, to me, and I at least six. Six doilies of lace, six battleship cannon, six old beerbottles, six thick steaks, six love letters, six clocks running backwards, six watermelons, and six baby teeth, a six cornered hat on six men's heads, six lovers at once or one lover at sixes and sevens;

(and then the poem moves into verse, which I will print here to show the contrast between my sense of delineated verse and prose poem)

> how I confuse
> all this with my
> dream

walking the tightrope bridge
with gold knots
over
the mouth of an anemone/tissue spiral lips
and holding on so that the rope burned
as if my wrists had been tied.

(pp. 45–46, Emerald Ice, Black Sparrow Press, 1990)

For me, the prose poem will always be not only one breath, but also descriptive, rather than metaphorical in affect. I also associate what I like to think of as a surreal narrative to prose poems. These pieces can contain the absurd logic often thought of as surreal, or they can emphasize explanations so fantastic as to seem poetic. I think, in our time, Russell Edson and David Ignatow have written the best prose poems that utilize this technique. My prose poem "The Beautiful Green Bird," which is section V of "Handbook of Marriage & Wealth," is an example of this. Actually it is what I call a fable. By that I mean that it is a story, somewhat fantastic in nature, with animals acting like people, and always providing an illustrative moral resulting from the actions of the characters. Over the years, I have written a number of these "prose poems." and I don't quite see them as poems but poem stories. Given how far-ranging the definitions of the prose poem have become, I suppose they are more like prose poems than like either poetry or fiction.

Extending this technique, I also have over the years written pieces that I call poem-lectures. They are almost all written as letters, and to me they incorporate the elements of line-driven verse and its orality into the one-breath paragraph phrasing and strong descriptive content of prose poems. I think the best of these is "The Emerald Essay," which is too long to include in this anthology. You can find it in my 1975 Doubleday collection, Virtuoso Literature for Two and Four Hands. It was originally written because I was, at a poetry conference in Virginia, asked to give a talk, specifically with the title "What Women Are Up To".

The difficulty of talking about these extensions of verse into the prose poem is that I do hear poetry differently. I hear it spoken, the poet's voice echoing both as music and as utterance. You could say that dialogue, in prose, is the spoken word, but it other people's voices. Poetry has to be one voice, even if there is dialectic intent, even if it is one voice with its splinters, vectors, resoundings and almost otherness. Perhaps the personal voice of an essayist is also important, but there the voice isn't required to speak and to sound musical. The prose of an essay is explanatory, and poems demonstrate rather than explicate. By titling my poem-lecture "The Emerald Essay," I wanted to acknowledge the attempt at explanation while allowing the power of poetry, the voicing of the images, the one breath of all the splinters of my voice that is channeled through the emeralds to become a maverick prose poem.

M. L. WILLIAMS

In the Tangle of Vines: A Practical Definition of Prose Verse

> … it's even in prose/I am a real poet. …
> —*"Why I Am Not a Painter,"* Frank O'Hara

My grandfather farmed in California, so I grew up with a strong sense of life on the farm, the dominance of seasons, spring's blessing of green, autumn's harvest and gold decay. My favorite field was the zinfandel vineyard, a little over an acre of 40+-year-old vines surrounded by even rows of almond trees in the Paso Robles hills. The vineyard, unlike the measured rows of trees over the hills, was haphazard—gnarled head-pruned vines squatting unevenly in a hollow among the trees, erupting in a tangle of vines and bud break each spring, sagging with black fruit on warm September afternoons, or hunched like scruffy travelers dreaming of warmth in the January cold.

Much like that outstanding vineyard planted seemingly as an afterthought, I often turn to prose poetry for a similar, freeing release from the restrictions of traditional verse's tyranny of the line. The prose poem, or prose verse as I shall refer to it here, is verse that erupts in an unmeasured tangle and turns through an elemental and occasionally wild blossoming of language into the fruit of the poem. Despite the fact that the prose poem refuses to take advantage of the line break to measure out its turns, it turns nevertheless, employing all manner of anti-narrative strategies, some subtle, some more obvious, to counter the narrative moment of the sentence. Quite simply, it is the poet's use of the turn, other than the traditional line break, that allows for the creation of verse in prose.

Every poet knows that verse comes from the Latin term *"versa,"* for "turn," in antique Latin a farming word that describes the tiller's move at the end of each row. This action creates an even, orderly measure across the field, assuring that every row is available to water and manure and sun and the meticulous order of the farmer's eye scanning for pests and thieves. This measured, memory-facilitating model has dominated verse for most of three millennia, and the resulting line break, the end of the row, has become the defining attribute of poetry, its turn against the sentence and its tyranny of time. And it is a beautiful, elegant assault on time when employed by our best poets. The plow turns up the soil; the poem turns time into a rich humus of language into song, row after row after row.

Finding an idiom for the prose poem has proved to be much more difficult, perhaps because prose verse lacks the graphological certitude that the line break affords. As Peter Johnson notes in his lucid consideration of the prose poem introducing the bellwether *Best of the Prose Poem,* much discussion of the form begs the question by devolving into "metaphor, trusting the analogical slices of our brains, which naturally embrace oxymoron and paradox." Many of the analogies Johnson offers are clever and, to a point, illustrative for those writers who already feel the beast inside. But how does one teach a talented poetry student to write a prose poem, something that is, as Charles Simic puts it in his analogy of someone chasing an imaginary fly in a dark room, ". . . a burst of language following a collision with a large piece of furniture"? Space here doesn't permit a more extended summary of the critical consideration to date or whether the roots of prose poetry should be traced back to the surreal subconscious or the French symbolists; Johnson has already given us that kind of summary. What concerns me here is more pragmatic. How do I explain to that talented student what happens in a work of prose verse? How do I develop a vocabulary that allows my student to understand how to approach writing a piece of prose verse? I've discovered in class discussions that my better students can innately sense the turns in a prose poem, and they can count them, just as a traditional verse poet can count accents in a sonnet line. Prose poetry is, after all, one of the forms of verse, and relies on methods of turning other than the line break to undermine the narrative impetus of the sentence.

To illustrate this consideration of the turn in prose, I will examine two poems that I had the privilege of publishing when I edited *Quarterly West* that use turns in different ways. The first is George Looney's luminous and playful "Finding Time," which I appreciated for its direct assault on time as it turns elegantly and devastatingly through a series of resettings. We begin on land and then find ourselves suddenly drowning:

Hunters of the muntjac, the "barking deer," say that if you kiss the horns of a female while stroking the soft fur on the backs of her ears without tranquilizing her or restraining her in any way, then you will find you have the time to get everything done that you need to do. Or you can take the advice of deep sea divers, who say the salty ink of the cuttlefish can slow time down. They say if you pay an old diver to take your watch down and pass it under the body of a cuttlefish as it releases its ink, and if the diver feels the pulse of his heart in his ears as the ink covers the watch, time will slow down for you, and you'll have enough time to be able to enjoy everything. Of course, they say, for this to work the cuttlefish must be protecting its mate, and the two of them must swim off safely together and touch tenderly as they swim. And the old diver must remember, as he rises a little too quickly to the surface of the water, the feel of a particular woman's lips on his bare chest and, in the memory, the woman must look up at him as her lips touch the hairs around his left nipple, and there must be a kind of joy in her eyes that he feels as the nitrogen begins to bubble in his blood.

The poem works by turning from one extravagant method for "saving time" to another, which turns again through a series of increasingly extravagant qualifications until the end, which turns against time itself as the diver is overcome by the bends and the poem is overcome by the lyrical eroticism of the diver's possible asphyxiation. One can count without too much difficulty at least six[1] turns, beginning with the turn from the title to the unexpected muntjac opening to the diver's increasingly elaborate qualifications that collapse into erotic memory and death (or loss of consciousness). The diver finds time in classic lyric mode, in the moment, while the "you" that needs to find narrative time ("enough time to be able to enjoy everything"), dissolves, just as the dissolved nitrogen begins to bubble. The turns here work directly against the narrative pressure of the sentences themselves and render line breaks unnecessary to satisfy the fundamental lyrical mode of the poem.

Peter Everwine's poem "A Story" uses prose verse both to explore and ironize its title:

---

1. Six is suggested as a broad number of turns here. As readers become more adept, they also tend to see them more readily. For example, some will count as a turn the shift from "Hunters" in the opening clause to the actions of kissing and stroking the muntjac that follow.

A STORY

A boy fell from a tree one day, and later one arm was shorter than the other and dragged at an awkward angle—like a wounded wing—as if it held in memory the accident of its origin, its difficult first flight. Thus marked, the boy gave up being a boy. He turned into a crow that croaked and flapped in the circle of those who had remained children.

In literature, this is not uncommon; people are forever turning into something else, and vice versa. What I am saying here belongs to literature. What a crow says is another alphabet and is therefore unintelligible. To us it sounds like Caw! Caw! It resembles laughter. Or perhaps choking.

Here Everwine brilliantly turns "A Story" into poetry by turning simile into the kind of metamorphosis common to classical poetry or, in prose, magical realism—a wounded boy looks like a crow and so he becomes a crow. Next, at the paragraph break, he turns on the story with his wry, dismissive gesture toward criticism and its take on the literarily overfigured tropes of the crow and metamorphosis. Finally, the poem counters the critical desire to categorize and interpret when it circumscribes the unintelligible, ineffable fact of the crow's "alphabet," and so the poem inscribes our inability to interpret the crow's cry as well as our desire to try to "read" it. In eight sentences, Everwine presents our problematic relationship with narrative, with language itself, as well as the fundamental inadequacy of similitude, and therefore with authority itself. "What I am saying here" cannot account for what cannot be said, except by circumlocution; that is, "as the crow flies"—direct, straight, without diversion—is a manner inaccessible to language, to story, and appropriately this "verse" can only circle above what interpretation misses. The crow's cry opens into an abyss only verse can approach, and this verse ultimately turns on two irreconcilable interpretations ("laughter" and "choking"), neither of which have meaning in the crow's alphabet and the failure of language to "resemble" the crow's cry. The poem turns in multivalent fashion around the nucleus of the crow's cry, its ineffable intention; the "story" is merely the outer, superficial shell the rest of the poem turns against and the literary theory becomes the necessary failure that falls into the pure lyric of the cry.

Rather than begin an exhaustive catalog considering all the ways verse can turn without line break, my hope is that this suggestive yet cursory beginning will serve to provoke a positive discussion of verse in prose: a discussion that considers what prose verse or prose poetry is, rather than what it is not, or what it is like—one that serves creative writing teachers who wish to find a way to *begin* to talk about prose poetry with students. Prose verse, or prose poetry, turns just as traditional verse does; it merely shuns the line break as its method of turning. And as any good farmer knows, whether the vines are set in neat, even rows or scattered in a hollow in the hills, ripe fruit from stressed vines is sweetest and gives the finest, most concentrated wine.

Works Cited

Peter Everwine, "A Story." *Quarterly West 36,* eds. Jeffrey Vasseur and M. L. Williams. Winter, 1992–93: 4. (Republished in *From the Meadow: Selected and New Poems,* University of Pittsburgh Press, 2004).

Peter Johnson, "Introduction." *The Best of the Prose Poem,* ed. Peter Johnson. 2000: 10–18. (Note: White Pine Press also issued an identical edition of this work in 2000.)

George Looney, "Finding Time." *Quarterly West 39,* ed. M. L. Williams. Summer/ Fall 1994: 9.

GARY YOUNG

The Poem in Prose

I have been asked on more than one occasion to defend the prose poem, and to explain in particular how a poem can be a poem without 'the line'. Curiously it is often poets working in free verse who make the most strenuous objection to prose poems, the same poets who argue for the legitimacy of free verse against those who champion poems written in formal meter and rhyme. Both arguments are absurd, and disingenuous as well. One might just as well be asked to defend the sonnet.

The prose poem has a history in the poetry of Europe and America that extends back more than a century-and-a-half. It was appropriated by many nineteenth-century poets who first experimented with other free verse forms, and in China the *fu*, or poem in prose, has a history that stretches back millennia.

There are certain formal elements the prose poem shares with fiction and creative nonfiction, and there are other elements that more closely resemble the tropes and strategies of verse. Brooke Horvath has suggested that poems written in prose attempt to "hide" the poetry behind the prose in part to reclaim an audience that has for the past two centuries been seduced by prose. He also suggests that the prose poem provides a home for fugitive content, and "may well offer a means of saying the no-longer sayable as well as the as-yet unsaid." Certainly the prose poem is enjoying a spirited rise in acceptance and practice. There are many lively journals dedicated exclusively to the genre, and several anthologies—*Models of the Universe: An Anthology of the Prose Poem* (**Oberlin College Press, 1995**), *The Party Train: A Collection of North American Prose Poetry* (**New Rivers Press, 1996**), *No Boundaries* (**Tupelo Press, 2003**)—are testament to the genre's vitality and acceptance.

There are those who argue that a poem written in prose is neither poem nor prose, but something altogether different. The distinctions, ultimately, are unimportant to the reader, though the writer may wish to position his or her work in one genre, or in one particular philosophical or theoretical camp. This raises the important question of expectation. What preconceptions does a reader bring to any given text, and how do those preconceptions alter the reader's apprehension and appreciation of that text?

Traditional poetic forms create an anticipation of the "poetic" that prose does not. It is this very lack of expectation that makes the prose poem supremely subversive and supple; the reader may be seduced in wholly unanticipated ways. The prose poem's flexibility is due in part to the fact that the form comes with so little baggage. The reader may be alerted that he or she is about to experience a poem, and yet they are greeted with comforting, unintimidating prose.

The reader's diminished expectation of a poetic experience also makes the prose poem an especially demanding form. There are no signposts that telegraph: this is a poem. Because it *is* prose, and shares more visual equivalence with the language we use to negotiate newspapers, contracts or personal correspondence, it must work especially hard to embrace the rapture of language we identify as poetry. Ezra Pound once said, "Poetry should be at least as well-written as prose," and we should expect prose poems to incorporate the best elements of both: concision, syntactical intelligence and rhythmical eloquence. By eschewing the ornamental apparatus of received poetic forms, the prose poem must rely wholly on the music and the honesty of its own utterance.

Charles Baudelaire's *Little Poems in Prose* was published in 1869, but even before the term was coined we can find hints of the form in Thoreau, Emerson and Hawthorne, among others. There are even traces of the form in the earliest literature produced in this country. In the mid-seventeenth century, Anne Bradstreet, one of the first poets in the Americas, wrote a series of short prose pieces titled *Meditations Divine and Morall*. Their brevity, allusiveness and their lyricism recommend them as prose poems:

> A ship that beares much saile, and little or no ballast, is easily overset, and that man, whose head hath great abilities, and his heart little or no grace, is in danger of foundering.

Walt Whitman may be said to have liberated the poetry of meter and rhyme with the ranging free verse lines we admire in *Leaves of Grass*, but sections of his prose book *Specimen Days in America* frequently approach the intensity and focus of his poems, and share more equivalence with his poetry than with his other prose works:

48

March 16.—Fine, clear, dazzling morning, the sun an hour high, the air just tart enough. What a stamp in advance my whole day receives from the song of that meadow lark perch'd on a fence-stake twenty rods distant! Two or three liquid-simple notes, repeated at intervals, full of careless happiness and hope. With its peculiar shimmering-slow progress and rapid-noiseless action of the wings, it flies on a ways, lights on another stake, and so on to another, shimmering and singing many minutes.

Whitman has pared his vision and his language to essentials here, and considers a single brief episode with precision, and without haste. He has created a text that is more poetic than prosaic, more poem than story.

Charles Baudelaire's affection for the work of Edgar Allen Poe is well known, and Poe's *Eureka: A Prose Poem* no doubt influenced Baudelaire's *Little Poems in Prose*. These poems, often moralistic and always a bit fantastic, heralded the modern prose poem in Europe, and were to inform the work of Arthur Rimbaud and countless others. Their fabulist quality has had a particular influence in America, the echoes of which we can hear in the work of Russell Edson and others.

Ernest Hemingway punctuated the stories in his collection *In Our Time* with short prose vignettes that also seem closer to poetry than to prose in their condensation, their impact, and their intention. The following piece describes a scene that could be part of a larger story, but it manifests its character, and achieves its power by standing alone. The reader must apprehend this unique offering with undivided attention.

We were in a garden at Mons. Young Buckley came in with his patrol from across the river. The first German I saw climbed up over the garden wall. We waited till he got one leg over then potted him. He had so much equipment on and looked awfully surprised and fell down into the garden. Then three more came over further down the wall. We shot them. They all came just like that.

Prose is characteristically literal, and we use it to describe, to document and to establish our hold on the everyday world. The prose poem subverts this quotidian use of prose, and employs it to retrieve or re-establish a connection to the poetry of our lives. Robert Hass, whose work is represented in this anthology, frequently combines prose and lineated verse within the same poem, stretching even further the boundaries between the two genres. The following poem is one of a series of prose poems from his book *Human Wishes*.

A STORY ABOUT THE BODY

The young composer, working that summer at an artist's colony, had watched her for a week. She was Japanese, a painter, almost sixty, and he thought he was in love with her. He loved her work, and her work was like the way she moved her body, used her hands, looked at him directly when she made amused and considered answers to his questions. One night, walking back from a concert, they came to her door and she turned to him and said, "I think you would like to have me. I would like that too, but I must tell you that I have had a double mastectomy," and when he didn't understand, " I've lost both my breasts." The radiance that he had carried around in his belly and chest cavity—like music—withered very quickly, and he made himself look at her when he said, "I'm sorry. I don't think I could." He walked back to his own cabin through the pines, and in the morning he found a small blue bowl on the porch outside his door. It looked to be full of rose petals, but he found when he picked it up that the rose petals were on top; the rest of the bowl—she must have swept them from the corners of her studio—was full of dead bees.

A Story About the Body telegraphs its resemblance to the short story with its title, and the poem possesses those characteristics of plot, discursiveness, and character development we might expect from a short narrative. What sets this poem apart from a short story is its compression, concision, and its lyrical intensity. This is another case in which the particular attention asked of the reader by the poem is rewarded by the poem's subtle movement and final revelation.

The paradox of any poetic form is that it simultaneously liberates and constricts. Any formal strategy will structure a specific logic, and every form accentuates or encourages a particular mode of thinking; I am tempted to say, a particular mode of wonder. Form is merely an architecture necessary to support the ceremony of the poem.

My own intention has been to quiet my poems, not to silence, but to equilibrium, where a calm voice need not interrupt itself with self-consciousness or artifice but speak simply in the knowledge that the breath propelled represents a faithful utterance of the heart.

I have found it more difficult to lie in prose, either through omission or amplification. Poems written in prose encourage—at least in me—a stricter honesty, and as a result the mysteries they reveal seem more genuine and profound. I have tried to write with as much clarity as I can about those brief, disquieting moments that define our lives. Where the impulse might be to reflect and elaborate, to draw a broader reality from the moment at hand, I have tried in my poems to pare away peripheral reflection to touch surely the moment, and to freeze it. The concept of a lyric moment is itself a conceit, of course; even the shortest poem takes time to read. But each instant understood thoroughly—understood as God might understand it—is of a caliber with any other, not because it has been demoted to some lowest common denominator, but because each is a kernel and a mirror of eternity.

My attraction to the prose poem is emotional rather than critical. The prose poem is a maternal form. It is comforting and embracing, but it can also be smothering, constricting; once inside there is no way out, no place to rest until the poem is finished. It is a clot of language, and must convince through revelation.

But in truth, what I treasure most about this form is the moral pressure it exerts. The prose poem encourages a particular kind of modesty. It might even at times achieve a certain humility, a humility which may, through grace, be reflected back upon the poet's own heart.

Notes

A longer version of this essay appeared in *The Graceful Lie: A Method for Making Fiction*, Prentice Hall 1999.

Anne Bradstreet, *Poems of Anne Bradstreet*, edited by Robert Hutchinson, Dover Publications, 1969.

Robert Hass, "A Story About the Body," *Human Wishes*, The Ecco Press, 1989.

Ernest Hemingway, "Chapter III," *The Stories of Ernest Hemingway*, Charles Scribner's Sons, 1938.

Brooke Horvath, "The Prose Poem and the Secret Life of Poetry," *The American Poetry Review*, September/October 1992.

Walt Whitman, "A Meadow Lark," from *Specimen Days; Walt Whitman: The Complete Poetry and Collected Prose*, edited by Justin Kaplan, The Library of America, 1982.

Essays 2

Processes, Influences and Reflections

TONY BARNSTONE

Parable of the Prose Poem

There is an animal that is marvelous because it doesn't exist. Like the unicorn, when you look at it closely, it turns out to be a two-horned oryx seen from the side, or a deformed goat. And yet in the moonlight...

Although its meat is considered of dubious value, this is a product of ignorance. Those who know will go to almost any length to obtain it. The hunter of this beast will spend weeks in the forest listening to the trees until he has achieved the necessary silence, then will stand very still, his breaths as shallow as a Los Angeles conscience, waiting for the beast, and turning green. Two centuries pass. The cities crumble like bread into the seas. In another century, the transcendent and elusive (yet hegemonic) network of language and culture is infected with a virus that short-circuits certain areas in the cortex, so that people from Borneo to Kalamazoo break out in spontaneous laughter that is so painful that it makes tears rise to the eyes, makes the neck flush red as jewels of sweat appear on the forehead, and causes them to emit short, barking sounds, baring their teeth, their lips pulled back in a death's-head grin. The beast still has not come.

By now, the hunter is half buried in the forest floor. He peers out from a tangle of strangling vines, covered with forest grubs, his long hair rooted in the earth. For the first century, his thoughts had been rapid and filled with regret. Why am I such a fool? Even if I capture the thing, no one will care. They like the creatures that fit nicely in the cages at the zoo, labeled with the scientific names, with their well-studied habits and habitats, with children poking them through the bars and mustached janitors to clean up their feces. Even if I could capture it, what cage could hold it? The biologists won't know what to call it, and so they'll call me a fraud. And what of Mary? I told her I would be back in a week. In the second century, his thought slowed down to a slow cycling like the sap inside the trees. Warmed by the sun, they would rise, driven by some hidden hydraulic pressure, and in the coolness of night they would subside and harden into a thick dreaming. In the third century, his face is cracked and brown as tree bark, and his thoughts now have stilled and almost stopped, but on certain nights, as tiny full moons reflect in the dark marbles of his eyes, a great unspoken word ripples out as if from the ground and the trees themselves. It says, *come!* That's all, but each month it grows louder in its silence, *come! COME! COME!* The beast still does not come. And slow tears well from the hunter's eyes, crusting his cheeks with salt.

In another century, the hunter is dead. And, now that he no longer exists, the creature appears. It steps out from a fold in the air, like an actor from a stage curtain, and on long, silver legs delicately approaches the hunter's corpse. It parts the vines and hair with its slender nose, and licks the crusted salt from the hunter's cheeks. It is so beautiful, but who is left to see it? Only the great-great-great-great-great-great grandson of the hunter, who has wandered off from the campground and gotten lost in the deep woods. He stares at the great animal with its tufts of hair like frosted wind, its wild dark eyes, its form shifting and slipping in the mind, neither this nor that. He puts out his tiny hand, and in a cracked, trembling voice calls out, "Come here, puppy. Here, pup!"

CHRISTOPHER BUCKLEY

Influences

My first book, published in 1980, written between 1976 and 1979, contains a prose poem; it's a letter-poem to my friend Pete Sozzi with whom I had gone through grade school and high school in Santa Barbara. Pete came home from Vietnam, and we moved to San Diego to share an apartment while he completed his BA and I worked on an MA. I wrote the poem to him years later while we were both trying to make a living in different states.

Mid-seventies, I was in the MFA program at UC Irvine and we all were familiar with the work of Russell Edson, Michael Benedickt, Peter Wild, and Edson even came to give a reading. There were surreal days and nights those years and a lot of the poetry, especially prose poetry, reflected the disjointed experiences resulting from experimentation with psychic energizers, the reality of and opposition to the Vietnam war, and an actively oppressive administration in Washington. Those years saw the first "popular" emergence of the prose poem in the US, but I had no poetic or human response to it in the absurdist mode. Edson, though still a very popular poet, has never reached me with the arbitrary strategies of his prose poems.

Rather, it was Richard Hugo with his letter poems who was the catalyst for me to try my own prose poems. I wrote a handful and included that one to my friend Sozzi in my first book. Hugo was a poet of great heart, writing with compassion, introspection, and grit, writing to friends about what meaning he could wrestle from experience. His book, *31 Letters and 13 Dreams,* (Norton, 1977) collected his very popular letter poems from recent years, except one—"Letter to Berg from Missoula"—which was published in *The New Naked Poetry,* edited by Stephen Berg and Robert Mezey in 1976. In the *Naked Poetry* anthologies poets contributed a prose complement to the selection of their poetry, a statement about their concerns or practice, about the state of contemporary poetry as they saw it. Hugo's letter to Berg talks about the evolution of his letter poems and a notion of form he had for them: "Usually, I took a fourteen-syllable line, propped it up here and there with an anapest and fired away. Maybe a couple I didn't pay that much attention ..."

No one I knew recognized that hint of scaffolding, and the poems simply stretched margin to margin with a human and compelling voice in long rhythms. So far as I could tell or thought about it, that was a prose poem. In this same piece, Hugo comments on Eliot, how he felt Eliot was largely misunderstood, and says his poems "... are honest recordings of personal pain for all the literary devices he had to employ to render them." That statement applies, to my mind, to Hugo's letter/prose poems, and the qualities of humor and self-awareness should be added in. And so at times I tried my hand at prose poems that I hoped worked in a similar manner.

However, when I really think of the first influences that attracted me to prose poems—the longer rhythms, the more capacious structure allowing for more Voice, more litany and detail, a more intensive engagement with the immediate political world and yet conversely a more introspective world—I go further back to Ginsberg's "Howl" and Kenneth Patchen's *The Journal of Albion Moonlight.*

I do not recall then or now anyone I know classifying "Howl" as a prose poem. That poem and that book were still icons, totems, and compelling forces for us in the early seventies, and we were not all that far removed from the poem's explosion on the poetic scene in the late fifties. I wrote a paper on Ginsberg in graduate school at San Diego and again wrote a long essay on my MFA oral exam; in neither place did I take up the subject of the prose poem formally, but that does not mean it was not working on me. I think this was largely because—as the sport's cliché has it these days, "It is what it is"—meaning that it was such a charged, original, and singular piece of writing, that none of us ever thought to make a case for its structure beyond the free verse arguments which were just starting to die down then between our best poets (quickly becoming senior then) and some older second rate academic poets still arguing for end rhymes or nothing. But look at it. Especially section I; it's all paragraphs designated/initiated by the anaphor "who" sticking out on the left margin to note yet another litany, rant, prophetic riff and declamation. I knew enough not to try and imitate that, but all this time later, when I stop and look, I can see some blueprint from "Howl" supporting prose poems I am writing today, especially when they take on a social or political subject. Of course in interviews and essays, Ginsberg talked about his composition method, the "elastic of one breath" (a big, long breath!). And it was clear then to most that the voice/rhythm/engine of such writing could be found in the Old Testament prophetic/vatic voice. One of the things we talk about today re the working of a prose poem is the longer sets of rhythms it employs, the rhythm of the sentence. There is nothing new under the sun. I think someone said that before somewhere?

As well, I found Patchen's long anaphoric lists in "The Journal of Albion Moonlight" energizing and compelling. A good part of the brilliance of the poem is the result of Patchen's imagistic invention of course. But the form of that poem, the long lyric blocks of the writing, spoke more to a prose poem style or organization than any lineation, especially with the text/prose inserts. And of course, Patchen's *Selected Poems* from New Directions contains many prose poems. In Patchen's prose complement in *Naked Poetry* (1969) he says in part:

> Words have distinct values of relationships that have no bearing whatever on the relationship of line to line; if this is remembered, of course, we get a perfect relationship of line to line over the whole poem. There is such a thing as weight in words. A rhythm felt is a rhythm that has its own laws. It is an absolute mistake to ladle out stress like a cook measuring off the ingredients for a cake. We've got a country of cake-baking poets now...

Patchen is, I believe, here continuing the free verse argument of the times, but to my mind it goes a long way to explaining the possibilities and workings of the prose poem.

And I should not forget to mention Jorge Luis Borges's book *Dream Tigers* (*El hacedor* in its original Spanish, Buenos Aires, 1960). In 1964 the University of Texas Press published the book in translation with the new title. Half of *Dream Tigers* is in prose, half is lined poems. While some of the pieces in the first section can be called prose fables or narrative, the majority are prose poems—something that does not now receive much acknowledgement. Reading the book for the first time while in the program at Irvine, I was taken with the philosophic style of those prose poems and as well with the possibilities for the idiosyncratic view inward, for metaphysical speculation. My favorite is one of Borges's most famous poems, "Borges and I," and I still recall the poignancy of "Delia Elena San Marco" in which Borges examines love and fate and the afterlife.

One of my favorite poems, lined or in prose, is James Dickey's "The Eye Beaters" published in a slim, 64-page book, *The Eye-Beaters, Blood, Victory, Madness, Buckhead and Mercy* (1970). I think we have somewhat forgotten Dickey—publicly at least—and his absolutely first-rate and forceful poetic genius, due to his dissipation and the awful last books he published. Dickey should not be forgotten for his singular power and vision, for his ability to write and invent a great many forms and structures for his poetry, and for the shock and sensation of many of his subjects which he managed to bring off with complete authenticity. Such a memorable poem is "The Eye Beaters." In that book you can find many forms wherein Dickey orchestrates his lines and phrases about the page. "The Eye Beaters" is essentially a block of writing covering five and half pages in very small print. Somewhat characteristically of this period, Dickey adds in an extra space between words for pause/rhythmical effect, but we are reading one long prose poem. In the margins at the left there are narrative "stage directions" that give the reader context and plot to reinforce the relentless, almost incantatory recounting of children in an institution in Indiana who have beat their eyes blind, and of their visions that the poet connects back to mankind's earliest images. Few poets could ever command the long and symphonic poem with such intensity as Dickey, and in this instance the prose poem form must have seemed the only possible choice. This is one of the most powerful poems, in any form, I know.

In those early days, Robert Bly's prose poems in *The Morning Glory* were important to me for their concreteness and simple but elevated vision. Bly deserves a great deal more credit than he has received for writing clear and meaningful poems and championing the prose poem in a time when much of the aesthetic concomitant with prose poetry was frivolous or self-indulgent at best. And while no one today thinks of Charles Wright as a prose poet, his first book, *The Dream Animal,* (1968) contains a section of six prose poems titled "Departures," five of which are reprinted in *The Grave of the Right Hand,* Wesleyan (1970); the poem there that captured my imagination and showed me a lyric element was possible in the voice of a prose poem, was "The Poet Grows Older." Also a marked influence were the longer meditative poems of Diane Wakoski, some of which moved back and forth between prose and lines, such as "The Pepper

Plant" in *Waiting For The King of Spain* (1976). I noticed also César Vallejo's prose poems, the intense "I Am Going to Speak About Hope" foremost among them. And Larry Levis in *The Afterlife* was an influence as he mixed prose poem and lined poem sections in his landmark poem "Linnets."

I continue to admire Robert Hass, who goes back and forth between prose poems and lined poems discovering the most appropriate format for his subject. Another poet that I teach and read often is Mary Oliver, who moves from prose poem to lined poem with an equal mystical grace. I love her vision and character, her modesty in the face of creation. Had I more talent, perhaps my poems would show her influence. Gary Young has written prose poems exclusively for the past fifteen years or more; standing in nature, his responses are honest, guileless, and, in the Zen tradition; his style is accessible and direct and yet in fairly short poems he always produces the kind of illumination all poetry hopes for. Morton Marcus and Killarney Clary are two other prose poets whose work I read with great joy. Stephen Berg's *Shaving* is an important book of prose poems, demonstrating what can be done with lyric narration. And I am a big admirer of Mark Jarman. He has a stunning collection of prose poems simply titled *Epistles;* "In The Clouds" is a *tour de force* in that collection.

As for my practice, it depends largely on Voice, a particular longer rhythm and edge I hear as I begin which sets me off in the direction of the prose poem instead of the lined poem. My last four or five books mix them, and for me the prose poem is one more option open to the poet. Often, but not always, a prose poem for me is not as lyrically driven as a lined poem; it does not seem to call for as much embellishment. I generally find more elbow room for complaint, for political comment, as long as they are mitigated by some wit and humor; the prose poem more openly and directly engages the ironic, topical, political, social. While it is more capacious, the prose poem is not an arena for discursiveness. But more can be included, more associations can be drawn on; it is paratactical, but not self-consciously so when most effective. In fact, the ability to be direct, to be or at least appear to be less contrived, to appear to be more reportorial and therefore "true" (Forche's "The Colonel" comes to mind) is a virtue in the prose poem. I place value in what my friend

Gary Young has written about his practice: "I find it harder to lie in prose." And it seems to me that if what we are ultimately trying to do is make sense of experience, the world, our lives, then is is a good form to turn to. Sometimes, the prose poem better accommodates the more dramatic subject, a good deal of grit and much gravity often does best not dressed up in lines where it might seem clever, disingenuous, where the poem might be seen to be trying too hard for effect. Often in the prose poem, the facts are presented right next to one another, one necessarily leading to the next, no one turning the poetry machine up to ten for the big finish. The power of apparent understatement, the power of accurate observation and thought are also its virtues to my mind.

An analogy from my years as a tennis pro seems appropriate in explaining how and why I choose one form over another. In a tournament, in the middle of a match, you had better not be worrying about mechanics—the proper way to position yourself for a backhand, a half-volley, an overhead. You had better be able by that point in time to rely on your muscle memory and the many years of practice so you can do some dedicated thinking about the discrete strategy needed to defeat the opponent across the net.

So after thirty-five years of work, I like to believe the most efficient and appropriate form usually presents itself to me in the early stages. I don't have the patience I used to when I was young, or said another way, I am not as easily intimidated by those playing politics with poetry and in academia, and so I have become a bit more cantankerous in recent years. When I am feeling like that, it usually signals that I'm headed off in the direction of the prose poem to put more ironies and a humorous edge of complaint in play. However, much the same as in creative nonfiction, a poet needs to be onto himself in a prose poem, needs to be able to be reflexive and self-examining, needs to be sure the soap box is broken up into little pieces—so some modesty and self-mockery have to enter in to keep you from sounding like an arrogant fool. I have a couple of poet friends who read my work and who do not hesitate to tell me if I am doing something stupid re choosing a form, or subject, or line, or image. Everyone needs such friends. Everyone needs choices. I especially enjoy the modesty and directness of the prose poem, its capaciousness, and still its insistence on singing and discovering light.

TERRY EHRET

The Deep Rhymes of the Prose Poem

A woman I met at a reading in New Mexico asked me, quite earnestly, "How do you know it's a poem if it doesn't rhyme?" She was puzzled by the absence of end-rhyme in modern and contemporary poetry, which seemed to her like prose arbitrarily broken into lines she could see on the page, but could not hear.

One can't easily explain free verse lineation without delving into abstractions. But her question was even more challenging because the work she'd heard me read were all prose poems. Not only had I abandoned end rhyme, but even the lines on which those rhymes might perch.

In the years since she posed her question, I have given a lot of thought to just what does make a poem a poem, and I've begun to wonder if rhyme might not, after all, be a necessary ingredient. By rhyme, I don't mean simply the resemblances of sound. Consider the rhyming poems that get under our skin and into our breath hundreds of years after they were first penned. Even in those that have the most elegant rhyme schemes, we recognize something else that makes the sound effects resonate: images, rhythms, phrases that echo and reflect, thoughts and ideas that rhyme inside the rhyming, and the rhyming itself a kind of logic that brings far-flung elements of the world together in ways the rational mind might never conceive.

And below this lie the deep rhymes: those moments when you are reading or writing a poem, and an ordinary experience begins to resonate with a parallel, but unconscious memory, or with some presence in the world you can feel keeping step beside you like a *Doppelganger.* These deep rhymes are invisible and inaudible. They can't be consciously created, or easily explicated, but they can be felt. And for me, writing a prose poem gives me an unusually direct access to these deep rhymes.

I don't know how or why it works, but when I'm writing a prose poem, I feel like a tightrope walker, steadying myself with a balancing pole: on one side, the reality of experience, and on the other, the simultaneous and multiple reality of metaphor. I must be careful not to let one or the other dominate. One cannot become the meaning and the other the reference. This is a quality the Italian prose poet Italo Calvino called "multiplicity," and maintaining this is both exhilarating and tenuous.

The long, unbroken line—the prose poem sentence—this is the rope on which I cross the empty space of silence out of which the poem will emerge. If I were to break that line, the thread that keeps me suspended would snap. But if I trust it, guided by those deep, inaudible rhymes, then the sentence miraculously appears with each word, each footfall. And if I can manage to stay aloft—well, that's how I know it's a poem.

JOHN OLIVARES ESPINOZA

Blood, Sweat, and Leaves:
On the Writing of "No Weeds, No Work"

Anyone who has spent hours performing the same repetitive action, as I have as a former gardener, knows that often they will fall asleep and continue doing their job in their dreams. That activity for me was raking up ten thousand leaves a day. I had done it so often for so long, that even six years after I had stopped landscape work, I dreamt I was raking and picking up a pile of self-replenishing citrus leaves.

The opening first third of my poem, a lyrical narrative entitled "I Go Dreaming, Raking Leaves," which first appeared in *Dánta: A Poetry Journal* out of University of Notre Dame, read like this:

> It's been six years
> since I've strangled
> a rake & dragged
> its green teeth across
> grass, & still
> I'm raking leaves
> during my sleep.
> The final third of the poem reads:
> The leaves never stop
> coming, the same way
> one cleans a wound
> & the blood
> keeps rising.

Inspired by a dream I had my third year into my MFA program, the poem was published in 2003 shortly after I had written it almost exactly as I dreamt it. Although the publication should have meant it was laid to rest, the poem still didn't seem to completely work for me, and I was unsettled by it. A year or two later, I had a revision; this time around I snapped the lines together like Lego pieces to form lines of approximately thirteen syllables:

> I rake a small pile, toss half into a plastic can
> And another pile takes its place. The leaves never stop coming.
> The same way one cleans the wound and the blood keeps rising.

And though this version appeared in 2007 in *The Wind Shifts: New Latino Poetry*, I continued to revise. The voice coming out of the poem, I then realized, directed itself to the prose form and I followed suit.

How did I know that this lyrical narrative was meant to be a prose poem? During the prewriting of any of my poems, I focus on story and its central idea. In the drafting stage I then pay attention to language and line breaks. But when the line breaks are not helping move the poem along, no matter where I am breaking, then the poem is trying to tell me it should be in prose form. By this I am not at all saying my prose poems are failed verse. I am saying this: a poem becomes a prose poem when it needs to be told in one shot without the artifice of line breaks. In the case of "I Go Dreaming, Raking Leaves," I traveled back, recalling when my workshop leader had said, "Prose poetry had a particular authority—an authority of believability equal to that of nonfiction prose." That was what my poem needed.

My first encounter with the form was in an undergraduate workshop entitled "Anatomy of Poetry." The poems that changed the way I wrote were the ones I was introduced to in that workshop: Richard Hugo's "Letter to Logan from Milltown" and "Letter to Berg From Missoula" taken from *31 Letters and 13 Dreams*. Richard Hugo established for me that a familiar and direct voice could be poetic and heartbreaking. Also, the prose poetry of Gary Young from his collection *Days* was very influential. The two poems of Young's I keep in mind are "Two girls were struck" and "The baby grabs." Gary Young's poetry captures what it *feels* like to be human. His poetry shows us how to celebrate life and its quiet moments like that of an infant reaching out to touch sunlight. Hugo's and Young's poems demonstrate that authority and believability my workshop leader spoke about. I always return to them for inspiration.

Yes, prose poetry can be narrative; yes, it can have characterization (like Richard Hugo's work); yes, it may have setting (read Stephen Berg's "Iowa"); and yes, can have dialogue or be written completely in dialogue (like my own poem "The Story My Grandfather Told My Mother a Few Months Before His Death"). Regardless of what fictive elements I use (character, "plot," setting, dialogue, etc.) my focus remains on the language, the discovery, and

66

the emotional turn. I work the prose poem as I would work any piece of verse, except that I do not worry over line breaks.

Since "I Go Dreaming, Raking Leaves" was a completely new poem, it warranted a new title. "No Weeds, No Work" was inspired by a phrase my father told me when I found myself landscaping with him again less than half a year after I completed my MFA degree. The new poem was a revision in every sense of the word; I had scrapped every line but kept in variation the parts of "the leaves coming" and "blood rising." The first half of the poem was about my frustration within that moment of dialogue between my father and me. The second half was still based on that dream I had so long ago. Even now, I don't remember if I my mother appeared in the dream or not; it sometimes comes to the point where I confuse what is dreamed and imagined. The images of the never-ending leaves and the superficial cleansing of a wound that needs constant attention ultimately seemed to me, for at least this poem, to work as metaphors for its writing process.

MARK JARMAN

Mine Own Prose Poem

The first version of the Bible that I remember reading, because growing up as a minister's son and a devout churchgoer I had to memorize a lot of scripture, was the Authorized or King James Version. The KJV was the standard text for the church my father served in Scotland when I was a child, and scripture memorization was the fundamental exercise in Sunday School, as it would be when I returned to the United States, where the Revised Standard Version was used. In the KJV, the poetry of the Bible is written in prose. The songs of the psalmists, of the prophets, of Solomon, and the great poetry of Job, all are written in prose. The prose does not undermine the rhythmical statement and reiterative parallelism of the poetry; it simply makes no attempt to acknowledge the verse line. So, the first poetry I learned by heart, the poetry of the Bible, I learned by reading a prose text. When I returned to the United States and was given my first Revised Standard Version of the Bible, I discovered that what the KJV had rendered as prose was printed in lines of free verse. Nevertheless, I had been impressed at an early age that prose could be a mode for poetry.

My first attempt at a prose poem was a lyrical paragraph in praise of the Northern California coast and called, with theological pretension, "Grace." I think I was sixteen or seventeen, and lived in southern California, where northern California was a mythical landscape. Frankly, I don't think I had even seen the northern coast by then, not beyond Santa Barbara, but I had read Robinson Jeffers. I left the prose poem form alone for several years, even after discovering the prose experiments of the French Symbolists, Baudelaire's *Spleen*, Rimbaud's *Illuminations*. Nothing about French prose poetry made me want to try the form, especially when it produced imitations like T. S. Eliot's "Hysteria" and Karl Shapiro's "The Dirty Word." When I was a freshman in college I looked with puzzlement for the first time at the prose poems of Russell Edson. I read Karl Shapiro's collection of prose poems *The Bourgeois Poet* and couldn't see the point. And yet another undergraduate poet, a classmate a little older than me, when she learned I admired W. H. Auden, advised me to read "Vespers," from his great sequence "*Horae Canonicae*." I did, but again I couldn't see the point, especially the point that this master of verse should want to write a poem in prose. Later, when I read Auden's own favorite poem, "Caliban to the Audience," also in prose, I couldn't see the point. Now, I do see it, and think "Vespers" and "Caliban to the Audience" are two of the splendors of modern poetry in English. But until I started devoting myself seriously to writing poetry, the prose poem appeared to be an anomaly, even for its masters—Baudelaire, Rimbaud—and as yet I did not recognize the mastery of Russell Edson, who worked solely in the form.

It was in graduate school at Iowa in the mid-seventies that the form began to push forward into my consciousness as a viable way to write. Charles Wright's prose poems from his first book, *The Grave of the Right Hand*, became available to me. The punning on the letter *a* in "The Poet Grows Older" and the long, loping sentences with their audible, yet unmetrical rhythm grew apparent and fascinating. I am still struck that among the poems in his first book Wright preserved only the prose poems for reprinting in *Country Music, Selected Early Poems*. Then there were William Matthews' prose poems, like "The Penalty for Bigamy Is Two Wives," with its praise for Janis Joplin, and his lesser-known prose poems like the miraculous but forgotten, perhaps due to its title, "Mud Chokes No Eels," which ends, "I have a good cloak, but it is in France" and speaks of "the big, chipped mug I use for coffee" and decries kitchens without windows. I was amazed at the capaciousness of the form, how it could include what Sylvia Plath once called lares and penates, the important small details of everyday life. I discovered that my teacher Donald Justice had investigated the form as end-pieces for his book *Night Light*, "Orpheus Opens His Morning Mail," and "Narcissus at Home." Sandra McPherson introduced her class at Iowa to the prose poems of Francis Ponge, the modern French writer of odes to the ordinary, who could make a horse the peer of a bishop and a cigarette something like the golden bough. The prose poems of Elizabeth Bishop must owe something to Ponge. The poet Vern Rutsala, whom I had met when my parents moved to Portland, Oregon, while I was in college, was working steadily in the form, in a vein not unlike Edson's, yet more intellectually satirical, without Edson's absurdity, but with a Swiftian sense of social commentary and outrage . His

69

book *Paragraphs* came out in the late seventies and also pointed a direction. And there was more Russell Edson to get to know, in part through a wonderful paean to the poet by Donald Hall in, I believe, *The American Poetry Review*, where Hall claimed, quite rightly I think, that Edson was a genius. I re-engaged the form myself, for a long poem I wrote while at Iowa, called "History." The poem, about the origin of my family and the family name, ends with two paragraphs of prose. The prose is not nearly as distinguished as the prose poetry I had been reading, but it includes everything from the King James Version's rendering of Biblical poetry to the long, loping sentences of Charles Wright's prose poetry in *The Grave of the Wright Hand*. "History" turned out to be the central poem in my first book, *North Sea*.

I left the form alone for several years after that. Living abroad in the late seventies, after my first book came out, and after I had more or less completed the manuscript of my second book, *The Rote Walker*, I tried a few short paragraphs, in the manner of Vern Rutsala, but never did anything with them except to show them to Rutsala, who said something like, "Ah, prose!" They weren't much good. I still have them, and once in a great while take them out of their yellowing folder to read over. One is about the exhumation of Lord Byron. As I have said, they are not much good.

So, years went by. The last time I had written a prose poem was in the late seventies. Then, in the early nineties, I was reading *Ecclesiastes*, in the King James Version, from a Gideon Bible I had accepted as a gift from a motel room some time before, and I began to remember a dramatic event from my first year in high school. Something about Solomon's stoic, yet lyric pronouncements got under my skin, and I found myself narrating an event, the suicide of a girl my age who went to my high school. At the same time I found myself quoting the Jacobean English of Solomon's translators and setting it beside the narrative of the event. As I wrote, I quoted a passage of Solomon, then set beside it a passage of graphic journalistic detail. In fact, my father, the clergyman, had been called to visit the suicide's grieving family the day she had killed herself, and I had not forgotten his account of his visit. Why it all came back, in this case twenty-five years later, I do not know. But it came back as prose. The poem that resulted, "Questions for Ecclesiastes," became the title poem of my seventh book.

This time the form of the prose poem did not lie dormant for as long as before. I was working frequently in the sonnet, and *Questions for Ecclesiastes* and *Unholy Sonnets* are dominated by the form. But I had come to see, with the poem "Questions for Ecclesiastes," that the prose poem could hold within it a variety of tones and modes, of rhetoric and diction, of nonmetrical and metrical rhythms. When I exhausted the sonnet, I turned to the prose poem, but not without being forced to it by a dramatic event. Strangely, it was an event like the occasion for "Questions for Ecclesiastes," but more immediate.

The son of one of my dearest friends took his own life in the early nineties. I did not know how to respond, but felt I must respond, and wrote a poem in the style of St. Paul's letters to the Corinthians, that troubled community. When I composed the poem, I even went so far as to designate chapters and verses, as if it were a Biblical text. An absurdity, of course. St. Paul never did such a thing, nor did any of the other writers in the Bible. Though I published the poem with its chapter and verse headings, I quickly abolished them. But what I noticed about the epistles in the New Testament, especially those of St. Paul, was how often they were given to metaphor, even of a pretty wild sort. In I Corinthians, St. Paul admonishes this unruly community as follows:

> For the body is not one member, but many. If the foot shall say, Because I am not the hand, I am not of the body; is it, therefore, not of the body? And if the ear shall say, Because I am not the eye, I am not of the body; is it, therefore, not of the body. If the whole body were an eye, where were the hearing? If the whole were hearing, where were the smelling. But now hath God set the members, every one of them, in the body, as it hath pleased him. And if they were all one member, where were the body? But now are they many members, yet but one body. And the eye cannot say unto the hand, I have no need of thee; nor again the head to the feet, I have no need of you. Nay, much more those members of the body which seem to be more feeble, are necessary: and those members of the body, which we think to be less honorable, upon these we bestow more abundant honor; and our uncomely parts have more abundant comeliness.

I don't know about you, but this sounds to me like Whitman making up his great metaphors of the democratic United States by the seat of his pants. And that is what St. Paul is doing for the early Christian Church—making it up with poetry. I know that there is

71

much that is objectionable in St. Paul's epistles and the other epistles of the New Testament, but in the mid-nineties, as a form of prose poetry, these great, poetic texts offered me a new direction and I set about over the next decade writing a series of prose poems which I called Epistles, after the New Testament books. Some of these poems are included in this anthology.

My aim was to write as if to a spiritual community, but not to one like St. Paul's. I wanted to write to a looser, less orthodox group, one that might wish to consider metaphors for mortality and eternity, for hope and despair, for grievance and forgiveness, for love and sex, for all kinds of things which, I believe, bemuse and beguile us in our everyday lives and sometimes exalt us and sometimes nearly destroy us. As St. Paul created metaphors for the early Christian Church to understand its faith, I wanted to offer metaphors for faith—any faith—in daily life. And I found that writing these poems, these Epistles, in a prose with the rhythm of the Bible, but also the rhythms of other kinds of prose, from Emerson's essays to self-help books, was the way to go about it. In the end, I wrote some thirty poems. They will appear as a collection, *Epistles*, from Sarabande Books, in the fall of 2007. When I think of the tragedies that led me to the form, I realize that what I have tried to create in the prose poem is an argument for life.

MORTON MARCUS

Riding the New-backed Beast

By 1990, I had published five books of verse poems and one novel. Before then, I had become mildly interested in the prose poem when I came upon Richard Ellman's *Selected Writings of Henri Michaux* in the San Francisco Public Library in 1966. I tried my hand at several prose poems, but desultorily, only half interested in the form during the ensuing years. My interest sharpened somewhat when I read W. S. Merwin's *The Miner's Pale Children* in 1970, and intensified in 1976 when I discovered Michael Benedikt's invaluable anthology of international practitioners of the genre, *The Prose Poem*. A year later, a young publisher asked me for a short manuscript, and I found I had twenty or so of my prose experiments that I thought suitable for publication. The result was *The Armies Encamped In the Fields Beyond the Unfinished Avenues*, with brilliant ink drawings by Futzie Nutzle, at that time a featured artist in *Rolling Stone*. The book came out in 1977, to no distribution and no interest.

Although I did not realize it at the time, the narrative impulse coursing through the prose poem had to be one of the contributing streams in my fiction writing between 1979 and 1980, when I wrote my novel, *The Brezhnev Memo* (1980), and it continued like an underground river in *Pages From a Scrapbook of Immigrants: A Journey in Poems* (1988), to emerge into the sunlight like Coleridge's sacred river in "a mighty fountain" in 1992.

The immediate inspiration for my undertaking new prose poems was a book of prose poems and parables by my old friend Larry Fixel, entitled *Truth, War and the Dream Game*. It was a selection of Larry's best work written over the previous twenty-four years. At that time, I was writing long feature articles about poets and writers for a weekly San Francisco Bay Area newspaper chain called *Metro*, and I persuaded the editor to let me write a 3000-word article on Larry's book. It was really a labor of love, since Larry had been the encouraging director of a small poetry group I was part of during the sixties and early seventies.

There is no doubt that my writing such a detailed piece forced me to look at ramifications of the prose poem I had been unwilling

73

or too lazy to see before. Many of the elements, I discovered, allowed me to verbalize my own practices and concerns and to recognize directions in my own poetry I had either half-developed or hadn't pursued.

Larry's engagement with the form of the parable made me acknowledge not just the narrative impulse in my work, but my reliance on storytelling. It further made me aware of the symbolic subtext I saw in the simplest everyday incidents, subtexts that assumed mythic if not archetypal proportions. As I said about Larry in the article, "Fixel's parables belong to a tradition that includes Kafka, Borges, Italo Calvino, Henri Michaux, and even Herman Melville. In their hands, the parable can parade as an imitation of everyday reality, but it is really made of the stuff of dreams, of the unconscious, of myth." I went on to say, "Fixel describes the parable in its modern guise as a narrative that provides 'a devastating illumination of a world split between psyche, spirit and material concerns, . . . [and is] especially suited to convey the distilled essences of a fragmented world.' Essentially the parable, as Fixel uses it, 'challenges our assumptions while, paradoxically, it evokes universal meanings.'" I went on to describe this situation as follows: "As we wish for and never get in newspaper accounts, Fixel's tales go beyond the surface description of events to their possible meanings. Fixel makes the reader aware of the significance of the words used to describe the happenings. These words become metaphors and symbols that lead us to a deeper and unexpected examination of the subject under discussion."

These thoughts made me realize that my work had veered toward the parable since I had first put pen to paper in high school. But as if I were driving a car, I had willingly, although unconsciously, brought my work back from a side road to the main highway—that is, to the main thoroughfare of American free verse lyric poetry.

At the same time, I realized that the freedom I thought I had achieved in free verse was an illusion, because if closed verse had determined my phrasing, the way I got from one line to the next, and even the structure of my poems—all of which, I came to realize, I had almost unconsciously learned from my readings of the old masters—then free verse, while giving me a latitude that made my voice more lively, still restricted my structures by the way

I advanced from one line to the next. However, when I gave up the line in writing the prose poem, I experienced new ways of seeing and saying.

As I said in an interview with Ray Gonzalez in the *Bloomsbury Review* in 2001, what I had come to realize was that the line had inhibited my thinking process, since my choice of words and sense of structure (in terms of word choice, syntax, and overall development of the poem) was determined as much by the line as by the way I conceived of moving from one thought, image, or metaphor to another, and how, in the end, I structured the entire poem. In other words, I found content was as much determined by my using or not using the line as free verse had been in releasing me from the tried and true ways of getting from one line to another in closed verse. Thus, in getting rid of "the tyranny of the line," I had also gotten rid of the baggage I had not realized came with it.

At the same time, the chains fell away from my imagination, and ultimately my greatest discovery in writing the prose poem is its ability to free the imagination. To me this freeing has everything to do with my vision as a poet, since I seek the level below consciousness from which to speak. As I said in the *Bloomsbury* interview, "My world is composed of funhouse-mirror distortions of reality, dream visions rooted in metaphor and symbol, which for me evoke a more resonant picture of the world than everyday realism does."

Looked at another way, my choice to abandon the line allowed me to pursue an unshackled phrase as my basic unit of rhythm, which at times extended to thirteen and even fifteen beats before a caesura, something that would be prohibitive in a verse poem. In a prose poem I could pursue "a sweep of words," as I wrote in *The Prose Poem: An International Journal*, "that in its unfolding opens unexpected vistas of content by releasing my imagination from conventional modes of thought which the line and other poetic devices, it seems, unconsciously dictate."

However, I also observed that I employed all the techniques of poetry, such as figurative language, assonance, consonance, and even internal rhyme to drive my rhythms and energize my prose poems.

The result of all this thinking and verbalizing was that several months after I wrote the Fixel article I experienced an eruption of writing unprecedented in it energy, and far surpassing my previous volcanic explosions of creativity.

The pieces seemed new, fresh, exploiting language, image, and idea as I never had before. My imagination constantly surprised me. I let my flights of fancy carry me along, not understanding what I was writing at first, but trusting the energy that was propelling my words forward. Many times I discovered that the fantastic situations and outlandish images I'd put on paper were the beginning of extended metaphors, or parables that themselves, in the end, were metaphors.

I had read Coleridge's definition of the imagination and the fancy, and abided by his pronouncements, but now the fancy was no longer a dirty word. As I said in an interview with Robert Sward in *Caesura* magazine in 2003, "To me, the fancy is a plaything which can be taken in hand and elevated to the level of the imagination—that is, it can be forced to be more than itself."

However, I pointed out that there were pitfalls in this thinking the poet should be wary of, since the fancy would allow his imagination free range and "weirdness for weirdness' sake is not acceptable, nor is the poet's indulging his facility for invention unless it is being used for specific purposes in a poem. The imagination's 'genuine' images and metaphors are the only route to vision, to the momentary glimpse we can get of the essential order of things, which is what the creative act allows the poet (or artist of any genre) to apprehend and through him the reader (or audience) to experience." The last part of that statement, which is really talking about structuring and craft, is what I take to be Coleridge's notion that in the end the imagination is more genuine, more solid than the fancy because it is also an organizing agent.

That wasn't all. By relentlessly following images that popped into my head, I soon came to believe that any idea or image that is manifested in the brain is not accidental, and should be developed seriously by the writer.

While all these elements were surging to the fore of my work, humor, more antic than ever, gushed up, spreading in garish colors over the poems. As I said in the *Bloomsbury Review* interview:

My predilections for the comic extend to my favorite authors: Rabelais, Cervantes, Stern, Swift, Aristophanes, Zhuangzi (Chuang Tzsu), the Rumi of the *Mathnawi*, and the folk hero Nasrudin. I'm drawn to the holy fools, the cosmic clowns, idiot savants, not just for their boisterous, fun-loving, and at times scathingly sardonic attitudes toward humanity and the bumbling ways of the universe, but because they upset our habitual ways of seeing the world, show us new perspectives by presenting us with the unexpected, and destroy our comfortable expectations and conventional values so we will once again encounter the world in fresh ways, renewed.

It is interesting to note that most of the writers I listed in that quotation speak in parables and extended metaphors.

In the interview with Sward, I talked about one of the ways the preceding statements allowed me to develop a poem. I started by saying that many times I begin a poem by imagining a voice speaking, a particular voice that is talking to me or which I'm overhearing, a voice whose rhythm and tone I let guide the method and structure of what I'm writing. I go on to say that images and metaphors present themselves in my psyche but that their appearances are unplanned and unexpected, and it is my task to pursue their meanings by following their development, which many times consist of grappling with their changes in shape and direction. Along with the notions of pursuing and wrestling with the images, and after reiterating that the poet should never consider such images to be trivial or "accidental," I concluded by describing somewhat fancifully my scenario for writing the poem by comparing my pursuit of the images and metaphors

> ... to riding bareback on a runaway horse, and what I had to do to survive was grab its mane with my hands, grip its flanks with my legs and hold on for dear life as it took me wherever it would. . . . To complicate the matter—and the metaphor—the metaphoric horse I was riding might at any moment change shape under me, as if I were riding not a horse but some shape-shifting, Proteus-like beast on the road to oblivion ... and that the imagination in this case is not so much "imagery" as "imaging," that is, it is not a noun but a transitive verb, an action, an act of becoming, the core of creativity. It propels the images and metaphors out of nothingness into being. So, as I ride the shape-shifting beast, I pronounce (intone?) both its twists and turns and the twists and turns of its route. When the beast finally collapses in exhaustion, I sift through and polish my memories of the ride and from them shape a verbal map from this formerly uncharted landscape, a structure the reader can follow for whatever reason he chooses. And that's the poem.

77

I published many of the new prose pieces in various literary journals during the second half of the nineties. Larry Fixel urged me to send some of the new poems to Peter Johnson, who had just started *The Prose Poem: An International Journal*. Peter, a fine prose poet himself, so appreciated what I was doing that he included my new prose poems in every succeeding issue of the journal, asked me to do a long review of Russell Edson's selected prose poems, *The Tunnel*, wrote an appreciation of my work that appeared in the seventh issue, and made me an advisory editor of the magazine. He also invited me for a three-day visit to Providence College, the university where he taught.

In what seemed quick succession, Hanging Loose Press began printing a number of my prose poems in their magazine and brought out a book of seventy-two of them in 1997 under the title *When People Could Fly*. New Rivers Press included two of my pieces in its definitive anthology of North American prose poetry, *The Party Train*, and one of the editors, Robert Alexander, who, I found out, had included a discussion of *The Armies Encamped* in his PhD thesis years before, asked to do a book of my selected prose poems two years later. That book, which came out with White Pine Press in 2002, is *Moments Without Names*, and includes thirty-five of the pieces from *When People Could Fly* and *Armies*, and sixty-five new prose poems. In 2006, Quale Press printed a volume of seventy new prose poems entitled *Pursuing The Dream Bone*.

Ever since embarking on the prose poem, I have felt like a moth who has risen from its cocoon to find itself a radiant butterfly, although, to tell the truth, I still write as many verse poems as I do prose poems.

CHAD PREVOST

The Power of a Prose Poem and Artistic Expectations

I recently gave a reading at Larry's Bar in Columbus, Ohio, and, having to read for two twenty-minute segments (at a bar no less), I thought I'd open with a few prose poems.

"I don't mean to be offensive, but can I ask you a question?" a man with a Walt Whitmanesque beard asked.

"Sure," I said, bracing myself.

"What is a prose poem?"

I gave my best brief answer, something about subject matter and no line breaks.

"Hard to find the poetry there."

He stated it as a question, but it wasn't. I assured him I wasn't offended, but shortly afterwards, I realized I was a tad deflated that whatever it was he'd experienced, didn't seem to be of the artistry he had hoped for. I thought later of the long and profound tradition of poetry, and how the many practitioners of its variant forms over centuries have established a strongly ingrained "metrical contract" between poet and reader. That is, there is an expectation—even among those who don't read much poetry—about what a poem actually is.

The prose poem simply tries to do what any poem does—only in prose—and that is to convey something memorable, intense or instructive in a short space. I like this definition, at least, because of its simplicity. The prose poem's strengths function very much like those of another hybrid form, the short short (a.k.a. microfiction and sudden fiction). That is, the advantages of the form lie in the brevity— the piece has to get down to the essence of what is most important, and is memorable as a result of the very intensity it produces. The boundaries do, no doubt, blur when one writes a prose poem with a strong narrative. How is it not a short short, especially if the piece is not autobiographical at all? In fact, as a case in point, Sherwood Anderson did write what many have called prose poems, but he always insisted were short fictions. So much for simple definitions.

While I'm muddying the waters, I might as well name a few prose poems that really do seem to blur the lines, but were early inspirations: "The Colonel" by Carolyn Forche, and "A Story About the Body" by Robert Hass. How can one forget the Colonel pouring a bag full of human ears onto a table, dropping one into a glass of water where it began to move, declaring that he was done fooling around and "as for the rights of anyone, tell your people they can go fuck themselves"? Not to mention, this prose poem is every bit as much a *story* as it is a poem. Further, in Hass' "story" how can one forget the young painter who thinks he's in love with an older woman painter until she tells him she's had a double mastectomy, and after he says, "I'm sorry. I don't think I could," she leaves a bowl with rose petals on top, dead bees underneath, on his porch? For that matter, Gary Young's prose poems often do just this: capture an intensely memorable moment in a very short space. One that really stands out in my mind from *Braver Deeds* is the scene in which the father ends up sobbing at the sight of his son's blood as he is in the middle of beating the younger one.

I do very much enjoy and admire the absurd world of Russell Edson, and the tradition of the surreal in the prose poem that is usually traced to Baudelaire and Rimbaud in France in the middle of the ninetenth century. And I do think the prose poem will always lend itself to wild subject matter for the very absence of its lineation. But the hybrid quality of the prose poem also offers opportunities for narrative, associational, descriptive strategies which will surely continue to excite both readers and writers of the form's possibilities. In fact, of the three poems printed here, each does have its own distinct approach. "After Punishment, Baptism" leans toward the narrative strategy with the repeated rhetorical device of "What I remember is…" "Stepping Inside, Mount Tamalpais" is, on the other end of the continuum, intensely lyrical. That is to say, the focus of piece is on images and association gathered together to form a kind of meaning (I'll let a reader decide what that "meaning" may be). "Fever" seems to blend both narrative and lyrical elements.

The truth of the matter is that any innovation in art has been met, at least at first, with scorn, fear and/or rage, because it often goes directly against our preconceived notions of what a given piece of art should be. Reactions to art of any kind that resist definitional category have far more to do with the cultural and aesthetic presuppositions of the audience than with the piece of art itself.

As I look upon the collection of prose poems I'm currently at work on, the most successful have tended to be those that have a comical element, and I usually layer that humor on top of one kind of contemporary cultural reference or another. Really, none of the following three poems do either of these things. Perhaps non-lineated verse (an oxymoron?) also offers an excuse to touch on subjects that one doesn't typically feel freedom to express through the typical/ traditional annals of the genre and its inherited expectations. I love the freedom of the prose poem, intuitive as the experience of writing it may be.

ROBERT SWARD

My Podiatrist Father and the Prose Poem

1. Like most practitioners of the form, I believe it is entirely possible to write prose poetry that has the musical attributes of lineated poetry, as my friend Peter Klappert puts it, and that "much good metrical poetry has a kind of prose rhythm—the rhythm of conversation."

2. Lately I have been working with dramatic monologues, poems inhabited by my deceased podiatrist father and spoken in his voice. In doing so I've discovered or, rather, re-discovered the rhythms of his conversation as, recent immigrant, he expounded on what he—an autodidact—absorbed from his readings, past and present and, of course, what he observed of life in the New World.

3. Leonard Cohen spoke once of how, performing in Paris, he felt himself to be well-received, in part, he said, because the French, understanding his limitations as a singer, still took pleasure in the result and responded favorably to what Cohen referred to as the "struggle in the voice." That is, the struggle of a singer or, indeed, any artist, to cope with limitations, whatever they might be and, at the same time, express subtleties of emotion, a range of passionately held and, at times, contradictory and even absurd ideas, and to do so with some degree of intelligence, wit, presence and musicality.

4. I agree with Gary Young: "Any formal strategy will structure a specific logic, and every form accentuates or encourages a particular mode of thinking . . . Form is merely an architecture necessary to support the ceremony of the poem."

5. I spent two years at the Iowa Writers' Workshop writing syllabics, sonnets, villanelles and free verse. From childhood on, I have taken pleasure in hearing poetry read aloud and, of course, delight in the music of lineated poetry. The prose poem, for me, is another genre, something new in the repertoire of possibilities. I'm a relative latecomer to the form. I'm not married to it, but I am at the moment fascinated and, so to speak, engaged.

6. Many of the poems in the podiatrist father–son sequence were written first in what I felt to be acceptable lineated form. Then, as an experiment, encouraged by Gary Young, Mort Marcus and others, I began composing new work, but also rewriting some of what I felt to be almost okay pieces, poems that I'd classify as near misses.

7. This I did by sounding them aloud, auditioning each word, each line, each phrase, editing as I went along, transcribing the work into prose paragraphs. In doing so, certain poems like "Melancholia," for example, seemed to find their natural form. I also found myself making cuts to remove "padding," unneeded words, lines and phrases. To my surprise, the work became tighter, more, not less, musical and the all-important voice of these poems, the podiatrist father, came through in subtly improved, clearer form.

8. I am not a naturally modest or humble person. However, the prose poem form helps me to back off, keep writer's ego in check, as my father with his wacky metaphysics, lets fly.

9. So it is I discovered "the moral pressure the form exerts." "The prose poem," Gary says, "encourages a particular kind of modesty. It might even at times achieve a certain humility . . ."

10. Humility? I don't know the meaning of the word. Yet here I am, half a century later, listening as I never listened before to that often impatient and demanding man, in effect translating for him, re-casting my perfectly adequate lineated lines into *his* extraordinarily self-involved, albeit conversational, albeit rhythmical, prose. And having to confess it was an improvement on my own.

CHARLES HARPER WEBB

How I Met the Prose Poem, and What Ensued

It was the seventies. In flared pants and angel-wing collar, I was browsing the U of Washington Bookstore, as I recall, wishing I had a book there. One of two things happened next. Either I pulled Russell Edson's *The Intuitive Journey* out of the Poetry section, or a pteranodon dragging a sign—WILL GRONK FOR FOOD— swooshed overhead, and dropped the book into my hands.

This wasn't The Virgin Meets Gabriel; still, it was a revelation. I'd been writing lined poems for several years. I'd even published a few. But I was baffled by the odd poem-stories I scribbled to amuse myself from time to time. These stories used "poetic" metaphor and imagery; but they didn't fit comfortably into poetic lines, and were too short to be short stories. They also tended to be funny (to me, at least), and very strange. One featured an animal with the face of a proboscis monkey and the body of a sea cucumber. Another concerned an air mattress that yearned to be a set of pan-pipes.

Writing these poem-stories was fun; but like cave-painting, there seemed to be no future in it. Now I saw that I'd been trying to invent the prose poem. Edson's book saved me the trouble. It also gave me models of excellence in the form, and from the credits, a list of magazines that might publish my attempts.

My next discovery—delivered by a man made entirely of Swedish meatballs, if memory serves—was Michael Benedikt's *Night Cries.* Seattle's nature poets and Roethke-worshippers had tended to find my work amusing, but not serious enough for real Poetry. For my part, I found their poems, and much poetry of that time, to be pompous, sappy, self-righteous, and hyper-serious. Many poets not only wore their sensitivity on their sleeves; they tattooed it on their foreheads and combed their hair back so everyone would see.

Imagine my delight to find a section of *Night Cries* called "Insensitive Poems."

Prose poems allowed me to indulge—and exploit—parts of my psyche that had felt off-limits to "regular" poems. It was as if several cylinders that normally froze when I sat down to write had broken free. My writing gained in horsepower, if not respectability. Prose poems exploded the over-formality and self-importance that I had found (and still find) laughable in poetry. I enjoy good line-breaks as much as the next guy, but to call a line-break "daring," "thrilling," or even "exciting" seems on a par with calling a well-made business card "orgasmic."

The possibilities that the prose poem opened for me, though, *were* exciting. And continue to be. Prose poems give me unlimited license to be imaginative, outrageous, surreal, obscene, politically incorrect, satirical, silly, seditious, scathing, and even sensitive, while being at the same time (I hope) smart, insightful, and emotionally true. Prose poems allow me to float lightly over sentimental reefs that would sink more formal poems.

Prose poems today range from little poem-stories to post-modern clumps of unlined, non-sequential sentences. L*A*N*G*U*A*G*E poets write L*A*N*G*U*A*G*E prose poems. Prose poems can be pure lyrics or solemn meditations. Yet prose poems lend themselves especially well to wit and humor. The form itself is humorous: an oxymoron; the duck-billed platypus of poetry. And humor is a device ideally suited to depict the absurdities, enormities, and pathos of contemporary life. Eliot said that to capture the complexities of modern times, poetry had to be difficult. I say it has to be, at least sometimes, funny.

Writing prose poems has lowered my inhibitions when writing lined poems. The result is that I write fewer prose poems. Subject matter and attitudes which once would have screamed "Prose Poem!" are, today, as likely to give rise to lines. I often try my poems in both lines and prose, moving back and forth until I find what the poem seems to need. Even if not orgasmic, good line breaks can add to the impact of a poem. If they add to mine, I use them.

Still, a prose poem can be paced effectively with punctuation. Sound, rhythm, and internal rhyme can be mobilized as easily as in lined verse. And there is a casualness to prose poetry which recommends itself to me as writer, and to readers—even the poetry-phobes. If a poem of mine is narrative, wildly imaginative, uses dialogue, and—above all—seems to read more naturally and easily in prose, into prose it goes.

To write even the most informal lined poem always feels to me a bit like dressing up. That's great. I like to wear nice pants and shirts, well-fitting jackets, well-made shoes, even occasionally a tux. But I still love to slip on a T-shirt, old sneakers, broken-in blue jeans, and to invite something strange—a computer named Bladdo, a self-dismembering guitarist, a woolly mammoth caught on a dry fly—to come and do what I think prose poems do best, which is (like any good musician) to play.

AL YOUNG

To Express What Utterly Needs to Be Told:
Reflections on Prose Poetry

In industrialized, colony-dependent nineteenth-century Europe, writers in France and elsewhere rebelled against poetry's traditional forms. French writers in particular began to kiss goodbye the grave, structurally demanding Alexandrine line. Rebels like Charles Baudelaire, Stéphane Mallarmé, and Paul Verlaine's *enfant terrible* lover Arthur Rimbaud rode not so much roughshod as shoeless over received structures. The idea was this: Uptight, cruelly restricted line measures and rhyme schemes could neither contain nor express the invasive, border-bashing realities of what has come to be called the modern era.

Prose poetry, though, even by the 1800s, was hardly new. Conversational and vernacular speech quiver with key-shifts and rhythm. Some of this came down to the Mississippi-born, seven-year-old me who sat in the Baptist church and listened to preachers whose score was the King James Bible. Music always came with the sermons, and the dancing that sometimes broke out. *God's Trombones*, the great James Weldon Johnson poem based on Negro sermonizing captures, as much as anyone can capture in text, the flavor and force of such prose-poetizing. Baudelaire's *Flowers of Evil*, Rimbaud's *A Season in Hell*, Walt Whitman's *Leaves of Grass*, Jean Follain's *A World Rich in Anniversaries*, Karl Shapiro's *The Bourgeois Poet*, Bob Kaufman's *Abomunist Manifesto*, LeRoi Jones's *The System of Dante's Hell*, Michael Benedikt's *Sky*, Xam Wilson Cartiér's *Be-Bop, Re-Bop*, Charles Simic's *The World Doesn't End* — all the vibrant varieties of prose poetry these works contain bust loose in ancient texts of every kind. *Bhagavad-Gita*, *The Iliad*, *The Song of Solomon*, *The Book of a Thousand Nights and a Night*, *The Pillow Book of Sei Shonagon* are tip-of-the-tongue examples.

For me the prose poem became a fun form to work in way back in the middle of the twentieth century, when I first began to try my hand at writing seriously. Reading widely, listening to music, paying close attention to painting and all the other art the city of Detroit offered (and then as now Detroit was art-driven), I realized that borders were drawn to be crossed. When Terry Gross, host of

National Public Radio's *Fresh Air*, asked drummer Elvin Jones if he ever got flustered when he was playing with John Coltrane and Trane's music turned abstract, Elvin said no. "I'm from Detroit," he explained, adding that he used to go to the Detroit Institute of Arts and look at all the Picasso, Matisse and Dalí on display. *"Abstract,"* he laughed, "that's no big thing, Terry. I can do abstract." I have always believed that the deepest, most moving poetry rarely gets set down on paper. But since we aren't privy to what those unknown to us utter to one another privately in ecstasy or out of joyfulness, anger, frustration, or in sadness, grief or heat, we have to settle for poetry that gets written, published, packaged and distributed. Speaking is natural; writing is not. Prose and poetry will forever combine and re-combine to express what utterly needs to be told.

GARY YOUNG

The Unbroken Line

I remember picking up the Kayak edition of Robert Bly's book of prose poems *The Morning Glory* when it was first published in 1969. I was moved by the simplicity of the poems, their clarity, economy and lyricism. I liked the way they sat on the page. I was an undergraduate at the time and hardly well-read, but these were not the first prose poems I'd come across. I couldn't imagine that the short prose vignettes punctuating Hemingway's *In Our Time* were stories—I assumed they were poems, and still do. Anne Bradstreet's *Meditations Divine and Morall*, Walt Whitman's *Specimen Days in America,* and of course my Peter Pauper Press edition of *The Jade Flute: Chinese Poems in Prose* led me to believe, naively it turned out, that the prose poem was a common and an accepted poetic form. Looking back, there was a genuine blissfulness to my ignorance.

In college I was introduced to the work of Francis Ponge, Jorge Luis Borges, Charles Baudelaire and Arthur Rimbaud. I fell in love with Russell Edson's quirky fables, and I read the prose poems in Charles Wright's *The Grave of the Right Hand* and James Wright's *Moments of the Italian Summer* with admiration and delight. I considered the prose poem only one of any number of free verse forms available to poets, and I recognized the prose poem's value as such. When I published my first book, *Hands,* in 1979, a single, long prose poem served as a fulcrum for the short free verse lyrics that dominated the rest of the book. There were no prose poems in my second collection, *The Dream of a Moral Life,* but while I was working on that book I was being drawn inexorably to the form, although I was unaware of it at the time.

I was experimenting with longer lines and longer rhythms, trying to write a poem of "equivalence" as I put it to myself. I wanted to negate hierarchy in my poems. I wanted to write poems with as little artifice as possible, poems that began and ended on the same rhetorical plane. I was fortunate that my work as a fine printer provided a confluence of this theoretical concept with its physical articulation on the page. I was printing an artist's book, *The Geography of Home,* a volume of relief prints stitched together with a single line

89

of prose that ran for nearly a hundred pages. This long typographic line served as a kind of thread upon which the many woodcuts and other illustrations in the book were strung. I found myself seduced by a form that literally embodied the semantic landscape I was attempting to inhabit. More importantly, it mirrored what I wanted from my poetry: a horizontal rather than a vertical structure, a poem that one might walk along rather than fall through. My subsequent book, *Days*, was composed entirely of brief prose poems, but in execution and conception I considered them to be very long one-lined poems. Despite variations in length, I still conceive of my poems as meaningful utterances playing out upon a horizontal field, and my poems continue to adhere to this form. My use of the prose poem is not based on any philosophic projection; it is a rather a matter of enthusiasm and practicality.

The prose poem's democratic itinerary, its horizontal rather than vertical trajectory, engenders a resistance to hierarchy and to inflation. Its fundamental nakedness may offer solace, but within a block of prose there's no place to hide. Karl Shapiro put it well in a poem from *The Bourgeois Poet*: "This is a paragraph. A paragraph is a sonnet in prose. A paragraph begins where it ends. A paragraph may contain a single word or cruise for pages ..." It is this suppleness combined with a certain brazenness that keeps me working in the form.

Although my last four books are comprised entirely of prose poems, I don't think of myself as a 'prose poet', and I have become increasingly uncomfortable with the term. Language poet, Confessional poet, New Formalist, prose poet—I see little benefit to this Balkanization of the art. It's true that I am a poet who writes "prose poems," but like most terms employed to describe some aspect of aesthetics, the label is convenient, but inaccurate, limiting and doctrinaire. I am poet, a lyric poet, and my fundamental project, like that of most lyric poets, is to stop time. Among its many virtues, the prose poem allows me to write lyrical narratives that hold within their knot of language a world, a whole story. Some poets exploit the prose poem for different reasons, and other poets will find nothing of use there. In any case, the poem will find a way, with lines or without, and whatever form is most conducive to the poet is the one that he or she should take advantage of.

90

Robert Frost once famously said that writing poems without meter and rhyme was like playing tennis without a net. One wonders what he'd have said about poems that have abandoned the line as well. With the prose poem you don't need a net; you don't even need a court. You just hit the ball as far as you can, and follow wherever it goes.

Poems

TONY BARNSTONE

Parable of the Cracked Man

The homeless man in Starbuck's is speaking fiercely to himself in a woofer-without-tweeter voice, an incoherent bass wave that startles students from Berkeley who've come with fold-up wooden book holders to cram for exams in the pleasant wash of talk and roasted reek of coffee, milk-steam, chocolate dust. They sure didn't expect this growling bass-guitar of addled humanity staring avuncularly into the middle air where the Devil is supposed to dwell, Prince of Air and pride and lies, man of a thousand faces, the Lon Chaney of the Medieval theater; they sure didn't expect the black tobacco and nightsweat and shit and poverty and pure crazy street living blended into this foul and strangely sweet reek, exotic as rotting tamarinds; and so the blond woman studying law rolls her eyes dramatically toward the door and her Asian boyfriend slams his textbook shut with a gunshot *crack*, and they edge carefully between the window and the back of his woolen army coat, leaving him at the long wooden table drawing angles and loops and equations on a scattering of blue lined sheets. I note his blue ballpoint, crabbed notes on the notebook pages spread before him, coded spirals and points of intersection, the fractured math, froth of steamed milk on his stiff bearded chin, and see he is here to study too, that the dead eyes fixated on nothing are not disconnected from the sea roar of the voice and the blotched body hunched within the army jacket. What microscopic fright would the biologist have to see in his tiny glass; what depth would the lawyer have to fall to in his Ray-Bans and Italian shoes; what sort of test would you have to bomb to end up this damaged, this foul, mumbling and staring at some geometry of horror while the mouth articulates basso profundo that freeway rumble, that music of disaster, ocean waves bursting and pulling the world under?

Parable of the Burning House

—for Maxine Hong Kingston

We could have burned to death in our sleep, my roommate says, then brightly asks will I drive her out to see the flames at the edge of town bounding through grass and up eucalyptus trees, each tree a torch that lights the next so it relays itself across the landscape into the hills above our house, a river of black smoke roiling overhead, splitting the sky into blue halves. We drive to the park, where a little crowd watches blazes lope through the valley then leap the freeway towards us like yellow lions. I am still in my head, thinking of Heraclitus, the fire philosopher, who says all things are made of fire and will change back into fire, but when a light voice asks, *Mommy, is our house going to burn down again?* and a heat-blast prickles our cheeks I shout *Let's get out of here* and we ricochet to the car in cartoonish fear.

Oh, it's easy to talk about the baptism of fire, about the forge of the spirit, the purifying flame, but when the sun is a bloodshot planet in the smoke and the sky fills with orange nebulae, people watching on porches start to run. When we get home, my roommate packs and flees but I'm on the roof with the garden hose watering the house down as fire spills downhill into the graveyard across the street, the trees like brushes painting the sky red above the sleeping dead. I'm gauging how much time I have before I must run, too, when the wind shifts and I stand on the roof with the limp hose, watching, guilty, relieved, as other peoples' houses burn.

Here is a woman riding out of the hills on the handlebars of a young man's bicycle while her house flames behind. *Wait,* she says, *my novel is in the house.* It is ten years' work, no other copies, but the young man doesn't understand. *Don't worry,* he says, *it's only things.* California is burning and it makes the eye burn, the nose burn, the tongue burn, and as the matter of the world goes up it makes the mind burn as well, since all things of the world are on fire, with the fire of lust, fire of suffering, fire of attachment. But it isn't easy to be a Buddha and let go of the world that houses our things, the mind that houses the world, of the women who loved me for a while, of even these words for which I've had such hopes. It isn't easy at all, and even if it were, what would be the point of being that free, of standing alone when the fires die, like this bathtub on claw feet in black stubble, this field of chimneys without houses?

Parable of Aladdin in Oakland

"Would you mind minding my store?" asks the Persian woman in Piedmont Lighting, and she's out the door in a breath leaving me alone with giant lilies that bend brushed steel necks long and tapered as a swan's over a desk. I duck my head not to catch my hair in the solar system dangling from the ceiling, blueberry and custard planets, the halogen dwarfs and incandescent giants, and soak in the brilliant milk of this paradise of lamps. Here a standing lamp lifts its burnished face, and here a reading light concentrates on a book, and other shining eyes bathe me with such gentle attention I feel the bulbs of my eyes bloom light, as if someone has flicked a switch and made everything I see shimmer bright, releasing all the genies with a single *let there be light.*

I worry where the owner is, if she's all right walking alone, looking Persian on the street, in these days after the Twin Towers went up in flames and then came down, since people need someone to carry their blame. These days it's hard not to worry when it will all give out, our president trying to stop fire with flame, the oil in our tanks turning to cancer in our brains, the weapons waiting underground in silos to give off their great light and send the planet spinning through space like a dead bulb towards a trash can. I think of all the lamps in this marvelous altar, each one a luminous tongue giving out a shout of praise, and wonder if the world will end in fire. From what I've seen I'd say it's just as like to end like this, with a finger flipping a switch.

September, 2001

Slowly, Slowly, Honking a Lot

Screaming into his beard behind the glass, the man in the SUV next to me bashes fists against the leather wheel, but the traffic has the ancient indifference of the universe, which carries on its ordinary chaos with no theory, intelligence, or design, and I think of it as slowly forever rippling away from some original big blast like the wall of molasses that rolled through Boston in 1919 when the great tank burst, cooking and drowning the people in the street or sweeping them into the Bay. It killed them with the machine calm of the Terminator crushing a rose beneath his boot. On display in my own glass case, tapping fingers, I strive for that kind of Zen patience, like a mindless cloud carried on a wind, like that old haiku: Climb Mt. Fuji, O snail, slowly, slowly.

Whatever speed we go, the past keeps passing into the past, though years ago when I was married and saw the years opening before me like rooms in a pleasure palace, I used to corkscrew through traffic, helmetless on my motorcycle and savage with speed while people at a dead stop watched from their stalled cars, and maybe that's why when we rented a dune buggy on the island of Naxos and drove eroded roads to see the colossal kouros lying on its back in a garden hung with jasmine and hibiscus, the woman behind the counter sized me up and told me in thick English, "Go slowly, slowly, honking a lot."

Now around me the motorcycles weave free while I slowly nose towards the source of trouble, black smoke flung into sky like crows fleeing a burning barn while below flames fly forty feet high from a blazing truck canted on its side. Slowly, slowly, we pass it by, each of us taking our turn to study what could have happened to us on the road, and some of us are happy enough that the big burn is still around some other turn, while others scream behind glass, honking a lot, then hit the gas and swerve off to spit gravel on the shoulder and speed away from it, as fast as fast.

FOR MOST OF MY LIFE, I have been fascinated by world literature texts that exist on the hyphen between prose and poetry, religious text and literary text. I have been a fan from childhood of the prose poems or prose parables of Jorge Luis Borges and Julio Cortázar. I enjoyed the way that they blended scholarship and literature, philosophy and the fantastic, and I have often sought to find a way to achieve such effects in my poetry. In recent years, I have found that the prose poem format is more hospitable to such blending of genre. I also love the way that so many Japanese texts, such as the military epic Tale of the

Heike, are composed according to the basic 5-7-5 syllabics of waka (poems), and yet shift into prose and into musical chant. I love the haibun, in which a prose passage is followed by or internally punctuated with haikus. I love the zuihitsu, or "random jottings," of Kenko and Sei Shonagon, in which parables and stories blend with diary and reflection. I love the Buddhist parables of Japan, China and India, and the poem-studded nested story cycles of the *Panchatantra* and of *King Vikram and the Vampire,* which gave rise to Aesop's fables and to *The Thousand and One Nights.* I love the great Chinese erotic and martial arts novels, in which moments of climax are lyrically expressed in poetry. And so, in my own poetry, I find myself writing a wild variety of sutras, chants, hymns, codices, parables, testaments, and apocalypses. Some of these are lineated poems, and some are in prose poem form, and in some cases I go back and forth between the two, taking out line breaks and putting them back in again, looking at the piece from every angle, trying to see what sort of animal I have created. I don't consider it a betrayal of the prose poem to lineate it, or a betrayal of the lineated poem to publish it as a prose poem. Rather, I see all my work as shifting back and forth across the hyphen, from magical to mundane, from lyrical to narrative, and like the great writers of Asia I am happy to exist in this realm of hybridity, in which the beast has the hindquarters of a hippopotamus, the claws of a lion, and the head of a deer.

POLLY BEE

140 Crandon Avenue & Other Points of Interest

The house shrank in the time between when I was a kid and grew into a grandma, but my son says it's important now to show his son where I grew up, so here we are in Niles, Ohio (a crumby place then and still) standing in front of the home of my youth which I've deliberately avoided for 60 some years, and to my surprise find I'm glad to see the old place upright—shabby & shrunk for sure, but plumb with a defiant elegance in spite of neglect and the For Sale sign in the yard . . . just like mother would become when dad took off and I was 9 . . . but before that event there were laughs and belly-flops on sleds in snow, and summer nights playing kick-the-can under streetlights with Bobo, Peeky and Imogene Van Wye, their homesteads still there on Crandon Avenue as we drive by in search of the haunted house, cemetery next door, where mom and we five kids lived after the divorce and gloryhallelujah the damn place has disappeared—poof! but the cemetery stretches far beyond the rock walls wherein I learned how to drive, stick-shift and brake on narrow roads between the graves that I've been told now hold my mother and my dad, but no map or directory to tell us where, so we look for them, grandson John and I casually zig-zagging up the hill on one side . . . **hey, kid, you're 9 and I turn 81 today!** . . . while his parents diligently search the other side, and the sun is bright, the air crisp, the leaves brilliant orange, red . . . **autumn always was my favorite time of year** . . . and we never find my folks . . . **ok, my goodbyes said years ago anyway, to mom with gratitude/respect, to dad with win-a-few/lose-a-few attitude** . . . but in our quest we do discover a rabbit, preying mantis, cement dog guarding a grave, an 18-wheeler truck carved on a marble slab and an Italian poem etched on stones—Giacomo, Comoletto, Lupino, Petrucello . . . **my dead Jane a Cazavela, Flora her middle name . . .**

On Losing A Horse & A Friend
& A Poem That Went Its Own Way

I promise Stellasue, a woman met at poets' retreat, if she comes to my house we will look into a horse's eyes to rid her of her fear of them like she saw an actor do in a picture show but I have no horse now, just an artificial hip and a surgeon who says not a good idea to ride anymore, so I worry about where can I find a horse with the right kind of eyes, my ex-husband had several but he died, so can't go there instead I'll go where I used to be with my horses and one day ride up into the hills on a mare no one can ride but me because I know about her mouth, how she needs to be coaxed gentle with feather touch, *I just know how she is* & mount her alone, no one to restrain as the boys who try to ride her do, guys on each side hanging on to that mare with all their strength, instead when no one is around I quietly walk up to her ignore those dark suspicious angry eyes & when she moves away, coo sweet low to her, gather the reins, let them dangle loose on the bit, let her circle around no attempt to make her stand, obey, just let her tell me when it's ok to put one foot in stirrup, ease other leg astride, feel her respond to pressure of my seat, thighs, *we get along that mare & me*, even one day when way up in mountains I dismount to let her breathe after long push to the top then attempt to get on again, she still full of high from the climb not willing to submit, me not willing to wait and when I almost am aboard she runs backwards, blindly, takes us nearly over precipice but I get her turned, ride her home with belly full of fear *that mare can kill me & I do not wish to die* just want to love her more than any horse on earth, and one day watch her birth a foal, nicker, nuzzle it & bleed & stagger to her feet, stand up & bleed & drop down to her knees & bleed & lie down & bleed & die & her eyes, oh her eyes & Joan, on the morning of your last day alive I visit you in a hospital bed in your own room at home where you want to be your love at your side & the therapist & the nurse & others who try to prop you up, make you do things you don't want to do & you too tired to oblige and for brief moment our eyes meet, yours dark bewildered, a bit bemused that ask without a word *Why?* & I keep seeing your eyes, oh your eyes

The Psychologist

My empty house bulges full with wilted blankets, tired chairs, crumpled papers; their heavy weight crushes me, no friggin' place to sit where warm and safe, no mate to touch and bid me dance away the bad blues holidays—a season I've tiptoed through each year since Jane died, covered my eyes, counted my blessings and all that shit, but this time I'm damn near paralyzed, sunk into an abyss of alone . . . *gotta get the hell outta here before the muck comes up, sucks every last breath out of me like it did my brother and a couple of friends recently* . . . but, croakin' ain't in my plans yet, and my kids have been notified there'll be little left when I do & for some time now I've been eyein' a different RV, one with a real bed for me and the pups and a bunk for who-knows-who-or-what, so, I head for the RV store, trade the old rig in for a bitty bit bigger one—*god J love the way she handles barrelin' down the freeway and damned if J don't feel better*—so, stop to pick up wine, chicken-off-the-grill, cranberries, coffee, thick-crust bread, then swing by the house, throw in the dogs, head for the lake where we rent a space, hook everything up *how in the hell does that work?* never do get the TV goin' but the radio, oh the radio and all that glorious music on classical KUSC just about blows the sides out of that new RV & I wallow in the sound, taste it, roll it in my fingers—dig under double down comforters with those radiant hounds & glory be to whatever, whatta Christmas eve—temps at 40 degrees but our fluffy cave cozy, big windows on two sides so we see the stars and sky and early morning watch ducks paddle across the lake, a great white heron fly & remember Jane, that day in dying when momentarily she awakes, looks at me and says *Jt always was about control, wasn't it?*

PROSE POETRY FOR ME is a runaway horse which I ride scared to death wherever the hell it goes, one long sentence on one 8.5 x 11 page, uninterrupted energy from beginn ing to end. I'm exhausted when I get off. It began unbidden, after I'd written a lotta stuff stripped of "a, an & the," lineal form, staccato beat, get-to-the point, no embellishment & then I wanted to write about a horse I loved and my brain took off, wrote the damn thing as a prose poem. Been hooked ever since. Used to be a reporter & love a good story. Prose poetry lets me be reporter-poet.

LAUREL ANN BOGEN

Visibility Report

You cannot gaze into the divisions of a heart or the pulse that separates this world from the next, but I have seen the eyes of others drawn into themselves, a face pinched shut; in the half-light even need itself is obscured. Come closer—I am slate. Who will scratch their name on the empty stone with a penknife or erase its ridges from the template? The unopened gift is still a gift. It is given like a forecast or traffic report—background to common cash and carry or extraordinary good fortune. There's a high pressure front ahead: A hand is offered.

Take it.

The Virginia Woolf Guide To Rock Collecting

Small hard pebbles can be as effective as rough boulders. They may lodge unobtrusively in kidneys and gall bladders. If deemed necessary, their growth may be accelerated through gastric intake.

He sat in the alley behind the house in Santa Monica where he lived with his parents. Birds screamed in his ears. A striped yellow cat rubbed his leg hungrily. It growled deep and throaty. The boy found a stone in his hand. He judged it to be of the right dimension and weight as he smashed it again as he smashed it again as he smashed it again on the yellow cat's head.

She said that it was too hard. He had left her heart jagged and cleft like a stone artifact. She was rock and he had made her cold. He had made her cold.

Virginia Woolf stooped pearl grey and dun against the sea. She gathered stone children to her breasts. She tucked them in pockets like secrets. Face like slate, she straightened and walked into the waves.

Pigmy Headhunters and Killer Apes, My Lover and Me

Pigmy headhunters and killer apes play basketball at the Y. The killer apes win but the pigmy headhunters are not sore losers. They take the basketball home and boil in your cast iron pot.

Hair. Lots of hair. Hairy devils those pigmy headhunters and killer apes. Vidal Sassoon chewed on this dilemma for awhile.

Pigmy headhunters and killer apes had flannel cakes at Musso and Franks. They were very hungry and ate three helpings each. But they wondered about the flesh beneath my flannel.

Pigmy headhunters and killer apes were homesick for Africa. They watched Make Mine Maltomeal on TV. They especially liked the part where John saved the world with gruel. It reminded everyone of home and they all had a good cry.

A cup of coffee is an honest thing. More honest than I am now. Its velocity in my veins throbs with need. I need to tell you this. You make my head hurt like sutures. You make this silly fist a killer.

Bone, hair, water, food. It is morning again. Last night the jungle used my fractured jaws to spear a message. Pigmy headhunters dance while killer apes beat their chest forget about you forget about you forget about you.

THE THREE PROSE POEMS chosen for this anthology were written over a period of twenty years. Something about the unorthodox nature of prose-poetry inflamed me as a young poet. In the early eighties I read a "slim volume" of prose poems by Margaret Atwood, *Murder in the Dark,* which fit nicely with my predilection towards experimental/literary writers such as Richard Brautigan, John Yau, Lydia Davis and Diane Williams. I believe I chose this particular form to express my outlaw/outsider point of view because the form mirrored the content. The form—No Boundaries or Rules. Content—Personal Struggle with Mental Illness.

NADYA BROWN

*She Reads the Classifieds
in an Alternative Health Magazine*

So here were the "inspirational" stories. "The Green Stuff, Super Blue-Green Algae" by Pearl. "A Vessel Waiting to be Filled" by the Avatar Master. With this she could get a holiday gift package—buy one, get one free! "The Love Temple," by Lumina, where she could mingle with beautiful, healing love goddesses, ecstatic temple priestesses dancing, and full moon drumming. And here's "Experience the Wonders!" by Charles. Well, he looked jolly enough in his photo, with his blue suspenders, his moustache and Real Estate teeth. What about "Awaken Womyn"—women, spelled with a "y" by Seradwyn, spelled with a "y." She could get this in beautiful and peaceful . . . where? West L.A.? west, convenient L.A.? Forget this one. Convenient always meant next to a freeway.

There was also "Inside Job." This sounded a bit more promising—particularly if it was coupled with "Acupuncture Face-Lifts." Maybe an inside-job and a facelift would get the job done. Hmm . . . with a name like Ricardo Miranda, one could hardly lose could one? Then there was "Awaken and Experience Your Intuitive Self Through Intuition." Well this sounded a bit redundant, didn't it? How *was* she supposed to develop her intuition—by putting silver cones on her ears? Exotic seaweed wraps from France folded and pearl-colored between her peach-colored upper thighs, bonding, veneering, crowning, bridging, in Sexual Herbal 99, Sinus Herbal 98, Skin Herbal 97 on her most delicate parts, pulling out mucoid layers in lengths of 2 inches, 2 feet, eliminating as much as 10 to 30 lbs of toxic waste and parasites, while learning how to project her voice, her art work, her sexual fantasies onto a wall in a rose pink building, mid-block, 5 streets west of Fairfax on the south side, under the rising sun logo—the one with the warm, safe environment with a blue carpet and a piano player?

Maybe if she went to that 40-acre semi-wilderness site at the foot of the majestic Los Padres Mountains where she could sweat it out with Flocco's Food, Hand & Ear Method—Flocco, Spocko?

Get some Extra Terrestrial Abduction counseling while she was at it. Yes, sweat out all those E.T.s by using illuminated pathways leading to private hermitages and sweat lodges dangling from purple ropes that were dotted throughout the forest. *But wait!* There was always the Growing Edge of Abalone Gulch. Ordinary time would dissolve, and poised on a cliff overlooking the Pacific, she could sit cross-legged, her blue hair fanned out, electrically charged, singing the body electric, emitting electrons, and sulfurous light, left, right, and center by swallowing electrical cell food—and concentrating on the arts of the burning bowl, discover the energy in her toenails, in the wind and the water, and how to arrange the furniture.

Did she want powerful fun, fast ways of making changes, safe self-hypnosis and fear-free flying using dreams, soul reading, new juggling with Robert, understanding that her teeth were connected to all parts of her body and that 100% of universal philosophy and wisdom of the ages could be taught in a five-day inner-bonding journey, involving a step-by-step Karmic trip by Commander August Starr, (legal for the first time in California)? She had to admit that coming and meditating with Mark and Hard Light with kundalini in his wake, sounded more—what—awakening? Plus, for the rare opportunity of this thunderous awakening, she could get a light meal included. All she had to decide was which Sanctuary of Revelations to choose ... the one on a remote mountainside in Bakersfield, or perhaps the retreat in the desert, where there is one of the only three Earthgates in the United States, two energy vortexes, Frank Lloyd Wright architecture, and some of the freshest air on the planet?

This information was strictly confidential and came with a code number, useful if she went into Real Estate too. This way she could remove interferences, like a misplaced rug, and a cat litter that was too high profile in the hallway, and dark entities, possessions and attacks. All this could be facilitated by wearing a black hat. Luckily, she had several black hats, including a beret she had bought in Paris, so this was OK. So, if she presented her blue shield, which was a sure sign that she was ready to be healed, she could gain all the insights of furniture arrangement, best prosperity abundance, big consumer extravagance, (ooh, yes, and time for lunch and little shopping)

106

and lonely pillow problems. So, for four office visits to Bruce for $95.00—you are saving $135 here, an offer which expires at the end of the month, (he wasn't giving her much time, was he)—she could work with Sukhari, Fire Star, Dr. Yoo Hoo, Bob Merrill, and Linda-Loo, Dan with his palm tree, Victoria Loveland, lovely Allan of the Miracles, and have conversations with God....

She Reads the Personal Ads in The Berkeley Barb

So, who to choose? She should pass on the large vegetarian, the one looking for Pocahontas, and the joyful, love and sunrise, philosophical hiker retired, 54 like her, and who had all his own teeth and hair. Well that was a blessing! Here's one who's at home in his tuxedo on a horse, whose motto is, "The essence of the Indigo plant is bluer than the plant itself," and who's in pretty good shape as he has already had his mid-life crisis.

On the other hand, a Gentle Straight Tiger, who is actually a young older man, a gentle Teuton, cultured perfect in every way of course, but who likes—what?—fireplaces? No, he's new to the area and pretending to look for financially secure Jewish ladies with brown spell-binding eyes. No, she didn't want any winter specials, huggable Grizzly-Adams types, down-to-earth knights without their armor looking for hidden treasure in the candle light while on the cusp of time-travel....

Then a Wild One, a Christian rock-n-roller, seeking a Titanic love affair, lonely with just his teddy bear in Lompoc, who likes to argue about the nature of the universe, with a bang and not a sizzle. A Sophisticated Dirty Old Man who says, "Fax me darling." Well, that's not curious and witty. An armchair adventurer looking for a little laid-back hootchie-cootchie. But, she wasn't a vampire waiting for the next millennium or for a gathering of Divine Humans who were going to interpret the Bible while taking sexy photos, that were very discreet indeed, that would make her feel sensuous and glamorous all over again, so that she could connect with that part of herself she needed for her soul-mate. That part of her that was still sunken as in a secluded patio, bubbling like quick silver, a renaissance woman, cerebral, arcane, nocturnal, who loved cats and Wolf role-playing. That side of her, the Nordic Lady, the Sleeping Beauty, who was waiting for sparks to fly on extended Viva Gorditas Pacific Adventures, while wearing high heels and a mini skirt, over her wily, willowy, and winsome moon-colored body—who was sincere, creative, fun-loving, intelligent, had no tattoos, wanted to be spoiled rotten on the beach in the sunset with her orchids and champagne, and her "Romeo, Romeo" who was genuinely aware and creative, and walking warmly, brightly, and with briskness and integrity towards her at the Karaoke bar.

So here she was, ready for Dancing Martini Madness, some midnight fishing under the sign of Sagittarius, life in the fast lane, on a Harley, in a canoe, no, not the ballroom, more like the simple pleasures of the surf and stars so she could settle down with—who? —Harley-bad-boy, a single fireman, a passionate ophthalmologist, outdoorsy, attractive, artistic Republicans who'd had the famous two-thumbs-up Scottsdale transplant now only available in Dubai, or an Asian navy pilot who would guide her to health, wealth, and an elegant home with a sumptuous garden and a pathway that led to a romantic situation comedy that included images from the Hubble Telescope, and water foul at sunrise. Are we clicking or clacking? I don't believe in love at first sight, but is there anyone out there? If so, call me, call me anytime.

Rituals

So what was she doing on the edge of the Pacific? Was she going to pile more small flowers from her walks around her small, grey-speckled, stone Buddha crouching serenely in the middle of her large white platter? Or, would she place her hollow bronze pyramid in the dark space below her bed so that it could glow dully in the dust—the one that had the brick pattern engraved on the outside edges, gouged by a dark hand after the bronze had cooled? She could imagine the molten orange metal being poured into the mold, the brown wax melting away in the heat, to somewhere, in a foundry just outside Heliopolis?

Would she continue to shuttle up and down 101 between Santa Barbara and San Luis Obispo looking on the cliffs for a white gazebo casting a long shadow in the sunset, on the grass; a stone house with a steep blue slate roof, radiating and reflecting the ambers and golds from its mullioned bay windows; a small windmill idling up there behind a dark, spreading umbrella pine; a good place to crouch in the long dry grass and throw yellow roses into the foam that ebbed and flowed quietly at the base of the cliff, between there and the island?

She remembered that winter, parking her car up there next to the fence posts, armed with a T.J.s baguette, a carton of hummus and a can supposedly filled with the very essence of mangoes and guavas. She opened her window and he appeared from nowhere, his eyes focused on her as he tipped his head sideways, listening to the small sounds of the bread breaking, barely audible below the tumult of waves. His gaze rested on her fingers. His large golden feet gripped the top of the fence—his grey, black, and white feathers rising against the wind, his beak with a scarlet splash from red and glistening entrails. He was waiting patiently while she thought about the food chain, stared back at the bird, and closed the window. "I am not dead yet" she said through the glass. He flew off, and she picnicked alone.

A FEW YEARS AGO, I took up a project of filling several large journals with dream imagery, images from childhood, and images from my everyday life. I wrote prose journal entries with almost every image. Going back through the entries, I found that in most cases, the writings were prose poems, working in those longer sentence rhythms, and on the associative level that all poems work.

CHRISTOPHER BUCKLEY
Dispatch from Santa Barbara, 2001

Mid-summer, July Fourth in fact, but I'm not in town for the fireworks display from the breakwater. I'm here on errands, an emergency trip to the dentist, in and out before they crowd East Beach, Ledbetter, and the harbor, packing in on the sand thick as grunion under a phosphorescent moon.

I have an hour before I have to be somewhere, and I stop in Alameda Park where my mother first brought me as a child. There was a pool of shade under some trees and no swans drifting a little lake, no roses, no hedges in the shape of a heart—precious little except the wood bandstand that even then was no longer in use. Little but that block of shade—Anacapa to Santa Barbara Street, Micheltorena to Sola—courtesy of Morton Bay Figs and Spanish palms, and the creamy, book-perfect, fair-weather clouds of the '50s going over the Figueroa range—since age 4, the clouds and trees carrying off my thoughts....

And today I think of Thomas Wolfe, the sad line anyone knows about home. He knew about time, the quick dusty path here below the clouds. Perhaps he knew what was coming with real estate on the California Coast, way back when everyone lived in bungalows.... Now, making more money than I ever imagined, I am nonetheless dispossessed, can only afford to live an hour north in the wind and fog. I stand here, my feet on a sidewalk worn rough as beach sand, pavement I've walked off and on for 50 years, looking up to the blue or to the old clear stars, and it's hard to call it mine.

My work is 3 hours south of here, and so I'm driven in all senses, past what I love. This morning, I'm taking time off from the world to be in it, to turn back—in star time—an instant, to 50 years ago when my mother took me after a nap out to the free, green republic of the park, from our turquoise stucco apartment on Micheltorena. We had just moved here and no one had heard of Santa Barbara, no one cared it was here an hour-and-a-half above L.A., a sleeping arboretum even angels overlooked, where we had next to nothing, and everything, where father worked nights, and my mother and I ate fried bologna and tomato soup in the Formica kitchen in front of a GE plastic radio. I had this life beneath the cool plush oaks and I didn't know to ask for anything more.

The Bandstand still standing . . . the small metal harp at the top, the cupboards for dwarfs all around underneath . . . the criss-cross walk corner to corner, the honorary wino in this black thrift store suit and white tennis shoes, smoking alone by the chained-off steps leading to the platform where I raced around in circles when I was 4 . . . the 2 obligatory people passed out on the grass, newspapers over their faces, the early silent heavy air going by, slowly it seems. . . .

Beneath the star pines and magnolias, the voluminous pittosporum, the 1 jacaranda pushing out for sun, the 5 paltry redwoods, the single eugenia grown exponentially beyond hedge size, older than me . . . I'm counting trees, so I keep it this time. And I want to name the St. Joseph's candle thrown out thick and twisted, to appeal to Our Lady of Sorrows with its washed-out pink walls and bell tower across the way, as if this, or any of these lost listings could help me reclaim or hold my home.

This park, this place, as full and spare as I remember it at 4— no adornment but the leaves, the carved top of the picnic table, someone's initials sunk beneath the brown paint, from Catholic High up the street in 1954, the bare civic patches raked, and sprayed with a hose—part of the world that doesn't miss me, where, if I could, if I had more time, the simple wherewithal of dirt, I'd be here all my days, content as the trees for all the sky to see. As the acorn woodpecker laughing at god, and his good fortune, at the same sparrows and rogue pack of pigeons claiming the earth or whatever is left of it here alongside the 1 picnic table and the grass as they peck at the grains of light. . . . I join them again today, holding on to everything the wind has left to offer. . . .

Dispatch from the Garden at 57

I love the red-winged blackbirds taking their places on the phone lines for the falling light. And the squads of crows rowing home out of the far blue after a day in the broccoli and artichoke fields—I love

111

them and all that high, unheard music, the intuitive cantatas slip-streaming along up there. If I look back past the canyons sunk off shore, past the plates of shale cantilevered against the sky, even past the two royal palms reaching up from this mesa—rustling, tilting back and forth with their invisible knowledge—what deeper realizations really await me?

So I praise the purple bottlebrush, my bed of double delight roses, the thick, rouged cheek of late afternoon. I love each deep breath I take here, away from everything, love looking up along side the pomegranates and pittosporum, the ornamental plum—one more thing still breathing. I love the yellow grass of January I don't have to mow, and the self-sufficient sandstone hills, life still at every turn as the bronzed atmosphere mists down.

The sky glazes over with opalescent clouds, and my cat, Cecil B., charges across the yard after shadows and the come-ons of gusts among the weeds. I fan my fingers like the sheet music of the light, I think a little about a poem escaping on the air. I pick up my dialogue with the hard-skinned lemon tree and do not worry about the wind, the separation of clouds and bones, the smoke drifting away like my aspirations. . . .

I'm lighting up my last *Cubano,*—a *Romeo y Julieta* my student gave me, hand delivered by his father from the island—I'm celebrating with an Italian bar glass full of double-wood Single Malt, a gift from my old friend, a Chicano who lives up the street—somehow, even back of beyond in Lompoc, there's an almost international atmosphere today.

But it's cold for California. The humming birds have gone south, far, I'm sure, past Santa Barbara where no one can now afford to live. I throw on my grey-blue Rugby shirt and thus match the winter light wearing thin over the west, shining like the knees on my good pair of slacks. It's a Ralph Lauren Polo, $2.95 at the Salvation Army Thrift—Rugby and Polo, two sports I've just recently given up. But the shirt fits, and so I wear it—pride and irony dispersed in equal parts when you can afford not to ask, How Much?

You hit plateaus in life, you think you know things—but at any level, there's been no salvation in sight. And, given a liberal arts education, when I think of how I might improve my station in life,

Aristotle comes to mind—how, puzzled by the inexplicable current off the coast of Boeotia, he jumped into the swirling water for enlightenment; or Empedocles, who, nearing death and wanting to be thought a god, vanished into thin air by throwing himself into the fires of Mt. Etna. There are, however, some things self-defeating with regard to career.

Like Cecil, I've adjusted to the friendly confines of Lompoc. He loves the inexpensive brand of Chicken Feast and at 16+ pounds could care less about irony. When he's cleaned his plate, he just wants out the front for a punch-up with whoever has it coming, a pursuit which, more often than not, damages advancement—I let a thought about work and department politics dissipate. I'd give him a dram of my single malt if it would calm him—it works for me in the twilight these days. For now, he's content on the chaise lounge, keeping me company on my birthday. My wife is at Yoga class, and I again assume the position, Sea Lion at Rest. I have salmon filet and yellowsquash for dinner, but no cake, not a crumb of carbohydrate—on this diet over a year now, everything I try works as well as prayer....

57 today. Firing up this *puro* and watching the smoke drift heavenward, the starry flow chart unfurl, still unreadable. Today, it's inconsequential that I am older by a year than yesterday—always, there are the same number of bricks to hoist up hill. Still, no matter what God's left unfinished, I've done my work. So I'll leave everything to the sea that, like a bill collector, is never far from my door—the dark sea, where today, alone or not, I've decided I will be happy, drifting in the small boat of my heart.

Eternity (being a condensed spiritual and aesthetic biography)

—for VS

No one says I look 55—no one says I don't, except my new friend Virgil. He has two catholic daughters and like me, hates to fly, but there's no other way to get home in time for the youngest's first Communion. I almost remember mine. . . I've been scared ever since—of Death, of course. You tell me why. . . . In second grade, the nun lectured us about Eternity, which almost arrived later from Cuba in the early sixties, Cuba where my friend Virgil was born, which has at least one entrance to hell and exits in Spain and L.A. In the afterlife, I don't think anyone is rolling cigars while someone reads them Don Quixote in the original. Anyway, we were going to spend Eternity in hell if we did not do as we were told. Sister explained that Eternity was like an enormous steel ball, the size of the earth, upon which an eagle, gliding in from the cosmic starry dark beyond Cleveland and the east coast, once every million years, landed and took off again. The time it took that steel ball to completely wear away from the friction of the eagle landing and lifting away was less than a second of Eternity, the time we'd be burning on a hot rock for cussing, eating hot dogs on Fridays, not making our yearly Easter obligation of communion and mass, or having impure thoughts about Belinda Sanchez. Go figure.

What if, on the practical side, the universe—and so time-space—does curve back on itself like a huge quesadilla? We're going nowhere. What, then, have we been suffering for all along? More specifically, what have I been doing with that image like a fish hook in my brain for 48 years? Nuns, with their psycho-spiritual hammer-locks, were terrorists, and they did not discriminate among ages or ethnic groups. Death, darkness, and sure damnation were there equally for us all if we didn't stop talking during mass and go out and finagle quarters from relatives and folks on our block for the pagan babies. Dear God.

I don't know what angel brings me these lines in the middle of the night after I'm up and down the hall to the bathroom, brings them every few years like a palm tree and a pool of water appearing after sands have shifted for no reason, like some metaphysical crust of light. Some angel sweeping down with dust, one in the back of the chorus singing hosannas like nobody's business who has a little time to spare, an angel who every now and then hands off a few imagistic granules while I'm flaming away here in the flesh, in darkness where I might not know the source but would know a gift when I heard one.

Once I'm half awake and the cells are ticking over like new stars, I lose track of time and switch the lamp on and off and write down phrases, losing sleep—what does it come to? The door of a '59 Chevy swings open like a vault and lets out some earlier, more sprightly version of me, only a few blocks from happiness, or the sea, which ever comes first—with my papers and a new poem in hand—more than I arrived with. Who knew where I was headed? The nuns were sure: Hell. Virgil and I voted for Spain, even southern California if that's the best we could do to breathe cool salt air. Maybe I could do this forever, who knows? As I was taught, worse things could happen to me. Outside of Time, will poems matter? Why ask now—I'm not an academic, an administrator, slick in a Republican suit. We're not for long, not forever. Death, of course. And next? I hope it's not hell, or anywhere near Pennsylvania, where I already served ten years for my sins.

Dear God. Thank you for the gift of the eccentric brain, this associative jelly. Thank you for this moonraking poem which keeps me alive in prayer, in doubt, and in hope. This poem which for once did not take 5 months and 50 drafts, though I would have waited patiently as always—like salt dissolving from the sea, like air gathering to be somewhere else, like the last flake of rust outside of time. . . .

The Sea Again

The sky is anchored to your feet, the stands of eucalyptus moored against midnight; it doesn't look like anyone is going anywhere. Wake me in the dead of night, before I can clear my head of the dark swells, and ask me what I truly need. I will answer, *A handful of birds*, or, *God Made Me*—both are true. Western blue bird, sunset red breast, my arms empty but for the equivocating fabric of the air, the old notes always up there above us. We filter the present through our memories of the past, and, strictly speaking, we live there. Our brains take time to process what we think—the present happened some time ago.

Rote memory and the feedback loops to the pig-iron sentences in the Baltimore Catechism: Who Made You? Why Did He Make You? And I sang back the answers, but what I knew in my breath and in my blood was *Kickball, Thistle, Oak Tree, Wave*, and, as God himself would not appear, I accepted substitutions in the sky, and took in equal parts of oxygen and doubt.

Whatever the oceans once dreamed washes away or is flayed in the caucus of the sun. The fish can't breathe. No architecture of light, no revisionist history is going to change the now and the then. Nevertheless, my fifty-sixth winter, and any day is a good one.

If the soul has a window, it looks out on spindrift, salt, our little life aimless as the old ostentation of the stars—the earth imperfect, eternal—the red planets and spiral galaxies rising up like orange peels on a dark tide.

I don't care, finally, if God is terrible, or vengeful, an old God. Let there be something sturdier than the sea of grasses, the diminished plains. Some days I think the waters turn white with His worry, some days with the torments we've invented. Who could blame Him, if He's grown disinterested, if He's given up? No matter what I think, I just hope there is some there, there—beyond the clouds, the waves, the shadows on the empty surface of the sea.

ELENA K. BYRNE

from *Voyeur Hour*

Out: A Perfect California Distance: 1 pm

Overhearing:

She said what she had to say, though it came out of her mouth wrong, a dozen cherry beetles and he was leaning toward the wall for protection. This is the repertoire darkness, answer-ellipse. Knowing is always the opening out, like the hands of the just dead. The level horizon keeps on leveling out. The stars are just tiny stick pins in the voodoo doll of the universe. Twelve palm trees.You've been in a glass-bottomed boat with no air all year.

Market, 12 pm

The rust shopping cart looked as if it was sent out to sea, its wheels underwater for the count, sixty others, their bodies shoved, joint-geometric, into each other, still unmoving, one small child running so fast, smelling like fresh-cut yard grass, his arm lifts the sleeve of my pants as he passes, attaches both hands and mouth to a giant glass jar of eye-marble candies, giddy in their colors, trips on the infallible dead tongue of the one loose lace screaming to his mother into the glass smashing, spheres rolling out their random deep space pattern, my heart set in reverie on one man, not mine, looking down: *I want one, I want . . .*

11 pm TV

"... there will I be, waiting for myself"

from the painted porch of that house you are not building for me, that could be mine. It was my body that survived your Amazon obsolete course, flight of green stairs down the waterfall, survived the carjacking turn of events caught on tape, my blood-trail. I can hardly see until you open my eyes with your one eye, sugar on the mark. I hate you because you gave me permission. I'm all leather in the saddle. You're in the horse. Through the window, I hop in the passenger seat next to you driving down the LA street, your sideburns on fire. Fear has everything to do with it, but I don't have to be afraid for long, do I? The weight of water holds my new voice upstream. It moves like an epitaph to my future. Whoever swallowed that drink, gave me thirst. Whoever gave me music, knew silence. Swine eat pearls. Clouds fall down and drown themselves in the soil, in another state. I am reading other women like myself in a Venetian metaphor, subsequent orientation on the verbal page. Billboard images bully each weakness until your ribs hurt like metal crowbars. Rabbits breed like the violence in the mind. Humpty Dumpty falls down inside of me for a few hundred thousand dollars. I can see myself there, bearing the mark of the real world where they are making up what comes next, in me.

Place Fable
L.A. Mythology

… where he appears annually, whoever outs the year one folklore at a time. Take Pilgrim's Way, the Puritan route there, as far as appeal, this pre-eminent unholy boat & ground pilgrimage west, west as further west where ocean & heat meet lying down, where the cat's among the pigeons. In the pink kind of place, pleased as punch, gold-double goldfish out of the crystal bowl, as unfaith as in the Italian Judy and Punch allegory giving us Ennui, in odd shape of a dog, Death, who is certainly beaten to death, Disease, in the fair guise of a doctor, and, subsequently weeded & outwitted, the Devil himself, a dialect in poker face. Return there, the blood-place for exit, narrow escape as a bag-man, member order of dervishes, call-boy on Plough Monday, with a pick of the basket, shine of shells & plum & oranges, drunken sunset mask, feet in the ash-ink sand, so ready to eat a calf in the cow's belly, to be beautiful.

THE PROSE POEM enacts a doubling of consciousness, the full-wing span over your head. In doing so, it takes on a long exhale quality that forces the reader under its skin, under the water of consciousness, holding you there, deep beneath its water. Because the measure is different, the intent therefore, is also different . . . a paradox of movement within the poem and its thinking on the page.

I believe in the celebratory doubt and the intimate impersonal created by a prose poem's center of concentration. The form, as another kind of "poem," at once, does what Susan Sontag describes when addressing painters who use words actively: it works "to undermine the image, rebuke it, render it opaque . . ." until perhaps it must be seen in its full narrative dynamism. There seems to be a semantic security in the shape of the paragraph, yet the prose poem's guile is its cleave/tethering forces from one image to the next, a resonance on the edge of chaos; therefore, within the containment of form, often one feels a contrasting lack of discipline, a need to break free, "for our souls live on treason" (Rilke) and so, in this case of creative treason, the country is the body of the poem, self- contained and sovereign.

The prose poem takes hold of a continuous present-tense and pushes it forward, future, all the while in a rhythmic rush toward the truth which is never really quite discovered, though always implied. Without the visual markers and cues, the prose poem seems circular, insular, an ontology of one gesture, cat's cradle open and close, open and close weave. . . its destabilizing cluster-attention, its Hockney-like accumulation of image, its self-voyeurism, its hunger . . . After all: a poem is a cannibal; the prose poem pretends to be far more civilized, though its mouth is left wide open.

MAXINE CHERNOFF

Lost and Found

I am looking for the photo that would make all the difference in my life. It's very small and subject to fits of amnesia, turning up in poker hands, grocery carts, under the unturned stone. The photo shows me at the lost and found looking for an earlier photo, one that would have made all the difference then. My past evades me like a politician. Wielding a flyswatter, it destroys my collection of cereal boxes, my childhood lived close to the breakfast table. Only that photo can help me locate my fourteen lost children, who look just like me. When I call the Bureau of Missing Persons, they say, "Try the Bureau of Missing Photos." They have a fine collection. Here's one of Calvin Coolidge's seventh wedding. Here's one of a man going over a cliff on a dogsled. Here's my Uncle Arthur the night he bought the prize peacock. Oh, photo! End your tour of the world in a hot air balloon. Resign your job at the mirror-testing laboratory. Come home to me, you little fool, before I find I can live without you.

A Name

Suppose your parents had called you Dirk. Wouldn't that be motive enough to commit a heinous crime, just as Judies always become nurses and Brads, florists? After the act, your mom would say, "He was always a good boy. Once on my birthday, he gave me one of those roses stuck in a glass ball. You know the kind that never gets soggy"—her Exhibit A. Exhibit B: a surprised corpse, sharing a last name of Dirk with the mortician. And Dad would say, "Dirk once won a contest by spelling the word 'pyrrhic,'" and in his alcohol dream he sees the infant Dirk signing his birth certificate with a knife. Still, Dirk should have known better. He could tell you that antimony is Panama's most important product. He remembered Vasco de Gama and wished him well. Once he'd made a diorama of the all-American boyhood: a little farm, cows the size of nails, cotton ball sheep, a corncob silo, but when he signed it Dirk, the crops were blighted by bad faith. And don't forget Exhibits C, D, E. The stolen éclair, the zoo caper, the taunting of a certain Miss W, who smelled of fried onions. It was his parents' fault. They called him Dirk.

Nomads

Since I've moved to California, I always worry about my mother's plans for Thanksgiving. It's not that she can't join me out here—she can if she'd like—but she rarely feels up to traveling. There aren't major illnesses in the way but her own habit of reclusiveness. This year, I'm happy but somewhat surprised to hear that her bus driver has invited my mother over for Thanksgiving dinner. He's not just any bus driver, she tells me, but a nice man named Ray. She'll be a guest along with the bus driver's girlfriend who is sixty but looks forty and her two grandchildren. I tell her to bring something to dinner. This is knowledge that an eighty-year-old woman should possess but somehow my mother may have missed in life. I can't remember my parents ever having had friends. I thought that friendships stopped at some exact age and spent my early thirties wondering when friends were going to desert me. When they didn't I became peevish to test their loyalty. I tell my mother to bring wine. She wonders where she will get it. I tell her that Walgreen's has a decent selection, knowing that it's in the course of her limited travels. She wonders if she should bring Manischewitz. I tell her that only she likes sweet wine and that her bus driver probably isn't Jewish. Even when she was younger, my mother would add sugar to wine, even to champagne. I tell her to buy a Chardonnay, but I can tell she is losing interest. Maybe she should bring something for the children, she says. What children? The nice lady's grandchildren. The girlfriend. She's smarter than he is, my mother adds. Almost passed her CPA exam three times. This impresses my mother, whose husband was a CPA. Maybe you can bring them chocolate turkeys or snowmen, I suggest. In Chicago, seasons are a cold or hot blur. Thanksgiving and Christmas are interchangeable, as are their icons. Leaves are gone from trees, the world barely alive by early November. Turkeys or nomads? she asks. Where will I find chocolate nomads? S-n-o-w-m-e-n, I spell. What? S-n-o-w-m-e-n. Snowmen, she says softly, as if our conversation is making her run out of breath.

I BEGAN WRITING prose poems at the age of 21. I was at first influenced by the Latin American prose poets, especially Julio Cortázar and Clarice Lispector, and French poet Henri Michaux. Prose poems were my main form for the first decade of my writing career. They led me to longer narratives, short stories, and then novels, then back to prose poems for a time in the eighties. Another brief visit in the nineties. Mostly now I write "verse" poems, but the prose poem is an interesting elastic form that I might use again.

MARILYN CHIN

Why Men Are Dogs

A long, long time ago in Hong Kong, a man and his dog died side by side, both asphyxiated in a hotel fire. The Goddess of Mercy, who happened to be jogging by with her pedometer, decided to bring them back to life. She examined the man's body and saw that his heart was shriveled and diseased by smoking and bad eating habits, but the dog's heart was still in good shape and was red, plump and healthy. She discarded the man's diseased heart and replaced it with the dog's heart. For the dog, she made a beautiful vegetarian heart with soy paste and wheat gluten. She said some mumble jumble New Age prayer and the dog sprang up and wagged his tail and barked in gratitude. The man, instead of thanking the Goddess, growled, scratched his balls, and tried to bite her head off for manifesting too late and for not serving him *steak tartar* for dinner and not saving him from the British Empire in the first place.

That Ancient Parable about Nanzen's Doll

Moonie and Mei Ling were fighting over a Barbie Doll. *The church ladies gave it to me!* said Mei Ling. *No, they gave it to me!* said Moonie. Grandmother Wong grabbed the doll by it's platinum ponytail, pulled out her big cleaver and hacked it straight down the middle. Here, she said, *The lamb and the host,* and went back to the stove and sautéed some day-old turnip dumplings.

Gutei's Finger, Redux

Gutei cut off his student's finger, put it in a bowl of chili, sued the restaurant, got two million in a settlement, divided the booty, 50/50, with his freaked-out pot-head student and called it satori. Twenty years later, on his deathbed in Macau, flanked by beautiful tanned boys, he issued his last email to the world: The finger, the finger. I give you the finger. Ha ha ha ha!

123

Lantau

While sitting prostrate before the ivory feet of the great Buddha, I spilled almost an entire can of Diet Coke on the floor. I quickly tried to mop up the mess with my long hair. I peeked over my left shoulder: the short nun said nothing and averted her eyes; to my right the skinny old monk was consumed by a frightful irritation of his own. He was at once swatting and dodging two bombarding hornets that were fascinated by his newly shaved head. "I hope he's not allergic." I chuckled softly. And beyond us, was the motherless Asian sea, glittering with the promise of eternity.

Impermanence

When Grandmother Wong gave Mei Ling her one-month-old haircutting party, she invited her old cronies from the village. Auntie Lu said, "Look at the baby's long fingers: she is going to be an accomplished violinist like Sarah Chang and Midori!" Auntie Lan said, "Look at her alert eyes, flashing left to right, already weighing evidence; she is going to be a fine counselor of law. She will be the Johnny Cochran of Chinese America!" Auntie Wu said, "How sad— we humans and our delusions. The only certainty about this child's future is that she will die. She is already a soon-to-be-dead person."

To this remark, Grandmother Wong grabbed Auntie Wu by the ear, dragged her out the door and kicked the door shut.

I HAVE BEEN WRITING prose poems/short shorts for at least twenty years now. I write them for a variety of reasons. I am a lyric poet who likes to tell tales ... and often, I feel the need to transgress the line to do so. That prose block is a flat and square canvas with many possibilities. And within that canvas, I have room to formulate arguments and expand on ideas, create characters and have a respite from lyric autobiography.

This group of prose poems includes re-imagined versions of ancient Buddhist and Zen tales. I've taken the Zen anecdote to a post-colonial, new world, Pacific-rim, Californicated interpretation. To be a true Buddhist, we must be able to laugh at the Buddha and to see the wild contradictions in contemporary life.

KILLARNEY CLARY

A smudge of cloud on the horizon, then the pale halo in the night sky. Quiet on the water, in the bare trees, tinsel rain.

A bright, silent wheel turns on the bayside where the secret flag is raised at midnight. Skiffs push off from docks in the fair harbor.

I don't want to hear, again, *Are you tired?* That's why I bought the boat.

⁓

Clouds of birds rise above the upper bay, slant into the white sky then bank, black and full; of bees in the ashes in the pause of traffic in the lull of afternoon; of fish, silver, solid then gone, masters of camouflage by light. Swells of kelp, of cloud, of leaves in the new wind from Palm Springs, of ochre dust on the dry edge of idleness. The stores are open and the sun angles harshly onto the window displays, insulting coats on sale before inventory. Even the moon is skittish, up early and pale but whole as the sun. Old, and of a plan.

The upper bay, the glitter of it, the heavy pelican that soars only inches from the surface are an hour away through Riverside and Garden Grove. The dust is carried there in a thick haze that gathers itself between Balboa and Catalina and packs down and hovers and drones on. It's trapped and embarrassed and won't stop excusing itself with all the elements of bad luck, except to claim with pride it stands undressed.

Out there in the calm, exposed, I might look back toward home. Everything, everyone is out of place, moving or turning again, able to see both sides of any argument. And I am there. On shore, a woman sweeps her toddler off to the parking lot for reasons weak and distant to me; but I understand—some discomfort or foreboding, fatigue from blowing sand or the glare, maybe tired joy. I drift away from the determined ones on solid ground. And I am here.

An hour away. I've lived within a two-hour drive all my life. The Santa Anas cease as abruptly as they blew in; the air deadens. After it rains in these mountains, I figure the silt will cloud the channel and fan out where it, too, can remember as it leaves the peninsula and Corona del

Mar. Nothing will dissolve, not boredom or urgency. The weather and moves we might have made nag like a child, "Watch me. Watch me. Look at me," before another ordinary, spectacular dive into the country-club pool.

⌒

Near four o'clock the daylight changes into a way of leaving. Spring, and across the city heat rises into attics, lingers, and grows tired. I tell myself not to go home in the afternoon and I think hard about a leaf on the concrete, the sound of tires rubbing the curb. Children in cars. Anne is waiting up the sidewalk for a station wagon. Under the trees. The game is just a sound for us, of a bat and ball above the field out on Waldo Avenue. Anne is so quiet I don't need to watch for her ride. She seems all right as she moves her eyes along the row of wooden houses, up the guy wire for the telephone pole, down to a sore at her thumbnail.

I know you, Anne, through high school, past this part of the city into another. We grow up this sadly along with the spay-painted "Ogre" and "Stinky Felix" that watch from the La Loma and even taller bridges, names placed for danger. With their quick power, they are certain they won't be covered.

Anne waits with the gradual shade. Her life is more confused than mine, so she carries her place in her clean skin. I tell myself not to go home in the afternoon when the air has no time or smell, to a place where I can imagine the interruptions are unvaried, dependable. It is so close to being true. Anne won't call goodbye as I leave; she'll become the afternoon, with a face that moves little.

I will go home with my mother; on the way we drive past other things I know. They are so close to being with me whenever I want. If I can make myself sad, I can be sure. So when my mother apologizes for being late, I don't answer her but think of Anne sitting on the low wall on Bellevue Drive. She is still there, and my mother is sad and I am sad and we are almost home.

⌒

She lied. *What you have made is good.* So many gray clay pots were proudly collected at the school gate. *There is no one like you, My Darling.*

Thin clouds hold the sharp heat off. Rocked in shallow swells, a drift of minnows pulses. Suspicion hangs in monsoonal moisture. A swirl of pale hair in the bay; pressing forward keeps the weight suspended.

Powdered, loose skin gives, cool against a kiss; receives, *I love you,* which veils with a sheer fabric—I love you enough to lie.

At the edge of the Pacific, a speedboat wake taps the shore. The speckle of shadow disperses, castles collapse into their tunnels, and a woman shakes her sunburned boy, *Where's your sister?*

⌒

Through a panel of controls in the Post-Panamax crane-cab, he raises the container from the ship, sets it on a trailer from which it will be transferred, at the intermodal yard, to a train through the Alameda Corridor. To another yard just south of downtown, switched through to the Inland Empire and beyond—the clothing, electronics and toys from Asia are on their way.

To the warehouse in Sparks, Nevada, to fill a catalog order in Emmett, Idaho—a blouse for a woman who will be better when the package has arrived. Summer coming. She slits the tape, unfolds the pale tissue, lifts the thing.

Dust on the dresser, powder on her throat, a fine quiet glow on what she has gathered, a riffle in the blinds, heat leaning on the outside wall of the dim bedroom. The color is different from what she expected. She pulls her shirt off, feels a tingling surge of shortfall behind her eyes.

⌒

White sand, tall grass. This strip of ocean is a thin bit of deep blue as if the earth bends suddenly out there, beneath the dark storm moving, pushing shadows on the surface of the sea which presses in close and rushes away. A cold wind feels impatient, too, as it returns in force with each break, again. And the sky that splits is a surprise, sending a straight shaft of silver to claim its town of luck. Doors blow open with a crash, close gently a ways away. They would close.

The sun is faith and will be for so many months of empty houses, linen closets, shelves of cold glasses, while the unending sand in the undying wind heckles the clapboards, blasts the paint.

Sometimes everything is all right except my ears are cold. I think, if only my ears were warm again. If only again, want. Away. A whistle in the wind. If something changed it all forever . . . It is all changing always forever. Certainly the fish must swim deeper and birds leave for a while. In the back of a school desk a scrap of paper learns its folds until they are weak, and the penciled joke is lost in the creases, graphite dust.

There is no imitating the weather, no remembering but a dullness I think is near my heart. And when I am asked to carry out the one fine thing form the burning house, I'll know what reflects me is arbitrary; I am invisible. Won't my habits be undercut while the paces across a familiar room are smoke and ash, distance no more? I don't know myself without these clothes—the buttoned coat of answers and shoes of home.

FROM THE NEIGHBOR'S garden steps at dusk where I have come to sit in the dampening air, there are no reasons. The hum of why a thing was done is silenced; there could be no other end for it. No one knows I am here. The drop of water on the lip of the hose lifted by its coil above the cool sod has this familiar contest with me. I will move first.

WANDA COLEMAN
Footnote to an Unfinished Poem

—after Hayes after Lorca

Carmel-by-the-Sea is a lonely tree overlooking Pacifica twice eternity. That was the time I was in the process of discovering that I was rediscovering Borges, if that's not too complex? It was the mid-80s and I was doing kamakaze watch over Berkeley and The Bay. "Bitch, I told you to cease-and-desist!" Dig, Big Sur, it was long over at Big Sur (damn, I do so miss that pastrami) although Nepenthe's was still a gas-gas-gas and for a longer time after that. But you see, it was truly a matter of urgency as I dived-bombed on City Lights and found out that Melville was still alive and workin' the docks. Please don't get me goin' on about all them unfree radicals, but Tor House just broke my heart, so you can understand why we blistered when Jean Arthur made us move our tore-down Skylark out the front of her crib.

1959

it is the year of love-eyed vixens with paper cheechees, plaids, pleats, and Hawaiian-print polished cotton. bus rides on the red line, south to Gompers Junior High. oxfords are good for hopscotch, or scuffles at recess, or long walks home made longer by gossiping with girls named Dee, Jill or Nancy, or twisting fingers with boys named Oscar, Wayland or Red. (white or black patent leather is reserved for church service and concerts)

   i engage in scopings for mange-free strays to adopt, or the scooping up of broke-winged birds for burial, stopping for a soda a burger a comic book, wasting a week's allowance in stingy quarters and dimes—'cooling it' on the porch when summer scorches the sidewalks, admiring the whoosh of big-finned convertibles & coupes

   on dinner duty for Moms, as she does a last-minute shop (morning screams from the hallway still in my ears, awakened to kill the earthworm trapped in newswrap. bruises from spankings like blueberries under my skin. the marks white teachers never notice. how can such an angel-faced creature be such a violent bitch? and here i am her bittersweet spit)

on phone duty for Pops (ever absent without leave), collecting maydays from the ships that never sail, living on books, in this revisiting, sometimes leaving loneliness for skate blisters and the laughter-and-shouts of neighbor kids between ooobopshebop sways and swings between bike rides, foul shots and hikes to the corner store for milk, bread and syrup

a cooking ironing mopping scrubbing sewing washing fool the fragrance of wet grass ever rises on breezes, sates my nose as i hose our lawn every evening at sundown. it will permeate those dreams ahead. for now, i am content to watch the western sky go rose go violet blue as all rainbows vanish in the spray. . . .

Union Station

the remnants of a free-wheeling expanding democracy are revealed in the high polished wooden beamed ceiling, and only the vague spook of a crowded downtown thoroughfare. it's all squirreled down by the miserly greed of a cheapskate generation

plastic, Formica & Styrofoam quick mean political fixes & a pill for grandness

listen. there's the sure brace of a woman's high-heeled step, nearly a march, hips swinging, the confident swish of a skirt, on her way to round up late-night arrivals by train

above, there's the gravel & grate of wind through age-worn pipes. the shallow whistle of air through conditioning ducts

i sit in the tan leather-upholstered high-backed chairs made for monarchs and for children who get a thrill when their feet can't touch ground

there are a handful of students, weary commuters, but mainly impatient drivers eager to get on with pedestrian routines. to close it down for the night

behind me sit two wood-colored men who smell of backrooms & bourbon in slag-colored duds and work shoes. they mark time, suppress their nicotine fits "smoke these days and they'll put yo' ass in jail" laugh-broken, they assess the "stupid young muthafuckas," with a "they must be out of their mixed-up don't know what to do minds."

that could be said of the city officials who have allowed this magnificence to decay (as better the best go fallow & fail than to let us have it or any true say in it) and uh-huh at the irony. me and brutha men whose tone i echo would not have been welcomed on these premises in that heyday one mean lifetime ago.

Going to Blazes

when we set out on the train to Nowhere, i thought, we are going to be the greatest of lovers but it was a tour of the grave of his first. the trip lasted twenty years. i was tired when we reached the station. he could not find a taxi to take us anywhere, let alone home (our bodies cleansed in public restrooms) we wandered the city like beggars, making love in alleyways by moonlight, white cement against the cobalt sky. "our essences have penetrated this ground, we are bound to this place forever. it is holy," he said

there, beyond our endless walk, i saw the spires of the Harbor of Pleasure—the jetty of a thousand pelicans where cabin cruisers, kayaks, catamarans, powerboats and yachts leisurely take the marina armed battleships silhouetted on the horizon, reminders that terror is a mere plane flight away....

we made our way to the viewpoint in an abandoned vehicle. magically, i began to conjure picnic lunches from my fingertips, food fit for an Emperor and his Empress. we contemplated our escape from poverty, hour upon bittersweet hour, praying devoutly to The Lord of Pigeons and The Guardian Crow

picture us this way: he is returned to beauty, the boy giving way to the man, bike rider to bowed walker. she, especially devout (quick to offer amusement), wears tatters as if they were the satins and taffetas of youth. on Saturdays when the open wounds run blue, they descend from the joshuas, flying dreams and jazz, imagining escape even as they race backward seeking a return to their salvation

placed in storage—there, above the vista, they stumble the profusion
an ideogram of silhouettes joined

I FIND THE PROSE POEM one of the most delicious forms for exercising one's powers of evocation, seduction and mystery. With greater density than the vignette, yet its cousin, it often demands a painterly delicacy, an aesthetic sensitivity comparable to an artist making brush strokes on canvas.

SCOTT CRELEY

Skin

I left a shred of skin on the inside of my wrecked car, the windshield scraping off the frill of my knuckle like a chef's knife separating a piece of dough. The tatter of knuckle skin hung there like frayed gauze, the limp discarded flag of a ghost ship. It lost its color while I watched, changing from watercolor pink into a kind of mummified grey, severed from the blood and heat of my hand. Uprooted and dying with the slow regularity of a puddle growing stagnant.

The Jetta rolled four times in the rain, gaining its tires and losing them again like a wounded animal who is not quite yet dead. Although I saw the ground rushing up from above, although a rock wedged into the open door and yanked a handful of hair from my skull, I had not been hurt until I brushed the inside of the windshield.

Now fluttering from the limp sheet of safety glass that droops inward above the steering column, is this veteran patch of my skin. Skin from the same knuckle that broke Brian Haster's nose with the sharp sudden motion of someone splitting firewood. The same knuckle that has brushed the insides of parted thighs and sometimes moved deeper, sending incomplete and mysterious messages from beneath skirts and pant legs. This same wrinkled thimbleful of finger that moves along the gentle lunar incline of my girlfriend's face in the dark.

This overlooked piece of myself is hanging from a shard of glass the size of a carpenter nail, finishing the parched business of dying, and I am regretful. This knuckle that has brushed away tears, has been cured like leather in paint chips and motor oil. Now it will be replaced by something smoother, by the pink skin of new growth that cannot entirely be trusted, skin that I will have to build from scratch, that may not turn out as well.

And somewhere on the side of the freeway is a clump of my hair, maybe dyed black, covered in transmission fluid and tar, wrapped around rocks and tied into knots by the turbulence of passing cars. I hope that a few strands have been buffeted to other places, carried by the contrails of big rigs up into the Cajon pass to rest with the ashes of my cousin, wrapped around an axel and brought up north where a blue jay will put it into her nest, tucked inside the latticework of the Golden Gate bridge.

These dreams are important because this skin is not going anywhere—it will be towed away with the car frame once I clean out my possessions. A secret bit of humanity tucked into the crushed hulk such places make of cars—hidden inside the wreck we make of the world.

Leukemia

"This Laryngitis is killing me, Scotty," says my grandfather, lashed to a hospital bed with plastic hoses and paper blankets. He says Laryngitis instead of Leukemia because of the morphine. I know I shouldn't try to correct him but I'm confused and too young to believe someone when they tell me they are going to die, so I do.

Leukemia, I tell him, It's leukemia. The word has the weight of impending weather, it almost darkens the halogen lights for a moment. He looks frustrated, his skin turned yellow tissue paper wrinkling between his eyes. Then instead of arguing he just squeezes my hand with a hesitant kind of softness, as if to remind me that he loves me even if I didn't turn out so bright. Whatever you want to call it, he says.

Sitting on the hood of my father's car, the night before the funeral.

The desert above Rancho Mirage is so dark because there are so few city lights. We sit on the hood of the car, my father and I, and talk like strangers, groping for every word. It is too cold, the frozen ground is insinuating itself into our bones until they are no warmer than the shattered rocks heaved up through the sand around us.

I am twelve and I want to ask my father about Heaven. Instead I ask about aliens, flying saucers, if they could be real. He says yes, looking at me for only a moment longer than he probably meant to, lingering just a little because he knows what I am really asking.

So I watch the sky for a while. Although I cannot tell the difference between stars and satellites, I know that I do not see any spaceships up there in the bleeding mess of nebulas that is the reservation sky. Nor do I hear any angels down here, picking their way over the rocky ground.

I am afraid for my grandfather, fearful that nothing will find him and carry him away. That it is too dark despite the stars and the frostbit desert moon, that he will be too heavy with the cold earth. I am worried that in the morning he might still be in that box, that he might have to be buried closed-coffin beneath the gloating Palm Springs sun. I would rather have him taken in the cold, before these very same rocks become embers and cook him into the clay forever.

UNTIL THIS LAST YEAR all of my poems were in verse. After being introduced to prose poetry I found it to be a method of writing with an absolutely stunning capacity for depth and the communication of subtext. The deceptively plain style that prose seems to encourage in my writing helps me to describe a scope of emotion that I would not dare approach in verse because it might seem too sentimental or melodramatic. The absence of line breaks causes me to rely upon my voice for control and emphasis.

BRAD CRENSHAW

When Don Was Serious, Like a Hyacinth

I

we spoke in French about his maudlin intrigue, a first adventure, since repented, among the Iroquois. One of her names—Mary something—I remember. Born to the Monster people, she was scarcely tattooed at all that I could tell, and sure enough, Don later gave me details. She really could dissect the white bear of the north. But he was in the Peace Corps then and practiced languages that spoke of his immense designs, the holy land of his ambition. Once a whiz in trivia about the suburbs, he'd hang with the mouthy L.A. gangsters that kept him strange.

II

I don't miss much—like Mary something's soft, huge soprano's boobs. Just kidding. I'm never shy about exaggeration. He lost an eye in time to some disease—a tremor in one cornea—which risked his point of view about his mother lost in time to heart attacks; I read her Blake's introit to innocence to keep her spirits blind to the world before her. Don lay like a drowned sailor by her bed, and mutilated people found forgiveness right there, down around their feet. When friendly Mary dated Irish heroes, Don perused in memory his reckless places with that one dark eye.

III

Write *this* down: eventually he wouldn't let me in his house—never seen again inside by literate men or women. I'd fret in the shadows looking lucky and unplanned while I peed on his shrubbery. I had to go. The crows of destiny flaunted up and down the pink light glad about something as I climbed undaunted in my father's truck and left. Fallen catholics were on the road and followed me away from Don's place, thin as his excuses were. I know, I know, I know, I am an unbeliever. Sorry. I've lost my confidence in friends and big money.

IV

The question is to what extent he's in his natural element. I wish you could see him dancing at that secret club for men in publishing, waving his most saintly Tiparillo at the other revelers and journalists. *Oh lighten up*, he might have said, justifiably. It occurs to me he told me that before, at night on our drive to Santa Cruz that perfect August. We took my truck. The grains of paradise were warmly glowing overhead in the dust of stars. *That one's Changing Woman rising*, he said in that impatient way of his coyote spirit—a voice I seem to miss.

I think of poetry as first a voice, an utterance that is temporal, sequential and dramatic. It is also inherently rhythmic and composed quite literally of *sounds*: rhyme, assonance, consonance are integral to the voice. Before they were ever written down, poems have existed for millennia as oral traditions in the fabulous Homeric epics, *Gilgamesh, Beowulf,* the religious stories of the Navaho, and on and on the list goes. For the convenience of preservation these voices can be codified by the tools of our notation: the alphabet, marks of punctuation, even line breaks. But I do not think of poetry as essentially a visual *thing,* anymore than I would grant the score of Bach's cantatas the primacy of place over Lorraine Hunt Lieberson's singing them. Languages like music are auditory, and they too like poetry have existed for whole eras before written forms were created to represent them.

I know there are languages that are not auditory—American Sign Language for one—but I am not composing poems in them. And let me admit I have nothing truly against the written word—I'm actually glad to have the alphabet. But I don't choose to accentuate its visual presence over the auditory being of language, and so I present my poems as prose: the invisible format. I have conceived of my poems here in this anthology as spoken aloud to someone dear to me. It could be you. I have also composed these poems as formal Shakespearean sonnets, after which I then dissolved the lines into their basic sentences. As I've said before, the rhythms and aural characteristics of language are integral. Visually breaking the flow of speech into lines is not. As prose, I am presenting poems with the metrical and auditory sophistication of the sonnet but embedded within the sinuous poetry of personal utterance.

ALBA CRUZ-HACKER

Hustling Tamales in Crestline, California

Sitting in my ten-year-old Honda Accord at Goodwin's parking lot—waiting for my oldest to end her shift of bagging groceries—surrounded by Cherokees and Explorers of the new year, or the year past, I see Luisito standing by the glass doors, slinging his mom's tamales in the cold. In this town, the sight of brown flesh thrills me to my toes, makes me want to run and touch a skin shade like mine, talk in the language that I still sometimes dream in.

His red coat hangs to his knees. And from under river-skipping and washed out jeans, brilliantly white socks bunch above scuffed and cracked tennis shoes the color of wet sand. He chases each customer crossing the threshold, pushing a cart, lifts his Aztec-chiseled face, framed by black hair with a cowlick on its crown, and tries to meet the blue, green or hazel eyes that peer ahead. Even if no one turns his way, he speaks his lines: *Do you want tamales? They're fresh.*

I see some lifting eyebrows, tightening thin lips, heads turning as if a fly had buzzed around those winter-reddened cheeks. Some shake their heads and smile, but others simply rush past, gripping the handles of silver shopping carts, making their knuckles whiter than they are, and search the lined cement toward cloned SUVs. My own fingers on the steering wheel slow the blood's flow as my knuckles pale too. Something warm and heavy settles somewhere behind my ribs.

The Warning of Flies

En boca cerrada no entran moscas.
—Spanish Proverb

Mom claimed a million times that *flies don't enter a closed mouth.* But I know now that if you're tuned to their buzz, the shit left on the shag carpet can be spotted before you cross the threshold. And maybe I could've stepped around it without smearing my pink between-the-toes sandals.

138

But at nine I swatted flies dead and kept my trap shut—a good girl inside that house with locked doors and red curtains drawn up tight. Yet the stench of sweat on wrinkled hands and thighs and grandfather's pasty, yellowing tongue made me want flies to hatch howling out of my throat.

I've learned that a fly's compound eyes receive light from different points in space: they have a six-sided view propelled by wings that beat 10,000 times per second as the fly roars from a rotten orange to the putrid plantain on the dining room table—so it's my best warning system. Back when I kept my lips pressed tight, flies never entered, but then nothing ever came out of my sealed mouth.

This Tug-of-War of Two Tongues

I live with two tongues in my head. One vibrates, curled against the roof of my mouth, rolling purrs. The other steers its pink tip and attempts to slow the rumbas of the first.

The one that breeds restraint wants to train these fast-talking hands to lie, have them rest on my wide hips so I can speak and navigate this maze in downtown L.A., and the one-way arrows veering left in San Francisco—all towered by glass and steel built at right angles.

I am round, a ripe papaya. Split, this deep red-orange pulp cradles a crowd of small, black seeds wrapped in their own, lucent sacs. I won't know which way they'll lean until they sprout and vie for space.

So in my brain debates and brawls go on. One tongue wants imposing straight lines and commands: *follow right angles and climb.* But the other fights back, stabbing its roots deep, to cling wild, as a bougainvillea, along my Spanish island's curves.

ALTHOUGH I HAVE BEEN writing poetry for many years, the prose poem is a relatively recent discovery for me—and what an exciting discovery it has been! Given my personal and professional journeys across geographical, linguistic, racial and ethnic landscapes, I discovered that the prose poem could provide the perfect venue to express a blurring and/or an amalgamation of these boundaries. I mainly write line-poetry, but believe that certain poems demand a hybrid form—one that merges some of the traditional techniques of the poetic craft but also embraces the expansiveness of prose. For me, on the page, the prose poem can embody the hyphenated self and the multiple allegiances that define it.

MARSHA DE LA O
To Go to Riverside

Picture a boy, exactly before the action, a smooth stone cupped in his hand; he's the boy David, or maybe it's a gun flat against his palm, and he's an archangel, aiming for the darkened windows of the church. First the blast, then the shattering, the slap of running feet; he never turned to see them fall. The windows fell inside solder lines, inside lead lines unless the caliber was too small and left only a bunghole of white light.

It could have happened that way. That's why my father went to Riverside, out past Rialto for the first time because a saint had been shattered or pierced, a woman kneeling with oils or a man reaching for the wounds, the five glorious fountains. Our father took us with him to the Inland Empire where groves were laid down in all directions like the careful quilting of God. Robber barons built their mansions and the fields of the Lord were planted in citrus. Churches reared straight up and were shot through by boys. We spent our first vacation at the Sleepy Bear while our father ministered to a fallen window and we threw ourselves over and over in the bleached water of the pool, hot dirty light shafting down on our heads.

I went back years later to college and met a black man who took me to his house. He'd been shot in the chest, a large caliber weapon, and when he took his shirt off, his skin was still surprised, an epicenter and ripples, all of it scar. I wanted to see the exit wound, but couldn't ask him to turn around.

I wanted to see the actual damage, the way the body took it, the light in the church when no one is there but the glazier and his small daughter, a girl not left behind to throw herself against the flat slap of water, eyes rimmed red with bleach, a plume from the steel mill over our heads, one great chimney called Bess, and many coking ovens without names, the leaves of the orange trees in Fontana had already turned black; first a kind of oil, then a kind of ash. They harvested the last grapefruit during the second World War; after that the trees couldn't give.

To go to Riverside when churches were stoned and men were shattered. I imagine my father on scaffolding, his careful hands, the way the three women were tender taking down the crucified Christ and their tenderness made the soldiers afraid. At college we were frightened by the murder of a coed. Someone met her in the groves where wind trembled and darkness rose through capillary action sweating oil on the underside of leaves. He killed her there. When they found her, her eyes were open, but empty, a cathedral with darkened windows. Someone had blasted through the rose. I remember a small shamed faith in my safety, as if her death assured my life, but I was scared of the groves of sickened trees where her body had been abandoned.

I wanted to trace the ripple line, the scar circling wider, but couldn't ask. In class students whispered details of her death. I wanted to touch the man who'd been shot. At first they'd thought heavy industry a good idea for the Pacific slope. Fleets of diesel trucks shuttled Fontana plate to shipyards and a plume spread in the groundwater. I didn't like them talking about her, casting lots for her last moments. The body can't forget a wound; it ripples out forever. I don't know why.

I was afraid to stay in his house in Riverside. They say it used to be paradise, but a dead girl lay too long, and a plume of fear spread, so many parts per million; we drank from that tap all our lives.

The Northridge Quake

Not the stopped trains, not the ants streaming out to read the invisible, not the way the city struggled to restore coverage so the camera could zoom the crack from chimney to base, not the marriage of fire and water as the main and the line crumpled together with a sudden understanding, not the clock face that grinned and went numb at 4:31, not the jolt of his body thrashing up out of sleep as the flesh of buildings fell from the architecture of bone, no, the chest is as close as I ever get to what happened in the Northridge quake. First a lunging resonance, layers and layers of thunder. And yes, the swell of a wave, water's surge, as of a girl in a wooden chest on the rolling seas, waves not capped or foaming, the chest drifting. Then, the dead air of the house when it stops humming its secret mantras and we're the only ones left with our little scalloped breaths. *I've broken free,* I whispered to the dead air.

142

Mother described that chest many times, each with its suave dangerous stranger, pockets full of sweetmeats, out there, trolling in silent concentric curves, all the strangers she ever spoke of. *They all have a trunk large enough to wedge in a child's body.*

She predicted our colors and postures in those chests, a phrase like *cut to ribbons* in the mind's eye of our dime store where spools of grosgrain with looped edges all pulled down wildly off their spindles and criss-crossed, wound about the children of the May cramped in their trunks. After the burning and cuttings, we might look like motley, like bright rags, like the stamps of foreign lands pasted one across the other in a hodge-podge of destinations. And the cigarettes would be welcome compared to *other things.* Oh, they lit us up in a way we could understand as she gestured in the air and mimed stubbing them out on child's flesh. *And then what,* one of us would breathe. *They lock the chests,* she'd hiss, turning an imaginary key, *and throw them in the LA River.*

Our mother could cleave to a tenet; our mother could hold a faith. For years we'd crane our necks, press our faces to the window glass, peering down a flood channel where a trunk might snag on a mudbar or wedge against a stand of rushes. There was never enough flow to carry them out, but they must have wanted that, swollen or roseate, they wanted to reach the sea by San Pedro where the longest thoroughfares end in cliffs and refineries, and children could be lifted and floated west. Never returned. She made that clear. But eased somehow and carried, and I wanted that too.

Is there something to the stories massing in the atmosphere and the shape of a life? The way each shock wave lifted the barge of our marriage bed and gliding down into the trough, I knew I would have to leave him. The video only confirmed it; rebar orphaned from its cinderblock, skeletons left standing while fallen flesh invented itself inside the disaster. By the first night fever clouds had formed over the valley sifting musk on all our heads. It was ravishing, that sense that fate was upon us.

What else could it be but the workings of desire when, after the fire turns the hills to ash and the sky passes through its whiskey colors, the rains come, rushing down through culverts faster than a man can run? St. Francis Dam only needed a small quake; concrete is supple like skin, it suppurates, bubbles and bursts. Something slips inside you, nose down, the chest slides a watery slope just as though you are that child and free because you finally reach the sea.

Loving with an Old Man

We are lovers, the old man and I, but not with each other. We are lovers, the old man and I, of the same beloved. He is mottled with age, looking fiercely ahead beyond the edge. Death does not frighten him. Not being here leaves him shaken.

The old man loves this land, the rockshelves beneath. The Cuyama Valley crumpled like a hand. Badlands dotted with pinones, rilled sky, ghostly delicate moon in the blue before dark. The old man loves by knowing, by speaking the names of rocks, tongues of earth that slid across ancient sea beds, lifted and broken by the force that raises up mountains.

He is an urgent lover. In his urgency he peoples the backcountry with lonely ranchers, with cattle. He peoples the land with its past. He knows all the old boundary lines, knows cathedral sandstones covered with figures, ochre and rust and chalky limestone. He rolls the images in his mouth, tastes the names like sweet fruit.

Ernesto Reyes in 1879 picking his way through the boulder-strewn gorge on horseback, with buckets balanced precariously, full of trout, living still, their flat wild eyes, their opalescent sheen. In order that the Cuyama River may run with trout, Ernesto Reyes, strange apostle, carries trout through the pass.

The old man recounts his stories, each word formed and released in love. He talks, I listen. He is filled with knowledge; I am inchoate. Both of us are hungry.

We climb, lapping the stillness like sucklings, passing silver tip firs, the spring on the mountainside. Birds shriek, rancorous in argument over water. We go on climbing toward the top, past a tree hunched in the wind, lightning-struck. The tree clenches its flesh, a scar running fresh and white down its length into the ground.

From the summit, the old man waves his hand out across the whole Cuyama Valley, the Carrizo Plain, Topa Topas beyond, the *Iwihinmu* where we stand, mountain that once was the center of the universe. "That's a lot of country out there," he says.

A PROSE POEM HAS the shape of water; it spreads out. Some poems are that expansive, that open and fluid, and their shape needs to reflect their nature. A prose poem puts a different type of pressure on language by its insistence that poetry is happening outside the structure of line break. Since it's indistinguishable from prose visually—what makes it a poem remains invisible, and that too, I think, is one of its propositions—the essence indivisible from the experience, its intensity and depth of meaning.

ANA DELGADILLO

Deaf Eyes Walking Through the California School for the Deaf, Riverside

All around me they walk with silent ears, black holes siphoning sounds . . . I walk and they don't notice how I cower to their hands as they weave hellos, goodbyes, and tell about the boy who loved them or the one who said he lied about his first kiss. I watch and hear nothing— my eyes blind to the rhythm of their sentences, each child finger spelling a life I've never known. Each sign different from the rest, and yet so similar that I become confused, but it doesn't faze them, so they move on. Little by little I close my ears; my voice turns off as easily as turning a dial above my larynx, and my lips are pressed tight as if in a tantrum, locked and the key thrown away. In the school's dormitory, Leslie asks me how to spell "interesting," her right and left hands pinching away from her chest, but I don't recognize the gesture. I don't know how to spell a word I cannot see and so she moves on, upset that I can't "hear" her, while I turn inwards until I can no longer hear myself. My eyes close and their fingers float on like origami swans caught in an autumn breeze.

"No Quiero Ser Quien Soy"

—Jorge Luis Borges

I don't want to be who I am, this nothingness of cells, connected by a glue that thins with each movement I make.

I'm sitting at the kitchen table covered by a mango-green tablecloth, I look beyond beige curtains and stare out at nothing but a blue jay, wishing I were it, perched on the fence, blending with the azure paint that peels away like water when it rains.

I don't want to be this tasteless recipe of meat, created by my mother and father, that'll only spoil in time, my father's nose, my mother's eyes, both their tempers that flare like moonlight during a coastal storm.

I don't want to be just me, sitting, writing, listening to the whispers of my *abuelita* telling me stories—of a lovely cockroach who buys

146

herself a red ribbon with a peso she found while cleaning beneath a chair, she later sits and waits for romance outside her door, and finds it in a young mouse named Ratoncito Perez, who she'll always love, and whose love will tear the feathers off sad pigeons when they fly away after they hear her cry, when he dies.

I am only the nostalgic little girl who cares, breaking her only water jar to the cries of a lost love, the sadness of the pigeons and a prayer that God would hear her anger within the shattered clay.

Surrounding My Birth in Veracruz

I'm sure I heard the plane's roar through my mother's abdomen, hitting my small upside down ears. My parents waved their goodbyes through the coconut palms of Veracruz. My uncle was flying north with the geese. Sometimes I can still feel my head throb where it bumped into the crest of my mother's pelvis, as she got into the car to leave the airport. She was anxious to get home, to get away from the fumes. I ricocheted clumsily within her like a pebble during an earthquake in Oaxaca that marked the day of my birth. The car crossed the city line and headed over the bridge where the Jamapa River's mouth tastes the saltiness of the sea, reaching the road canopied by mango trees, from Tinajas to Tierra Blanca. Oaxaca's only an hour away but still too far from home. My mother scrunched up in the back seat felt our connection, a pearl within an oyster in a smoked metal can. A truck passed by as another truck overtook us. Shots broke loose like cannons from the truck, fired at the men fleeing. My legs touched the tip of my nose as my father thrust my mother's head between her knees, all because the poor were just trying to get away from being poor.

My mother says she could feel me searching for an opening so I could see. I wanted to see. I wanted to know. I pushed my head through, opening her womb like a window. My mother still remembers the pain. My father rushed us to the nearest hospitable, where seventeen years later I would watch my grandfather die. The hospital floor remembers me. It remembers my father's worried steps, his snake skin boots bruising the linoleum tiles. It remembers the earth shaking.

The Muse

I work best alone, in the scent of sandalwood, in the scent of rotting fruit, but more so, surrounded by air that smells of roses withering in the rain. I work the best at night. When the cars stop passing by my house and wait like corpses along the street, a shadow or two resting on top of them. I work surrounded by the buzz of a small room heater at my feet, the whistle of the water steaming away on the stove dissolving fragments from my past, like the broken plate in the kitchen I dropped when I burnt myself. I listen for the voices walking on the street, cool with death, covered in scarlet silk that hides their tattered skin, rags within rags. And there is a girl among the crowd, her face, young, like grapes before they're laid out beneath the sun. She wears a black skirt that slips loosely above her hips; I imagine it isn't hers, for she's so small and it tents around her, tied at her waist with a red camisole. I look at her one last time, before my heart skips, before hers detonates. I look at her and feel my lips touching poisoned flowers, each petal like a fingernail cutting through my skin, cutting through her veil.

AS A CHILD, I grew up to my grandmother telling me short stories filled with lyrical qualities. I've loved prose poetry since reading Carolyn Forche's "The Colonel", Jorge Luis Borge's short prose pieces, as well as works by Neruda, Luis Cernuda, and other great poets. The liberties inherent in prose poetry allows for more of that childhood-influenced lyricism. It allows for the story feel, but has a way of developing in a more imagistic manner than having the formula constrictions that fiction has. The content of the poem is emphasized by "proper" line endings, but the continuation of the traditional line poetry into prose allows for both language and content to weave the poem together. I've come to depend on the form when the story and theme need more room to breathe. I've come to learn that sometimes when a poem isn't working with the usual line breaks I need to fill in the gaps and let it take its course in prose and vice versa.

JUAN DELGADO

Weather Reports

Clouds, cartoon-like, float across his TV screen, then yellow blots rush over a map of freeway routes. Another storm is coming.

His hand plunges into the sofa's crease. Where's the control? Nothing clicks between the weather's plot and ads announcing close-out sales and year long warranties.

He's missing the lights dimming around the visiting team and its star player running onto the court with a cocky smile, the self-assured entrance of a winner. Thunderstorms are expected. His house is sealed by double-pane windows, but the Doppler radar is closing in, surrounding his town. Over the TV's hum-dumb-consciousness, he says *I am lucky* that he's not on the freeway that crisscrosses and slows, reducing him to a pulse, a tapping on the dashboard, waiting to reach his off-ramp, his relief. *Lucky*, he says, but where is it?

He could test the sidewalk's icy cement, watch the leaves begin to flutter in schools of brown, and spot the tips of branches leaning with the wind if his wall was a green screen, a screen where his hand could direct the weather's route. He could click everything off and point to a blankness, giving him a clearing, a chance to watch a fox plunging its nose deep into the snow, sniffing the ground for a scent. Another storm is coming.

Wood Stilts

Early on, I knew there was the childhood I wished for and the one I had. In the city park, I roamed among the families enjoying their all-day picnics. They started their barbecue fires, fanning them with paper plates. Their charcoals turned grey by night. Junk stores were also my playgrounds. I met other kids, kids who could also waste whole afternoons. I would make my way to the bicycles they had hung by their handlebars. I would spin their wheels to see how fast their spokes could whirl the air. I would go and try on the discarded eye glasses, picking them out from a large wicker basket. The heavy frames that distorted the afternoon light coming through the store's windows were my favorite. I got dizzy. I rubbed my eyes among racks of blue jeans. Children would dart across the aisles of clothing. Often I stopped to stare at the jewelry. Back then, I was no thief. I knew Sunday afternoons were for lying on someone else's mowed lawn, daydreaming. Once I imagined I strung together two tin cans and had a conversation with the father I had lost. He kept his promise and made me some wooden stilts out of two-by-fours so I could walk around, shouting: "Look what he made for me." The other kids who lived on my street ran after me, watching me wobble with excitement across their lawns, waiting for me to fall and wanting to try out my home-made stilts. But I kept on going over their front yards as if their houses were abandoned. They couldn't catch me.

Astray

Why leave a grocery cart of belongings like this? By the freeway, it leans against a guard rail, loaded with bags. One has its mouth open to the Santa Anas, speaking nonsense. The cart's handle is greasy. Where is its owner? I get going. At a corner, I wait for a boy with a backpack to throw down his skateboard and glide. Then a man wearing two sweaters steps off the curb. Under his arm, he carries a rolled up sleeping bag. His hair is long and unkempt, covering his face. While the street pole chirps for him to hurry, he stops, finding something of value on the street, then he crosses. The driver behind me gently taps her horn. I clench my steering wheel. I try not to turn around to face that look of *hurry up*. In my neighborhood, who was first to notice the swelling of cars in my driveway? Again, I see my reflection the day I stepped in front of my answering machine's red eye, the voices of a funeral. I found a suit for my friend that still fit. I tapped his stiff shoulder and prayed. I get going. Under the freeway overpass looming over me like a fairy tale vine, I hesitate and stop, thinking about my off-ramp. The overpass straddles me like a giant spider with gray legs, and I stand captive under its long shadows, staring at the patches of sky while a horn blares past me in a gust of wind.

150

El Tigre Market

As apparent as the rest, the weeds crowd the asphalt cracks with green, the rust goes beyond metal, the abandoned lot's rails, battered by carts, blind and dumb bumpers, cast bars on the unsuspecting visitors, and the flower pots' opening bouquets are arranged for buyers who never come. As apparent as the rest, El Tigre walks upright and wears a sombrero and serape while pushing a grocery cart of food—there is the usual bounty for the ghosts of women drifting to a wake, another empty lot on Third Street by the train station waiting to be retrofitted for the big one. The spotlight on the roof guards no one. The lot frames the warning sign against criminal trespassing and the cardboard beds of the homeless brought in by the tracks. As apparent as the rest, the overturned grocery cart is a cage, openmouthed, freeing the jubilant buyer who moves to a bigger market, manicured and inviting for now.

I FEEL I HAVE AN added freedom to carry on when I write a prose poem, though I know this is not quite so. I start out not choosing to use line breaks, yet somewhere in the middle of writing my passage, I start wondering about the choices I am not making, wondering what would happen if I did break here or there, but I push on, trying to write through the distractions like a man with a fat check in his front pocket who wheels a grocery cart through a supermarket of choices. I pause, mouthing a self-imposed refrain, lost among the options.

DAVID DOMINGUEZ

The Bridle Paths

Carmelo Dominguez, b. 1814, Ures, Mexico

My great, great, great, grandfather, a Yaqui Indian, harnessed his mule team in the barn before dawn and packed the wagon with horse-hair rope and boots—goods he hoped to sell as far north as Fillmore, Piru, and Santa Paula. During the journey's hottest days, he dreamed of hills rolling with oranges and waxy leaves, not of the Sonoran granite that jolted his wooden wagon wheels and made his jawbones ache. This was before the Mexican-American War, so nothing stopped him but hunger and thirst. Along the Sonora River, he found a place under a flowering *palma blanca* and unrolled a mat made of fronds. The mules munched on tufts of weeds, and he ate egg and nopal burritos and drank coffee. The coffee tasted good as dusk disappeared. Stars. A breeze. And so he stretched his limbs before removing the bits from the mules' mouths, before unpacking his blanket, before feeling the round earth in the small of his back under the white flowers of the moon-lit bridle paths.

The Sunlit Barn

Esteban Dominguez, b. 1844, Ures, Mexico

When my great, great grandfather was a child, his father moved the family to Fillmore where they bought a cattle ranch among orange groves and oak trees. One afternoon, while unloading the wagon, Esteban knew that he didn't want to work on the ranch among flies and manure but in his own shop over an anvil and fire and rods that he could bend into hooks and chain link. These thoughts crossed his mind as his father, Carmelo, entered the barn. Carmelo commanded the mule-team's reins with a scowl, but today, his face was soft, and he said, "Son, this is for you, for your hard work," and it was a wooden box containing a horsehair brush, polish, and a rag. He showed the boy how to remove dust from his boots, how to polish them, and how to use the rag to buff them. "Treat things with respect, even the rag," he said, folding it and putting it in the box. Esteban stared at his father. The silence in the barn seemed to soothe even the gnats as Esteban searched for courage so that he could tell the person he feared and loved most, "I'm going to be a blacksmith"—the words, "Dad, I'm leaving the ranch forever."

Greeting His Fold

Esteban Dominguez, Junior, b. 1880, Piru, California

On the corner of Nebraska and Sheridan in Selma, California stood my great grandfather. The year was 1927, and he was wearing a black suit, holding a violin, and singing hymns in front of the Mexican American Methodist Church—the mission he founded amid the fields from where the *campesinos*, their knees embedded with dirt, came to worship singing the hymn "Hay Poder." The foundation sat high. One ascended many steps to enter its hall. I wonder if, as he sang, "La sangre que Él vertrió," if he thought about his father …a blacksmith who, unable to feed all his children, gave away his namesake son to a couple who sent him to seminary school in Mexico to learn the Bible and the violin? Perhaps he had made his peace before becoming a man of the cloth, before finding this plot of earth, before building this church—this boat in a river flowing west through grapes and nectarines and dust. Perhaps he thought not of his father and not even of himself as he greeted his fold like a shepherd and not like a scared boy who had become a sacrificial lamb so that the rest of his family could eat.

Evening Ritual

Moses Dominguez, b. 1915, Santa Paula, California.

During World War II, my grandfather worked for Bethlehem Steel building Naval war boats, in the Bay at Hunter's Point, with a rivet gun that shot threadless bolts through sheet metal … Liberty-vessel bows South Pacific bound. "Loose lips sink ships," the men said, so, after work, Grandpa said nothing as he strolled with his children on Ord Street, strolled wearing a hard hat, a blue Oxford, Frisco jeans, and steel-toed boots. At night, he practiced the trumpet as my father, age six, watched. And this is how it was—a man and a boy—the boy's eyes ablaze as he watches the man clear the spit valves; put away

153

Arban's Trumpet Technique; and sit on the couch; now, the boy takes the trumpet and polishes the bell and hands it back, his eyes still ablaze as he studies the way his father puts the horn into its black case lined with blue velvet and snaps it shut. . . .The father thinks not of work but of only his son, who is sitting on the couch and humming the "C" scale like a dove, perched on the edge of the roof, wanting nothing more in life than to celebrate the wild sun weaving together the clouds and the light.

Sitting in the Masonic Auditorium
Moses Dominguez, Junior, b. 1937, Madera, California

My father, a field laborer by the age of eight, played trumpet for the Sixth United States Army Band. Stationed at San Francisco's Presidio, he earned $72.00 a month and saved enough money to see John Coltrane at the Masonic Auditorium atop Nob Hill—its avenues smelling of the honeysuckle and bougainvillea hanging from the mansions' brick facades. In his pocket, he had $1.00 to spend as Coltrane said, "Good evening" so resonantly that my dad thought about only the miracle of being there and about the winter he hitchhiked home to Fresno and watched, through windows dripping with fog, the cotton fields lining the highways, fields whose ghosts had left his back tangled muscle, fields he knew he'd left forever as he watched Coltrane conduct his band with the dip of his horn. Coltrane and Dominguez . . . searching for something other than what they knew, not the usual run of chords, not the furrows infested with yellow jackets, black widows, and snakes. Something different and beyond reach but there and real and hiding in shadows of quivering jasmine climbing up the magnolias along the curbs of Nob Hill.

Gardening in My Backyard
David Dominguez, b. 1971, Fresno, California

This morning, I'm scooting between two rows of vines, tying stalks to wire so that come spring, my eyes will fill with blossoms. For now, the wires need tightening, so I pull them taut, with a pair of pliers, and recoil the slack around the nails in the posts. My nerves calm as I hum "Liebestraum" by Franz Liszt, a piece I'm memorizing on the piano, but the fingering slips from my memory unlike the blackberries that I'm going to eat with scrambled eggs and nopales and coffee. The woody thorns draw blood from my skin, but I don't care. In minutes, I'll be at my desk and writing, and with me will be a muleskinner, a blacksmith, a Methodist minister, and my grandfather and father. They are with me *now* . . . and everyone is sitting on the porch of a cattle ranch and talking about working in the orchards, about who can best tie a bowline knot to secure the crates in the back of a wagon so that the nectarines never bruise. . . . And now they are singing a *bolero* that Grandpa wrote, "Que seas para mí . . ." They sing as my father's trumpet makes the lyrics rise up out of the dust, and the words are clear and bright as gold.

I ENJOYED USING the prose poem for this series of works. Eliminating the line break encouraged longer sentences. These longer sentences were perfect for recording history. As the sentences unfurled freely so did nearly 200 years of family history. Thus, the prose poem helped me write about the years in which my family left Mexico and settled in California. If we want poetry to be read by more people, we must write poetry that is clear. One can not write clearly without knowing oneself first.

TERRY EHRET

World in Need of Braiding

This time of year our hands reach for the ends of things, twist patterns out of reflected light, out of water, loaves of bread. We lie down on the grass beside those we have disappointed, dry, unforgiven. We are supposed to be eating, preparing to sleep, filling the storerooms with enough color, dividing the universe into light and dark. But the dry grass, the purple thistles, the burrs in our socks want our attention. They are old. They are dying. They need us to listen to their stories, the same as last year.

"Not much breath left," say the grasses, and the brittle gates of the hill swing open. We love this season of loose connections, excess of prepositions, the long shadows of the corn. And now the carriage of darkness rides into view, bright yellow wheels and spokes like unfriendly laughter. Now the long carriage of night gathering speed.

Take us slowly down the wind-sea, this plenitude of death. Slowly, slowly run the last of the daylight, riding away the sun. We come wobbling, void of course, shaking in our inadequate clothes. We need time to lie down in the evening shadows we love, to stretch our heart beyond its cage of silence, to pull what grows, richly and abundantly, towards us.

The Dialectics of Outside and Inside

> In this drama of intimate geometry, where should one live?
> —*Gaston Bachelard, The Poetics of Space*

Yellow. Even here in the west where color is not the signal, some trees stopped being green. They got tired. They shook and rattled halfway up the hill from the schoolyard and I don't know if anyone was paying attention to them. I did. I did because I had always read about those towns where fall bathed the world in vivid oranges and russets and colors with names I only saw on crayons. My world was evergreen and pavement. Nothing dried up or swelled with rain. But those poplars bordering the mansion, near the convent grotto behind the boiler room, once an old livery stable, those poplars I watched shake and undress. They dropped thin yellow leaves, then

stood bare and stark through the chilly winter rains. It wasn't much,
I knew this. Poplars don't do anything in a spectacular way. And I
probably didn't even know their name then. I knew only live oak and
pine in my evergreen pavement town. From the asphalt schoolyard
to the flames of my imagined worlds, poplars halfway up the hill.
Poplars shook. I held onto them like anchors, like the only hope,
the possibility of change, the chance of dying as I knew I would. As I
knew I was. We had that in common.

Dark Birds

Dark birds are circling over the lines we live on, under a grey sky,
folding and unfolding. This sky comes to us from Alaska, dust motes
stirring in Africa. The difficulty of standing still, of finding a place in
the house to stand still, opening the cupboards, opening the drawers,
hearing the voices of women, their voices circling.

Watch out for the man in the office; no, listen to the man in the
office; no, it's clear you must forget the man in the office; he is only
a man and you cannot tell if he is really a man or only a bad smell, a
bad feeling, an arrangement of dark lines so much like the ones we
live on, only standing up and walking. He doesn't know where he is
going, and so if you follow him, your heart will shrivel up and you will
have this horrible thing inside you, this shriveled seed of something
once living which you no longer recognize as your own heart. Your
whole life spread around you, a landscape of holes, and each time
you look at them, they disappear, so that you must keep your head
very still, looking straight before you, with your wishes bumping
against you, bumping inside your ribcage like the heart you once
had. You know you are tethered to the future, tethered to this man,
so that to cut yourself loose would be to flap about making obscene
noises like a balloon suddenly losing its air, something ridiculous.

This is what they tell you, or what you tell yourself, and so you
go back to the beginning, back to the cupboards and the drawers,
studying how everything is arranged like weather patterns, not
lines after all, but circles moving out from a center you have not
yet discovered, though it must be near because you just caught a
glimpse of yourself circling back across the space between you and
something incredible, something unbearably bright.

JOHN OLIVARES ESPINOZA

Mrs. Flores's Oranges

It's Friday. A slow dusk after school. Anna enters my backyard when she notices me watering the pots. I shut off the faucet. My hands, wet and cold—fingers stiff as jerky. We talk of geometry, Beowulf, and flavored sodas. Anna is the only Mexican at school with red hair. Red as the shades of autumn. Freckles ember about her face. She wants an orange from Mrs. Flores's tree. Its branches eavesdrop over the wall. Setting my father's ladder by the wall, she climbs as I stare at her behind, plump as a pumpkin. She takes about four oranges in her hand and gives them two squeezes each. I feel every one. We hide under the blossoming grapefruit. She pulls out a folding knife as wide as two fingers that her father gave to her as protection from our streets. She says orange juice is good for the skin and slices the orange in half. Anna walks up to me and, vampire-like, tilts my head, squeezing the orange over my neck. The juice disappears into my shirt. She unbuttons her blouse halfway, throws her collar over her onion-white shoulder and squeezes some juice over her own neck. The pale orange strand of fluid running into her shirt tickles her, so she asks me if I'm going to let it run and let it stain her blouse. I pluck a grapefruit leaf and sweep it off. She buttons back her blouse. We finish our halves with talk of P.E., homecoming, and Pac-Man. She leaves, tossing her half between some pots. I'm left picking the pulp caught between my teeth.

No Weeds, No Work

If there were no weeds, there would be no work, **Dad says.** He's a machine sliding his hula-hu through the weeds carpeting the rose bed. I lag behind, raking, collecting weeds in dusty mounds until they are too heavy for the rake. My sore hands struggle to drag it another inch. The sun burns my nose, the tips of my ears. It will be hours before we quit and months before returning to the cool air of a classroom, more sleep, and fewer lunches for Mom to pack....

   I'm raking citrus leaves in my dreams again, even years later. I rake my first pile; toss it into the receptacle, then another one appears. The leaves never stop coming. My mother in shorts appears on her knees, helping me scoop leaves into the can. I tell her, *If there were no fathers, there would be no work,* as if somehow this was her fault. Her knees are scraped and bleeding now. The leaves never stop coming. I clean her wounds but the blood keeps rising.

Westbound

The rear tire blows out. Its puncture—the mouth of a swimmer coming up for air. Christmas week. No Triple A. No jack to lift my car like a dog raising a leg to piss. No jack to lift my spirit. I wait for a tow truck and it arrives with two Mexican men from Sonora huddled in the back. The truck tows their Ford Bronco, lame as a horse with a broken leg. Inside the cab of the tow truck it is cold and quiet. The heater offers less warmth than my own coughs. I ask the men what they'll do tonight. Sleep inside the car until the shop opens, they say. My car gets hauled to my parents' house in Indio. It didn't occur to me to offer the men shelter and some comforters laid on top of a tiled floor for the night. In bed, I think of the truck driver who pulled over to help before the tow truck. I remember declining his help, afraid maybe he would drag me into the saguaros, thrust a screwdriver in my neck. I think of those men inside the design of the Bronco, bodies undiscovered like the contorted dead. They will count stars through the windshield before dreaming of their wives smoothing the sheets after they've made love, in a town no one knows the name of, where no one stops for a cup of coffee. A town like mine.

The Trouble with Frankie Avila

He remains calm in his chair. I call his name and he looks over his shoulder. When I make eye contact, I call him again. He approaches my table, holds a steak knife to my throat, and asks how I know his name. I tell him I knew him once and say my name twice. He doesn't remember me. I mention the old friends—Tiaga, Boomer, Pérez, and Lomas. I mention the trashcan fires at school, the shattered windshields from the road reflectors he chucked, the drugs inhaled like desperate last breaths; I mention the bullies and their blunt fists he kept away from me; The shopping carts he pushed like a train to nowhere after high school. I mention the armed robbery and how there is nothing to forgive because I'm in no position to judge anything.

He withdraws the knife. He says he can't remember anything as part of his rehabilitation. I tell him I could help him. That no one should grow up in prison. I could teach him how to write, after all this time that's all I've learned how to do. I offer that maybe it will help him make sense of things—those neckties so difficult to knot.

I'm at some Melrose restaurant when I spot him. His face smoothed down from the raging fires of acne. He's wearing a dark suit woven with metallic thread, a maroon tie falls crooked down his torso. The knot is as round as a small plum. A blonde in a blue dress dines with him. A cream napkin is dropped on his table, smeared with lipstick the color of bougainvillea leaves. The blonde in the blue dress excuses herself from the table, insulted with something he's said. He hasn't changed a bit, old Frankie....

PETER EVERWINE

A Short Novel

A woman was courted by a man, but things did not go well for her.

She would be digging in the garden. "Worms in the cabbage!" she said.

"The bright horns of Moses," he replied.

She would be banging pots in the kitchen. "The cracked dish," she said.

"The princess is dancing in the ballroom," he replied.

She would be darning socks by the fireplace. "The rip in the seam," she said.

"Two birds in the bush," he replied.

She would be opening the door. "I'm leaving," she said. "The wind in the orchard," he replied.

The woman went off to the next village and was courted by another man.

"Worms in the cabbage," she said. "No doubt," he replied.

"The cracked dish," she said. "Just as I've always thought," he replied.

"The rip in the seam," she said. "And not a moment later," he replied.

The woman took the man for her husband. They prospered, raised a family, and grew old in the even tenor of their days. The man died with his eyes tightly shut. The woman died looking out the window. Their children gave them a grand funeral and took a different name.

A Story

A boy fell from a tree one day, and afterward one arm was shorter than the other and dragged at awkward angle—like a wounded wing—as if it kept in memory the accident of its origin, its difficult first flight. Thus marked, the boy gave up being a boy. He turned into a crow that croaked and flapped inside the circle of those who had remained children.

In literature this is not uncommon. People are forever turning into something else, and vice versa. What I am saying here belongs to literature. What a crow says is in another alphabet and is therefore unintelligible. To us it sounds like *Caw! Caw!* It resembles laughter. Or perhaps choking.

The Banjo Dream

One morning Earl Scruggs sits up in bed, reaches for his famous banjo, and plays nine consecutive wrong notes to a tune he's known all his life.

What's happening? he cries, holding up his hands, which he no longer recognizes. Meanwhile, thousands of miles away, I have awakened from a disturbing dream to discover that my hands—they no longer seem mine—have become thick-veined and tremble on my quilt like small horses at the starting gate. I am suddenly overwhelmed by happiness. Everything lies open before me: Limpid days. Blue distances. The song that will unlock the gates of paradise.

I RARELY WRITE a prose poem, and I have little more than a passing acquaintance with the form and its history. To use the form one must abandon any notion of poetic line, and I have difficulty doing this. Early in my writing career I wrote in traditional meters, so that even now, having long abandoned them, I still hear "metrical ghosts" informing the way words and syntax move from silence into speech. The few prose poems I've tried to write came from the dilemma of having a potential subject matter but no sense of line with which to develop it.

In short: my prose poem begins in failure.

Having said this, I should also add that abandoning the line for the paragraph is like having a large but definite space in which to roam about. I have a sense of freedom, though I still look for compression. Recurrence, expectation, surprise: these are as important to the prose poem as they are to the lyrical poem. So is silence and pacing, as ways of impeding the rush of sentences And there's another bonus for me: I get to try out another side of my temperament, something looser, more playful or ironic, than when I'm writing what I call "my poem." That I can count my prose poems on the fingers of one hand may suggest, alas, a different sort of failure.

ANN FISHER-WIRTH

Reading Dinner

we called it, when we'd each bring a book, prop it open under the
edge of a plate or balance a salt shaker on the pages, and read while
we cut our meat, passed the sugar, scooped out peas or mashed
potatoes. We sat at the cherrywood dropleaf table, in the alcove with
yellow organza curtains, turning the pages of a mystery, or history
homework, or *Glamour* magazine, and ate in silence. Oh, sometimes
the phone rang, that ugly brown wall phone with its long snaky cord
that got dirty and tangled, that you could pull to its full length to go
whisper in the hall, but then our mother would say, "Dear, call back
when you've finished your dinner."

Sometimes the cups and the sorrow would be very small, and
our mother would just sit, silent. We were near her. Near her. Mid-
American cooking, nothing special, but every night we ate together,
even when there was nothing to say, when to begin to talk would
have meant starting down a black staircase, backward, still gesturing
with the hands.

So those winters after my father's death, my sister and I helped
our mother through those long Berkeley dinner hours, reading,
passing the salt, our hands warm if they brushed each other. And
outside, dark coming on early in the roses he had planted, in the
wormy apple trees, the azaleas and fijoas. Dark coming on early
across the Bay, fog spilt through the Golden Gate, little drops of rain
beading the window glass, licking the spiky leaves of the olive tree.

Five Terraces

John Welpton (1903–1962)

He terraced the back yard in Berkeley, sweat-drenched, hacking
out blackberry vines all that summer. To me he was invisible, just a
presence down there somewhere, and at dinner our mother would
say, "Girls, isn't it wonderful, Daddy terraced the hill today with
railroad ties he carried himself."

But is this possible? I know he worked with no one, I know
there were railroad ties, because there they remained long after
his death, dividing what had been an eroding weed-choked

hillside into five terraces. First, at the bottom, the badminton court with its white pagoda where in 1961 Billy kissed me. Then the level of bushes, what kind I don't remember. Then the level I loved, where white spider chrysanthemums spilled their feathery petals and draggled in the mud of October, November. Then the level of apple trees, and finally the level of sundial, roses.

Curt, he ordered my sister and me to pick up fallen apples. And how we hated the sweet stench and squlch of bruised or rotten apples in the tall grasses. How we hated him then for making us touch death, making us pile soft wet slush and squoosh of brown apple flesh in buckets—touch what was not lovely with our nearly adolescent fingers, while our parents did the clean work, pruning: she happy to be near him, holding branches, he lopping and shearing.

I knew him that summer, that fall, and not much longer. One day he was in bed. The house was quiet, darkened. "Daddy strained himself in the heat," our mother said. What, exactly, was wrong, we never knew—or whether it was connected with his collapse one Christmastime, his death the next November.

I know him down there somewhere: after the war, after Japan, after his retirement from the Army, those brief Berkeley years when my parents thought at last they'd have a life together. He chops out weeds, cuts back briars, digs terrace levels and smooths the clay. His muscles rope across his back, sweat stings his eyes, as he hauls the heavy railroad ties, terracing. He makes the earth stand still.

Pathétique

We have all been in rooms we can't shelter in, rooms where the clocks go to twenty-four hours and the blue walls offer no harvest of sleeping. We've all been lost in a chair, trying to tie our shoes as mother calls, "Come to the charity." Even small we've watched the garden through our window, sucking on broomstraws, fumbling with shoestrings. How lonely the little benches with their umbrella men. How lonely the mushrooms far away beneath the pine trees, where lovers come to gather wet wood. The unaccountable fire of their beauty causes the scholars to murmur, "O the cherubim, the cherubim." But where we sit and think, rain wipes its nose on the streaky window. Still, we've been here before, juggling a tennis ball. Tomorrow fifty years ago, the baker and the milkman will make their magic deliveries. The dog will steal the doughnuts on the doorstep. Gleaming bottles with red cows and print will greet us when we step into the day.

EVERY CHILD AND ADOLESCENT should get to live in Berkeley as it was in the early 1960s. We moved there from Camp Zama, Japan, in 1957, when my father retired from the US Army; my parents got to choose where to live from anywhere in the whole wide world. Though my sister and I tried at first to convince them that the babysitters, movies, and ice cream were better in our former home of Camp Hill, Pennsylvania, once we settled into the house on LeRoy Avenue, Berkeley became our cherished place, too.

My mother always said that after "the girls" grew up, she wanted to ride around with my dad in a little red sports car. He would wear a beret, and they'd stop at coffee houses or walk beneath the eucalyptus trees in Tilden. My parents' engagement had endured World War II, and their marriage had endured the Korean War. They loved each other completely, and these were to be their years together. But in 1961, my father collapsed at his office in San Francisco, and on November 23, 1962, he died of the brain cancer a team of doctors had not been able to excise.

After my father's death, I would sit in my room overlooking the Bay, high in the Berkeley hills, as if I kept watch on a ship all night as it carried my family through storm and sorrow. Those were rough years; they included the stillbirth, three years later, of my first daughter.

I don't ordinarily write prose poems, though it's a form that intrigues me. There are, however, moments in a life that resonate and deepen over long periods of time—"moments of being," Virginia Woolf calls them—and sometimes, it seems to me, these can best be explored in prose poetry: a world in a little room. Also, as in "Pathétique," the prose poem offers a great space to play around with the alogical; image and language are foregrounded, when one doesn't have to think about the line. (I should add a note to "Pathetique": it may not seem to be a California prose poem, but that little old milk bottle is from the organic dairy at Point Reyes Station; I wrote this at The Mesa Refuge while resident there.)

I think that poetry, trees, the ocean, saved my life. Then and later, Berkeley held what I needed, accepted whatever I gave it.

DIANE FRANK

His Emotions Were Slippery Like an Avocado

It rained between conversations. We were in a café on Judah close to the beach where sand dollars pile up after the low tide. He bought me breakfast—avocados and eggs before a journey into the underworld.

When the rain stopped, the light turned green at the corner, reflecting green on the puddled streetcar tracks. "I'll be keeping the light on inside for you," he said.

I told him, "I'll remember that," thinking inside to myself, "table crumbs," wondering how he smelled inside his shirt.

He paid for my lunch, which is a signal in this part of the country. He said he'd been painting all morning and explained to me what the fumes do to your nose. I could see it—green paint on the hairs inside his nostrils.

On Friday night he kissed me on the street, gave the half-Japanese man two dollars to buy himself a beer and go away. We talked about how strippers in West Palm Beach are like the geishas in Kyoto. He should know. He was there. He told me men like to give up their power to these women and let the woman be in charge. I told him about the Noh actor in Kyoto who thought I was a geisha. He took me out for tea late at night, which is expensive, because he needed to tell his secrets to a stranger. Someone he'd never see again.

American men don't tell you what they mean. They give signals. They think about seducing you in airplanes but pretend they don't care. They don't tell you the truth until you are gone.

Later that night we walked on the beach, where I found a slice of a conch, the fractal spiraling to the edge of my emotions. My palms felt like sand dollar fossils—etched orbits of the pentagram pressed to stone between sand. I wanted to put my nose against his skin. Then my lips.

I remembered the night in San Francisco when we went to Ebisu for sushi and got a little bit drunk on sake. That was my first signal. The wind was strong that night around the ATM machine and the telephone booth in the Inner Sunset. We tangled around each other on the streetcar and loved each other for hours that night.

His plane left at six o'clock in the morning. I let the hug he gave me imprint like oak leaves. Bamboo over a koi pond, his eyes eggshell blue full of messages. My emotions—spider webs on leaves tearing apart. And what does it mean to have a man inside you? I act like Sheherazade. I tell him stories.

Every Monday I Put Herbs in His Water Bottle

His grandfather is a Yemenite herbal doctor. He is an astronomer or a satellite engineer, but he is obsessed with herbs. I always dance with herbs in my water bottle, and if he asks me, I tell him the formula. Sometimes we dance together, when his wife or his dance partner doesn't come. A dance partner is like a wife in these circles and you can't interfere.

Sometimes we dance together, old couple dances like *Rachel* and *Shnei Shoshanim*. Usually his dance partner pulls him away from me. On nights when she is unbearable, I stand next to him in line for dances like *Debka Inbar* and *Al Salsalim*. I have to touch him, even if it's just his hand.

There's something unbearably sexy about muscular men who dance. Israelis have endorphins in their muscles—it's from their time in the army. The studio where I don't live anymore has the scent of a paratrooper who used to do push-ups with me curled around his back. Easier, he said, than a soldier on his back with a heavy pack on. The memory has molecules of endorphins.

American men on the dance floor can look at you in a way that you know they'd like to go to bed with you. Israeli men look at you like they're already in bed with you. Even when I'm standing next to him in line, he looks at me that way. His skin speaks to me in the language of an olive tree. His voice is my history.

When my desire is too strong to be appropriate, I dance with other men. But I know exactly where he is on the dance floor. At the end of the evening, I put aphrodisiac herbs in his water bottle and say, "This is for your wife."

He says, "What are you doing to me? You have no mercy. I won't be able to walk tomorrow." His skin is the same color as the paratrooper. They know the same form of deadly martial arts.

On the way home I listen to *Debka Inbar*. I play it over and over. By now he is in bed with his wife, but his eyes have no mercy. The music is inside me and reminds me of his skin.

Between Two Languages

Keeping silent is a tactic, but really I want to talk. In Hebrew the letters look like animals or doors to a different life that I won't be going through this time.

When I was in Jerusalem, I could not talk because I didn't know the language. The family I stayed with wanted me to marry their eldest son, but I couldn't tell them if I was tired or hungry. I danced with them in the space between two languages.

All I want to do in my dreams is dance. If you want to control your dreams, Castaneda says to look at your hands. I choose to fly instead, to take on the body of tiny, delicate animals without gravity.

All of my dreams are about breaking rules. I seduce a Chinese friend, which is against his culture. I have dinner with my therapist in the basement. You understand my letters even though they are in a different language.

If I could control my dreams, you'd come and make love to me instead of walking away. I'd abolish distance and the airport.

I was up in the air like a bird when he dropped me. My delicate frame could not withstand the impact, and I shattered between two continents.

My dreams bring me messages. At night something large and silent wraps itself around me and puts its hand over my heart.

I LOVE TELLING STORIES and using a narrative voice in poems. As a musician, I'm highly aware of rhythm, the music of language, and how that functions in a poem. When the rhythms feel more like prose than the condensed cadence

168

of a poem and the line becomes so long that a line break is arbitrary, a prose poem is the natural form. I was introduced to the prose poem by Stephen Dunn, my first poetry teacher, when I was nineteen years old. Robert Bly's prose poems, with their shaman voice and non-linear leaping style, continued to open my writing that way. The idea of a prose poem was mysterious, but a few years later, I found myself writing that way. San Francisco continues to be a huge influence on my poetry and my prose. I grew up on the east coast, but San Francisco was the first place that felt like home. It's a place of intense freedom and permission, full of beauty, music and mystery. Poetry is easier for me than playing cello—music is my edge of discovery. It's also a huge part of my San Francisco experience and spills into my poetry and prose.

JULIE GAMBERG

from *California*

Grapevine

Every summer, the wooden posts burn, and I return to eschatology. Thick black smoke smothers the hills like a mover's blanket. Sometimes in winter I am impassable too, and there are signs for miles away announcing this fact. Still, no one believes it. Still they come toward me, as if in a dream. As if running toward water and being unable to stop.

Sun

First there are brown glasses stacked like ladder rungs at the drugstore. Fire in the mouth. Then there is dry grass. Open a box. Intonation in the heart. Swelling. Lizards with tiny flicking tongues.

Spanish

Preserved sounds, packed in chocolate. *Why do you never speak?* Fully translated into time rings cut from branches. These utterances exceed their material construction. You have to open your mouth wider.

Ocean

I ignore the colony of missiles. They are as unfriendly as a high school student, shaky fingers clasping the popularity cliff. We have the body of the mind. The mouth in a fine O, the lips standing still. The voice must be saying something. The language of evaporation. Air posing as air.

Mexico

These skies are sung by longing. When I was in love, a vibration of coral, teardrop-thick. Shadows cast on radio waves stutter and start. Blue like curtains of glacier, something to do with sunlight and oxygen. Dividing land by language.

Disneyland

Kabuki pale. Parking lot aria. You stand at the podium and tell me how life should be. I sell hot dogs for more than you have in trade. They are made of the intestines, ears and anuses of pigs. Neither matter nor energy can be created nor destroyed. Nothing is ever wasted.

Market Street

I do not run at an angle, but rather the streets around me scoot and shift when they see me coming. I scare them into apathy, with my long track marks and my giant Safeway. I could swallow up whole this entire state and no one would see it coming. Sometimes I'm tempted to fold up like that, to just give away my remains and leave behind this orderliness. In the wayback of my memory, I ate kumquats at tea time.

IN THE NOVEL *Everything is Illuminated* the hero's grandfather is a freak baby. He is born with a full set of teeth. When I chose to write these poems in the form of prose poetry it was because in the process of their birth, they made clear that they come with their own set of internal line breaks and rhythm, their own logic, and a horizontal layering that creates, as Sarah Manguso writes of the prose poem, their own "aggregation of meaning." The prose poem, by ignoring the one irrefutable way to tell a poem from anything else, is nothing if not highly subversive. I delight in these beautiful, subversive freak babies, and rock them just the same.

RICHARD GARCIA

Ponce de León and the Ten Milkshakes

My father claimed that his side of the family is descended from Ponce de León. That would explain why the men in our family have always been considered immature.

Ponce de León's birth: No one knows how or where or when Ponce de León was born. But it is said that he cried in the womb. Those who cry in the womb are sometimes able to know the future.

That is why members of my family sometimes know what is going to happen. When I was nine I knew days in advance that I would win a ham playing roulette at the Saint Agnes Church Easter Fair.

Why was he called Ponce de León? Would it not have been better to be roar of the lion, or claws of the lion? My father said it was because he could eat as much of anything as he wanted and his stomach would not be upset, hence, belly of the lion.

Even as a child Ponce de León knew that he would do something no one else had done, some feat or adventure that would make him legendary. When I was ten years old I knew that I would be famous for drinking ten milkshakes.

I announced to my friends, "I can drink ten milkshakes!" This was way back in the nineteen-fifties when milkshakes were milkshakes. The challenge was accepted. Chocolate, vanilla, strawberry—each cold chrome canister filling three tall glasses with a little left over. I drank that too.

Historians have written that Ponce de León was not looking for the Fountain of Youth but for natives to kidnap and sell as slaves. My friends thought that I could never drink ten milkshakes.

Because I am descended from Ponce de León, I knew I would drink nine milkshakes and that the waitress and my friends would plead with me to stop before I exploded, right there at the counter of Glendell's Sweet Shop.

Historians have doubted that Ponce de León ever found the Fountain of Youth. No one doubted I could have drunk that tenth milkshake. Not my friends who carried me home, held above their heads like a hero of old, not my father when he saw them carry me up the stairs with milkshake dribbling down my chin. He had known that I would be carried home by my friends that day and was there to greet us.

"Ponce de León!" he exclaimed in triumph, pounding his stomach with his fist, "Ponce de León!"

Could Ponce de León have drunk all he wanted from the Fountain of Youth and never gotten full? Could Ponce de León have drunk ten milkshakes? Ponce de León's death: nothing is known of Ponce de León's death.

The Poetry Lesson

for Charles Webb

Charles and I are painting a wall in my childhood room. This is how we teach a poetry lesson at Harvard. A minor official from the Dean's Office comes to see us. He can barely suppress a smirk, as he tells us, in his fake British accent, that the Dean is not pleased. Our paint is peeling after it dries. The spackling is showing through under the paint; obviously, we did not prime it.

And the wall was supposed to be Navaho Pink, not Bone Yard White. In short, bad poetry lesson and our services are no longer required.

Well, I remark, feigning indifference, I bet those Greeks forgot to prime their temples and statues too. So that's just hooplabumky. And in case you don't know what that is, Mr. Minor Functionary, that is when you feel all alone, abandoned like a country bumpkin on a basketball court but the squeegee of indifference wipes the window of your mind clear and dry.

Charles, being more experienced in academia, says nothing. We gather up our tools and climb out the window, over the fence, down the alley and into the street. It is San Francisco in the late forties. Technically, Charles hasn't been born yet. But hell, we're poets, and as the wind blows right though our bodies, we wish the wind well.

Postcard from Lake Manzanita

The trees here are made of glass, and they are alive. Actually, there is only one tree. It rises out of the lake, a huge scarlet red and yellow tower. It feeds on air and plastic cushions that float in the water.

When we arrived I was alone. How is that possible? I must have, in our haste to pack, driven off without you. I can picture you standing in the driveway in the predawn light, surprised, or perhaps amused, as the taillights of our car recede in the dark. Did you turn and go back to your puzzle?

Tomorrow I will try fishing. They say the fish here are also made of glass. The only bait that works on them are tiny, triangular mirrors, each with a number or letter etched into their surface. Figuring out which number or letter is effective at which hour can be a challenge. But locals say that a small #1, trolled on the surface so it creates a V, always works for a few brief but frantic moments, one hour after sunset.

A Hero in the War

The Japanese, aware that Americans have short memories and learn all their history from the movies, are buying up the Hollywood studios.

Gradually, they are changing the endings of World War II movies. Eventually the Americans will come to believe they lost the war.

A used car salesman wakes up with the night sweats and reaches for the gun he keeps by his bed. He was a hero in the war. Or was it a movie he saw?

Maybe he was a hero in the war and he wrote a book about it, then starred in a movie about his life. But he is confused. It seems the last time he saw the movie on late-night TV, he died.

He grabs his gun and runs outside screaming, "I am not dead!" But nobody in the neighborhood pays much attention to him.

Not at the all-night convenience store. Not the police who bring him home and put him to bed. He has done this before and his gun is only a cap pistol. Besides, he was a hero in the war.

174

THERE ARE TWO WAYS by which I know a poem I am working on may work better as a prose poem. The first is that I just can't seem to get the line right, either as a short line or a long one, and either way just seems wrong. If I open it up into prose, the line seems to flow better, to actually be more lyrical. The second, which is often combined with the first, is that the poem has a fable-like narrative.

"The Poetry Lesson" came in a dream. The locale, as in so many of my dreams, was my room in the house where I grew up in the Haight-Ashbury district of San Francisco, and the alley and the fence I used to climb as a child, and still scale in my dreams. "Postcard from Lake Manzanita" was written while looking at a postcard of the glass art of Dale Chihuly. It also has to do with days I've spent fly-fishing on Lake Manzanita in Northern California. "Ponce de Leon" is based partly on a bet I won when I was about eleven, that I could drink ten milkshakes. An article I read about Audie Murphy is part of the basis for "A Hero in the War."

AMY GERSTLER

Upended Lament

> "You see, casseroles can shout too. Everything can."
> —*Pablo Picasso*

Seeking relief from the tide-like pull of dark thoughts, I took some household objects into my confidence. O useful friends, I began. What am I to do? Marooned and wounded, I'm in the midst of an extended stretch of celibacy. Each time the last man I dated and I got to the brink of sex he'd go pale and whisper, "Let's just cuddle." My boss takes great delight in making me cry. The troop of toothless parolees next door opened a car repair shop in their driveway. It's busy from midnight to 5 am with jobs that require chain saws and rivet guns. Police helicopters swoop back and forth over my block all night shining searchlights into bedroom windows. My brain is a smoldering train wreck, full of sinister information and . . . The waffle iron yawned greasily. "It's your own damn fault. Why didn't you move to a better neighborhood when you could afford it? Oh, for Christ's sake don't cry. I was only joking." The faded tablecloth looked ashamed. Its fringe continued to fray. "Quit whining," rasped the cracked glass pitcher. She was feeling a bit choked, as I'd cut a bunch of begonias and jammed their stems into her open throat. I poured myself some club soda to settle my stomach. "Water's for sissies," the tumbler mumbled. "After all you've been through, what you need is vodka, pronto." The light of day mocked me. "A couple of slaps in the face, a few fresh setbacks and suddenly you're numbering yourself among the slain? Give me a break." During a lull in the conversation, a hand painted china plate explained, "You suffer the trials and transformations of middle age. Yes, there are annoyances and betrayals. Yes, loves fall away. That doesn't mean you give in." For several minutes an atmosphere of gravity and forgiveness seemed to prevail in the kitchen. Pink and black peppercorns nattered happily in their grinder. "We who are about to be pulverized salute you!" Down the long hall, the bed was remarkably welcoming. "Come to me," it whispered. "Climb aboard and drift for a spell. We'll find some windswept piney islands and you can go ashore and colonize them if you like." I thought about the soul's wilderness, still unexplored at this late date. So began an unmapped and provision less voyage. I threw my clothes overboard and watched them sink. Immediately I felt lighter, like a woman whose health has been recently restored. Peering over the edge of my barge, I could see a beautifully appointed ballroom at the bottom of the deep water, complete with coat check rooms, mirrored walls, and lounges carpeted in a bold pattern of red and yellow quarter moons. There were rows of round tables with candles aglow on each, and beyond that, an oblong mahogany dance floor. People were dancing the lindy, the shimmy and the mambo. The bandstand was lit with colored spotlights as though a show was about to begin. Can you fathom the serene feeling it gives to float over a drowned ballroom? And now everything slows way down. We must wait patiently to see who steps out on stage to entertain us, to warble and croon, struggling to attain his or her perfect form, clad perhaps in dark green sharkskin or a silvery gown encrusted with pearls.

Introduction to a Now Lost Lecture on Disposition

This afternoon, despite the extreme heat, I hope to address those of all temperaments: the thin and the thick blooded, wearers of polyester and leather, hyper types and gloomsters, those with unlimited sympathies, dupes and rubes, flatterers, bright excitable types, sulkers and drunks, brooders and the cruel, cold fish and committed party-ers, those who believe life is a to-the-death contest of their urges pitted against everyone else's, kingly types who demand the rest of us kneel and kiss their rings, the kindly ones who think they know best, the threateners and frighteners, those who know they see and feel more deeply than the common throng, those who just want to be left alone so they can finger-paint all day or tinker with their cars or repair broken toasters in their spotless garages, that anointed tribe who thinks of nothing but where their next fix is coming from, the gregarious ones and the bad mixers, the ones who plan elaborately but never act; and the exhausting ones who croon, "I love you, I love you . . . I want to stay up all night exchanging whispered intimacies with you, till the milk is delivered and the newspaper comes thumping on the doorstep"—the breathless ones who won't let you get any sleep and won't stop talking your goddamn ear off. (yawns)

177

Interview with a Dog

Q: Why on earth did you eat that ten-dollar bill? It can't have tasted nice.

A: Don't be gruff. Anything that falls on the floor is mine. Can I have a cookie now to change my mouth lining flavor? Can I? Can I?

Q: What does it mean to be runt of the litter?

A: Stomped on lowest rung. Everyday fear-bath, nonstop bow-down. Wreathed in terror-reek that broadcasts you are last of the last. I don't like to talk about this stuff...

Q: OK. I just gave you a bath. Then you went and rolled in manure.

A: Will you barbecue soon? Will you let me lick the grill when it cools?

Q: No, really. How come I get you all nice and clean and you immediately roll in something stinky?

A: Humans don't get true grooming, which only takes place using the tongue. Toothpaste, mouthwash, and deodorant are what's "stinky." Soap's revolting. Terrible invention. Why have it in your lamplit, carpeted, doorlocked lair? Dung is informative, complex—full of news flashes from the body's interior. Shit's an encyclopedia, volumes of urgent correspondence your organs wrote if only you knew how to read. What's learnt from smelling shampoo? It just causes sneezing, erases articulate fumes. Bulldozes olfactory signposts. Washing is book burning.

Q: How come you chew window blinds during thunderstorms?

A: Must break hard things with teeth—bite/crunch/tear when scared. Need escape hatch fast. Eat my way out.

Q: Well, that makes a certain sort of sense. But why did you roll in the carcass of that dead seal when we took you to the beach at Morro Bay?

A: To transfer ghost-cloak of invisibility, silly. Death-smell lends protection. Winner of ripest warm day decay contest is not challenged by pack peers—billowing putrefaction blasts inspire respect and great kill-pride! Meat rot bouquet is prey-smell's best medal. What don't you understand in that?

Q: Hmmm. And what motivated you to eat that postcard from Alex and chew up several of my Catholic saint statuettes?

A: Doesn't make a lick of sense to me. THERE'S THE CAT! GET HIM! (races out of room.)

THE PROSE POEM is an attempt to try and fuse the angelic and the tawdry; the holy and the lowlife; the earthly and the celestial. This particular marrying of seemingly opposite elements is an abiding interest of mine for a number of reasons, not the least of which is that such a fusion is central to my sense of what it's like to be human; to be a seething container of the mystic, the quotidian, and the sinister, among other things.

JANICE GOULD

The Lesson

Just beyond the hairpin turn on Del Mar Avenue, three blocks from home, my ankle twists on an edge of asphalt, and my right foot smashes against hard-packed soil. Stumbling into a parked car, I almost drop the slim, black oboe case. Pain spikes into a gasp of shock, sending my books with études and exercises flying. A sudden, violent ache in my foot makes sweat bead at my hairline. Should I return home? That would mean facing my mom's wrath. It would take twenty minutes to walk back up the hill, only to have her yell, "You came home because of a turned ankle? I pay good money for those lessons, and you haven't touched that instrument all week! So if you think I'm going to drive you, you're out of luck!" Leaning against the car, I remove my loafer, empty it of grit and pebbles, and gingerly dust off the instep of my bare foot against my left calf. I squeeze my eyes shut against the pain. I don't dare look. Straightening my skirt, I gather my books from among the weeds and clump ahead, trying out different methods for proceeding without bearing down too much.

The steep road is shady beneath the eucalyptus along Glendale, but La Loma is bright with plum and apple blossoms and the forever view through the Golden Gate. On this Saturday afternoon, the bay looks steely beneath the pale sky. Despite my foot's excruciating distress, I work at denying it. A pair of mourning doves perches cozily on the phone lines above the oblique walkway. I can smell the pungent fragrance of acacia trees. After Buena Vista, I take the short-cut down the paved back steps of my old elementary school, Hillside, bracing myself against the iron rail. The air is moist beneath a canopy of lilacs and bare madrones. Reaching Hilgard, I wait to cross busy Euclid Avenue, then Scenic and Arch. Limping, I force my weight onto the metatarsus and my big toe. *It's not that bad,* I whisper, *I can make it.*

The streets are no longer precipitous, the grade hardly noticeable. Here's Oxford and the horticulture station where my high school friends and I joke that UC scientists devise experiments, growing huge cauliflowers in nuked-out soil. I can see Mrs. Forrest's old Victorian on Shattuck near Virginia. She owns the music shop down the street, but Monsieur LeRoux—first oboe in the San Francisco Symphony—has arranged to give lessons in the living room of her home, which he prefers to the cacophonous rooms in the music store. I hobble as quickly as I can along the sidewalk, stumping like Chester from "Gunsmoke," afraid I'll be late. At the top of the steps, Monsieur LeRoux greets me kindly, and offers me a café au lait, which he makes on Mrs. Forrest's gas stove. We work on breath control, and he demonstrates again how to fill the diaphragm with air and release it slowly, aspirating so carefully the flame of a candle hardly flickers and will not blow out. All this time, my foot is throbbing mercilessly, but I am too shy to say anything.

After the lesson, waiting for the bus by the drugstore on University Avenue, I finally slip off my shoe and examine my foot. The bone juts up alarmingly beneath the skin, a knobby sponge, darkly bruised. Tears spring to my eyes. I consider calling home, but that would mean using some of my bus money, and if Mom refuses to come, I'll have to walk back up the hill. As it is, I hoof the usual half hour from where the bus leaves me off at Grizzly Peak and Shasta Road. When I get home, dusk has fallen. From the street, the steps are shadowy because no one's turned on the porch light. Is Mom still mad? She seems calm when I find her in the kitchen, preparing a chicken. "Look," I tell her as I stumble in, "I've hurt my foot."

Flu, 1962

It was a cold decade, mostly black and white, but occasionally capable of the sweetest color—pale pink blossoms on the Japanese plum, apple trees laden with white flowers, and north of Sebastapol the vibrant yellow of daffodils on slender, pleated stems. After five, shadows were lengthening, and we sat stuck in traffic just beyond San Rafael with night coming on. We were headed to the Bishop's Ranch, a weekend retreat for Episcopal Young Churchmen in the hilly country that would someday grow superlative grapes for expensive wines; their garnet hues would stain the inside of a glass.

I was queasy from the lurching of the car, the stops and starts, the smell of exhaust. I felt a chill on my neck but was too shy to ask the lady, the mother of one of the other girls, to turn on the heater. It was a decade of odd fabrics, synthetics, which is why we were never warm, and even men wore polyester, their suits shiny like the armor of certain insects. The next day I shivered in the warm sun, but that evening, when a fire leapt in the fireplace of the big lodge, I felt flushed. The young, recently ordained curate (we were not to know he was gay till some years later) had asked me to bring my guitar, and now he wanted me to sing about the girl who decides to sleep next to her mother instead of taking an unfaithful suitor. After the song, I slowly, tiredly went back to the bunkhouse under an inky, star-filled sky. The downhill slope swam before me and, stumbling with dizziness, I almost fell headlong unto the clipped and dew-slick lawn. I had the sensation of being lifted slightly out of my body. Late in the night, I awoke, flesh aching, in the shuddering cold of the dorm room, feeling homesick. The usual fear and dismay resurfaced in me that I had failed my mother. The secrets of my newly adolescent life were beginning to strangle me. When I arrived home, the Sunday fog, hardly a mist, was gathering in the tops of the eucalyptus across the ravine while a blue notice lay open on the dining room table—the classes I was about to flunk. Mama harangued, chastised, humiliated me, and I retreated to my room, having earned her scorn, her fierce, upright anger. "I don't care if you don't feel well, you'll be in school tomorrow!" That night was the last time I came to parents' room, seeking their bed. Unable to stay warm, trembling uncontrollably, I stood, moaning, till Mama woke up and let me under the covers, where she tried to warm me with her body. Weeks later, we learned that one of my classmates, a robust girl who shot baskets as well as any boy, had succumbed to the illness and had died. That night, Mama placed her hand on my forehead—her smooth palm, her touch, complete and gentle—and said to my barely awake father, "This child has a raging fever." Like a miracle then, it seemed as if I was alone with my mother, and I was still a child. So, comforted, I slept.

Easter Sunday

Easter Sunday and my father plans a visit to one of the old missions along the Camino Real. After church we get on the highway and begin our journey. It is late March or early April. The sky is azure and clouds scud in from the Pacific, thick and white. They break apart as they pass over the coast range, and the broken fragments, still large, move swiftly over the land. The land is green, not the green of Germany as I have heard it reported, but a green full of sunlight and rapid change. If the winter and spring rains have been sufficient, the presence of last year's grasses will be hidden, their gray stalks covered by fresh growth. This spring the sturdy flowers have opened, and my mother reels off the endless list of names as we pass them by: lupine, California poppy, clarkia, larkspur, Indian paintbrush, owl's clover, buttercup, vetch, trillium, forget-me-not, columbine, fairy's lantern, pearly everlasting. The species are so mixed we hardly know the indigenous from the introduced, the native from the volunteer, the survivor from the parasite populations that have sprung up in the friendly habitat. This is California with its rich, false history. Whatever direction one goes. north or south, the flowers mark boundaries, the possibility of their appearance determined by many things: hills or gullies, rainfall or drought, ranches or subdivisions, the presence of other like-minded plants and trees.

We drive far south to the mission in the Los Padres Mountains. Here, at the far end of a long, fertile valley, the military has established a base. It is difficult to understand the need for weapons or to feel cheered by the hard-faced, uniformed men, armored vehicles, and what appear to be the underground houses for missiles. No one wants to talk about the war, which explodes somewhere else with wearisome regularity each night on television. It is Sunday, Easter; the family is enjoying a rare peace. The day is beautiful and the lulls sacred. It is hard to imagine destruction. At the mission, the enclosed courtyard is dry and warm, bees buzz among the cactus and purple roses. In the small adobe cells, opened for our inspection, are the accoutrements of the Franciscans, solemn crucifixes nailed above their skinny beds. In other rooms the Indians worked, tanning leather, shoeing horses, cooking the padres' soup. In these troughs, the Indians were fed. Beyond the mission are the remnants of *hornos* and corrals, the fields of wild bulbs and clover the Indians longed to eat. Under the portico, a shiver moves up my spine: the dead, I know suddenly, are buried in the walls, among the arches, and beneath this well-tamped earth.

Across the mountains, not far as the raven flies, lies the ocean, the jagged edge of the continent.

THE FORM FASCINATES ME. What I like about the prose poem is the compact narrative combined with the lyric qualities of poetry. Like a poem, it offers turns and surprises and depends on compressed language. Like prose, it offers a narrative but seems more interested in the story's kernel.

C. G. HANSLICEK

Meditation on Mockers

I know the mockingbirds in the maple are sitting on eggs. I know this because on Sunday they exploded from the tree and drove away a pair of crows who returned twice more for scrambled eggs, but who got nowhere but to the very tip of a deodar, tossed by the bewildering wind, cackling quietly to themselves. And I know this because on Monday one of them chased a squirrel for fifty yards along a power line; the squirrel looked like a drunken ballerina, legs whipping every-which-way, not at all *en pointe*. And today both of them swooped down and pecked the tail of a portly cat until he loped off, bereft of dignity, utterly uncatted. Soon a half-naked, downy choir will sway in rhythm, open mouthed, begging for bugs.

Prague, Late November, 1989

One quarter of a million people are gathered on the square. After seven hundred lost battles for Czech freedom, they can feel in the air that the time may have come to win one. They light candles at the base of the statue of Wenceslas on horseback; candles, like ardor, burn even in this cold. The tricolor, which must only be flown side by side with the Soviet flag, waves all across the square in sudden solitary dignity. When Alexander Dubček appears on a balcony and throws out his arms in an embrace that enfolds an entire nation, a giddiness rises among them, as if they are breathing laughing gas. They chant, "Jakes to the garbage, Jakes to the garbage," and then, "Dubček to the Castle, Dubček to the Castle." The Party twitches, but it is dead. Privilege is dead. The professor who has been stoking boilers on the night shift for twenty years may teach again. A man who closed down his newspaper in '68 is passing out free copies of today's revived edition. A voice over a loudspeaker calls for attention, and the crowd instantly falls silent. There is an urgent message: a nine-year-old boy named Honza has become separated from his mother. "Be brave, Honza, be brave," they chant. No Czech can be truly free until Honza finds his mama.

The Grove

Off Highway 46, two hills, in perfect symmetry, slope into the straight-line ravine between them. Planted in the notch is a heart-shaped grove of trees, a green tribute to a simpler time, when a piece of one's land could be dedicated to whimsy. Was this a newlywed's grand gesture to his wife? If so, she must have been touched to see the heart grow in synchrony with their affections. For decades, driving to or from the coast, we've been cheered by the grove. The man who dreamed it and then placed it in the world is no doubt gone now. The grass on both hills has been stripped away, but the newly planted vineyard keeps a respectful distance from the heart. My eye, fond of landscapes, has aged in its own way; it expects a new depredation around every curve, but this vineyard bows to boundaries.

I'VE ALWAYS BEEN a fan of the prose form called the *feuilleton*, which comes from *feuille*, meaning "leaf," as in a sheet of paper. The implication is that the *feuilleton* should be brief enough to fit on a single sheet. These brief essays or chronicles became very popular in Middle Europe in the nineteenth century, where they often appeared in newspapers, sometimes serialized, when newspapers still had literary aspirations. Jan Neruda (yes, Pablo Neruda took his name from a Czech romantic poet) was a master of the form, and in the early twentieth century, the novelist and playwright Karel Čapek wrote hundreds of charming pieces, and toward the end of the century, the form was again revived by Ludvik Vaculík. The pieces are most often very intimate in tone, and they sometimes have an ironic or humorous turn at the end. My prose pieces are even shorter than the norm; I guess they could be called mini-*feuilletons*. I hope they carry a feeling of intimacy, and I suppose half a leaf is better than none.

JAMES HARMS

Union Station, Los Angeles (the Reagan Years)

So often the man scraped to bits by his latest try at walking through
daylight trails sheet music from a pocket, as if the song forever
dribbling from his mouth has origins in the world. He stands too
close to the tracks, though the porter is gentle with him, guides him
behind the broad yellow line on the platform by touching softly
the one elbow unexposed (the other scabbed and bruised blue, the
shirtsleeve frayed and flapping in the easy wind blowing up from the
tunnels).

The problem is the way sunlight slips through holes in the
evening air, the sound it makes, like a child choking on water. Union
Station never closes, though three times a day it's swept two ways:
a man on a rider broom motoring through the tunnels, swerving
over bottles and paper napkins; the transit cops nudging to life each
sleeping pile of rags and plastic sacks, shooing them through the tall
tiled archways toward the parking lot, toward the alleys off Oliveras
Street, the 6th Street underpass, to Chinatown or City Hall, the
fenced yards beneath the Hollywood or Harbor or Santa Monica
Freeways.

It hurts to climb from dreams and shave and dress, to work all
day and wait for rush hour to end, to meet Tom and Bob and Jeff and
Dwayne in Little Tokyo for a drink before dinner, another after. And
then to Al's Bar near the tracks: the Blasters on at ten, the Plimsouls
at twelve. The night ends late and everyone is tired but trying not
to say so, just walking slowly in the early morning emptiness of Los
Angeles, wondering if it's time to give it up and go home.

We'd known him in college: he stood in the drip of a rusted drain
pipe somewhere east of Al's, took off his shirt and smiled. "Hey, guys,"
he said. "Long time no see, etcetera."

It's where you find it: public policy and smaller government, the
trickle down effect, a gray face recently excavated, all those years of
thinking it's enough, hard work and straight dealing, all those years
lifted like dust from an artifact, the wind a soft brush across the lips.
And then the rain of rusty water, memory: part agent, part solvent,

breaking down to bone the irretrievable, the stripped and bruised-through, the shame. "I'm taking a slow shower," he said. "Now please …" he turned around and spoke over one shoulder. We were looking for my car. I'd parked it somewhere near the station. "Please," he said again. "Could I have some privacy?"

Gridlock

Even in Los Angeles the traffic eases up at noon, particularly heading north toward Palmdale on a Wednesday, since no one goes where there's nothing to do when there's a chicken-salad sandwich nearby, the midweek special at Barney's, coke and french fries included.

But something's wrong. The usual river-hum of cars on the Hollywood Freeway has been hushed to a horn blast now and then, the stream of traffic slowed to a standstill, a twelve-mile-long parking lot. Someone rolls away his window and leans out to see what's going on. Drivers exchange looks, the *What's up* of raised eyebrows, shrugs instead of smiles, though a few just shake their heads as they inch their cars politely to the right, to the open shoulder, the offramp just ahead: freedom. But there's always one, in this case a battered Honda Civic, that moves in fits and jerks, the driver beshaded and oblivious, cutting off the more cautious, his insurance long lapsed. He's given the room he needs, the indignity of a cracked windshield his red bandanna, a symbol of the city's largest gang—not Bloods or Crips but the resigned and dispirited, those who've given up and just drive.

The freeway has been closed at Melrose so the men from Brinks can do their job. Red-faced and stoic, forced to wear orange vests, they kneel and rise on the freeway's sticky tarmac picking up over and over what seems to be light, flecks of sun shining on the asphalt. Around them it's just road and blue sky, the oleander and eucalyptus audible in the new silence, California's ubiquitous wind break whispering in a breeze, nearly laughing, though really it's the motorists snaking up the ramp, pointing and snickering, witness at the end of hours and miles of traffic to this latest urban inanity: three men—the driver and two guards—on their knees on the 101 northbound.

And of course, the road north leads to promise say the angels fleeing home: the fertile valleys near Modesto, the emerald forests of Marin. The road north is paved with hope for those tired of breathing ozone, of waking with trembles in a doorway, beneath a desk. The road north is littered with coins, dimes and quarters to be exact, for at last a truck has spilled money instead of oil, a bank's worth of loose change just beyond the temporary sign—FREEWAY CLOSED. Someone once said (perhaps it was Tom Hayden) that to solve all its problems L.A. should get its citizenry headed in one direction. But someone else (perhaps Tom Wolfe) answered with the literal and obvious: that if all of Los Angeles hit the roads at once there'd be a used car lot the size of Austria, a good idea he said, since then it would be easy enough to pave over the cars, the people, the whole damn city. But if all of Los Angeles heard there was money on the Hollywood Freeway they'd laugh it off as another empty promise— a call back for a sit com, an agent who *loves* the screenplay—though they might drive by for a look.

Song of Sand, Song of Sea, Song of Leaving, Song of Leaves
"Here Comes a Regular," Balboa Pier

I own this song like a buffalo nickel, carry it around to offer the air every day or two when I'm alone in the garden, the shower.
*
And now it drifts through the parking lot and out beneath the pier, a bit of musical tulle fog lapping at beach towels, a song so secret I'm sad to hear it leak from a low-slung El Camino.
*
The bubbling edge of a broken wave is singeing Walt's ankles, his first time by the sea.
*
Beyond him a line of pelicans shoots the pier heading north, wings wide and still in the inch of air above water; Walt turns to yell, mouth full of wind, his words torn apart by the wake of Pacific waves.
*
The El Camino leaves the parking lot and leaves behind my song of leaves: *First the lights then the collar goes up, the wind begins to blow. . . . First the past then the leaves that last, here comes the snow.*

189

*

Catalina floats in the deeper distance like a cloud settling on the water as Walt breads himself with sand, rolling toward the ocean, singing.

*

I walk down to the water to hear his new voice, changed by the sea, to help him wash the beach off his body.

*

And Walt wants to know did I see the birds.

*

And Walt wants to splash me, the cold Pacific: he's laughing and so am I, each of us someone's, each of us fearless, within reach.

I HAVE TO ADMIT I don't always understand why the prose form seems right for certain poems. Sometimes I'm just trying to solve the problem of the poem and lines fail me; when I get rid of them the poem seems to work. Other times I find that lines are trying to impose a rhythmical (or even incantatory) sense on the poem that seems inauthentic or misleading. To be honest, I believe many prose poems would work just fine in lines but that, for some reason, they work a little better with margins. I don't believe in formal destiny. But for the sake of argument, I could say that, having grown up in the Los Angeles area, all the time I've spent cruising down the freeways has found its way into my work via the horizontal drift of the prose poem; maybe I'm driving for the horizon in certain poems. Maybe.

LOLA HASKINS

Fourth Grade

We pick up eucalyptus nuts and put them, sweet-smelling, in our pockets. In the art building we file, not talking, up the stairs past where the nuns live. Some of the nuns haven't been outside in years. I've heard that in one dark paneled room there's an old nun who crouches over a sewing machine all day, making aprons for convent children. Maybe she made this one. I suck its corners when no one's looking and they comfort, like my sheet would comfort when I was small. Miss Mayberry looks over my shoulder at the apple I'm drawing. That's good Lola, she says. Keep it up. Then she tells us again how she went to Europe last year and when she said she was from San Francisco, the people all fell at her feet and said tell them anything, and she told them about us.

Tamalpais

When I was a little girl walking up Mount Tam with Daddy, what he didn't know was that the switchbacks didn't exist because I was straightening them with my wings. When the troubles began, I'd learned to fly, first in dreams then awake. I'd skim the surface of our potholed road until my foot-soles were air and I was looking down on our gray house with its curls of cigarette smoke wafting from the windows, down on the poppy-smeared hills with their lichened rocks, down on the fire roads Daddy and I used to walk when my limbs were stretching every day and my cheeks were bright as spring from Mother's slaps, down on my own small self as I'd stumble blinded past the red geraniums at the top of the drive to run away again.

In Tide Pools

Lavender-spined urchins reside. And anemones with wavy mouths. And periwinkle snails, full of themselves because they have been given such a beautiful name. And over these low-dwellers, fine-haired grasses drift, as if underwater there were always a wind. And since these communities, not touching, are like language groups that have grown apart, it is not surprising that each has its legends. In one, it is said that the Maker, taking pity on the rocks' empty cups, filled them. So the rocks, once beggars, became kings. In another, that certain stars, unhappy to be among multitudes, found solace in these smaller skies. Elsewhere, it is said that long ago the dwellers in these valleys lived deep. But slowly and slowly, the rush of the waves drew them upward. And now they are visited every day by her who, breaking over them, leaves parts of herself, which they drink and want for nothing. It is not only humans who have religion. On the edge of the sea, the finger limpets see the Almighty, and cling.

I FIND PROSE POEMS work for me when I want to tell a story in which imagery looms large. Because I'm *telling*, it's prose, but because the point is really its stealth subject, the boat, not its ostensible subject, the fisherman, it's poetry. Also, prose poems sit more strongly on the page than lined poems do. They're compact little chunks, like toddlers, and sometimes, especially when I tire of the pretentiousness of certain kinds of lineation (including my own), the lack of self-consciousness of the prose poem format just plain appeals to me.

ROBERT HASS

from *The Beginning of September*

Here are some things to pray to in San Francisco: the bay, the mountain, the goddess of the city; remembering, forgetting, sudden pleasure, loss; sunrise and sunset; salt; the tutelary gods of Chinese, Japanese, Russian, Basque, French, Italian and Mexican cooking; the solitude of coffee houses and museums; the virgin, mother and widow moons; hilliness, vistas; John McLaren; Saint Francis; the Mother of Sorrows; the rhythm of any life still whole through three generations; wine, especially zinfandel because from that Hungarian vine-slip came first a native wine not resinous and sugar-heavy; the sourdough mother, true yeast and beginning; all fish and fisherman at the turning of the tide; the turning of the tide; eelgrass, oldest inhabitant; fog; seagulls; Joseph Worcester; plum blossoms; warm days in January.

A Story About the Body

The young composer, working that summer at an artist's colony, had watched her for a week. She was Japanese, a painter, almost sixty, and he thought he was in love with her. He loved her work, and her work was like the way she moved her body, used her hands, looked at him directly when she made amused and considered answers to his questions. One night, walking hack from a concert, they came to her door and she turned to him and said, "I think you would like to have me. I would like that too, but I must tell you that I have had a double mastectomy," and when he didn't understand, "I've lost both my breasts." The radiance that he had carried around in his belly and chest cavity—like music—withered very quickly, and he made himself look at her when he said, "I'm sorry. I don't think I could." He walked back to his own cabin through the pines, and in the morning he found a small blue bowl on the porch outside his door. It looked to be full of rose petals, but he found when he picked it up that the rose petals were on top; the rest of the bowl—she must have swept them from the corners of her studio—was full of dead bees.

Conversion

Walking down the stairs this morning in the bitter cold, in the old house's salt smell of decay, past the Mansergh family coat of arms on the landing, I longed for California and thought I smelled laurel leaves: riding an acacia limb in the spring, rivers of yellow pollen, wild fennel we broke into six-inch lengths and threw at each other in the neighbor-hood wars or crouched in thickets of broom, shooting blue jays with BB guns. *Oiseaux,* I read last week when I picked up a volume of Ponge in the bookshop on rue Racine and thought of blue jays and so bought the Ponge, thinking I would write grave, luminous meditative poems. And walking across the bridge later past Notre Dame, I remembered Jack Kjellen who lived with his mother the telephone operator and who always wanted to pretend that we were the children of Fatima having a vision of the Virgin, and 1 would have to go along for a while, hoping to lure him back to playing pirates. Vision of Jack kneeling under the fig tree, palms prayerfully touching, looking up awed and reverent into the branches where the fat green figs hung like so many scrotums among the leaves. Scrota? But they were less differentiated than that: breasts, bottoms. The sexual ambiguity of flowers and fruits in French botanical drawings. Oh yes, sweet hermaphrodite peaches and the glister of plums!

The Harbor at Seattle

They used to meet one night a week at a place on top of Telegraph Hill to explicate Pound's *Cantos*—Peter who was a scholar; and Linda who could recite many of the parts of the poem that envisioned paradise; and Bob who wanted to understand the energy and sunrise of its music; and Bill who knew Greek and could tell them that "Dioce, whose terraces were the color of stars," was a city in Asia Minor mentioned by Herodotus.

And that winter when Bill locked his front door and shot himself in the heart with one barrel of a twelve-gauge Browning over-and-under, the others remembered the summer nights, after a long session of work, when they would climb down the steep stairs that negotiated the cliff where the hill faced the waterfront to go somewhere to get a drink and talk. The city was all lights at that hour and the air smelled of coffee and the bay.

In San Francisco coffee is a family business, and a profitable one, so that members of the families are often on the society page of the newspaper, which is why Linda remembered the wife of one of the great coffee merchants, who had also killed herself; it was a memory from childhood, from those first glimpses a newspaper gives of the shape of the adult world, and it mixed now with the memory of the odor of coffee and the salt air.

And Peter recalled that the museum had a photograph of that woman by Minor White. They had all seen it. She had bobbed hair and a smart suit on with sharp lapels and padded shoulders, and her skin was perfectly clear. Looking directly into the camera, she does not seem happy but she, seems confident; and it is as if Minor White understood that her elegance, because it was a matter of style, was historical, because behind her is an old barn which is the real subject of the picture—the grain of its wood planking so sharply focused that it seems alive, grays and blacks in a rivery and complex pattern of venation.

The back of Telegraph Hill was not always so steep. At the time of the Earthquake, building materials were scarce, so coastal ships made a good thing of hauling lumber down from the northwest. But the economy was paralyzed, there were no goods to take back north, so they dynamited the side of the hill and used the blasted rock for ballast, and then, in port again, they dumped the rock in the water to take on more lumber, and that was how they built the harbor in Seattle.

ELOISE KLEIN HEALY

Asking About You

Instead of having sex all the time I like to hold you and not get into some involved discussion of what life means. I want you to tell me something I don't know about you. Something about the day before that photograph in which you're standing on your head. I want to know about softball and the team picture. Why are you so little next to the others? Were you younger? Were you small as a girl? What I want most is to have been a girl with you and played on the opposite team so I could have liked you and competed against you at the same time.

In the interests of examining the connection

to the lives we are living we must ask does the bond run in the blood or is it as some believe directed by the power of the moon or as others say by the power a woman effects on your angle of vision but of course some don't bother to say or didn't say but even in casual photos the distinctive tilt of the chin speaks volumes and the incredible glance that lives on in the one standing next to you who has as well included as a personal style just the most impossible shading of arrogance which indicates and welcomes an understanding that goes beyond cultural boundaries as when the lights go off and one fingertip after another gauges the dimensions of sensation on the surface of the naked skin or under cloth or leather or beaded and gathered stuff arranged ever so wonderfully you can't believe in looking at the photographs and the paintings that nobody thought anything of the display and took no opportunity to comment on the distinctive manner of ornamentation and posture which acts almost but not quite as an affront to the received and applied rules of behavior while making a territory alongside of or just out of reach of the norm in which she and whomever she wanted to be with simply blossomed

Oh, Dr. Surgeon

cuidado

because what if my wrist locks in place like a rusty gate and whatever I have in mind can't get through, whatever I try to hold can't catch. What if the hinge there is too old to repair and forever after all my shirts will not tuck right, drying off with a towel will hurt me hurt me, drying my hair will hurt and pulling the covers up hurt, and worse, everything I go to touch will have to be thought through, thought through even when there is a vocabulary of impulse right there in the air at the end of my fingers, stories spun by the little bones in their tiny dance. It is not enough to speak, you know. It is not enough to have the words to say. There is that moment when something has to hang in the air. Hang in the air for a moment, and turn not on the tip of the tongue, the pointed slippery tongue, but here en *el dictionario de mis dedos, las palabras huesudos* clicking cumulative as a litany, running repetitive and desperate to find a saint still awake to this gesture, someone who in the past has worked miracles with the touch of her hand and can still identify with the little needs of the living, a saint of small things like The Little Flower, who understands dusting and folding, who probably hurt herself and dipped her hand in Holy Water or cried out just a little and then only in private. if I could pray anymore I would return to the rosary because even with a simple string you can fashion one if both your hands work, and when I can't sleep I fall back on its prayers and its mysteries attached to suffering, to joy, to memory, to the blessedness of what comes around again, familiar and whole

For me, the prose poem is a very distant cousin. I know quite a bit about her, and when she comes to town for a visit, I am very happy to spend time talking in that very "cousin" kind of way. Our conversations come out all in a rush— there's a passionate exchange, a kind of breathless back and forth as though a lot of history needs catching up on. There is a feeling though that we really aren't speaking in our first languages but the intense connection that is blood and background makes up for it. I have another cousin, the sestina, with whom I have the same kind of conversations, but they are much more driven and dense. It's unspoken, but true, that we would die for each other.

JUAN FILIPE HERRERA

behind the storm this life

behind the storm this life flutter this exchange that stillness
everything again wide thin brimming the felt the edge the fuzz then
the knees the breast so so white so thin the membrane when you
meet the circle between here and there the paper appearance the life
around the wrist how you point to the easel then the freeway rivers
pure chalk viridian cadmium thalo red the syrup waters lonesome
apartments lilies inside the forehead the various folds the inside
topaz monet manet picasso's hairy chest the minotaur his tiny legs
in the warehouse a plate with sardines

ripped mandibles it is about this war

ripped mandibles it is about this war continuous as this line more
continuous since it is not a line rather rather ten directions at the
same time if only your breath this one became love the way breath
is bread full of nothings and everythings it is love love at the same
time brown hills adobe maize sheaf leaf falling the lovemaking is
continuous but it but it is not in the papers that is the loving of the
lizard the tiny eye going green to black the limp cat the leg the edge
again the fur again the mirrors on this hat the legs falling through
time four quadrants the ancient tree the night this desert is all there
is this final explosion the explosion

my mother meanders when she sees me skipping
across avenues

my mother meanders when she sees me skipping across avenues
glossy there he comes with one hand lacquered full of tints and the
other empty empty one up one down one moon one clown one dry
so so abandoned long ago before she died long before I sang sang
could you see this guitar strapped across my back one string one
song made made of crystal one performance that followed another
one shadow that became real a man a man that is who walks here or

there at a time when war continues and destroys the starry breath
the color scheme the flat panels of young miracle it is a man a laugh
a tenor the voice is new the gait is long

the shrapnel that is what the palette knife
is pushing moving stripping

the shrapnel that is what the palette knife is pushing moving strip-
ping doing smearing across the space the space again the empty slate
canvas again this rugged wash this jagged water this unfashioned star
the living night of veils and velvet panoramas gone astray furious as
you may note yourself the path is wooden wet rainy snowy distant
the path is lost for the moment the moment stands withers whispers
freeze and dissolves this hand in yours this soft powder between the
lips the fingers the parable becomes clear it is the glazed posts the
wintry roads that come together the oils that spill waves thighs all
the movement of the arms the stillness of the clouds

IT PROVIDES AN ideal canvas to paint, that is, to mix colors, images, designs,
depths and perspectives into a tremulous, fragmented whole. A story can
be entered with more clarity. The prose poem is the most direct guide to
the stuff of the poem itself. It is a bit more rebellious, more elusive, more
precise. Contradiction, synthesis and ordeal find a unique conductivity in the
prosarama, that is, the expansive yet collapsible structures of the form.

JANE HIRSHFIELD

Tears: An Assay

A great philosopher is born, walks his lifetime's allotment of footsteps, and dies, but while he is living he has the demeanor and body and voice of a great clown. Each of his propositions is heard, but met with snorts, guffaws, and the wiping of tears of laughter from the eyes. Or perhaps it is the reverse: a great comic is born, walks the earth, and dies. But her demeanor and body and voice are such that people listen gravely, they nod in silence at her words, are moved to weeping by the feelings her thoughts cause to rise. The composition of tears of laughter and tears of grief are not, it seems, the same, though the tongue cannot tell this. Different still the tears of outrage, or the tears that come from a misplaced dust mote, errant eyelash, or flake of soot. Each brought to the earth a great if different pleasure. Each died unsatisfied and angry, though this too is not perceived. And where does the mistake lie, if a mistake is granted at all? In the person who refuses an inescapable fate, or in those who shed at his words their tears of subtly erroneous composition?

Ryoanji: An Assay

Wherever a person stands in the garden of Ryoanji, there is always a stone that cannot be seen. It is like the sliver of absence found on the face of a man who has glimpsed in himself a thing until then unknown. Inside the silence, just before he begins to weep. Not because of the thing he has learned—monstrous or saintly, it was always within him—but for the amplitude he hadn't believed was there.

Between the Material World and the World of Feeling

Between the material world and the world of feeling there must be a border—on one side, the person grieves and the cells of the body grieve also; the molecules also, the atoms. Of this there are many proofs. On the other, the iron will of the earth goes on. The torture-broken femur continues to heal even in the last hour, perhaps beyond; the wool coat left behind does not mourn the loss of its master. And yet Cavafy wrote, "In me now everything is turned into feeling—furniture, streets." And Saba found in a bleating goat his own and all beings' sorrow, and this morning the voice of that long dead goat—which is only, after all, a few black-inked words—cries and cries in my ears. Rilke, too, believed the object longs to awaken in us. But I long for the calm acceptance of a bent-wood chair and envy the blue-green curve of a vase's shoulder, which holds whatever is placed within it—the living flower or the dead—with an equally tender balance, and knows no difference between them.

"Ah!": An Assay

When the Greek gods would slip into the clothing and bodies of humans, it was not always as it appeared—not always, that is, for seduction, nor to test the warmth of welcome given to strangers. The sex—like the sudden unveiling and recognition—was not without pleasure. But later, they would remember: "The barley soup offered one night in the village of ———, its wild marjoram, scent of scorched iron, and carrots." "Ah!, and the ones who turned away from us, how their eyes would narrow and wrinkle the tops of their noses." "The barnyard odors." "And afterwards, sleep in that salt-scent, close by their manure hoards and feathers." "Sleep itself!" "Ah!"

For this soft "ah!," immortals entered the world of bodies.

"Of": An Assay

Its chain link can be delicate or massive. In the human realm, directional: though one thing also connects to another through "and," this is not the same. Consider: "Science and elephants." "The science of elephants." "The elephants of science." In nature, however, the preposition is bi-directional and equal. The tree that possesses the roots is not different from the root-possessed tree. The flashing red of the hummingbird's crest is the bird; the crust of a bread loaf, the loaf. The interior nonexistent without the external, each part coequal. And so grief too becomes meaningless in that fortunate world.

Sentence

The body of a starving horse cannot forget the size it was born to.

POETRY, FOR ME, is experience that exists in the concentrating, alchemical admixture of word, thought, feeling, and music. Without sound's activating presence, the cupboard of poetry stands empty. This is as true for prose poems as for poems in free verse or form. A prose poem's music and carriage lean towards prose, but it is not prose. It is a wondrously hybrid creature, chimerical and hippogryph in its eyes, ears, and gait. That extra dimension declares poetry's presence.

I've never set out to write a prose poem; certain poems simply arrive in the sound-shape and musical notation of paragraph rather than of line. The difference is hearable from the first phrase, and they are, it seems to me, doing different work. They think with feeling, perhaps, rather than feel with thought. They look, almost always, at some single thing, which opens and changes under their gaze. They meditate, ruminate. Their epiphanies throw a slow, deep heat.

One might as well ask a horse to feed on stone as ask a prose poem to breathe in the rhythms of free verse. This can be tested. To place a verse-poem into paragraph form extinguishes much of its meaning and lustre. The reverse is true as well—a prose-poem set into lines becomes rickety, lifeless, an unbalanced chair. Prose poems want all four legs on the ground: they think and move better that way. But they are not without tension, not lying belly-down in the grass: they stand and walk within and upon their own music, as any poem must. Yet the prose poem's particular voice-tones and way of traveling pry open the world differently, as if a sudden slant-light began throwing new shadows, revealing corners not even existent from other angles.

SANDRA HOBEN

Dumpster

Huge and yellow, it's parked at the base of the drive. I'll fill this vessel with what I've got: the rattan table unraveling like a bad sentence; ladders whose rungs will never again hold my weight. Flowerpots, dog shit, spelling tests. I heave a full-length mirror, murky as the bay after rain. Brooms matted with weather, rakes without teeth, the blank spaces in the latticed fencing. I've carried this baggage from one century into the next.

I'm giving away the sound of stumbling on the stairs, the white peonies exploding with ants, my suede purse a stranger stole in Oakland. All this I fling over the edge of the metal walls into that mysterious classroom I can't see into or remember, like sleep or death.

Even so, there's room for more. The neighbors gather—the opera singer and the mayor, the artist and the fireman, lugging hoses and gavels, canvasses swirled with black paint. Together we celebrate our failures, the left-out-in-the-rains, the stars and the moon rusting on the patio.

Gopher

I've never seen him with his fur-lined purses filled with coins of dirt, though we've been neighbors for years, rich neighbors who don't like each other and keep to ourselves. Even when patches of grass turned gold in early summer, dirt banked against the fence, I turned the other way.

But now, in August, when the tomatoes have swollen and begun to take their color from the sun, and the basil has captured the smell of the earth, he is burrowing under the rows, untying each package before it's wrapped. He's smashing the light bulbs burning in the tight petals of the marigolds, devouring from within the stars of jasmine.

I was weeding when the ground began to swell beneath my bare feet—it made me feel sick and afraid, the earth shaking out its fur like an animal, pelt of peat moss and bark. That's when I saw them:

the long trails, the tunnels and freeways of gopher winding through the garden, the one place I wouldn't have them. I took a shovel and raised it up and stabbed the earth again and again, until my fingers tore and I came back to myself inside the fence of my own skin.

He is down there, burrowing, eating the soft, tear-shaped roots. Eyes closed against the wet earth, mouth and cheeks full of dirt, dirt in his bowels and under his claws that shine like the husk of the moon, he breathes.

Nothing moves in the garden except the wilted leaves of the tomato. But past the oak, where the yard widens and grows wild, a new vault opens. He is there, laboring painfully, one paw maimed, the moon broken in rough water.

Parallel Lines

By definition, parallel lines never meet. This fact makes it possible for birdcages to exist, and jails of all sorts—railroad tracks, picture frames, director's chairs. And we can walk to the store and back, water the garden, watch our shadows lengthen on the lawn.

But parallel lines meet at infinity, which makes it possible to get to Coalinga, build fires, tame animals; and we have eggbeaters, hammocks, the hulls of ships. We can tune banjos, swim, read books more than once. Folk dances can be passed down, and rings.

If parallel lines meet at infinity, it is also true they never meet; conversely, if they do not meet at infinity, it is also not true they never meet. And so we are lonely and confused, our dreams have coins in them, our pets die. There are eclipses, earthquakes, falling stars. And although we can see the spiral within shells, and the delicate double circle within flowers, we will never understand what we already know, and, even if we did, there would be nothing we could do about it.

As part of completing my Masters at Fresno State, I chose to translate some of the work of Juan Ramón Jiménez. The poems were short, celebratory, and reverent; while I admired the poems, they were not work that could worm their way into my own poems. Then I discovered Jiménez's prose poems in *Diary of a Poet Recently Married.* He had traveled to America and was appalled—the money, the fashionable apartments, the billboards. While his level of sarcasm and disdain was a little sour for my taste, I found delight in the combination of the strong narrative and images. One prose poem, in particular—"Poe's House"—had lightness, a sense of history, as well as a sense humor. For the piece to work in prose seemed to demand even more mystery, more images, than if it had been written in verse. Other prose poems I've return to over the years include Zbigniew Herbert's "Period," "Armchairs," "Hen," "Episode in the Library." The form seems to encourage me to take on subject matter I might not otherwise approach.

GARRETT HONGO

Cruising in the Greater Vehicle/A Jam Session

"Well, goddamnit, Lawson! Whyn't you play in key and keep to the rhythm? First you say you wanna go back to Fresno, back to the fish store and Kamaboko Gardens on the West Side, and then you say, forget it, I take it back, let's go to the Sacto *Bon-Odori* instead."

"Yeah. And this ain't even *shoyu* season yet, chump!"

"Awww, hell. What's wrong with you two? Can't you improvise? You know, I'm just laying down a bass, man. Just a rhythm, a scale, something to jam on, something to change, find our range, something to get us going. Once we get started, we can work our way around to Weed, put on some tire chains, or break down in Selma, refuse to buy grapes, raisins, or Gallo, do a pit-stop at a Sacto sporting goods, pick up some air mattresses shaped like pearl-diving women, and float all day downriver to the deltas, sipping Cokes and *sake* in the summer heat."

"Shit. Whyn't you just solo and forget the rest of us? You start chanting and pretty soon we're hearing the entire Lotus Sutra."

"You two Buddhaheads just a pair of one-eyed Japs with dishpan hands and deadpan minds, man. This is the Champ Chonk talking, and we're playing Chinese anaconda. Eight-card, no-peek or *pak-kai*, roll your own, hi-b, three for sweep, four for hot-sour soup stud, and neither of you's put down your ante yet. So shit or get off the *shu-nai*, fellas."

"Calm down and watch the road, Alan."

"Who's driving this heap, anyway?"

"I thought you were."

"1 thought Lawson was."

"Don't worry. This is a dodo-driven, autopiloted, cruise-controlled, TripleA-mapped, Flying-A-gassed, dual-overhead-cam, Super-Sofistifunktified, Frijole Guacamole, Gardena Guahuanco, Chonk Chalupa Cruiser with Buddha Bandit Bumpers, Jack!"

"Where we going, Alan?"

"Where do you think? We're going to Paradise."

Body & Fender/Body & Soul

At the grill, the Indian girl with buckteeth and dimples serves us a round of coffee and sweet rolls. We're waiting for the guy at Henley's Texaco, down the street, to find us a fan belt that'll fit. It's early, the sky's still in the john, shaving, and the sports page has to wait to get in. Everybody's grumpy. We sit around, jab at raisins with our forks, and try to look as tough as the waitress.

Her name's Rita. Her brothers jump fires and pump oil in Alaska. Her sisters string beads and make babies back on the Res. Her ex is white, a logger who threatened never to come back and didn't. She doesn't hold any grudges. That's why she's so nice, why she pops her gum filling the salt and pepper shakers, why she adjusts her girdle so we can see, why the egg spot on her dress doesn't show.

Outside, the sun eases up over the parking lot, scrambles across the freeway, and runs for cover behind a pile of pumpkin-colored clouds. 99 starts shuffling its deck of cars and pickups, getting set to deal a hand of nine-to-five stud. We don't watch. This is Redding, and ain't nothing thing going on besides the day shift.

Alan says, "Look, there's Venus," and points to a piece of light draining into the sky. I want to order a countryfried steak, talk about the Dodgers, but there isn't time. Lawson hums a few chords, stirring the changes with his coffee spoon.

Rita cruises back like a bus bound for Reno, starts dealing some ashtrays. She says, "How's it going, boys?"

I answer for all of us—"Hey, Rita. It's almost gone."

Bugle Boys

As I am Kubota's voice in this life, chanting broken hymns to the sea, so also am I my father's hearing, 55 now and three years shy of his age when he died, my ears open as the mouth-shells of two conchs, drinking in a soft, onshore wind.

In the fall of '63, at the end of our first year in Gardena, south of L.A., electrician that he was, he built his own home hi-fi speakers out of parts from Scandinavia, an amp kit ordered through the

207

mails, the glittering turntable, brushed gold aluminum, a drivebelt, and an inboard motor—each component meticulously laid out on a bedsheet soon after it arrived, jigsawed cabinet boards with serrated edges, yellow capacitors and rectifiers black as tar, shining and glossy as aquarium fish under living room light, and the miniature crystal towers of vacuum tubes, steel pins scaly as aged platinum, Erector sets of grey plates and haloed getters intricate as space stations under sparkling glass.

In shapes like Coke bottles, potato mashers, and—my favorite—the tiny rockets with arrowed heads he called "Bugle Boys" for the labels of white-line cartoons, anthropomorphized tubes blowing trumpets stamped on each of their sides.

"They make electric sound come sweet," he said, "Like no can b'lieve…"

He'd spend evenings in the garage, soldering circuitry and studying schematics—blue zigzags and squiggles on grey paper that folded like army maps—checking his work.

Once the speakers were set in their walnut cabinets and the amp out of its gold-mesh cage, he asked me to listen while he balanced the stereo channels—a marvel—and swapped input tubes, pulling pairs from the sagging pocket of his aloha shirt, the glass of them making a gentle clatter like tea or sake cups as they knocked softly together when he dipped and swirled his fingers in, pulling them out like fancy fish from a bowl.

He couldn't hear.

Or, rather, he couldn't quite hear, losing it from a lifetime of cumulative, small misfortunes: a fever as a child in McCully, guns and canons while away at war at 17, the job holding down a jackhammer, the job under jet engines at Kaneohe Marine Base.

I knew every reason, though he never gave one himself.

"Sit here," he'd say, pointing to the carpeted floor in front of the beige sofa we never used.

He'd throw me a zabuton to sit on, tell me to concentrate, and I'd hear measure after measure of Big Band tunes filling the room like airy clouds of brass cotton lofting around the lamps, ashtrays, and coconut curios around me.

"American Patrol," "Ciribiribin," and "Shake Down the Stars" took turns with lush vibraphones and strummed ukes—50s hotel music from the islands.

"Tell me whatchu hearing," he'd say, and I would, my father taking notes, smiling over our evenings of pleasurable work, string basses and horns in my ears, kickdrums and toms reverberating through the floorboards, Sinatra swaggering a tune, just behind the beat.

What did I know of travail or passion then? My father trying to beat the clock, hastening to hear or not hear each spinning A-side he ever danced to at the Black Cat in Honolulu before the world closed its cave of cotton around him, cymbals become a silent splash of metallic light, snare rolls a strobe of sticks with no sound, a song only a murmur without scale, and music a birthplace he could never return to.

"No ka ipo lei . . . manu," sang the Sons of Hawaii, and so I said they did, my father jotting it down, Bugle Boys jousting in the pocket of his shirt.

MY FEELING FOR the prose poem is scanty, but rooted in my admirations for those of Melville (his dense, brief cetology and metaphysical passages in *Moby-Dick*), Rimbaud, de Chirico, Ponge, Neruda, and Beckett. Like them, I hope I try for arresting imagery, but even more, an aura of mystery and also the unfulfillment of the implied narrative of the poem. The hard thing is to avoid merely being sly or fey in tone. For me, the prose poem is at best cinematic—suggestive, jittery and jump-cut—an interrupted slice from a longer arc of narration carried along by imagery, character, or tone.

ALTA IFLAND

The marvelous child

On the threshold of adulthood I began to dream of a little girl who
followed me everywhere and who was myself *and* my child at the
same time. She was light and joyful, wise, yet sensitive, close, yet far
away. As soon as she came into my life, I banned from my soul all
desire to ever love a man again, all desire to love, all desire ("All" is a
way of speaking, of course). I gave her all my blood and the marrow
of my bones, and I saw my reflection in her eyes as if into a bottomless
well, and the marvelous child grew, and the more real she was, the
more unreal I became.

Light

In Europe, light is as sad and weak as the old continent. But here, at
the other end of the world, by the ocean, it seems almost material,
ceaselessly renewing itself out of a sky of untouched enamel. Under
the line separating sky and ocean, the waves are an iridescent blue-
gray, and it is impossible to watch them without being wounded by
their blinding clarity. The light waves stream through the trees, and
arrive soaked in maternal tenderness on the wooden terrace. There,
their rays like spread braids linger on the surface of things, and the
wood seizes their heat, and gorges on it, and light suffuses the boards'
grain, burrowing deeper and deeper into silence.

Ocean

In front, some green bushes, a patch of gray land—the beach—and
the ocean. Remember all the exotic dreams about seas and oceans
impossible to reach during a life equally impossible to imagine now, a
life that was yours and that now belongs to no one's past. Remember
and rejoice in this marvel. Light broken in waves, blue sea mixed with
green ocean. Blue flow tinged with white, black depth with a child's
face. Brightness streaming in the night of dreams. Bottomless peace
murmuring in the depths of all things rhymed: waves, rain, trains.

Rain and fire

To listen to the rain falling on the roof, its voices like loose hair, its liquid voices, to watch the fire dying in the hearth, to feel the veil of heat crumbs on the closed eyelids, to open your eyes on the almost dead embers, and to hear the crackling wood exploding in small sparks, and to feel the heat advancing in sleepy waves and settling in the white of the eye, and then to listen again to listen to the rain that keeps falling above our heads, and to gradually disappear in the rain with long, thin fingers, in the fire with red, coppery tongues.

THESE POEMS ARE from a bilingual volume of prose poems, *Voice of Ice*, written between May and December 2004, immediately after I moved to California. I initially wrote them in French, but soon afterward, I decided to do something I had never done before—translate my own work into English.

If there is an esthetic vision behind these poems it is a vision that refuses to separate reflection from beauty, or thinking from sensorial experience. This separation often manifested in contemporary American poetry is artificial and is a result both of an ideology-driven culture and of a "specialization" of discourse. I find this divorce extremely puzzling and sadly comical, as it would be hard to find a philosopher or a brain specialist who believes that one can truly split thought and feeling.

Coming from a Francophone tradition, I am of course indebted to Baudelaire's prose poems, which are literally short stories with a narrative line and characters, or prose fables with a moral or a twist at the end. The poems selected here, however, are image-centered rather than narrative, but even in them the description of the gazed-upon thing is intertwined with the reflection triggered by that image.

I believe that the prose poem, as an "in-between" genre, is the space where two different kinds of discourses are likely to intersect: poetic and narrative discourse; or poetic and reflective discourse. If the first combination is best represented by Baudelaire, the second harbors a conflict between the poem's desire to protect its mystery (it describes something without "explaining" it) and its desire to lay it bare (it includes a critical reflection).

MARK JARMAN

For the Birds

When you wake up, raising the film over your eyes, in a hollow of boughs or bark, you are always hungry. And you all talk at once. Each twig has an opinion and holds a singing fabric sewn with discussions of lice, offspring, height above ground, eyesight, mates, one night stands, best routes to Canada once the warm weather comes, the taste of this bug, that bug, spittle needed to mat human hair, mud's pliancy, the housework of the sky. We think that none of you has an insight into the afterlife. But you all remember birth and the cramped translucent dark before the break-out.

I am bored. I need birds. Not flight but activity, not serene detachment sailing but intense engagement hunting. Look me in the eyes, frontal, head on. And I admire you. Study me askance. And I adore you. Even the moa in the museum case. The trinket hanging from the Christmas tree.

Incurious witnesses, feathers dabbled in blood, poking your noses in the wounded hands and feet. What did St. Francis tell you? Be yourselves, little ones, and you will praise God.

For how many of us were you the first word?

Trouble sleeping, I think of you in the netted aviary. There among reaching fronds and green blades, you hovered at my sister's washed floating hair, patient to take a single sand-colored strand that, buoyed by static, reached out half-limp to be taken. She felt it go with a little cry when the root broke from its anchor of scalp-skin.

And this morning, there's an oil smear on the sliding glass door to the patio, and in it, dangling gray breast feathers—five of them, like milkweed fluff. One of you caromed off the hard sky and left this pattern, as precise as fish scales, scalloped on the glass like a record in rock. Veronica's napkin. The Shroud of Turin.

Woodpeckers, hairy or downy. Red bellied. Pileated. Flickers. Cardinals. Brown thrashers. A single rosebreasted grosbeak. Once, a tumbling flock of drunken cedar waxwings, chirping like crickets. Red tail hawks with breasts like lampshades. Great horned owls conversing at dawn, in January. Screech owls in their red phases. Mockingbirds copying mockingbirds. Chimney swifts back from Peru to the same elementary school chimney. Kingbirds on powerlines. Blue birds in pairs. Blue jays in gangs. To be a man who surrounds his house with birds. To be a woman visited by wings. To say to the turkey vulture overhead, "Sister." To say, "Brother," to the starling in the swirling flock.

If your call and response first thing in the morning make us hold hands and smile in the dark, as we lie in bed, it's because we're not alone in the world. And when letters like this one are written, it is because we are.

To the Trees

How do you feel as you rear up or hunch over to seek sunlight? When young, as pliant almost as water, when old, second only to rock. I think you must feel that roots are better than roads, that the avenue to the sky is best straight up or crookedly up. That whatever happens around you is no more than rain or snow, even the building that embraces you, even the saw and stump remover that eat up all trace of you.

For the present you are stone, but let the wind rise and you sing and dance like bamboo. Your children are the dapples of sunshine in shade. Your ancestors bask on the mossy facets of your bark. And within is a coming and going of thirst and records of thirst, of flesh that fire would love to taste. You know the math that sends the fire branching upwards. You know the myth that lights the candelabra. Planets and stars gleam on your smallest twig ends.

You have held back the body of the wind. You have held back the onslaught of the heat. You have given me the idea of depth. You have revealed the nesting of microcosms, all while staying in one place. We came down from you and stood upright like you. Because you will not rush along with us we cut you down.

It's what's inside and outside that counts. Hollow with ant meal, your blossoms and leaves still come. Solid as granite, you can stand deadgray for decades. You bleed, you break, you rot. The massive inner framework fades, and there's a limp limb, a branch of brown leaves among green, a bridge across a stream, a back-breaking fall on a ranch-style house. You rot, you break, you bleed. You go up in smoke, sideways in fire, down and down and down.

In my metamorphosis, she appears in the doorway, wet from the shower and looking for a towel. We catch each other by surprise, goddess and little boy, and we are both changed. At times she is a row of eucalyptus, where the trees and the sunlight between them are the same smooth color. It is my fate to hunt for her everywhere except where that tree grows. At times I am pyracantha under her windowsill, burning to speak. It is her fate to believe I have nothing to say.

You are life to those who hold fast to you, but standing apart on the lawn, don't you all long for the forest canopy? To join and blot out the sky, with a dancing floor lifted to the sun for hawks and monkeys and orchids in the higher parts of shadow? Don't you all long to rise up and erect your shade?

Let me be neither branch nor leaf but one facet of your bark, deeply incised on all sides, gray in dry sunny weather, and in rain, showing a face of turquoise.

Through the Waves

If I spoke to you through the waves, which one would catch your attention, the ripple that wet your knee or the beach-pounder shaking your bed? If I spoke to you through the waves, would you remember what I said as a series of glittering, nostalgic video images, far from the ocean, each as harmless as cotton floss?

Small, gray, glassy, like a pleasant hour reading, transparent to its heart of jellyfish and seaweed. Large, swift, green, opaque and grinning whitely, asking for a quick response. Unanswerable, coming down startled, all bulk and foam, which you must dive under. Each bearing a message. Lovely swelling blue, giving you time to move into position, just as it peaks and you feel its force behind you. Black, making her arms glisten as she swims at night, belly and face like candles of phosphorus. Colorless, dismal rippling, coming to shore over shingle, cold enough to turn fingernails purple. And the warm giant that beckons before it sweeps you under to toil among churning roots.

If I spoke to you through the waves, would you see your face reflected in the upthrust wall of words? If I spoke to you through the waves, would your revery before their arrival ever turn into understanding?

To quiet myself I used to remember being lifted and carried by them, buoyed as they broke around me, and standing up in the shallows among the frothy rubble of their collapse, then wading back out, swimming out to meet them as they continued coming to shore. That would help me to fall asleep when I first began to live apart from them. As years passed, and I moved deeper inland, I would dream of them. In one recurring dream I walked along a sea wall and they broke against it, and I saw in their explosions, they were made of pigeon feathers or anthracite or my parents' faces or red oak leaves. Though enormous they broke slowly and benignly, their spray drifting like confetti and dissolving in air. But once I began to dream of them I no longer tried to remember them when I couldn't sleep: to do so only made me more wakeful. A time came when I no longer dreamt of them and they ceased altogether to have any reality for me. They had been lifted and shaped by homesickness. They had emerged composed of dreamstuff for reasons I could never fathom. Now they are a single idea: the image of body and soul together as one.

If I spoke to you through the waves, would you see that I mean more than the moon and less, more than the wind and less, more than the sea floor and less, more than more, less than less? If I spoke to you through the waves, how many times would I have to repeat myself?

Out of chaos, beyond theory, into a life that peaks and breaks, the wave emerges. The shore where it dies lies ahead and waits, unseen. A life must peak as it rides up the shallow approach, steepen, and break. I want you to think of yourself like that, of your body and soul like that, one flesh traveling to shore, to collapse, all that way to end by darkening the sand and evaporating. Where do you go? You repeat in other waves, repeat and repeat. Each bears a message. Each has a meaning.

If I spoke to you through the waves, I would continue to bring them to life until, looking at how they laid themselves at your feet, at how even the greatest ended as film on sand, you said, "Someone is trying to tell me something." And I would not stop.

A Fall Evening in Berkeley, 1970

Brautigan was the draw and read last. Duncan, wearing his elf cloak, read and conducted his fractured narrative of murder and Tarot cards in Santa Cruz, where we were in school. Snyder came on stage, bowing to fellow yogis with palms pressed, flashing a significant presence, a turquoise stud in his left ear. He read from *Turtle Island*, the future Pulitzer, about America's stupidity and the tough old stars. And also one in which rain drops each bore an image of the Buddha. We worried the Buddha image on the jitney back to school.

But Brautigan was the draw and appeared with a quarter ream of mimeographed poems, each no more than four lines long. They were all introduced by a local nabob, who was most pleased by Brautigan. Brautigan read his purple jokes, as Snyder winced and Duncan, eyes on the long ago, looked off.

God, it was wonderful! A fall evening in Berkeley, feeling superior to one image in Gary Snyder, and everything Richard Brautigan wrote, and not even mentioning Robert Duncan, so far beyond us, though liking his cloak of roots and branches. We rode back to school to write poems that would make them blush, and we kept writing and loved poetry.

In the Clouds

Simply by thinking I stood among the clouds. They surrounded and passed me, being and becoming. Blood released into clear water. Breath into cold air. Formlessness entering form, forced into form. Breathing felt huge then smaller than a cell. And I thought, "Don't the clouds themselves feel ambivalent between heaven and earth, hardly more substantial than their shadows? They come into being as randomly as we do. And they disintegrate. They go. What is the lifespan of a cloud? We want to float among them, loving the colossal, shot through with crooked pins of fire, towering side by side."

How did I get up there? I was thinking about changing my life and wanted to talk to a cloud, since clouds are always changing. And the clouds said, "How long has it been since you felt completely happy? Because you are always dissatisfied, always disappointed—it has been a long time. Talk to us. We are admired and disparaged. We are less than everything you compare us to except nothingness. We are not nothing. Talk to us. Our silence, like the new shapes we are forever assuming, will be sympathetic. In the clouds, you will understand yearning as you never have and come back to earth changed, who knows how? Surrender your skin, your bones. But we will not hold you up. We are as ineffectual as cattle, turning steep white faces beside the road, to watch you spin out of control. Placid as the love of God. Fall out of the sky, go sliding down the icy face of the air, we will watch, a little lightning might flicker in a distant bulb of fiber glass. Come to us as the exhalation of your speech, the spirit trapped inside your webs of flesh torn free. We are the embodiment of detachment. You know us best when we are most distant and you are least afraid, when we are most moving and you are unmoved."

Brothers and sisters, consider the taste of cloud in a Sherpa's mouth, of fog in a surfer's throat. Consider the flocculent muscle of the cumulus. The icy elevation of the cirrus. But especially the thunderhead, full of zeal, hurrying in with its bevelled wind, white slanting rain, its electric personality, its aftermath. Consider how the clouds predict one another and how they break up, pulling a new body behind them. The farmer's wide open perspective. The office worker's sidelong glimpse. Weeks of drab overcast. A single afternoon of separate sailwhite drifters. Clouds flat and dull as lampblack, clouds with the contours of the brain, clouds like sheets of paper. I have read that even in an empty sky there exists water vapor enough to make a cloud. Belief enough to make a God.

As they change, clouds grow neither better nor worse. They alter because it is their nature to alter. They can fill us with joy or cast a stagnant sorrow over our days. Such is life under the clouds. In the clouds it is different. But if we live in the clouds, we have to take the earth with us.

JANINE JOSEPH

The Undocumented Immigrant Poem #79

It's Lent again and this year I've given up mangoes and Whitman.
I've stocked the freezer with thirty-minute fish sticks, and set the old
photos taken during my father's diving years next to Hikmet's prison
poems, the highlighted pages proving that I, too, have journeyed
nowhere beyond the immediate dust. It's been ten years since I've
stopped dusting for God beneath my bed or writing prayers to
him in the steam on the bathroom mirror, but, nevertheless, I'm
still fasting on Fridays. Somewhere between fish and the Catholic
Church, I think I strayed, entered a house where ritual overwhelms
even atheism. Tonight, I'm eating my dinner of no red meat in this
bedroom, in the dark, so I can see the silhouettes of the birds that sit
on the telephone wires during a rainstorm. And I don't know what
to make of those birds like hitch knots on the wires, or the bells of
clouds that move behind them like jellyfish. I just know one day I will
leave this house where mirages of street vendors I remember from
Manila still come, still call me with their carts of fish balls, stamping
me into the passport of my departing blue memories.

Second Lesson (Circle Inn)

When my father's bail was posted, my mother made me run across
the school quad, afraid he would come for me first. She had filled
and Pentel-penned three days worth of underwear and coupons
into a bag zipped right to left across my lap.

As we drove down the 60 freeway, she told me we had no choice;
he wouldn't hesitate to lug her again by the back of her shirt, to drag
her over the front yard like a bundle of firewood. I cracked the
window and could smell the horses, the saddle leather and manure,
as we sped past the dairy farms. I thought, Oh god, everyone at
school will know.

But at the Circle Inn, she watered the fake carnations. I spent the
day out of school, high with candy cigarettes and Astro Pops while
she watched as I jumped on the bed. She let me leave shoe marks on
the motel sheets.

Junkyarding through the Great Moreno Valley

S. was always looking for a carburetor and I'd hang around to get some sleep on the bench seat of his Ford. When I was awake and not browsing the glove compartment, I'd help comb the rust edging the lots, finding nothing shaped like a such-and-such all day. We'd split up—he called it double-timing—and I'd poke around at alternators and engines under the corrugated hoods. If I got lucky, a cat or possum would skedaddle out a trunk, or I'd find a cassette tape-song we'd jammed to at the skating rink a few years back.

Once when I was leaning against the open door of a stripped jeep, he proposed with a pipe clamp too big for any of my fingers. I still wore it around, every so often forgetting what it was and calling it a gasket. We were always getting it wrong, he and I. He'd tell me to look for serpentine belts, but to stay away from the rattlesnakes, and I'd come back swinging an inner tube or two on my arms. It was good.

Sure, not much happened, but those things we'd holler one after the other across the junkyards, weekend after weekend, well, they became something like a language passed between us, our own long American sentence.

PEOPLE OFTEN ASK ME why I turn to the prose poem and, in most cases, I've found no other way to explain the impulse than to bombard them with examples, beginning with Carolyn Forché's "The Colonel" and Gabriela Mistral's "The Body." Needless to say, I quickly tire each one of them out until I am left alone with my photocopies. Someone once argued that there could be poetry in prose, but no prose in poetry. All's fair, I thought; but I had to wonder where that person grew up, and under what conditions. In my experience, I've found that the freeways and desert landscapes of Southern California demand this form. I've found that lineating sentences from one margin to the other is what best captures what it is like to drive past curfew with only the dividers and freeway guardrails guiding me. The very breath of the prose poem—how it can speed and slow and speed again—is likewise the only one I've found to match almost perfectly the gusts of the Santa Ana winds.

RICHARD KATROVAS

The Super Rich Are an Oppressed Minority

that has no choice but to defend itself against the machinations of hoi polloi, the kidnapping and lying, the acts of theft and destruction and gross bad faith, but especially the inept service and envious glances. "The eye of a needle," scholars tell us, was a portal into the city large enough for a donkey to pass through. So may all rich men and women and their progeny pass in single file from the Free Market Wastes into the Heavenly City, where commerce is unregulated and taxes perfunctory and meager. May those of us unconnected, unmotivated, disinherited, unfocused and clueless, those of us lacking talent and drive, we who were born with plastic spoons in our mouths, learn to express compassion for all who possess the means of production and therefore also the will to fuck us. And when they do, let us only shyly insist that they also hold us close and kiss us.

The Liberal Arts

are where you bring a lot of articulate people together to compete for relatively meager resources. It is the rubric under which the chasm between information and knowledge contains at its bottom the bone yard of Youthful Exuberance, and where the high-minded and petty dance slow, close and dirty through the crumbling stacks of the Library of Babel. It is where the dreamy bothers and sisters of scientists and technicians are kept out of the flight path of real thought, a kind of holding tank with soft walls and benches, or a leper colony with soft walls and benches, even gardens and fountains. It is where you scoot off the otherwise uneducable young to, and where all others must pass quickly as through long aisles of rocks under glass. And is not the "canon" just rocks under glass? Objects of dispassionate scrutiny, though also potential, if primitive, weapons?

George W. Bush Was Very Nice to Me

as Bacchus rolled down St. Charles, and I chatted with him about politics, local and national, especially the eleven-fingered idiot running against David Duke for the Republican nomination for Führer of the Suburbs. I told him flat out I hate the Republican Party and still he was nice to me, stood next to me, in the back of the ten-deep crowd that yelled for trinkets, and chatted for several minutes as though he really liked me, and didn't mind at all that I'd ripped a fine white string of beads from his grasp when he grabbed it from the air at the same time as I. As we chatted about Duke and New Orleans apartheid, about my having recently lived in the French Quarter and about how the trees on St. Charles seem for months after Carnival—indeed on some stretches all year round—like bearers of many-colored fruit from where the bead strands get caught in the branches, I knew I would one day write about meeting the president's goofy son, a nice guy, which is to say someone you shouldn't mind standing around shooting the breeze with on a peasant spring night in New Orleans, though not someone you'd want to be cooped up with on a long ride, say, from El Paso to San Antonio, or certainly not from one paradigm to another.

I CALL MY TEXTS herein not prose poems but *feuilletons* (though certainly they're as much prose poems as anything else!); the *feuilleton* is of course a French form of ephemeral journalism, though before 1989 in Eastern and Central Europe many dissident writers adapted it to the weightier concerns of "samizdat," the underground network of literary dissemination. My *feuilletons* are actually much briefer that those of, say, the great Ludvik Vaculík, who says a *feuilleton* should be roughly three typed pages long. Whereas the analogues for most prose poems are fairytales, myths and dream narratives, the analogue for my *feuilletons,* and almost all others, is the acerbic, ironic personal essay.

CLAUDIA KEELAN
Everybody's Autobiography

1.

At the end, the only thing left in my parents' house was the piano and an oversized portrait of them on their wedding day. At the end, he died in my house, in Las Vegas, and I called *I love you Dad*

through moments struck open, a lid on a trunk that was our life together, struck open, in his dying. At the end, the firemen and paramedics, the coroner from Chicago smoking on the porch, and the captain saying

would you like to pray? At the end, we did, struck open, the bed that was his tomb still in the guest room, and yet no angel telling me of the risen Lord. At the end, I kept returning to the room

to look at my father. In the end, they placed him in a bag, I heard the zipping and though I didn't watch, I heard the effort they made lifting, and he was gone, no sirens, before my son woke.

2.

In the beginning, in 1924, Lenin died, and Stalin ruled for 29 years. Calvin Coolidge was president and there was no vice president. Clarence Darrow, a man who, unlike my father, believed in law, helped Leopold and Loeb to escape the death penalty for the murder of their 14-year-old cousin.

In the beginning, Ruth Malcomson from Pennsylvania was named Miss America, and George Gershwin's *Rhapsody in Blue* debuted in Paris.

On April 3rd, 1924, my father Edward Thomas Keelan Jr., was born in Compton, California to Marguerite Keelan *née* Kearns and Edward Thomas Keelan Sr., the boy between two girls, Peggy 2 and Patricia, the baby.

This is the autobiography of everyone because all lives and books begin and end.

> This is the autobiography of everyone and is for all of us still alive in the broken middleness, mouthing our stories. My father fell into this world from a woman's body. And yours? This is the autobiography of everyone

Because it was my father who taught me to distrust distinctions that separated the simple subject from the compound subject, particularly, and to begin with, the subject *I*. *I'm hungry,* I told my father.

The world is rumbling he said, and placed a piece of bread in my mouth.

I'm thirsty, I repeated and he pointed towards the split in the dream and handed me a hollow stick.

3.

Of death, Gertrude Stein writes in *The Geographical History of America*:

> Now the relation of human nature is this.
> Human nature does not know this.
> Human nature cannot know this...
> Human nature does not know that if everyone did not die
>   there would be no room for those who live now.

This is true. Almost everything Stein said was true. I know because I've felt it happen, human nature. Human nature is interested in itself. One day, human nature finds a place—a room, a table, a field, a site of becoming—where human nature loses, in a flash, first distinction, and finds itself suddenly something other, one's whole understanding of a glorious singularity disappeared in an instant.

How large the world has become in your loss! You have understood the purpose of death. Having done so, you understand the purpose of life. You must give your self away. Then you can sleep.

Stein: "This is the way human nature can sleep, it can sleep by not knowing this. The human mind can sleep by knowing this." I have spent my life asleep, standing by the window year after year with my mother, waiting for my father to come home safely. This is the autobiography of everyone asleep in one room or the other. Natural mind, have you seen my father?

4.

In the beginning, Walt Disney created his first cartoon and another invention, the Teapot Dome Scandal, debuted in Wyoming, and Elk Hills, California, not far from where my father worked the oil wells years later.

Harry F. Sinclair of Sinclair Oil Company was sentenced to prison for contempt of the Senate and for hiring detectives to shadow members of the jury in his case.

I liked the dinosaur in the Sinclair oil sign, just as I found the oil wells themselves, perpetually making love to the edges of Interstate 5, oddly comforting, though a little sad.

In the years before my father was born, the Southern Pacific Railroad monopolized California. William Hood was the chief assistant engineer who saw that tunnels were the only clear route through the sometimes impenetrable mountains. He envisaged eighteen tunnels in twenty-eight miles of track

climbing down from the Tehachapi Mountain to the San Joaquin Valley below. The Southern Pacific Railroad was as merciless as it was inventive. When a town denied access to the company, it simply built another town.

The farmers too felt the brunt of the railroad's power. Allowed to settle on isolated land, in Tehachapi, in Boron and many desert regions of the state, many farmers had cultivated the barren land into lush fields.

5.

In 1878, the Southern Pacific Railroad took titles to the land and appraised the land at twenty-five to fifty dollars, instead of the two dollars and fifty cents originally quoted the farmers.

Outraged, they went to court where they lost every case; by the end, eight farmers died and two hundred families were evicted from their farms.

Earlier, in 1881, the Southern Pacific joined the Atchison, Topeka and Santa Fe Railroad at Deming in New Mexico territory to become the second transcontinental railroad.

My parents sang the song as we drove along, and so did we, along with "I've Been Working on the Railroad," "Give Me a Ticket for an Airplane," wanting I suppose now that I think of it, to be anywhere but the car.

For all their invention and cruelty, the founders of the railroad obviously had a vision of shared beauty built into their machine. The dining cars of the early railroads were elegant meeting places where travelers

met over fine china, eating roast pheasant, exotic relishes and drinking California wine as they gamboled together towards different destinations. The gilded age of the railroad ended in 1910 when Hiram Johnson was elected

governor of California and methodically broke the political hold of the Southern Pacific Railroad. A United States Senator from 1917 to 1945, Johnson was the Progressive party's nominee for vice-president in 1912.

6.

As a senator, he was an isolationist, opposing membership to the League of Nations and the United Nations. A large state on the edge of the Pacific, California itself is contained, isolated, and like all things in isolation, it has no

concept of boundaries. Apotheosis to the "bedroom community," the suburbs of Southern California are predicted in the next century to reach Las Vegas. The golden state, *El Dorado,* California was the destination dream spot

of millions of immigrants from the 1800s when pioneers traveled the California-Oregon trail, to the present day when Mexican émigrés are smuggled across the border, camouflaged as part of the car's seat.

It can be no mistake that in the years during Johnson's political career, the oil companies laid the foundation for the state's eventual enslavement to the gasoline combustion engine. With the downfall of the Southern Pacific Railroad,

the oil barons took, and continue to hold, the transportation realities of the millions of Californians who now inhabit *El Dorado* alone, or commuting, and mostly in traffic jams, in automobiles along the state's freeways.

225

7.

A Brief History of the Major Oil Companies in the Gulf Region

1889: Standard Oil (Indiana) founded as subsidiary
of Standard Oil Trust

1911: Standard Oil of Indiana founded with the dissolution
of Standard Oil

1910: Standard Oil of Indiana purchases
Pan American Petroleum

1932: Standard Oil of Indiana sells Venezuela operation
to Jersey

1954: Pan American and Standard of Indiana merge,
new company is called American Oil Company (Amoco)

1957: Begins joint venture with Iran independent
of Iranian Oil Consortium

1959: Amoco signs agreements with Shah of Iran

1959: Jersey strikes oil in Libya

1972: Jersey changes name to Exxon

1972: Saudi Arabia, Abu Dhabi, Kuwait and Qatar
acquire 25% interest in Exxon's production operations
(in country), with right to increase stake to 51% by 1982

1981: Exxon sells Standard Libya to Libyan government.

Along with Amoco, Getty, Exxon, Ashland Oil, Chevron, Conoco, and many others continue to operate in the Gulf Region.

8.

"But there is no remembering in the human mind."
—Stein

My father died on July 21, 2001, and on September 11, 2001, fourteen boys in airplanes crashed into the World Trade Center, the Pentagon, and into a field in Pennsylvania, killing themselves and thousands of people.

This has something to do with my father, with oil, with me. My government and with you.

Since my father's death, I've slowly begun waking to my childhood. It's mostly full of other people's words, as is time in general, the specific a rare event, relying as it does upon an individual member being awake.

I'm waking to my childhood in my own child's life, the driving he loves on video games, a version of the driving I loved, asleep in the backseat. May all his crashing be virtual.

In remembering is re-membering. Heart and mind, body and soul, time and space, father and daughter, we are separate; we are attached.

The mind knows this when the heart pulses freely, dependent on its own muscle. The soul itself is a muscle, both housed and independent of its own body.

I'm aware of its contraction now, in the arc it's making outside me as it follows the automobile's whine, which is a pulse too, surrounding each moment of modern life.

Time is eternal in space. Trapped radio waves prove it, as does my dead father's DNA wound through me.

Heaven, then, spirals in a dragonfly's hovering, look, just now, and in its vanishing.

STEPHEN KESSLER

Long Story Short

Mother, I was born half-way here. My head was in the new world, my knees and stomach in another. You were gone before I knew who you were. Rumor is that you were beautiful. Father was a worker who disappeared into a factory, executing merchandise for the masses. There were slaves somewhere in the ancient distance, maybe our relations, I'm not sure. Nobody told me anything. I'm figuring it out myself. I hear there may not be time to write this down.

The streets blur. There were several, and several cities. Once we arrived we were always moving, even when we had our own place. Room had to be made, so we edged over. The neighbors kept changing too. First the Egyptians, then the English, Chinese, Indians and so on. The world was a wheel.

From my littlest moments I loved horror stories. It must be in the blood, the immune strength, the endurance vision. One of my grandfathers held my hand as we watched the images of terror flicker. We felt the fear from a distance and kept close together, leaning the other way. We imagined ourselves immortal, like the story characters, dying over and over forever, always admired, remembered, honored by new voyeurs.

Ballgames raised me to a full boy. Bug guys in uniforms on green grass. Even from the stands you could smell their breath: they spat tobacco like prisoners of a rude zoo. In those days the pros were tough and mean, lovable just the same without the replay. We saw their faces from afar, wore them in our minds on our own fields, spitting in the dirt in neighborhood parks, kissing girls through the chain link. I caught a bad hop in the forehead once and tripled in the same game, tackled my other in a brotherly embrace, stole a ball running a fast break and got the assist. Those were as close as I came to heroism.

When war came, or seemed to, we hid. Kids then thought they were too young to kill, though everything's different now. Our patrols were inward, crawling under a car, retreating behind a school, barricading our ignorance with books. I prayed for safety, believed

228

my general, followed the teacher's orders, sang each morning "My Country 'Tis of Thee." Singing in unison felt good, it powdered the fear, made us more sure of ourselves, our gods.

Then bright flashes showed us our bones in retrospect. Something shattered. Glass flew. We fled the shelters, gave back our prayers, left our guardians for dead. The streets were alive with refugees. No one knew where they were going, only that we needed to get lost. I must have been nine or ten—in my prime—I could have done anything I tried. I enlisted in a preschool for comedians.

We had some laughs while our cousins were carried off in trucks. What else could we do. The other guys had the guns. I fell in love. She laughed at all my jokes, I laughed at hers. We turned the howl of sirens into ironic screams. We were happy for a time in the laughter academy, learning each other's lines. One day a bomb hit and we scattered. My love went underground. I emigrated.

I went back to the old world to find my roots. It was shut, everybody'd moved, the government was new and they threw me out. I decided just to travel for a while, working odd jobs. I did a stretch as a jockey, a standup delinquent, a chauffeur, an adult impersonator. I was fourteen. I knew show business was the future. I was getting my chops, paying my dues, learning the ropes. I even worked as a hangman for a while. I was a gypsy scholar, reading the texts of the dead in my spare time. A scout from one of the networks found me and offered me a gig holding the flashcards for a famous actress.

That's how I got to Hollywood. I could speak Romance languages out of both sides of my mouth, turn the other cheek and duck at the same time. But I didn't last. The producer my leading lady belonged to didn't like my looks. I was too cute, I had a smart answer for everything, my background was suspicious and I had a crush. I was kicked out. I hitched a ride out of there in a Volkswagen bus full of Central American beatniks playing James Brown tapes, wearing bandoleros full of pens and pencils.

We drove for years, stopping often en route to pick up pilgrims, pitching camp by the highway and eating mushrooms. By campfirelight the typewriters were taken out and we worked on a collective translation of the Sears Catalogue. It was 1969. Free love, free thought and free trade were our bottom lines. I got tired of making decisions by consensus and dropped out, setting off in the predawn hours toward a distant light in the west.

My tapes got erased in a metal detector at the first shopping center I crossed. Transport helicopters passed over, stewardesses wobbling on their high heels. Girls in bikinis parachuted out of the clouds. I looked for cover in the lettuce fields, eating what I could find. Winter fell. A laundromat was open so I climbed into a warm dryer to cop some sleep. When I woke it was spring; my sweetheart from comedy school was folding me into her clothes on a plastic tabletop. Kiss me, she crooned, and I was born again.

We settled down on the coast to raise some orphans, open a gourmet cooking school and train blockaders. I took up herbs and surfing, shaved, gained weight and became a healer. One of my clients is an older man who claims to be my father.

Autumn Rhythm

So where do you go when afternoon blazes a hot blue and eases slowly all day into a pink-and-white haze around six o'clock and you begin to get pleasantly sad as the sun goes down, angling its fine light between trees, across the corners of office buildings and through the braided parabolas of bridges—do you just stand there wondering how one more day could be so gorgeous, gifted with insights no postcard could touch?

Maybe once in a museum you met a painting that spoke to you, swooping off a wall on waves of its own energy to stop you smack in the midst of a city: a great canvas dripping with the shapes of a season, days dropping off like leftover lives across roads, in woods, descending in elevators, yellowing and falling casually in softening loops whose every turn tells a going-away story to your eyes where tears are beginning.

Study it long enough and grief will laugh, embracing its best losses like little brothers gone off to battlefields, hills of no return against long odds. You knew they were lost from the time they left and you become accustomed to the silence behind them, admiring this late light like a love letter: I love you, yes indeed, the sun says, disappearing.

And how easy it is to crave the new cool nights with crickets repeating their national anthem and those mornings curling with the first smoke. Even the city feels clean one fall dawn before the trucks get started and the terminals start ticking and the stock market spits up its figures. Each sidewalk shines with its own transience, mean and ironic under the streetlamps. You breathe. Coffee is roasting by the docks and some dog is inaugurating a lawn. Dreams seep back into the pillow's mind and you see what you forgot, believing.

There are piles of fresh newspapers to ignore, layers of civilizations frozen for the moment out of sight in lava, to be discovered when we blow away and be turned into dissertations. More leaves let go as you stroll out into the transforming morning: you smell school, you are rehearsing for Halloween, amazed at the sweetness increasing in your young lungs. All the swallowed smoke that's built its home in the internal tissues takes pity on the flesh and disperses into the keen climbing light.

Emptying your heart into a fading hydrangea you remember a baby you never were, witnessing her beauty from a distance in disbelief. "I am destiny," she whispers, and soon you are both giggling, growing with all you've got out of someone's grave. The garden droops into its deepest fruit. Mature women are blooming.

Along the coast cafés are doing a brisk business, hotcakes and eggs and sides of nostalgia for the visions unrealized, a flick of regret into the sea breeze followed by a strong appetite with coffee back. A day for savoring, getting things done before the flood. It was how many years this fall when events overtook you and you took on historic hallucinations: brute truth picked you up bigger than King Kong and carried you high into its empire. In those days you could be put away like Nietzsche for hugging a horse in public, no one but you could know who the beast really was—but now the animal is us, we park ourselves in the street waiting for the embrace.

And right around midday every day, amid bites of lunch, through rising fatigue, distracted by bad news or music pouring from a horn, invisible hands are felt caressing your face as if to confirm who you are—anyone, alive someplace, looking out for everything you can't quite see except with intuition. Headlines and mascara blur in daily lies. You are linked with it all despite the breaks and you sense undeniable alliances.

All day they move through you in pulses hooked up with the next ones, all moving the same way, time measured in arterial miles in bloodstreams' bright meanderings. Flights of chance take you across frontiers into new jobs, into rendezvous beyond under-standing which pay in endless non-negotiable gold.

It's warm. There's skin to burn under a thin moon. Always the same winds, same replayed flames and devastations, same birthdays weeping for what they wanted, aching with gratitude.

Desire lingers in moving life. That surface should be so beautiful always, and it is.

Final Exam

What's eating you—the freeway, the keyboard, the TV, the deep freeze? Do you breathe wrong around the diesels, as if defending an island of air violated in the depths of your last lung? Is every day a factory for you, a deconstruction of the never-was? Are you discontinuous to a fault, nonlinear in the light of relativity, relaxed in the face of annihilation because you can't keep from remembering the flash-in-the-pan your life was microwaving an irony in your mind's eye?

Maybe everybody's days are like this lately: in the moon's grip—gravity's—which swamps your body in bogs of black radiance. And as you sink you swim, whistling in the dark because your homework is overdue and you're graduating this week but you heard some tune while Frenching your sweetie and its beat keeps thumping overtime in you, begging the question of accompaniment. Or because you lost the big game and came home to a cold barbecue, sour roses rotting in the compost, the snails ate the leaves of the seedlings, the cats have worms and the ruling junta has rejected your application for active duty—and so you are reduced to a kind of tango.

Grief is melting in Tierra del Fuego, feeling its way upward toward the Tropics of Atrocity—neonazis running electroshock

232

machines on dissident Jews and genitals—stories you wouldn't believe if it weren't for the glare of your own hardware. Walking along the aisles of Torture Supply you may charge your freedom against the repression used to preserve it, and wonder. Are you shocked that you secretly admire the erotic violence of alien pain? The power to inflict suffering is a famous aphrodisiac. Nothing is beneath you these days, the radio told you so.

But a deeper reading of your chart reveals a karmic slug, a boomerang of some shit you ran on somebody coming back. It's like throwing the *I Ching* to the wrong base and bringing the tying run around. Behind you, leftover alliances with lovers who never leave; before you, whatever you can imagine except an ever-after. All those hours in downpours gazing into a face whose legs were yours disappear like distant relations gone away with the Gestapo.

Is it morbid to be reminded of the blues without end trailing from fuselages moaning over the Earth eternally? Each pilot talking dutifully into his tape is taking dictation from the future, pulling us that much farther away from the farm, arming our adolescence with complex hungers for destruction: *conquistadores* driven to acrobatic extremes via Coke and cinema. Everyone craves. Everyone flies and crashes his own Christ. The talk of the town is a nameless angel that landed unannounced in what well known café?

Freedom of freedom? Dreams some guy with wooden teeth and a wig entertained while warming up to throw the first pitch across the Mississippi? Which thug did you elect? This is a pass/fail exam, an either/or beyond yes and no. But only a test. We are prescribing a paragorical solution whose painkilling powers may be dangerous.

Picture a war of numbers, a war of papers, of chemicals, of newlyweds and celibates, of barkers, strippers and booksellers battling it out over rights to the ice cream concession at the South Pole. Trends are set and zigzagged before you can get in the groove, the nerve gas you thought you'd got rid of turns up in your own Jacuzzi, your masseuse doubles as a succubus. Luis Buñuel is using your last telephone call as grist for a script. The worship service you meant to attend was cancelled for the sake of a weapons convention. There are singles bars beckoning which refuse to close because purgatory knows no curfews.

And grinning images slither from the magazine rack. The tools of actors hang out in ads pushing video-anesthetics for the home. The secret sex of the starlet beats for gossip's regret and ex-nuns take up arms to avenge deprivation. The hourglass is upended and time runs out, accumulating in a pool at the foot of an automatic teller: *The time is . . .*

Do you speak when you hear the beep? Those games on screens are early warnings of a plague we may never live to see—delinquent smoking limbs allowed to fumigate the night with ceaseless *boing-boings* and blips to drive dogs mad. Was that Billy Graham we heard banging out a refrain on his own bandwagon? Evangelical commandoes have stormed the sanctums of the lapsed, claiming refugee-sensitivity to the promise of promised lands. Millions of rafts are seen bobbing and subsiding just beyond the embargo. Their signals got crossed along the color line.

So what if generals won all the elections? Quit thinking only in critical terms and positivity will conquer. There are no mirages in a deluge—just pure oppression, fear in a jar like a salve for the disappeared. Your reading habits have been shattered by hallucinations tantamount to a tragic artifact. News dies for you every day and its pulp gives birth to tomorrow.

THESE TEXTS WERE originally written as newspaper columns in the early 1980s for the *Santa Cruz Express*, an independent weekly in the days before the "alternative" press surrendered to a more formulaic corporate model. As a columnist I had the liberty to infiltrate, subvert and confound a journalistic medium by throwing a curveball every so often in the form of a prose poem.

As a way of reporting the psychic news as informed by current events, this kind of composition was an ideal vehicle because of its relative looseness and flexibility. Many of my verse poems start as notebook prose before they're broken into breathing lines, so from there it was easy to dispense with lines and let fly with a more relaxed sense of the sentence, which in poetry need not obey the formal logic of normal prose. I was able to tell little stories or riff on whatever was in the air while experimenting with different kinds of syntax and associations than would otherwise be permissible in that context.

The openness of the form creates its own exacting demands, just as free verse requires a self-created technical and stylistic discipline that is imposed more mechanically from without in fixed forms; like field composition à la Robert Duncan, the writing of poems in prose calls for a comparably subtle and finely tuned rhythmic ear and a feeling for the breath of natural-sounding speech. For me, the hybrid form of the-poem-as-journalism proved an excellent mode for things I couldn't have said in any other way.

CHRISTINE KITANO

Lost in the Move

Photograph: My Ballet Recital; age, 12.

The applause has stopped, the mothers and fathers have ushered their daughters home, draping crushed velvet coats over pink leotards. Waiting, alone under the empty lights, I crouch down to the stage and collect shed rose petals. My mother clicks the camera by accident, trying to wind the film.

Photograph: My Aunt Chizu, age 22; Topaz Internment Camp, Utah; July, 1944.

Her smile is wide and sun-bright on the black & white film. She points to the laces of her saddle shoes. "Tar," she'd say, sixty years later, shaking her head, "it melted in the sun—sticking our soles to the ground." She'd smile again, to herself, and laugh. "Your father brought his trombone."

Photograph: My Seventh Birthday.

I am pinching the pigtail of a large orange balloon, and smile despite the fear I'm feeling—that at any moment the balloon will break free, slip away, disappear up a chimney of clouds. In the background, my father leans against the yellow porch swing and tips the lip of a glass tumbler, swallowing his medication with wine.

Oxnard, California; August, 1989

I am three years old and standing at the entrance to the gift shop in the lobby of the Casa Sirena Hotel & Marina. My mother dressed me that morning—light blue overalls, pastel pink blouse with ribbons tied in neat bows across the collar, white socks trimmed with lace, and brand-new sneakers.

The stiff shoes are too big and a rubber toe catches on the checkered carpet. I fall onto the track of the gift shop's sliding glass door. My forehead splits open like a baked potato. The memory of the fat stitches across my small skull lingers, a picket-fence scar shadowing my brow.

It isn't until I am twelve and want to enter the Junior Miss pageant that my mother tells me she cried for a month after the accident, terrified I would be ugly, scarred. This fear is what she remembers most.

What I would rather remember is sitting in her lap on the way to the hospital. The taxi's black leather backseat collects the day's heat and when I reach down with my sunburned hand, my fingers stick to the melting duct tape stitching the seat together. That's what I want to remember most—the stickiness of the leather, the tape, my blood, and my mother's sweaty skin against mine.

On Losing My Identity in Fourth-Grade Art Class

Mrs. DeHaven passed out sheets of paper and placed a coffee can filled with crayons in the center of each group of desks. We were drawing "self-portraits," she explained. The best artist would win a prize.

I was small and shy and didn't move quickly enough, and when it came time for me to color in my eyes and hair, the black and brown were already taken, the purple crayon the only one left. I figured if I pressed down hard enough, it would darken from the pressure. So I leaned in and rubbed hard against the paper.

The mark grew bold—a rich royal-blue bruise before the paper wrinkled—then tore right down the center, the wooden desk's glassy grain splitting the make-believe eyes like a lightning bolt. My face in ruins, I hardly looked like a person at all.

The Hour After Dad Left

The doctor hands me a plastic drawstring bag. Inside are my father's khaki Dockers (size 37 waist), his white undershirt, and a pair of brown socks, the elastic around the ankles pulled loose. His shoes are gone and so is the cash from his wallet. I leave without them.

I empty the bag onto the carpet in my bedroom and pull the undershirt to my cheek. It smells of shoe polish, just the way it had when he took me on the carousel at the Santa Monica Pier. He hugged my waist so I wouldn't slip from my seat on the wooden white horse, my small hands clinging to its gilded mane. Every time the flushing horizon came around I would point, and he would look.

Inside the pocket of his khaki pants I find a half-eaten Hershey bar. The chocolate is melted around the wrapper's torn edge. He always broke his candy in two, saving half for me when I came home from school. This half is mine. I peel the melted paper from the chocolate and break off a square. The sugary syrup stings my back molar. I breathe in, and both my tooth and lungs feel hollow.

Birds of Paradise

My father believed in gardening, and planted tomatoes under the study window so he could watch their progress, strawberries outside the bedrooms to favor sweet dreams. He'd protect his plants to the death, kept a cheap pellet gun in the bottom drawer of his desk that he'd point, now and then, rotating his wrist so that the pistol waved, side-to-side (one eye open for *those damn rodents*), almost friendly.

My mother loved flowers. She'd stand, absentminded, at the kitchen sink, anticipating the rush of white irises and morning glories that would encircle the house like a fog. I'd cup the canoe-shaped bract of a Bird of Paradise in my hand and pretend I was an African queen, the stunning orange bird my companion, or Sleeping Beauty, the flower's sharp stigma a poisoned spindle. I knew, before blooming, the stem tips would swell, harden into full calyces.

My father swam every day of summer, and he'd take me with him to the community pool. I'd sit on a bench with my crayons and watch. He dives in, pierces the surface with his fingertips and spreads his hard arms wide beneath the surface, a white spray erupting into wings. He swims with such power I almost forget who he is.

I draw pictures of birds, of my father, of squirrels shot dead before they tear the ripe buds from his plants. I draw what I think I know about the birth of flowers, blooms diving out from wrinkled shells, unfurling thin petals, becoming pale, wet butterflies.

THE FIRST PROSE POEM I remember reading is Marcel Proust's "Wind of the Sea in the Country." I was attracted to the focus on rhythm and sound without the use of broken lines. As I experimented with different forms of poetry, I found that the structure of the prose poem allows the writer to capture a concentrated sense of restlessness, a fluidity of movement through time. A function of its form seems to be its ability to maintain a sense of honesty and innocence, making it well suited for poems that recall memories, especially.

RON KOERTGE

1989

Because AIDS was slaughtering people left and right, I went to a lot of memorial services that year. There were so many, I'd pencil them in between a movie or a sale at Macy's. The other thing that made them tolerable was the funny stories people got up and told about the deceased: the time he hurled a mushroom frittata across a crowded room, those green huaraches he refused to throw away, the joke about the flight attendant and the banana that cracked him up every time. But this funeral was for a blind friend of my wife's who'd merely died. And the interesting thing about it was the guide dogs; with all the harness and the sniffing around, the vestibule of the church looked like the starting line of the Iditorod. But nobody got up to talk. We just sat there and the pastor read the King James version. Then he said someday we would see Robert and he us. Throughout the service, the dogs slumped beside their masters. But when the soloist stood and launched into a screechy rendition of *Abide With Me,* they sank into the carpet. A few put their paws over their ears. Someone whispered to one of the blind guys; he told another, and the laughter started to spread. People in the back looked around, startled and embarrassed, until they spotted all those chunky Labradors flattened out like animals in a cartoon about steamrollers. Then they started too. That was more like it. That was what I was used to: a roomful of people laughing and crying, taking off their sunglasses to blot their inconsolable eyes.

Discarded Shoe Locates Owner in Los Angeles

This afternoon police confirmed that a brown Florsheim wing-tip had made the journey from San Bernardino and arrived at the door of its owner, Laurence B. Clay. Mr. Clay was still hospitalized at press time after a violent confrontation with the shoe. Witnesses said it seemed "angry" and "vindictive." "We're used to dogs and like that finding their owners," said Detective Mallory. "But this is a whole new ball game." Police would not comment on reports of roadblocks

240

outside the city. They claimed that the enormous dust cloud near Palm Springs was probably due to unusual atmospheric conditions. They forcefully denied that telephone lines from the that area were jammed with calls from people asking for help of any kind.

Bumper to Bumper

It's homey on the freeway today. Bronco shaves, those Jetta girls bicker, vanity plate asks for a room at the Hotel Tesoro and her deep-voiced dash replies, "Muy bien." We are lined from here to the vanishing point, but our collective idle is full of promise as a dial tone. In the blue shuttle beside me, a woman sleeps, her lips against the window. I get out of my Ray and french her through the glass. It's a perfect Los Angeles kiss: passionate but safe. Everyone applauds and the Corvette with the beard wants to option the concept for a sitcom.

The Chinatown Book of the Dead

Beside me is a box that says Candied Squid. Across the room a small shrine with oranges and incense. Eyes half-closed in concentration, a new Chinese doctor is taking my pulses. "Kidneys weak," he says. "Not serious." My old Chinese doctor used to ask about my sex life. "How power?" he'd say, raising his forearm and clenched fist. So I brought him a poem by a ninth-century concubine which began, "All you can do is mumble." Dr. Xi laughed uproariously and told everyone in Tin Bo Herbs & Pharmaceuticals. Even the old ladies leaning on their dutiful sons smiled. When I went back in September, he didn't stand up to greet me. He listened, wrote out another prescription, then put both hands on my forehead and said good-bye. I don't think he will have a hard time in the bardos, looking with mere affection at the beautiful young girls, with tolerance at the piles of silk and gold. Only one thing might tempt him to slip into yet another body, and that is the rheumy eyes and heavy breathing of the ill, our hands extended, wrists exposed, and beneath the skin the insistent pulse.

Cosmos 2219

I drive up Angeles Crest Highway, ease the little truck into #26 at Silver Moccasin Campground and stretch my legs. Lots of tents and fires. A family argues in Thai as they arrange blue Igloo coolers and canvas chairs. A couple of girls kissing at a bare table scowl at me, and the skinny one holds a flashlight under her chin so she looks horrible like some kid at camp trying to scare the crybabies. My wife's sleeping bag still smells like her, so I slip in and lie down in the back of the truck. A satellite goes over and I glance at the What's Happening in Heaven Tonight schedule. There's Cosmos 2219, right on time. Some people believe those satellites are monitoring our every move, just as God was once supposed to monitor our every thought. When He got to me I imagined Him frowning at Betti Page in her skimpy cat suit. When people died back then, our pastor said the good ones went to Heaven where everything was taken care of, nobody had arthritis, nobody had to get up at 6:00 to start a fire. Which sounded a lot like Hawaii because those who could afford it always said, "Oh, it's so beautiful and warm and we never had to lift a finger." I try to imagine some of the dead people I know in that heaven. Jack would get along fine. He liked sitting around while good-looking boys brought him things. I'm not so sure about Dad. Waiters intimidated him, but I think any heaven worth its salt would have a cafeteria. And I can easily see my grandma, who died changing a light bulb, sweeping the streets of gold in front of her mansion. All around me, people settle down. I hear the long zippers of sleeping bags. A baby cries. A girl laughs and says, "Stop that!" The mountain, full of amputated trees, sighs. Another satellite goes by winking like a weary roue. But no falling stars. So I give up and head home. I'm on the freeway when there's this meteor shower with a huge radiant drift. Wouldn't you know it: an hour each way and the big show goes on one minute from home. As I turn into the driveway, I imagine Jack and Dad standing on clouds like folks in a cartoon, but instead of Zeus-bolts, they're tossing meteors. Jack will always be young and limber, so it's easy for him to pinpoint the Castro and then Green Valley where his parents live. Dad's arthritis is gone, and he has a wicked sidearm that carries right over Collinsville where Mom can see it. Grandma is up on another ladder, a brand new star in her hand. But this time she doesn't fall. Only the star slips and lights up the sky over the garage. My friends at Moccasin Flats must see it, too: the ranger brooding in his green truck, the skinny girl who likes kissing, the Thai father smoking one last bitter cigarette.

The Pasadena Freeway

Originally Arroyo Seco Parkway, you were the first freeway in Los Angeles. Short-sighted people see you as the crucible of noxious progress, but others value your originality and pioneer status. We come to drive at all hours and we come alone, single peas in restless pods. Because you wind like a nature trail, you are the safest of all the freeways, nothing like those whose exit speeds are measured in g's. And your air quality is so sensational that careless drivers plunge into pollution as into huge, dingy marshmallows and are safe. Conceived in the Crown City, you glide ever downward, through a smudged and mysterious barrio. El Grande Jacinto's name is everywhere, and blue-eyed commuters wonder if the Giant Hyacinth will ever stalk their pretty streets. Then you skirt Chavez Ravine and plunge gratefully into the cool Harbor Freeway. Sunset Boulevard at the unfashionable end lures a few nomads or Hill St., kingdom of the No. 4 dinner. Every evening we lift our eyes and know that we are almost home when we cross the dry arroyo that was your maiden name until - like any luminary—you changed it, honoring the city you wear on your long and lovely self like a sprawling trinket. O, Pasadena Freeway, we have loved you from the beginning, all of us who can hardly wait to hold the sacred wheel and even in our dreams negotiate your movie star curves all night long.

THE PROSE POEM is a very congenial form for me, since I often write a long, loose line anyway and prefer a narrative spine in my poems. I remember seeing my first prose poem when I was in graduate school (1962+) and loving the solid look of it on the page. I was a bit of a blockhead myself and the form seemed meant for me.

STEVE KOWIT

Home

You arrive at the gates of Paradise feverish with anticipation, assuring yourself that everything will be perfect—no migraine headaches, no ambulance sirens, no goodbyes. & it's true, the view from your sitting room is breathtaking, the service impeccable, the food enticingly garnished, & although the water tastes slightly metallic, there is always the coke machine in the lobby. & the climate—the sort of weather you love, one glorious day on the heels of another. You stroll down the beach, much like those long, sandy beaches of Southern California, in love, as you were on Earth, with the word oceano, white seagulls, the bronzed & half naked women—women who are everything you have always dreamed, & yours for the taking. Truly a hedonist's heaven. Yes, everything's perfect, perfect by definition … till one afternoon in an unguarded mood you confess to yourself that the cuisine is without flavor & the wine flat, that the celestial Muzak piped into your suite, however mellifluous, jangles your nerves. How you wish you could turn on the radio & hear Monk or Dylan or even the six o'clock news. You long, if the truth be known, for a cup of cold water. As for the women, however lovely to look at, to the tough they are as lifeless as the pages of the magazines from which they were drawn & as weightless & predictable as the figments of your own imagination.

It is just then—at that very instant—that the thread of a name & face catches the light on what remains of the delicate film of your cortex, the wraith of a memory … & escapes. You call to it desperately over & over, but it will not return, though its residue lingers on your tongue. Such is the other side of God's marvelous amnesia. From that day forward you are lost. You pace in distraction along the Elysian beach obsessed with the need to recall who it was & what it must have been like. How insufferable, at such moments, is the glare of Paradise! & so it is that with only your foolish heart as witness, you begin to long bitterly for home.

244

Second Coming

Jesus returns, just as he'd promised he would, a decent sort of guy, friendly, smart, great sense of humor, just the sort of guy you like right off the bat, but because he's too unassuming to make much of himself, he's the sort of fellow you're never likely to think much about.

Until one evening, during a horrible rain, tooling down the San Diego freeway in his beat-up old VW bug, he passes one of those awful head-on collisions & pulls to the shoulder, leaps out, strides past the El Cajon cops & paramedics &, before anyone can think to stop him, kneels down & with a few encouraging words in some crazy language coaxes the dead back to life. The little girl gets back her severed right leg, & all that blood disappears like a bottle of trick ink. Then everyone starts waking up, even the drunk in the other car, sober & looking sheepish as hell. He knows he's done something dumb, but thank God no one was hurt.

Friend, do not be encouraged overmuch: no one starts suddenly loving his neighbors; the wretched of the earth are not suddenly fed. On the contrary, the sweet looking fellow with the scraggly beard is cuffed & thrown into a squad car, from the caged rear seat of which a huge attack-trained German Shepherd growls deep in its throat & bares his teeth. But twenty minutes later, when the paramedics have at last sped off to Sharpe Memorial Hospital with their dazed but grateful occupants, and the exhausted California Highway patrolmen make their way back to their cars, that big happy mutt is resting his head in Jesus's lap, the fellow telling him what a good little dog he is, & scratching him between his ears something that no one has done since he was pup. The cuffs, opened, are up on the dashboard.

The following morning a sanitized version of the curious incident is fed to the press and, not surprisingly, the odd, amenable stranger, apparently harmless, is asked to do an interview on the ten o'clock news. The anchor, a well-meaning pro who doesn't yet know that his beloved daughter—the light of his life—is to die in a few months of leukemia, asks, with an amused grin, how it feels to be the son of God, a claim the fellow apparently made on one of last evening's police reports, & instead of responding, the chap with the beard & tender smile leans forward, laying his hand gently on the anchorman's wrist, whereupon the poor newscaster starts to weep, inexplicably, right there on network news forcing the astonished cameraman to cut at once to the weather map: a composite aerial photo of the entire nation showing, as the network weatherman, taken aback, hastily improvises, a pattern of unusually fierce winds whipping around from the northeast, accompanied by a huge storm front that had moved in more quickly than anyone would have guessed, bringing torrential and at least as of now seemingly endless rains.

Curriculum Vitae

Exemplary patriot of long standing service to the state seeks employment as low intensity warfare facilitations coordinator, destabilization & coercive interrogations specialist, & extraordinary renditions & detention center plausible denial CEO for special assignments in colonial security & permanent counter-revolution.

Experience: Pyongyang depopulation program Command Center; management protocols traffic control for the SAVAK-Pavlavi genital-shock persuasion squads; Accounts Coordinator for termination of 12,000 Quiche Mayan expendables under White House mandate to keep United Brands investment skies sunny; Kinshasa deep cover Lumumba extirpation assignment with Larry Devlin & Sid Gottlieb; in-country PsyOps Nam pacification field command & oversight of Operation Phoenix tiger-cage-&-yellow-rain compliance center for termination of 30,000 potential unfriendlies.

With an assist from Tom Karamessines & Eddie Gonzales, it was I who brought down Che, I who trained the hit-man who offed Herbie Rojas, I who fingered Casla Morighelli in Brazil; it was I who was Frank Bender's point man in the Cuban penetration operation, I who conducted the Dan Mitrione Uruguayan torture seminars, led the first troops into Santo Domingo, directed the Paraguayan Indian

Dispossession Project setting up no-exit camps for the Guayaki-Aches, I who administered the Bolivian forced-Christianization program under cover of the Summer Institute for Linguistics.

Distinguished service as advisory liaison to Batista, Marcos, Somoza, Mobutu, Luckner Cambronne & the Tontons Macoutes; consultant to Augusto Pinochet, Pol Pot, & Arik Sharon. Oversight of deniability & liquidation operations in East Timor, Beirut, Shatilla, Haiti, Rio Lempa, El Mozote, Jenin & Fallujah. Current oversight of Team-Kadima & the Palestinian Final Solution with adjunct service as unofficial undersecretary of disinformation compliance & enforcement, orchestrating unequivocal mainstream media capitulation on all fronts.

Personal: California native. Married with children. Hobbies: duck hunting, surfing, off-roading, & slow-pitch softball. Health: Impeccable notwithstanding minor anatomical anomalies: i.e., two apiculated skull protuberances, flexible longicaudal tailbone appendage, bifurcated tongue & cloven feet. Not the least asset, your humble applicant casts neither shadow nor reflection. Discreet. Will travel. Undying loyalty to US corporate & colonial interests. No job too small or too dirty. References upon request.

AS FOR THE PROSE POEM, all I can say is that I love Zen & Sufi tales, epiphanic fables, those wonderful parables that Kafka composed—pieces like "A Knock at the Manor Gate" and "An Imperial Message." Are those prose poems? Are the final paragraphs of Joyce's "The Dead" a prose poem? & how about all those incandescent flash fictions, those one-page jewels so many writers are producing these days? Why can't we call them prose poems, too? I think of those droll & luminous moments of psychological revelation caught on the wing by Logan Pearsall Smith, the tiny pieces he collected in *Trivia*. Though they were done in the final decades of the nineteenth century & are far removed from the more surrealistic mode in which so many prose poem practitioners are working, they are surely the most savory & delectable of American prose poems. Yes, I know they are out of fashion. So much the worse for fashion. In the end, if the author of a splendid paragraph that makes my mouth drop open wants to call it a prose poem, who am I to argue or complain?

JUDY KRONENFIELD

History

He has only one arm, but he doesn't have none. He has only one ear, but he doesn't have none; he has one leg, he has one leg! he has no legs, but he has a trunk; he has no arms, but he has a trunk; he has a hole in the heart of the trunk, but he has his eyes; he has no eyes, but he has his nose; he has no nose or eyes, but he can hear while his armless, legless trunk plummets down hill on its little wooden wheeled platform. And let him not mouth *this is the worst*, should that trunk hang by the teeth of its head over frightful, sheer cliffs and unswept minefields, but salute his President with eyeblinks and await a rousing chorus of "Them Bones."

Oh cosmically-proportioned Human, spread-eagled over six of the eight compass points—you've already lost one of your four legs to crusades or jihads or whatever, one to "insurgents" on one side, one to "insurgents" on the other. One arm wasted away in unregarded famine and snapped like a twig, one flew from a blasted bus or targeted car, another was nailed, as a warning, on an enemy door. And one little bite of the brown recluse spider—blessedly created out of non-existence—just hanging out under your filthy straw pallet, and the two remaining limbs'll go necrotic and have to be amputated from their quadrants. What shall we say now, Mr./ Ms. Cosmo/a Little? *Thanks, but no thanks, we've already drunk from that cup?* Organ chords and seraphic choirs! Melancholy bugle calls! We want to stamp the blank check *insufficient funds*, but there's always more where that didn't come from.

But listen—please don't take his remaining leg arm nostril ear kidney eye lung, he is really grateful, he *is*, he is lighting this candle, carrying this feather, dropping coins in this slot, kissing your book, prostrating his body, spilling this blood, voting for God, inscribing Your Name on his still-beating heart.

In this heaven, the files are white, the labels darker white. The silver-white onionskin papers in the files, on which the records are kept are crisp as soldiers in dress uniform lined up for inspection. No clicking fingernails on keyboards break the labor-intensive silence. New information is added by an immortal workforce of gatherers and scribes who wear white gloves like antiquarians handling incunabula. Their work is infinite in infinite space and time and they are infinitely patient. Thus this heaven has something of the atmosphere of august old libraries, the ones with catalogues of folio size, into which titles are pasted—carefully inscribed in a fine hand on transparent slips of paper. Or of the scriptoria in which monks worked year after year after year on illuminated manuscripts. But it doesn't smell of book or parchment dust, and no one sneezes; the aether, in fact, has a faintly antiseptic scent, like the air in sealed-off sterile units of hospitals where those with compromised immune systems are kept infection-free.

Here the plots of all the books the immortals have ever read inhabit their minds like homing pigeons flown back to the coop. And all the flowers that have ever been pressed into those books—now two-dimensional works of translucent art showing pistil, stamen and leaf vein in delicate exactitude—are assembled and indexed. The invisible ties that connect friends who have "grown apart" or "lost touch" are revealed, and they snap back together like released rubber bands, to gasps of delight, and occasional consternation. The floor is covered—as far as the eye can see—by a maze-like carpet of silk, each strand of which memorializes what you forgot each time you went into a room and forgot why you went there; the path is yours to recapture.

And thoughts, like the ones I'm having now, that I'm not sure I want to pursue, that I could abandon when I go into the kitchen for a cup of tea, or when I look out the window and become mesmerized by the waving of branches, or a bird pummeling past—such thoughts, like all thoughts, are threaded on a great crystalline spool, and each thread-end has a white tag, labeled by hand in that darker white. Some immortals, with infinite access to or recall of time ahead, behind, and around them, pitch themselves into the well of forgetfulness. But it, alas, forgets forgetfulness, opening at the bottom and spilling them out on the silk carpet near the crystalline spool by the white on white files, where they are snapped into groups of people growing ever larger—*thwack, thwack, thwack, thwack.*

Resident Dead

I glimpse over the cemetery's stone wall the Hallmark seasonal window effect, as I slow, driving on a less than everyday route in my dusty suburban town: paper and real pumpkins all over the grass, a large scarecrow of raffia and printed cloth by one grave. I have visited my mother's in the small, largely unadorned Jewish section just once since she was buried there a decade ago last July. I cannot imagine bringing plastic bouquets, mylar balloons, butterfly pinwheels, porcelain lambs and angels like those I remember decorated most of the flat stones, or even a small July 4th flag like the few that waved over the Jewish dead—housewarming presents for the name-plated doors of death's local habitations. Yet now my mother's wizened corpse in her coffin floats over the stones into my mind. The skin is taut on her bones, brown and papery as the skin of mummies, the mouth drawn back, the few teeth exposed . . .

But is skin left? Pleistocene slowness or puffball speed?—I have no idea of the time to dissolution. Could she still be dressed as I instructed for the closed coffin service—neither in the customary white shroud, nor as if she were going out to meet her Maker in good viewing style: suit, jewelry, pumps—but as if we two were cheating the Angel and she were going in for a long hospital stay? The old velour robe, the hospital booties, the floral nightgown—already dust, or mildewed into juice? Dust the chipped pink polish on the nail of her dangling little finger, which I stroked that last night? Dust the fleshed finger? Yet "my mother is buried in Olivewood Cemetery," a *place* to stop, or not. Had she been whisked from my last glimpse of her on her hospital bed, her ashes scattered to the atmosphere, to whirl with rocks, and stones, and trees, would I like my dead nonresident? Or would I have felt a restless permanent unease, like hers—as she wanders through eternity—as some rabbis warn? I read somewhere the Romans cut off a little finger for burial—to ground the spirit?—before they burned the body.

I clasp that last glimpse, the whole body dressed for a night's sleep, before it slides under the lid of earth, because it seems easier for the resurrection I don't believe in to occur with the rudiments of bones and hair and teeth in the neat package of the coffin—a kind of erector set in disassembly, an eternal life kit—than with dispersed dust lifted and sunk on the winds, spirited into the heavens and falling again in the rain. As if re-assembly were an imaginable task for an only semi-great God-I-don't-believe-in: a jigsaw puzzle after tea in the retirement home rather than the mystery of the first carbon molecule, Jehovah bending close to breathe on some random handfuls of dust . . . A plume of which I leave behind, the convened atoms of my body accelerating, bound, right now, where I aim.

I HAVE BEEN WRITING lined poems for twenty-five years and prose poems only for the last few. Among the things I love about prose poems is the way they often allow me to get outside myself more easily than lined poems. Perhaps this is because of the surreal tradition that hangs about the prose poem and invites me into fanciful explorations (though, in truth, I occasionally do this in lined poetry as well); perhaps this is because of the little aura of the discursive essay that also hangs about the prose poem and invites me to develop and explore an idea a bit more intellectually than I might do in lined poetry. Perhaps this is also because the prose poem takes me away from the gravity and portentousness of the line, and into the wild and wooly rhythms of the sentence; I feel that I am twisting, twirling, sidestepping, jackhammering, leaping and flying with the sentence as I move horizontally across the page, violating it and, as well, discovering its tensile strength.

These prose poems are clearly not as place-conscious as many others in this collection, but there's a substrate of suburban California reality in "Resident Dead," and maybe one could argue that the proximity of Hollywood and the pursuit of eternal youth has rubbed off, a little, on "UnLethe."

DORIANNE LAUX

F-16 Fighter Jet

No arms, no legs. He was born that way. The TV shows a closeup
of his face, the short-sleeve's embroidered insignia, sun glancing off
the helmet's plexi-glass visor snapped shut over his eyes. He's safe in
the curved leather seat cupped like a human palm. Someone's idea
of charity. Gift for a boy who will never flail or fall from the sky, the
long way down onto the torn fields of war.

Blind Man on the 22 Fillmore

He is blind and she is beautiful. They are whispering and she tries
to soothe him and he is angry. She moves closer, smoothes his hair,
rubs his knuckles with her fingers. Her tenderness is lost on him.
When she laughs the whole bus lights up. He taps his cane, turns
away, slipping from one darkness into another.

What I Saw
(Olympic Valley, California)

3 boys in shorts and sleeveless sweatshirts running barefoot, single
file, across the damp expanse of morning grass. A snake with yellow
ribbons on her back. She sidled past our tennis shoes and sandals and
slid into the tall weeds. A tree so tall it scared me. A boulder shaped
like my husband's face. A man with a baby on his hip, stepping into
the elevator. Outside a hotel door, on a tray: a newspaper, a pair
of muddy boots and a tube of lipstick. The sexy bells of foxglove.
A woman wearing a pink shirt, pink shorts, pink socks, red shoes.
A blue ladder with a yellow top step and silver rungs, folded up like
an accordion by a man the color of Thai Iced Tea. A pond, seething
with wind. When it got still, I could see to the bottom. The rangy
trees swaying on the slopes like young boys at a school dance,
standing in the bleachers, waiting to be asked. A robin navigating
the dry riverbed, rock by rock. Grasses the color of my daughter's
hair. A poet who lifted his hand and waved when he saw me. When

I looked back he was leaning against a pine staring at the mountain. When I looked again, he was gone. Wind on exactly one half of the pond. The universe bending its kindest light over the valley. Gnats.

The Line

The line runs the length of the department store aisle—a mother grips a toddler's hand, hugs a baby to her hip, jiggles a newborn's stroller with her foot. Their nappy hair is woven, bright beads and bumpy cornrows. They're in various stages of crankiness. She's trying to find a practical way to fill out the form. She fastens the child's fist to the stroller, instructs her to hold on, shifts the baby to the other hip, balances the clipboard on the crossbar and writes as it teeter-totters above the newborn's head. Behind me a woman speaks to her children in Chinese. When she asks where the forms are I point to the front of the line, offer to watch her kids while she's gone. She fixes their fingers to my shirttails, hands delicate as wrens, skin tinted yellow beneath the brown. I finish filling out my form. I know my daughter's eyes are blue but I reach out, lift her chin, and look again. There is no word for this particular color. We've been here for over an hour, waiting to have our children fingerprinted, birthmarks and scars typed neatly on pocket-size laminated cards, their pictures in the left-hand corner so if they're stolen we'll have this card to show. So we won't be caught with our faces frozen, mouths open, unable to remember when we saw them last, what they were wearing, the exact color of their shoes. We're making our children stand in this line trying not to think about coffins the size of dresser drawers, the dragging of rivers. We're promising them the park later, rides on the plastic ponies out front. We're the mothers of the twentieth century and we stand in line at Payless, waiting to reach the front desk where men from the American Legion will take thousands of thumbs and fingers and press them into a pad of ink, recording the delicate whorls on treated paper. We're gratefully taking each folded towelette to clean the purple stains from their hands as they sit on the stools and smile, as only our children can. As if nothing were wrong in the new world. As if the future were theirs.

THE FIRST PROSE POEM I ever read was Forché's *The Colonel.* I was struck by the sentence, how it moved so gracefully through such difficult material, like a snake in the grass. And how it seemed journalistic, factual, undeniable. There's that same quality to Gary Young's sentence poems I have loved and admired for years. "F-16 Fighter Jet" was written quickly after seeing the image and hearing the story on the news. I just wanted to get it down so I drafted the piece to work into a "poem" later. Really more of a note to myself. When I looked through my files and found it, it seemed the form was trying to imitate that quick take I had when I saw the news clip.

PHILIP LEVINE

Old World

On the train from Copenhagen to Helsingor a tiny, deformed woman jerked on my sleeve until I stopped reading & looked up. "You will see there ahead the Royal Deer Park," & she pointed over my shoulder to the manicured acres of startling green that streamed by. Her cheeks, though powdered & rouged, looked dry as parchment; even her little darting tongue seemed too red, made up. "In your land you have not this?" she asked. Speaking slowly—still caught up in my novel—I explained that in my country we had no kings or queens and therefore no royal parks. "Exactly," she said, & her white-gloved hand abruptly closed my book. "Here in my kingdom you must not read, you must look."

Fixing the Foot: On Rhythm

For Lejan Kwint

Yesterday I heard a Dutch doctor talking to a small girl who had cut her foot, not seriously, & was very frightened by the sight of her own blood. "Nay! Nay!" he said over & over. I could hear him quite distinctly through the wall that separated us, & his voice was strong & calm, he spoke very slowly & seemed never to stop speaking; almost as though he were chanting, never too loud or too soft. Her voice, which had been explosive & shrill at first, gradually softened until I could no longer make it out as he went on talking &, I suppose, working. Then a silence, and he said, "Ah" & some words I could not understand. I imagined him stepping spryly back to survey his work. And then another voice, silent before, the girl's father, thanking him, & then the girl thanking him, now in a child's voice. A door opening & closing. And it was over.

News of the World

Once we were out of Barcelona the road climbed past small farm houses hunched down on the gray, chalky hillsides. The last person we saw was a girl in her late teens in a black dress & gray apron carrying a chicken upside down by the claws. She looked up & smiled. An hour later the land opened into enormous green meadows. At the frontier a cop asked in guttural Spanish almost as bad as mine why were we going to Andorra. "Tourism," I said. Laughing he waved us through. The rock walls of the valley were so abrupt the town was only a single street wide. Blue plumes of smoke ascended straight into the darkening sky. The next morning we found what we'd come for: the perfect radio, French made, portable, lightweight, slightly garish with its colored dial & chromed knobs, inexpensive. "Because of the mountains reception is poor," the shop owner said, so he tuned in the local communist station beamed to Spain. "Communist?" I said. Oh yes, they'd come twenty-five years ago to escape the Germans, & they'd stayed. "Back then," he said, "we were all reds." "And now?" I said. Now he could sell me anything I wanted. "Anything?" He nodded. A tall, graying man, his face carved down to its essentials. "A Cadillac?" I said. Yes, of course, he could get on the phone & have it out front—he checked his pocket watch—by four in the afternoon. "An American film star?" One hand on his unshaven cheek he gazed upwards at the dark beamed ceiling. "That could take a week."

Not Worth the Wait

"For twenty years I drove only Buicks," he said, gesturing contemptuously at his battered Mercedes diesel parked in front of the shabby little café in the Baxia. Buicks had given him a sense of confidence, of security, with their powerful grilles modeled after the jaws of a shark. We were seated at a small metal table from which I could catch sight of the port & smell the salt air. Once again he assured me we would find my father's hotel, the very room he'd called home in 1919. "Everything in Lisbon is remembered, everything is entered by hand in enormous ledgers that are preserved forever." My heart sank: I imagined myself like some sad & aged clerk out of Dickens spending day after day scanning the pages of funereal books in order to catch the name. "These people," & here he waved his hand in a circular motion that took in the dim waiter, the gray-suited man whose head was buried in a newspaper, the two passersby weighted down with enormous leather purses, "they remember the earthquake. Nothing is forgotten." "Why's that?" I said. It was simple. Nothing had happened for centuries. The navigators had all drowned. The whole country had drifted farther & farther out to sea to find its true weather, the perfect miasma in which we now sat. "Once upon a time we were Europeans," he said. His cell phone rang & rang. "You're not going to answer?" I said. No, he knew it was the colonel's wife wanting to be driven to the prison to visit her husband, who was perfectly happy working out chess problems & writing his memoirs. "If he lives long enough there will be a pardon, & the poor man will have to go free."

The Three

Rudi suffers a mysterious stroke that robs him of the power of speech & the use of his right hand. Still he plays the piano with his good left hand for which friendly composers write sonatas. With the help of a cane he walks the streets in all sorts of weather; if you come very close you will hear something like humming. Out of respect the townspeople—who've known him all his life—pretend he's not there. When we meet I speak very slowly saying as little as possible & stare into his eyes which answer with precision & wit the questions I lack the nerve to ask.

Jerzy's wife of forty-seven years sinks slowly into pain & drug-induced comas; meanwhile he translates the Book of Job into his native language, claiming it's his autobiography. His sons come to visit him; they bring bottles of wine & little poppy-seed cakes he later feeds to the birds in the yard behind his hilltop, California house. Alone, after half a century of exile, he goes back to the city of his youth. Deaf now, he listens only to seashells & clouds & speaks to the crows that accompany his awkward morning walks.

Louis writes from his rural farm house far from the city where he earned his fame. He writes by hand & from memory, for he can no longer see. The letters arrive in thick envelopes of a dozen or more onion-skin pages down which the words tumble & vanish. He has only a single subject: the glory of the physical world he's left behind. The doctors tell him that before long he will lose what hearing he has left. "I'm growing impatient," he writes, but does not say what he's waiting for.

257

Was it only thirty years ago that huge photographs of the three hung above the entrance to a great public theater in Rotterdam? I was among the crowd that later drifted out into the still warm air of late July leaving their presences hanging like smoke indoors. I cannot now remember a single word of all those I carried with me for years believing they had changed my life. The photographs I remember, three finely detailed portraits held firmly in place by something invisible, each one revealing the strong yet delicate landscapes of those faces that are nowhere now.

SINCE 1957 I'VE BEEN a Californian, but like many Californians I've chosen to get out of California a good deal in order to preserve my sanity or to perfect my madness. So I travel, but when I'm on a trip I make no effort to write poetry. I think this is due to the fact that on my early trips overseas I traveled with my wife & sons. For the sake of peace, I chose not to get hung up on a poem some morning while my kids were hungering to get on the road to Samarkand or Gouda. I learned it was a lot easier to wait until we were some place for a week or a month or—better still—a year. Nonetheless I still needed to write, so I got in the habit of buying a small journal or notebook in the first town I was in. I would fill it with details that seemed memorable or curious or often simply forgettable. When I was lucky I would write tiny prose narratives or landscapes or character studies. The first such worthwhile piece I wrote & published, "Fixing the Foot," was composed in half an hour in Vondelpark in Amsterdam in the late summer of 1969. The park itself—named after the Dutch poet Joost van den Vondel—is the largest & busiest in Holland. That Sunday it was full of people whose incomprehensible speech was a background music to my solitary brooding which crested that afternoon after some days of muffled growth. (Years later in a poetry text I saw this very prose piece employed as an example of a variety of syllabic verse. I thought of it then & still think of it as prose.)

I do not write these little pieces merely to keep busy; I don't believe in "busy work," I think it can drain energy from the real thing. I write these pieces because I love to write, & they seem present, percolating in my brain or itching in my fingers, urging me to pick up my pen—that is not a metaphor; I write by hand & hope to write with a pen or pencil magnificent words on paper but settle for whatever I get. If the words are ordinary it's possible they may tell a memorable story. At such times I'll accept whatever unexpected thing pops onto the page. Of course I throw a lot of them away. I do believe that such a thing as prose poetry exists; I've read superb prose poems by—for example—Baudelaire, Tranströmer, Zbigniew Herbert, Michaux, Simic. Of course there have been passages of amazing poetry in writing that has never claimed to be poetry. Poetry is there in Ecclesiastes, The Book of Job, The Letters of Paul, the sermons of John Donne, the meditations of Pascal, Antonio Machado, Juan Ramón Jiménez, & the fiction of Dickens, Joyce, Hemingway, Katherine Ann Porter, Elsa Morante, Gabriel García Márquez, to name only a few. What my efforts are I'm not sure; I enjoyed making them & since I still travel a good deal I expect to go on making them. I no longer travel with my sons, but the writing habit persists. If each of these is a prose poem all the better; if not—as my wonderful editor Harry Ford once said when I insisted on publishing a few poems he disliked—"They're so short they can't do much harm."

LARRY LEVIS

A Brief History of California

1. The drunken Apaches began circling Martha at dawn.

2. For little apparent reason, the huge Buick shot past the heavily breathing factories.

3. After they drove the Russians out of California, Carl and the Miwoks turned their attention, and symbolically at least, that of the Bear Flag Republic, to the pressing general question of "Greaser's Rights."

4. "This Rose Parade, in fact the entire Tournament of Roses, is getting real strange, Howard."

5. Dad's answer to the problem of too many "things" lying around was to dig a large hole and live underground, listening to the AM radio. He soon became expert at turning the dial quickly so that several announcers shared one complete, if disjunctive, sentence.

6. The silent hitchhikers we do not darkly stop for are all good guys. Forgive us. We mean no harm. We just hate to slow down our ancient car, a Buick.

from Linnets

1.

ONE morning with a 12 gauge my brother shot what he said was a linnet. He did this at close range where it sang on a flowering almond branch. Any one could have done the same and shrugged it off, but my brother joked about it for days, describing how nothing remained of it, how he watched for feathers and counted only two gold ones which he slipped behind his ear. He grew uneasy and careless; nothing remained. He wore loud ties and two-tone shoes. He sold shoes, he sold soap. Nothing remained. He drove on the roads with a little hold in the air behind him.

2.

BUT in the high court of linnets he does not get off so easily. He is judged and sentenced to pull me on a rough cart through town. He is further punished since each feather of die dead bird falls around me, not him, and each falls as a separate linnet, and each feather lost from one of these becomes a linnet. While he is condemned to feel nothing ever settle on his shoulders, which are hunched over and still, linnets gather around me. In their singing, they cleanse my ears of all language but that of linnets. My gaze takes on the terrible gaze of song birds. And I find that I too am condemned, and must stitch together, out of glue, loose feathers, droppings, weeds and garbage I find along the street, the original linnet, or, if I fail, be condemned to be pulled in a cart by my brother forever. We are tired of each other, tired of being brothers like this. The backside of his head, close cropped, is what I notice when I look up from work. To fashion the eyes, the gaze, die tongue and trance of a linnet is impossible. The eyelids are impossibly delicate and thin. I am dragged through the striped zoo of the town. One day I throw down the first stillborn linnet, then another, then more. Then one of them begins singing.

3.

AS my brother walks through an intersection the noise from hundreds of thin wings, linnet wings, becomes his silence. He shouts in his loud clothes all day. God grows balder.

Schoolhouse

It had one bell that you had to ring with a real rope, and if you were small, a first grader, you had to jump onto the rope and hang your whole body on it and feel the rope descend slowly until the bell rang once, and then jump off. Often the bell would get stuck, turned over, and one of the raw older boys who was already a car thief would have to go up into the tower and turn the bell over with his own great hands. Usually the boy would refuse to come down from the tower, and since he was older and fiercer than the others, and since his teachers were all women whose eyes trotted back and forth, he could stay up there all day. There was a rumor among us that at night these women turned the schoolhouse into a brothel, where workingmen came and drank. Each day I would look up at my teacher and imagine her secret life, her dress with the orchid print and the brittle 78 records she would play, afternoons, drinking brandy maybe, to get into the mood.

The Plains

I put down my detective novel and look out, over the plains. So much light. If anything was out there, I would see it. But there are only a few nervous farmers and their wives. It occurs to me that one of these families could be my own, lost in bitterness, like a sideshow at a county fair. This way they live and tell nobody. This way the few elms that are left get back their leaves. This way, whenever I look up, somebody else is missing.

In a Country

My love and I are inventing a country, which we can already see taking shape, as if wheels were passing through yellow mud. But there is a problem: if we put a river in the country, it will thaw and begin flooding. If we put the river on the border, there will be trouble. If we forget about the river, there will be no way out. There is already a sky over that country, waiting for clouds or smoke. Birds have flown into it, too. Each evening more trees fill with their eyes, and what they see we can never erase.

One day it was snowing heavily, and again we were lying in bed, watching our country: we could make out the wide river for the first time, blue and moving. We seemed to be getting closer; we saw our wheel tracks leading into it and curving out of sight behind us. It looked like the land we had left, some smoke in the distance, but I wasn't sure. There were birds calling. The creaking of our wheels. And as we entered that country, it felt as if someone was toughing our bare shoulders, lightly, for the last time.

The Selected Levis (University of Pittsburgh Press, 2000) shows us that, among many things, Larry Levis was a poet who commanded a wide range of forms—varying line lengths and stanzas to his particular subjects and the voice he was using to investigate his life at the time of the writing. Few poets show as much range, experimentation, mastery, and originality as Larry. As early as the early 1970s, Larry found subjects and occasions that fit the prose poem form. "A Brief History of California" is the earliest prose poem we know by Larry; it is from his PhD thesis at the University of Iowa, *Signs,* which was never published in book form. The first three sections from his well-known poem "Linnets" was published in *Field* and in *The Afterlife,* (1977) his second book; that book also contains "In A Country."

In 1980, Larry published a little-known chapbook with his wife, Marcia Southwick, *The Leopard's Mouth Is Dry and Cold Inside* (K. M. Gentile Publishing/Singing Wind Press, St. Louis). This modest offset production contained seven prose poems by each poet. "Schoolhouse" (no doubt drawn from Larry's early life in Selma, California, a small agricultural community outside of Fresno) and "The Plains" are taken from this chapbook.

In his well-known essay "Some Notes On The Gazer Within," Larry commented specifically about the second section of "Linnets" and on prose poetry in general: ". . . I fashioned the story into prose, where it belonged as a narrative, and cast it as a parable of sorts, or fable. But a fable with no values. Any ready-made significance would have made my poem pretentious, and silly. I quote below the second section of the poem, the fable of some kind of wild justice done to my brother."

—Christopher Buckley

GERALD LOCKLIN

The Dolphin Market

The Dolphin Market is one of the last of the privately owned neighborhood markets.

It is only half a block from where I live on Ocean Avenue in Seal Beach, California.

Its prices are considerably higher than at the supermarket; you are paying for the convenience. And the personal touch.

Also, you are at least able to feel that you are handing over your money to human beings, not a symbol of the stock exchange. Human beings will save your Sunday *Times* for you.

The very human beings in question are named Kenny, Charlotte, and Brett.

Kenny, the owner, once played minor league ball in the Cincy organization. He still roots for the Reds against the Dodgers, the Cowboys against the Rams. He races hot rods and is a steadying influence on the young kids who hang out at the store. He has a good sense of humor, which he exercises largely at the expense of my wife's aversion to cooking and my own attraction to a nearly liquid diet. I usually have a few words for his distinguished selection of wines—you have a choice of Gallo or Cribari. Kenny and I probably share as few political as athletic heroes, but as long as he doesn't start voting for Hitler or I for Stalin, it's not apt to be an issue.

Charlotte works days, so Charlotte sells me a lot of Excedrin. We discuss movies and *Masterpiece Theatre* and anything else that's in the papers or on our minds. She always has a cookie for my daughter. Sometimes the mail-lady joins our parleys. Since Charlotte has been married for a long time to a Navy man, it's possible we don't agree on every point of national interest either, but for some reason I can't remember us ever *dis*agreeing.

Brett is a sophomore in high school. He gives my daughter handfuls of cookies. He looks like a lover not a fighter, but when tough guys give him shit, he always gives it back. He's not a punk. The girls his age have started hanging around his shift. He likes to kid me, and with my long hair and beard and heft and absentmindedness,

I bet I do strike him as awfully strange. He works out with the crates as if they were barbells. It's just the sort of thing I would have done myself at his age.

The Dolphin is a square drab building at the corner of Dolphin and Ocean, with a collection of beer cans on a shelf above the counter.

I prefer it to Harrods, Les Galleries Lafayette, and Fortnum-Mason.

Of course those other joints don't cash my checks.

I Am Not Gerald Locklin

I have always hated the name "Gerald." I used Gerald when I was first writing because I thought a writer was supposed to use a formal name. I even, as only Marvin Malone and a handful of others remember, sometimes stooped to "Gerald Ivan Locklin" to lend a spurious poeticism to my fledgling literary productions. Today I still use "Gerald I. Locklin" on official documents because there are obviously so many "Gerald Locklins" running all over the place.

I was named after an Uncle Gerald who died young, before I was born, of tuberculosis. He was supposedly a very nice man, but, even aside from the consumption, I never wanted to be him. As a child I didn't even want to be "Gerry": I was given that name in school. At home I was "Jodie," a name I personally garbled for myself in the crib. Presumably I did not also give myself the female spelling of the name, but that never bothered me.

Today only two people still call me "Jodie": my only surviving aunt and Ron Koertge. Sometimes Ron calls me "Bear," which was given me by my first and only good karate teacher twenty-five years ago, just before he got busted in a hot car. "Bear" is flattering, so of course I don't mind it. Sometimes my wife also calls me "Jodie," but there is mockery in her voice. I call myself "Toad" sometimes, especially in poems, although that Toad is not always myself. John Owen also calls me that, loudly, whenever I run into him in public. George Carroll does too. And Paul the bartender. They call me that affectionately, I think.

I guess my favorite nowadays is simply "Ger." When people call me that they seem to be really getting a kick out of it. I have always enjoyed being a source of amusement for people. Frankly, I often find myself rather amusing. And "Ger" sounds youthful, boyish, as I frequently wish I were. Yes, just call me "Ger," and I promise to spare you all tales of white whales.

To Get What You Pay For Is the Least You Can Expect

I overheard how Bukowski had these incredibly reasonable mortgage payments on his very nice house in San Pedro and yet he had this constant worry that he wouldn't always be able to make them.

I can understand that. He didn't, after all, have a steady job, and who would not be a fool to count on the continuance of literary income, especially anyone who'd known the years when royalties were zilch.

So he knew well the way employers and the government can get you by the balls, and now he had a chance to learn, before dying, the way lenders can get their claws into you.

So why did he do it? No doubt partly for his wife, a woman whom he loved and who was giving him a better life than he had ever known.

But he also enjoyed the place, the garden and the view, a good place to raise cats, a bit of spaciousness, a little privacy, room to garden, room for a narrow lap-pool, some shelves to keep his books on, improved audio for Bruckner and Ludwig B., some neighbors and some distance from them, a little girl across the street who brought out the grandfather in him.

And who really wants to end up living in the gutter, dying in humiliation?

So, a little mortgage-worry wasn't all that bad a trade-off.

And anyone who thinks that you don't pay for what you get in life is either an old fool or a very young one.

How To Get Along With Charles Bukowski

1. Never call him on the phone. (I never have.)

2. Never drop in uninvited. (I never have, and I don't like ANYONE to drop in uninvited on me. I'm not crazy about phone calls either.)

3. If you must visit with him make it early in the day. (Bukowski, like the rest of us, is a little closer to docile when still hungover than when working on his next hangover.)

4. When Bukowski says, "So, here we are—back to the old literary chit-chat," it is an excellent time to leave.

5. Don't dance with his women. (Don't dance with mine either.)

6. But do not kiss his ass or accept abuse from him without appropriate response or he will have no use for you.

7. Keep your mouth shut when you don't have anything to say. (Come to think of it, these are not bad rules for life in general.)

8. It helps to believe he is a great writer. (I do.)

9. Don't hesitate to correspond with him. He is one of the great letter writers since Keats, and prompt to boot.

10. Bring your kids along. (When I brought my teenage daughters to his sixtieth birthday party he was the perfect gentleman the entire evening.)

11. If you allow yourself to be put in the position of taking responsibility for him, you are asking for trouble. (I did, twice.)

12. Do not betray his trust.

13. And most importantly, NEVER NEVER NEVER NEVER NEVER push your luck by writing HOW TO GET ALONG WITH CHARLES BUKOWSKI.

Do You Remember The Scene In The Godfather Where James Caan Says, "Now Make Sure That The Gun Gets Stashed In The Rest Room— I Don't Want My Kid Brother Walking Out Of There With Nothing But His Dick In His Hand"?

Because I knew I would be walking her through some of the meaner night streets of Downtown L.A., I reached in my glove compartment and slipped a fold-back knife in my pocket. And we did run the gamut of some fairly unsavory concentrations of inhumanity, but as each potentially tense encounter approached, I patted my pocket and felt a little less naked.

Safely back in the car, I extracted the weapon from my pocket and found us both gazing at a b-flat harmonica accidentally filched, years ago, from one of Fred Voss's dodecaphonic parties.

MY EARLY POEMS, and some of the later, have so often been accused of being "mere prose" that I sometimes have trouble not thinking of my poems and prose poems and some of my shorter stories and certain chapters of my novellas as virtually interchangeable in genre, even though I know their true similarity is that all my writing is governed foremost by the ear. I studied metrics intensely early-on, and while I seldom write sonnets or villanelles anymore, I would sooner commit a mortal sin than a cacophonic phrase. (I suppose I'm guilty of both nonetheless.) My definition of poetry has always been, like Coleridge's, measured, rhythmic language, although, for me, there are as many rhythms available to lines of words as to lines of musical notation. Thus, the format in which I write is simply that in which I seem most comfortable at the moment I'm writing that particular work—I certainly do not belabor my formal choices with theories of craft. Maybe I'm more a child of the Sixties than I realize because I do abide by a sort of aesthetic "If it feels right, do it." Or maybe that is just the result of having written so much. I've been known to retype a poem as a story, and vice versa, to fit an editorial need. My primary goal is to get things written, and a close second is to get them read ... by a few eyes at least. The quality of what I write matters greatly to me, but the categories into which others place my work matter little.

The chief advantage of lined poems is that they are easier on my eyes, especially as compared to single-spaced block paragraphs. The disadvantage of lined poems is that they look like poems are supposed to, which sometimes offends my contrarian nature. On those days I write prose poems.

PERIE LONGO
Cable TV Interview LA Style

The hypnotherapist, wearing a purple silk shirt, black leather jacket, and amethyst ring the size of a full moon, lavishly gestures how quickly he healed from his knee replacement only three weeks ago. His co-host, a sex therapist, with a shiny, bolero puff-sleeved jacket and dress tight as the skin of a kiwi, tosses her long red hair over her shoulder and asks if I have a brush, she was up all night, jazzed after doing a healing—what's my thing? The other guest, who calls herself a lymphomaniac, *haha*, rather than a lymphologist, says she teaches people how to get their lymph system moving after surgery, is her brown velvet shirt good enough for TV, and excuse her but I need more makeup or would wash out next to them. In seconds, she's smearing rouge all over my cheeks. On the monitor, I look like I've run into a wall. "Nice slacks," the hypnotherapist says, "really smooth," and all three start running hands up and down my leg chanting "Cool!" "Quiet," the floor director orders. I'm sent to the corner until it's time to talk about my brand of alternative healing, harnessing words to speak the unspoken, certainly not new, though I'm speechless, trying to find my tongue. But when I'm called, the poem I read helps, a bridge from darkness to a kind of lightness. Soon they're all arguing about what it means right on TV while I sit there in my plain Jane clothes, face on fire. "It's a take," the director yells and they burst with congratulations for each other, hugging and hugging and kissing about how well they did, I must join them for lunch, to help, you know, come down from their "high." The place is right across the street "where the show people go" and I'm elbowed out the door into the middle of the street where the hypnotherapist flashes smiles and waves his purple arms, limping on his cane, cars braking and screeching while they turn on cell phones, calling significant others about their success. Once curbside, I can't help but ask, "Who watches this show anyway?" A staccato snap of phones. The three of them stare at me. What a question, and no camera. The sex therapist, who can't stand lack of action, jumps in how happy she is, life just one big orgasm, so who cares?

270

The Raft

It could be a silent movie, grainy and gray, the raft floating on the lake just beyond the rim of cattails lining the bank, water lilies like scoops of vanilla ice cream on green plates glistening under drizzle, just past Labor Day. The father, white-haired and pale-bellied, has ordered his two adults sons to help him beach the raft, frost not far off. Not for awhile, but soon. Now is the time. Already he's wearing his plaid swimming trunks, gathering ropes, his face set, movements solid and brisk. The task ahead full of complications. They follow behind like snails, heads hid inside sweatshirt hoods, each with a separate mission, one working for the government in a dangerous country, home on leave. The other from across town seems to shoulder some invisible weight, come to mend fences and see his visiting uncles and aunts. I'm one of them inside the house behind the glass window two stories high that ends in a point. We're drinking coffee with their mother, my sister. She's promised her sons homemade chocolate chip cookies, even at their age. If they cooperate with their father. The house is new, their dream home sitting on top of the old cabin's ghost, demolished, where they once summered away from city sprawl. All three climb into the rowboat, make their way toward the raft that kept them safe, removed. There are words. The boys yank off their sweatshirts and jump in the water. Disappear. Come up again. More words. The older son gestures with vehemence. The younger nods. Even from a distance we see things are not going well, the boys under water again. The picture blurred, my sister says the anchors must be stuck in the sludge. Her husband seems to be shouting, but we can't hear as he ties ropes to the raft. We open the window, step into the scene and start cheering. The boys rise, thrashing, toss one anchor on top, then the other, help each other into the boat and row back to shore while their father holds the ropes. Like a belligerent dog, the raft follows, carrying summer, all of them, toward shore, where we gather, link arms for a picture in a frame of trees, hold on as if we're floating. And we are.

Grandma's Miracle

Grandma set me on my path with no deliberate intention, just sat there in her arm chair with the front door open to the church across the street to let the holiness in just in case a thought of murder might cross the track of her brain, a swath of white wiry hair strayed out like old train smoke from the knot on top of her head. She used to tell me how she rode a train in 1888 from Colorado to Florida all by herself back to help her foster mother steal back money from her ex hid under somebody's mattress in Orlando. It was never clear if she succeeded or not, but I was bound to her, the intrigue, her patience on the plains waiting rail repairs and her fierce love to do right by the Irish Catholic woman who raised her, her own dear mother dead minutes after her birth.

I didn't see Grandma that much, but she was my kind of woman, one who followed her nose, saved those she could, and confessed one day she was 68 years old, her rosary dangling from her fingers. When I said that was something, her son being 71, as that twirl of hair sprung loose, she quipped, "Well that goes to show, miracles will never cease."

SOMETIMES WHEN I type a poem, and the lining seems forced, or arbitrary, I mush the text together to start all over for a different look, or highlight the rhythm in a truer way, the flow seems right for what I'm saying, in a narrative, for instance. When I first presented "Grandma's Miracle" to my writing group, they suggested I try it as a prose poem. At first, I balked, but when I thought of how the words tumbled out when I originally wrote, the form seemed more honest. Not confined by lining or compression, there's a flexibility of language that often happens, I've discovered. In the poem "The Raft," I'd typed it three or four different ways, all lined, taking out details I couldn't work in. I finally gave up, pressed the "justified" tab and voila! problem solved. Suddenly the poem looked like the subject, a big raft, and I discovered not only what I wanted to say, but found the ending. Some poems just don't want to be hemmed in. They want free range to pick at whatever will feed them. "Cable TV Interview LA Style" was that way and I just rolled with the story, loving the telling far more than the original moment. Maybe that's what it's all about.

GLENNA LUSCHEI

Carpinteria

The first time I walked with Bill he put peppermint from the café into my palm and closed my hand around it. In San Francisco he chased my straw hat under the trolley. I knew he would take care of me. We loved Paris but we were California country. Like Colette I served our friends from unmatched casseroles.

We skipped back a generation to become our grandparents, walking to the post office by day, picking avocados for supper.

Bowl

My mother drove to California from Oklahoma. When she couldn't find work she sold the wheels from her jalopy to feed us.

We built fires at night from orange wood, we got up early every morning to snatch oranges before the pickers came. In the trailer park my first dresser was an orange crate. My first dress was muslin sewn on the treadle machine the owner's wife gave to us. One day she gave us chocolate.

Washing in the river I found a porcelain bowl and placed it on the sewing machine and thought of the Chinese girl who came here when her man worked on the railroads. I went to work in the lemon-packing house.

During the war: sirens and wardens, Japanese subs off the sand dunes. Mother worked as a welder. Sparks flew into her throat, changed her voice forever.

Feathers Everywhere

I loved my stained and smelly bathrobe as much as my scrap of blanket that grandmother, showing mercy, would rescue from the trash time after time. That summer the girl at Paso Robles Park took me to meet her parents in their jalopy, a cardboard suitcase roped on top. The mother nursed a baby.

Young as I was I understood their poverty. My friend introduced them as royalty. I understood family then. Next summer in Fresno I learned how chickens mate, and later about human sex, even more weird. Feathers everywhere.

Roads to California

My dream sets anchor in your arms. I water ski behind the moon skim the Missouri where I waded as a child. Though floods whirled up to our back screen, we children slept buried in sand. The goose-necked lamp ran with the ostrich. Grain bins blew apart. The highway swelled with rotting wheat.

From Ventura you wave, cross the berm from creek to lemon trees. I wake in the crescent of your flank. I first knew the ocean at thirteen.

SINCE I HAVE BEEN working on my memoir I find that I work naturally with prose poems. They are a good medium for dreams and past memories. I started out writing prose poems forty years ago and am now returning with pleasure and satisfaction to this form. I feel my subjects are able to develop without constraint in prose poems.

MORTON MARCUS

Incident from the Day of the Dead

Miguel told me he had been home alone for two hours, studying. It was in Guanajuato when he was twelve years old, on the Day of the Dead, and his mother and sisters had gone to tidy his father and grandparents' graves.

He didn't remember why he looked from his book on the dining room table to the sideboard in the corner, where his baby sister had surrounded the makeshift altar with the candies his grandmother liked so much and the small dark cigars his father and grandfather were so fond of. It was probably a sound of some sort, he said, a chair creaking maybe. But when he looked, there was his father, turned the other way, holding a cigar under his nose, sideways, like a flute, sniffing the length of it as he did when he was alive.

The old man was so intent on the cigar, his face serious, that he didn't notice Miguel at first. He was sitting on a dining room chair, in the black suit he had been buried in, and was leaning toward the altar, as if he had just picked up the cigar. Then he tensed and a moment later turned toward Miguel, and they sat that way, looking at each other across the table in the late afternoon light. And that's how Miguel knew, he said, that only a table separates the living from the dead.

"What did you do then?" I asked.

Miguel shook his head.

We had been talking for hours about one thing and another, sipping beer at my kitchen table, while the household slept and the night wind buffeted the tiny house on the northern California coast. Our talk had wandered onto the brushes we had had with the dead, and he had told this story about his father, and now it was clear he had said all he intended to say.

"That's it?" I asked. "Nothing more?"

"No. Nothing."

We sat in silence for several moments. *Just as he and his father had,* I thought, and I said aloud to continue the conversation, "How long did you sit that way?"

275

He shrugged. "My mother and sisters returned soon after."

"And he was gone then?"

He clenched his jaws and looked past me toward the window.

I knew that if I continued my questioning I would be invading a reserve in him that I had learned to respect, and I must admit that I was too timid or unwilling to hurl myself at the barricade of facial expressions he had thrown up between us, and there the matter ended.

But I also felt that I had somehow failed, failed in the same way Miguel and his father had failed with each other.

At the same time, I felt that the incident was not finished. Miguel had told me the story, and somehow the story and the telling and what had just occurred at my kitchen table were now joined in a single event. It made no difference if Miguel and I never spoke of the incident again, or if my insistence had destroyed our friendship, which, I'm relieved to say, it did not.

It was as though the story told me in a California kitchen by a middle-aged man about an incident from his childhood in Mexico now included me, was somehow mine as much as it was his and continued from that point, having less and less to do with our friendship, or even us. His reticence and my timidity, both our failures, and his failure with his father and his father's failure with him, were what the story was about.

And now, dear reader, just as I became part of the story Miguel told me, so you have become part of the story, too. It is as if we sat across from each other at a kitchen table, although I am no longer here and possibly wrote these words years ago. I may even no longer be alive. You, however, read these words as if I am sitting here with you, and that has allowed me to include you in the tale, a tale whose telling beyond this point I am either unwilling or unable to provide.

I Find the Letter

I find the letter in a drawer, still sealed, postmarked five years ago. A letter that when opened shrieks for help, but silently—like a hand above the waves, clutching air.

I've seen him a number of times since he wrote it, but never once in word or gesture has he referred to it.

I call him three minutes later. Remarried, no longer a drunk, he says, "Your refusal to answer made me see how foolish I was, and caused me to change my life."

In Autumn

In autumn on late afternoons, I stand at the window, watching the yellow cities collapse in the sun.

Prayers go unanswered in the corn's cathedral, and in the hallways of flowers bees are browsing with heavy heads.

Somewhere at the end of the house, a door closes, a room is dark.

The Letter

I found the letter in a book I bought at an outdoor theatre turned flea market every weekend. It was June 1995 in a small town on the California coast.

The book was Tolstoy, *Anna Karenina,* and the letter was tucked between pages 434 and 435, where a delirious Levin, the day after he's proposed to Kitty, visits her parents' home. The letter—pinkish, sealed, not mailed, faintly redolent of talcum, like a pressed flower—was from a Sarah Harris, dated inside October, 1939.

Yes, I opened it and read how fine the trip was from Des Moines back to Cincinnati, suspecting nuances and unworded passages I had no way of understanding—or, more accurately, deciphering—to go along with what I took to be the mute appeal to Carl Bigelow, 913 McKinley Avenue, Des Moines, Iowa, in the final paragraph: "There didn't seem time for me to say all the things I needed to. Do you feel the same?"

The Tolstoy was a book club's bonus edition bound in grey leatherette. Had Sarah Harris purposely placed the letter between those pages depicting Levin and Kitty's jubilant betrothal? I had no way of knowing, and refused to suppose. However, I resealed the letter, affixed fresh stamps to the envelope, and sent it on.

At Peace

Some nights the universe is a black stone millions of miles tall and eons wide, and balancing on its surface somewhere, a luminous drop of water is poised like a bird's egg on top of a black monument. But there are other nights when the black monolith's internal structure relaxes, and the drop of water sinks like a glowing pearl through its depths, illuminating veins and root ends, tiny skulls with empty eye sockets, fossils of ferns and fish fins, and I am at peace.

Into the New Millennium

Like a surfer expecting the years will build to a wave and the wave will crest into the next century, I feel the long pull of time catapult me toward shore on my coffin-lid board, forcing me to walk my individual plank with the weight of history, like a pirate ship, behind me.

Is it rapture, giddiness, or fear I feel as I swerve one way and another under the stars, keeping the difficult balance needed in such uncertain footing while I'm swept toward shore?

I'm a supple croucher, taking the wave as it comes and abandoning it before it splinters against the beach like a foundering ship full of useless cargo. By then, I'm paddling toward the next wave, still a hill, a ton of water that will never know it's a wave when it becomes one, nor that it's the wreckage of the wave that came before it.

Funny, but the shoreline is never the object; the ride is. Ask any surfer worth the salt he swishes through. The best of them don't look forward or back, and so cannot turn into pillars of even their own communities, whether or not they remain stationary on their rushing boards.

It's the rhythm, finally, that enthralls. The board points its finger, and I follow.

A Little Night Music

1

Through the miles of darkness outside the window, bird song, a lone staccato whistle, one bird calling and calling.

2

Sometimes, lying on my side, I listen to my breath coming and going on the pillow. I can hear the flowers breathe beyond the window, and the voices in the trees murmuring from the leaves. At such moments I am aware of the ocean, so far away, endlessly advancing and withdrawing.

3

Another storm tonight. It's been raining on and on for months. Everyone is sick of the gray days, the wet, wind-filled nights. Unable to sleep, I lie in bed, and think of the living and the dead, the eons of them beyond the window. The squall shakes the house, sloughing the rain in one direction and another. I sense the walls surrounding me, the rain beyond the window, the glossy streets, the marshy fields, the trees, and the river outside of town, where the homeless, huddled under bridges, watch the rain-spattered water rushing past.

4

Most nights, I sit alone after the household is asleep. I've done this for years, a sort of ritual to adjust the tempo of my days to the telluric rhythms of the earth. There is the house and silence, the timbers creaking around me, the city and the countryside stippled with sounds beyond the window. These are moments I cherish, when it is just me, the house, and the miles of moonlit chattering I cannot separate into individual pieces of noise, sounds that scatter from the grasses, the trees and the rivers beyond the cities, all of them rushing into a starry future where I am left behind and forgotten.

rife—in widespread existence or use, from the Old Icelandic *rifr,* abundant—"they're on fire," she thinks, of the slim trailside trees burning with green flames. A lush, new season! And she's practiced the theory all week, "abundance thinking." It's true; there's so much of so much: moss, stars, dumpster agleam with the worst of what an old man couldn't take with him.

⌒

shape—the outline or form of an external surface, from the Old English *gesceap,* creation—the blue shining (a starship from across the field), a plastic window. From up here, bedrolls of fog, grey swatch, green swatch, my own street, my own roof, how the town got created the way it did. Living down there, I know it's not perfect, neither the world nor we are; the match is.

⌒

creek—a watercourse smaller than a river, from the Old Norwegian *kriki,* bend—fallen, hand-sized, heart-shaped leaves cover the octopi and treasure chests imprinted on the plastic pool he bought for the dog. Everything's changing; everything's turning; soon the rains will come, and the dog won't want to cool off. Soon, everything will sail around the bend.

wooded or windswept

•

Whatever his natural inclinations, they are subsumed by this persona that doesn't get involved.

• •

What if the Stoics were right and that everything that occurs—if we could see it—is a necessary part of the whole?

• • •

In the sixteenth century, the Aztecs, who died by the thousands from smallpox, saw the Spaniards' immunity as further proof of their invincibility.

280

• • • •

For some, you can easily picture another life—if only they'd taken the wooded path or the windswept path. Overriding all their choices, a cloud—big, suspicious, burning.

being neither

•

She taught classical Indian dance to young girls. When she walked on stage, a man, who turned out to be her husband, said: "A beautiful woman in a beautiful dress," sliding his eyes from side to side, mimicking the dancers.

• •

A month after I'd refused to see my ex-boyfriend, who had decided to become a woman, a headless calf appeared in a dream, following me with its non-cow eyes.

• • •

Olivia determined that she must be more of a country girl than a city girl because she hates the smell of cow shit.

• • • •

His wife held him responsible for her fate. He forgave her so that it might change.

$\longrightarrow\!\!Q$

BOB DYLAN'S "If Dogs Run Free" comes to mind when I think about why I enjoy reading and writing prose poems:

> If dogs run free, why not me
> Across the swamp of time . . .
> Oh, winds which rush my tale to thee
> So it may flow and be
> To each his own, it's all unknown
> If dogs run free

For me the prose form allows a poem to run free and across time with a tale in its mouth that it tells with unexpected harmony and often with more breadth and subtlety than verse. Many prose poems attend to the particular with such devotion that the singular moment, like Blake's grain of sand, contains the world. "A house roof and the star growing pale above it held the glance of a man who felt himself caught again in the delicate play of causes." Unleashed from the patterns of verse, here Jean Follain's run swiftly to the profoundly universal.

Like many writers, I use the prose poem to tell a small story. The prose form, which might at first seem limited and narrow, often ends with a big, free idea. Marvelously, the prose poem has a discreet shapelessness. Sometimes it's circular—with a beginning, a middle, and an end that characteristically refers back to the beginning—but more often than not, it spreads outward like a fan, letting its details: a slanted roof, a pale star, a man's glance expand upon one another.

Many of my prose poems, begin with a specific place in a specific season—a dry creek in a California suburb or a grove of redwoods after winter rains—but no matter the terrain, the voice usually feels casually contemplative. This is not to say that the prose poem doesn't require close crafting, but that, despite its depth, the prose poem is at ease; it has doggy ways—sniffing here and there, weaving a tale. Or is it wagging its tail?

FRANCES RUHLEN MCCONNEL

Lament

The day is lonely as a mountain landslide where no one hears the crows' commotion.

In the curve of the empty riverbed the air ripples with heat. Who cares about my heart, clanging out of tune? Does the tumbleweed care, bounding down the bank of the arroyo? Does the tortoise care, snug in his medieval suit of armor, whooping and grunting and jousting shells with rivals, trying to tip them over to the broiling sun, then stomping out a courting dance so pugnacious he might get tipped himself by his lady. Or she by him. A drama so slow you'd think a chess game had stalled in awe at the upending of a queen. A drama that could take years.

Tell me about it—Little Alice, crying in a wilderness of restless stones.

Debris flows come with the first shower after the wildfire and the earth slips its shell like a dewy chick that has battered its way free of the old forms. If my heart says let me out, who will open the door? So long cooled, the fires; so held back, the rains.

On Highway 15 to Las Vegas

Along red cliffs, the prickly pears whir with wasps. Background whir in our heads above engine rumination, wheels fluttering with song. Pilgrimage highway with its caravans, its migration of hopefuls. And here come the marching Joshua Trees, arms up in surrender— bandidos, coyotes, border crossers. But we are the border crossers— two grown-up girl friends and the tumbleweed. Yucca rears its unlikely candles, ablaze in the shadow of a rockpile hill. A larva inside its seed has the singular evolutionary role of hatching a moth that will roll pollen into a ball and stuff it down the gullet of its flowers. But we're not *that* kind of girl-friends. Sun ricochets across our vision. Squinted vistas. Flutter, flutter—lashes against the East. Hypnotic lines cat-cradling with our minds. You da driver; come out of this spell! I fiddle with the radio. Static, though I'm hardly trying. Our breaths circle back on themselves. The AC throws up its invisible shield.

Ahead, in a silver mirage, trucks skitter toward us. Silver mirage of neon buzzing *Nevada! Two Hundred Slot Machines! First Stop! Turn your head—Last Chance!* On the steering wheel, you tap out a lonesome, nomad beat. I hand you the bota bag. Like a bee at a blossom, you tip up your face to our first earth-mother's milk, first and ultimate luck of the desert—water.

Sage, Tweezers, Hummingbird

At my age, near things blur in any manmade light, so, Saturday, I'm out with my tweezers between front door and garage, where there's still bright sun but no neighbors' eyes to reach me, plucking my upper lip, when a humming bird buzzes my head. He floats, wheels off, slicing the sky in two, zips back, hovers above my left shoulder, then my right. There's something urgent in his thrum.

What is it? I say. *What's the matter?* Again, he veers away, threading the liquidambar's leaves, returns. And then I see them as in a vision—the blooming sages my daughter gave me—one blue and one magenta—and the empty space beside the front walk where they sat in their plastic pots. Yesterday I took them out back to my garden—to draw bees I hoped, my tomatoes chest-tall and sprinkled with tart yellow flowers. But not yet even one tiny green bead, though I've shaken them, like the books say, gently tickled the blooms. Is this crone-witchery—playing West Wind to bring on a crop? Or tapping into the wavelength of birds?

I say I'm sorry. I tell the hummingbird where the flowers have gone. I'd show him the way—the narrow path along the fence—if only he'd follow. Or I'd signal it with my hand mirror. But maybe the backyard belongs to one of his many kin. He flies straight up so sure and fast I know he could leap the roof. But I'm beyond leading him that way, my bones gone brittle. Or so my husband says, who hates to see me on a ladder.

(But could John love me with a crone's moustache?)

I guess I won't find out. Or how this hovering millisecond bird could show me his worry. Or how to ask him my own questions: if growing old will make him settle down; how it feels to probe the dusty throat of a flower—does he mind the tickle to his tongue? And if he likes not only sweet, but sour.

I'M ONE OF THOSE people with a prized and yellowing copy of Michael Benedikt's *The Prose Poem* bound with scotch tape and rubber bands. I picked it up new at the end of theseventies and was dazzled but didn't dare my first prose poem until 1982. That poem was on the subject of learning to listen to jazz—my second husband was an aficionado—by listening to various versions of "Body and Soul." This is telling for several reasons: most of the prose poems that I write include riffs and all of them have a certain idiosyncratic magic that rarely exists in my lined poems, a magic I also found in jazz, particularly in jazz solos, when the music acknowledges and plays with a familiar, sometimes mundane, musical work, and magically transforms it to something startling and sublime. Sometimes a prose poem might begin as a lined poem. Take "Lament," which began as a ten-line poetry exercise I did with a class. The initial impulse came from the season—a time of landslides after wildfires—but other impulses came in. Students and poet friends alike asked what *Through the Looking Glass* was doing in the poem. Since I found myself unable or unwilling to answer, I decided to try the piece as a prose poem. One simply doesn't have to field such questions about a prose poem. Nor did I have to explain what was relevant about the sex life of the tortoise. Or, to be honest, what was originally the sex life of the armadillo. Though the armadillo got into the poem the same way Alice got into it—whatever way that was—once it began to gel as a prose poem, it had to leave. It didn't belong in the Southern California landscape. (Though it may soon, given that that critter is expanding its range almost as fast as the coyote.) You would think this would contradict my theory that prose poetry can support any incongruity and perhaps it does. But the advantage of writing prose poems is that you can switch theory mid-stream and feel all the more deft for doing so. The riff on the sex antics of the tortoise comes from some vein in some layer of self that gets tapped by my muse, not me. Or so I feel I am allowed to claim about prose poetry.

DEREK MCKOWN

A Theory of Flight

I was in the third grade and, having read the encyclopedia, knew everything there was about birds, that feathers are hollow, the delicate physics of perch and balance, even he ash-and-clay taste of worms, all except how to fly. The bones knitting my face throbbed with this rebuke from the God I was taught: little did I know.

I wish now I could have sat next to my father in his B-52 over Southeast Asia, to learn if not flight, then its debt—duty, the love that strengthened his hand. I could have wrapped my arms around his neck, bitten his ear, let him know that someday, someday Isaac would hand the knife back to Abraham, and whisper, I love you too, Father.

The Country Where He Grew Up

The creek was lazy and sweet again, the early summer rain having drained away, leaving the root-nests of water oak and redgum at bank's edge to shallow, sun-warmed eddies. I sat beneath the shrubby blue beech, raised the long stick of the .22 and waited for the cottonmouths to poke their triangular heads above the water's mottled surface. My father, nearby, nodded. It was his gun as a kid, and the snakes, cousins of those he'd killed. I might miss the shot of course, and fail this test. Maybe the rust-pocked barrel would explode in my hands. He sat and ate. We had pan bread, cheese, and a Vidalia sweet. He could wait.

One Note Music

Up onshore, the mother rings an old school bell for her men. She stands on top of the dunes, which are patched together with ice-plant, and the salt breeze reaches for her floral skirt, snapping it back like a flag. Oh! she hopes they do not hear her, so she can finish.

When she was a child, she chased a bell like this around white mimosas, into a straight line with the other children, heads bowed, behind Sister Cecilia. They marched, strung together like the rosary beads round Sister's waist, into the classroom and took their seats.

Years later, and wed to an Air Force pilot, she told her husband about a swaybacked girl in Golden Gate Park who handed her a flower and asked what she has done to save the babies who are burning under napalm bombs across the ocean. He stared hard at her, said he was only doing his job.

The deep clang of the buoy far offshore floats up to her. She begins to time her strokes, strong, echoes across the ocean. The sun is warm and fleshy, blinding. Her husband and sons almost shadows in the surf.

Sister held a globe of the world in her hands, and pointed to a pink patch in the middle of Africa. This is where the pagan babies live. They sleep in huts, eat only yams, monkeys, and parrots. They do not believe in God. She asked the children to pray for them.

Ringing the bell, the mother remembers closing her eyes, then being lifted up, flying past Sister as if cradled in an immense and invisible hand. A vague sense of panic flushing her face, she watches the boys take turns being thrown through the air, smacking against the waves.

Flying the Polar Route Toward Russia, the Crew of a B-52 Reviews Its After-Action Checklist: October, 1962

> The summer grasses—
> as if the warriors
> were only dreams.
> —Bashō

Watch the man—your father, or my father—untangle himself from singed parachute and quick-step into the forest line, away from the boiling sea.

Where the air grows cool and damp he squats under a fir tree and begins to dig a trench that becomes a box that becomes a room.

He crawls in, reaches up between the wrist-thick roots, and with his tired hands pulls the earth back, the tree breathing for the man— your father, my father.

They'd told him that after two days he could emerge for half an hour, stretch his legs.

After six days he could stay out for two hours, and if he were short of water rations, the streams would be safe again.

The did not tell him he would begin arguing with limping spiders and grave beetles, would cup his hands to catch the color bleeding from the ferns and tattered mosses, the world become all white light, night insensible.

Upon the thirteenth day they could not have known his new rank, or that he'd let slip the shroud of his flesh to reveal strange new bones and the stubborn ghost of his heart.

They did not have to tell him to climb the mountain above toward the parted curtain of air, toward the invisible cities, toward home.

The Whale

No doubt hours had passed since it beached itself. Vehicles aureate with eye-twirling lights sat sinking into the tumbled coast, while a dozen rubber-suited acolytes in wet-breath amazement tugged toward the carcass, a blue-black bag sagging around an architecture we all gravely wanted to touch, a pelagic cathedral. The smell clubbed my head, acrid and saline, laced with the scent of limes. It is a longing we all felt, the burial of ourselves, to slip deep into the imagined gullet of what we remember was the fish that swallowed the world, soft and slippery muscles pulling us down to a fetal darkness whispering, I am God, I am God, close your eyes, close your eyes, I am God.

Signs and Wonders

My mother clutched me by the arm, nails leaving tight red smiles in the tender skin of my armpit. She dragged me through the carnival confusion, into the flapping black tent painted with hundreds of crude red hands. It scared me to see my mother's face change when she read tealeaves at the sink, before she rinsed the cup. But this was worse. The old black woman opened my mother's hand like a brittle shell found mysteriously in a tree, divining its grooves and whorls. My mother, eyes unfixed, nodded in perfect rapture. Plugging my ears, I conjured my father kneeling, genuflecting over the hot tarmac, while her moon descended into the House of Jupiter.

IT TOOK LEAVING California for graduate school in central New York to begin really writing about the emotional and physical landscape of my birth and growing up. My lineated poems sometimes attempted to capture the dynamic I associate with the tumbled coast of California—broken dreams re-made and re-invented—transformation. But then, for reasons half-hidden from me (a repatriation to southern California?), I gravitated toward the prose poem's sense of containment: the roiling energy of syllabic and phonemic rhythm you must create and heighten with the absence of line-break, the enlargement of narrative (stanzas becoming chapter-like), as well as its curious and seemingly contradictory (given the recovery of the sentence as the primary unit of meaning) distillation of storytelling that encourages a fabulous tone. The prose poem, it seems to me, whatever its manifold forms rediscovered in the past ten or fifteen years, can foreground the communal mythology of California (*Westward Ho!* and *The Dream Factory,* for instance) and stimulate the writer's more personal mythology, as well as, most interestingly, knot these two threads.

CZESŁAW MIŁOSZ

Kazia

A two-horse wagon was covered with tarpaulin stretched on boughs of hazel and in that manner we had been voyaging a couple of days, while my eyes kept staring out of my head from curiosity. Especially when we left the flat region of fields and woods for a country of hills and many lakes, of which I was to learn later that it was shaped thus by a glacier. That country revealed to me something not named, what might be called today a peaceful husbandry of man on the earth: the smoke of villages, cattle coming back from pasture, mowers with their scythes cutting oats and after-grasses, here and there a rowboat near the shore, rocked gently by a wave. Undoubtedly these things existed also elsewhere, but here they were somehow condensed into one modest space of everyday rituals and labors.

We were hospitably received for the night in a manor by a lake. My memory stops at the very border of returning there but cannot cross it and the name of the place does not appear, nor the name of our hosts, nothing except the name, Kazia, of that little girl at whom I looked, about whom I thought something, though how she looked I do not know anymore, all I know is that she was wearing a sailor's collar.

And so it is, against expectation, that Kazia or another girl, a complete stranger, accompanies us for years and we constantly ask ourselves what happened to her. For, after all, we are able, by concentrating our attention, to raise her, so to say, to the square and to make her important to us disinterestedly, since nothing sentimental colors our imaginings. This is a meditation on one of our contemporaries, how she did not choose a place or time to be born into such and such family. There is no help, I entangle her in everything that has happened since that moment, thus, the history of the century, of the country, of that region. Let us assume that she married, had a child, then was deported to Asia, starving, infected with lice, tried to save herself and her child, worked hard, discovering a dimension of existence which is better left in silence, for our notions of decency and morality have nothing to do with it. Let us assume she learned about the death of her husband in a gulag, found herself in Iran, had two husbands more, lived successively in Africa, in England, in America. And the house by the lake followed her in her dreams. Of course in my fantasies I imagine a day and a place of our meeting as two adults, which has never occurred, perhaps our affair, her nakedness, her hair, dark I am pretty certain, our basic resemblance, of a couple having the same tribe, language, manners. We have been paying too much attention to what separates people; in truth we could have been, we the two of us, married, and it would have been fine, and our biographies would have faded in human memory as they fade now, when I have no idea what she really felt and thought, and am unable to describe it.

To Find My Home in One Sentence

To find my home in one sentence, concise, as if hammered in metal. Not to enchant anybody. Not to earn a lasting name in posterity. An unnamed need for order, for rhythm, for form, which three words are opposed to chaos and nothingness.

Autumn

Cathedral of my enchantments, autumn wind, I grew old giving thanks.

Alexandria

In my early youth I got somewhere a conviction that "alexandrianism" meant a weakening of creative impulse and a proliferation of commentaries on great works of the past. Today I do not know whether this is true, yet I have lived to the epoch when a word does not refer to a thing, for instance a tree, but to a text on a tree, which text was begotten by a text on a tree, and so on. "Alexandrianism" meant "decadence." Then for a long time concerns about this game were abandoned, but what about an epoch which is unable to forget anything?

Museums, libraries, photographs, reproductions, film archives. And amid that abundance individuals who do not realize that around them an omnipresent memory hovers and besieges, attacks their tiny consciousness.

A Polish Poet

It is only through great effort that a Polish poet overcomes in himself a heritage preserved through language—that of concern about the fate of a country squeezed between two world powers. In this he differs from a poet writing in a happier tongue.

A Kurdish poet is concerned exclusively with the fate of the Kurds. For an American poet, the notion of an "American fate" does not exist. A Polish poet is always in between.

From that clash of two forces pulling in opposing directions, the specific character of Polish poetry should emerge—visible in poems having nothing do to with history, such as the erotic poetry of Anna Swir.

A complete liberation from the gravitational force of the local and provincial condemns a poet to imitate foreign models.

A poet, thrown into the international bouillabaisse where, if anything can be distinguished at all, it is only lumps of over-boiled fish and shrimp, suddenly discovers that he sits firmly in his province, his town, his countryside, and begins to bless it.

Where Does It Come From?

Where does it come from? These lips, twenty years old, lightly touched by carmine red, this chestnut hair in sprays—too loose to say locks—these beautiful eyes in a frame of lashes and brows, proclaiming what? She was born at a time when I was teaching Dostoevsky and trying to cope with the realization that I was old.

There is no end to being born, and I, if allowed to continue to live, would sink again and again, dazzled by wonder and desire.

Watering Can

Of a green color, standing in a shed alongside rakes and spades, it comes alive when it is filled with water from the pond, and an abundant shower pours from its nozzle, in an act, we feel it, of charity toward plants. It is not certain, however, that the watering can would have such a place in our memory, were it not for our training in noticing things. For, after all, we have been trained. Our painters do not often imitate the Dutch, who liked to paint still lifes, and yet photography contributes to our paying attention to detail and the cinema taught us that objects, once they appear on the screen, would participate in the actions of the characters and therefore should be noticed. There are also museums where canvases glorify not only human figures and landscapes but also a multitude of objects. The watering can has thus a good chance of occupying a sizable place in our imagination, and, who knows, perhaps precisely in this, in our clinging to distinctly delineated shapes, does our hope reside, of salvation from the turbulent waters of nothingness and chaos.

Pity

In the ninth decade of my life, the feeling which rises in me is pity, useless. A multitude, an immense number of faces, shapes, fates of particular beings, and a sort of merging with them from inside, but at the same time my awareness that I will not find anymore the means to offer a home in my poems to these guests of mine, for it is too late. I think also that, could I start anew, every poem of mine would have been a biography or a portrait of a particular person, or in fact, a lament over his or her destiny.

BILL MOHR

Milk

A pail of milk. I stick my finger in. I hear lips moving. A purple line loops my fingers and wraps my hand until it's bandaged tight and round as the heart of a huge vegetable. My hand throbs as if it could split in half and form lips for holding swollen milk. I'm alone and old. The pail is empty. I hear lips moving.

The Alarm

for Pat Zeitlin

The alarm clock ticks loudly and I almost can't go to sleep, as when I delivered Sunday papers as a boy. In fact, it was accidentally set, with a pair of pliers, for the same hour as I used to get up then. I wake, startled, my fingers smudged with black ink from folding papers; huge moths swirling past my face towards the porch light. I was frightened, but never shot my rubber bands at them.

One time, though, I overslept. The man who left the papers stacked in the driveway pounded on the door. My father leaped from bed. He was waiting for a telegram about his dying father. He'd spent a week with him the summer before in his house in Milton, Massachusetts. When he returned, he said, "We never talked so much in our lives."

But now I think of my childhood visit to the church my parents married in, somewhere in Los Angeles, and I wonder if he said, "Father, I love you, though I married three thousand miles from here, halfway through a war."

Why the Heart Never Develops Cancer

One of the mysteries of the body is why the heart does not develop cancer. Every other organ in the body—stomach, skin, brain, lungs, liver—can develop cancer, but the heart squeezes itself again and again without the least trace of malignancy. It is as though the heart is a furnace and anything cancerous that enters is immediately

294

consumed by the heat of its pulse. On the other hand, the only pleasure the heart receives is imaginary. The skin, the stomach, the lungs—all these organs are capable of enjoying sensual life: the warmth of the sun, a feast of vegetables and turkey, a good smoke, and therefore they are more vulnerable. The heart has only our blood to be its companion. Blood, like the heart, receives no direct pleasure and it brings no relief to the heart, which denies that the body it inhabits means anything more than a warm place to work. The heart, like the life-force itself, is absolutely impersonal. The heart does not care what happens to the body. It is there to work as hard as possible for as long as possible and in return for the body's acceptance of its indifferent loyalty, it never betrays the body by consuming itself cell by cell.

I'VE NEVER ASSIGNED myself the goal of writing a prose poem, but once begun, I don't ever remember reversing course. My practice of versification involves revisions in which line length and the proportions of stanzas go through numerous mutations. Prose poetry, however, seems to align itself with a commitment akin to peripatetic sculpture. My pen seems more like a chisel: each tap with a hammer is decisive. As soon as my imagination has decided that the subject of the poem will be the relationship of sentences to the spatiality of spontaneous meditation, I abandon the influence of prosody, and focus on the necessity of making the path I've chosen more visible at each specific step. Prose poems are more intimate and less idiosyncratic than poems, or at least that's my aspiration.

FRED MORAMARCO

Six Traumatic Scenes from Childhood

1

My mother never let me bring any of my friends over to the house because they might mess things up, so I was thrilled one summer when she took a trip to Italy leaving my father behind to watch out for me because I knew he was a soft touch and would relax the rules. Imagine my surprise when my friend Lefty and me come trotting up to the front stoop where he was sitting out in the sun, smoking his Camels and I say real casually, *"We're going inside to play"* and he looks at me sternly and says *"Oh no you're not—just because your mother's gone don't think you can get away with anything"* and just then the sun dips behind a cloud and the sky darkens.

2

Something must have been bugging my father the day I asked him for fifty cents in the upstairs kitchen, because although he was always a sweet and gentle man and gave me most everything I asked for, this time he turns around from the sink where he is washing dishes and starts swinging at me fronthand and backhand, again and again, his face contorted with a rage I never saw before or again. I shrivelled into the chair by the kitchen window sobbing and begging this stranger to stop. Eventually he does, and the silence of the rest of our lives swallows the moment forever.

3

Here I am at age eight playing triangle, a Brooklyn street game, when somebody shouts "Freddy, look out for the car" and I turn around and *pow*—nothing but the grill of a '40 Ford staring me in the face. The next thing I know I'm in the back seat of this guy's car and somebody's holding a greasy rag to my head to stop the bleeding. I don't remember much about this but somebody told me that when Pete LaBarbera told my mother I was hit by a car she dropped her bag of groceries and started hitting him with both hands. This whole thing had happened before. I was her second Fred. The first Fred was hit by a car at age eight and killed.

4

I'm helping Pete on his newspaper route. It's a big one—route 4711—and on Sunday the Long Island Daily Press is thick and Pete piles the papers in a baby carriage and we go down Bainbridge Street then up Chauncey Street and down Marion, me working one side of the street and Pete the other. We're at Mr. Little's house at the end of Chauncey and the smell of rural Georgia wafts out from his vestibule and just then I'm feeling used and cheated by Pete as he tells me he'll have to pay me less than what he promised because I couldn't collect from Mr. Little and he knows as well as I do that Mr. Little never pays. So I take the change he hands me and hurl it against the stone steps. My eyes are watery as I scream, *"Keep your goddamned fucking money."*

5

The guys are getting together to choose up sides for a stickball game and it's Brother DeRose choosing Jimmy Sorice because both these guys can hit and better not be on the same side. DeRose says, *"I'll take Carmine,"* and then Jimmy says, *"I'll take Emil,"* and DeRose says, *"OK, I got Lefty,"* and Jimmy says *"Ronnie,"* and DeRose comes back with *"Pete,"* and Jimmy counters with *"Junior,"* and DeRose looks around and says, *"I got Cosmo,"* and Jimmy, looking totally disgusted but resigned to his fate, says, *"Oh shit . . . OK, I'll take Freddy."*

6

It's somewhere around Easter time and my mother bought me a pair of new royal blue pants but they're too wide at the cuff and I can't wear them like that because all my friends will laugh. So she agrees to "peg" them and unstiches the seam from the knees down, the tapers the width so they fit tight at the ankles. But it doesn't come out right. When I put the pants on they look like they're bunched up around my ankles, but my mother insists I wear them because they cost plenty and she put a lot of time into them. I do wear them on Easter Sunday. My friends laugh.

MELISSA MUTRUX

Sobralia

> "Time held me green and dying"
> —Dylan Thomas, "Fern Hill"

I was walking home today when I saw a bee half-smashed on the bottom of my porch, its stripes erased and one wing torn off, and I was suddenly sad because I didn't know if, on my way to a job that pays only half my bills, I had carelessly killed it. Now I see stripes of fading color in the air above a sunset and think it must have been my fault.

I had thought I was young, like the orange of a sunrise or a newly opening flower and not the flame-brief amber of autumn leaves already dropping from the tree. I had thought the young couldn't be at fault for anything, not even for a stupid bee smashed under my heel when I was too hurried to notice. And this evening, I'm thinking of philosophy and age, wondering if some bearded old man ever said youth is never responsible because it can only end. Time may have held me, but I think now I was never green, only dying.

I think I must have been pale blue or lavender, like the color of a twilight sky. I was the purple of a newly opening Sobralia bud, ready to bloom and wilt and die before the sun fully left the sky, or the shimmery white of a star, half-dead to start and already gone lone before we realized.

The Star

San Bernardino, California, 2003

They lit it every year at Thanksgiving, and it burned on the hill through the nights of December, five crossed line of fluorescent lights so vivid in the dark you could see them fifteen streets down and maybe from the freeway if you tried; you could watch the star rise and expand as you got nearer and nearer, could follow it as if following the star pointing home. At night, I would climb up to the roof of our garage, watch it gleam in the air like a nightlight, and make a wish.

That year, blazes flared through California like the firefly embers that leapt through the sky above a lop collapsing in a campfire. They

298

stormed through the hills and spread veils overhead, until the sun and land alike shone tiger-lily orange. We swathed our faces as if we were doctors going to surgery and watched ash fall like snow and cloak our cars like a sheet. We set out belongings at the door, just in case.

That night, we climbed the ladder and stood with our eyes torn to tears by the wind and hot ash, watching as curled ribbons flamed their way across the hill like the incandescent tail of a burning, falling star.

The Margins

I walked along the tidelands once, along the bottom of a cliff. The shoreline arched like the back of a seal caught in fishing twine and seaweed between the mussel-encrusted rocks, and I could see behind me the tumult of red and orange and yellow where the crowd slumped across the beach. Ahead, there was only the cliff and the sea and a shard of beach where seagulls roosted and sandpipers tracked the tide, echoing their cries against limestone and basalt and a setting sun. Caves cleft the rock, and bleached driftwood, silver like old bones scoured clean beneath old moonlight, like a Tu Fu poem, littered the empty stretch.

I sat, watching the water crawl closer over bubbles in the sand, over the tops of my shoes, and when the clouds rose from the sea, the night was dark, so wild and quiet that not even stars could breathe.

While all the concision, the attention to sound and word placement, and the encapsulation of a poetic intent involved in lined poems still applies within the prose form, it seems to allow for more situational meaning. Where the broken rhythm of lines and the impulse towards the compact in vertical poems make them better suited to poems centered on singular images, the prose poem for me leans towards the use of anecdotes and moments which place imagery in a more detailed context. This lets me create poems that are less about making statements, even indirectly, and more about searching for understanding.

MARICELA NORTE

And I write, "going home—listening to Cannonball Adderley's version of 'Autumn Leaves' from the 'Something Else' LP. This is so good someone needs to grab the mike 'probando probando probando' and introduce the band with one small addendum 'and sitting in on Pentel Rolling Writer—Marisela Norte.' Applause applause applause . . . and with that said, a light sprinkle, a drizzle of rain falls over the streets, the smell of wet pavement almost as good as it gets in public . . . think back— it's as good as that first bite from a sandwich from Cole's in 1983 with the rain outside and a couple of lite beers on the table and always that anonymous row of men at the bar, already drinking past the white lines too early in the afternoon. An overcast sky works wonders—alters time—makes you think of downtown L.A. like one giant 3D View-Master card—time—mood— the atmosphere thick inside of a sixth street restaurant where you find yourself with your lover at the time, you're sitting comfortably somehow in your twenties and perhaps this is/was that particular Thursday when you tried to quit smoking because he was growing tired of kissing your ash-stained smile.

"But you spend hours inside that restaurant, crazy, nervous hours inside a basement restaurant and except for Mr. Cannonball Adderley and his band who are responsible for making me remember that moment, there is no soundtrack—none exists, at that moment, you are in it and it's just the sound that your voices make when they're deep making a conversation, words overlapping and embracing over the sound of a wooden stool as it's dragged across the cement floor to sit next to you.

"Love.

"And the conversation drops, the tones are hushed, mellow as Art Blakey's brushing on snare.

"I stand before you, bare-boned, with heart open wide, as big a threat as a chocolate cupcake sitting on a dashboard waiting for the sun to go down."

It was the summer circa 1965 when my aunt decided that after a short stint with the Pentecostals and after having moved away from

300

the Catholic Church she was now indeed ready to step into the Kingdom Hall of the Jehovah's Witnesses. That just happened to be the very same summer my five cousins and brother all signed up at the Plunge on Atlantic Avenue for swimming lessons.

Across the grid that is the city of Los Angeles, another neighborhood was already being set on fire.

I chose to forgo the swimming class; the idea of having to force not only myself but all of my neuroses inside a bathing suit in my pre-teenness was too much for me. Instead, I opted to accompany my aunt on her spiritual journey and together roam the streets of East Los Angeles in search of souls to save.

Back in the day (think early sixties), neighborhoods were tighter, they just were, you knocked on doors and people opened them, you rang a doorbell and a voice came from the kitchen and welcomed you inside. For a budding peeping tom-tom girl, I had indeed struck gold.

My Aunt carried around copies of *The Watchtower* in a big black handbag she used to sell Avon from. *The Watchtower,* with its sadly illustrated pages printed on that cheap newsprint—you know the kind of paper that has poorly translated into English instructions for building poorly assembled tin space ships from China. Inside *The Watchtower* there were these black-and-white idyllic scenes depicting man at one with nature, always outlined with a kind of eerie science fiction halo; lions and lambs cavorting in the Edenesque setting on one page but on the next, it was always some downtown nameless metropolis engulfed in flames!

Men, women and children running for their lives just like scenes out of every B movie I'd ever seen at the Center Theater. Meanwhile, the Family of Witnesses walked blissfully toward the pale beams of orange light that poured from the sky like a kind of heavenly carpet that was rolled out for these saved souls to make the climb toward salvation and eternal life.

I asked my aunt, "OK, one more time, what are we looking for?"

"You see those houses?" she'd ask, pointing to the rows of neatly trimmed, rose-bushed, yerba buena growing in a coffee can, tricycle-strewn front yards, "You need to try and imagine that those houses, they're all on fire and we have to go in and save the people who are inside."

"You and I have to save them?"

"Marcello, who will save me? Everything is so difficult . . ."

"Marcello, I'd like to be somewhere else—alone."

I develop a fascination with of all things, the Albanian Embassy after my first look at Godard's Band of Outsiders on the big screen at the New Beverly Cinema notorious for great double bills and the worst seats in Los Angeles.

Little did I know that in twenty years I would find myself seated at the American Embassy in Mexico City for a Thanksgiving dinner with all the trimmings.

But, that was the early 1980s, 1983 to be exact, and we were the new unofficial Band of Outsiders winding in and out of dark Chinatown bars, taking those notorious walks from Philippe's (also known as the unofficial ASCO Club house, our very own Cub Room if you will) all the way to Clifton's Cafeteria on Seventh and Broadway downtown—taking a long walk in a narrow skirt and not to mention trying to make art along the way.

This was my continuing education or maybe it was just continuation period.

Lessons were learned, poems were written, hatchets were buried, more lipstick was applied, lines were drawn, "We don't last that long" he would always insist, and the reds only got deeper and the Lady and the Ginsu Knife, I emerged from a half-shell on a downtown street with a Nino Rota soundtrack to tie it all together.

Some nights, there was no official ringleader and we all took turns at orchestrating a piece of the evening. These were the 1980s, when artists could still afford the cheap rents around Rose and Traction and it was just like that scene out of *La Dolce Vita* where we as both gate crashers and special invited guests held make shift candelabra and we made our way through iron stairwells up to rooftops and another view of our city. My love affair with the city of Los Angeles was in full swing and there was no turning back.

Back then, there was never any question about how and when I would be getting home. These days, I make sure to take that last sip before another Unhappy Hour comes to a close.

"Marcello! Amo la vita di notte!"

But sadly, he was no Mastroianni and I, I was hardly Anouk Aimee. My head had grown used to doing the 360-degree spin so as not to have to face his endless parade of infidelities. These indiscretions, all of them always in the name of art—his art. At that age and stage of my life, I preferred the role of "You're the one he really loves, I mean, you're the one he always comes back to." The one he always comes back to until I asked him to just stop coming.

My stiff upper lip had finally had enough and I gathered up my Ginsu knives and cut myself loose.

So, I took up with a side man on congas and bongo and faced the audience right in the eye, lost in Los, I let myself spill like little pearls of mercury onto the page.

But together, we will always have the shared experience of movies, of leaving the dark theater, completely devastated, changed forever by a particular scene, a close up, these few lines:

> "Sometimes at night, the darkness and silence weighs upon me. Peace frightens me, perhaps I fear it most of all. I feel it is only a façade hiding the face of hell. I think, 'What is in store for my children tomorrow?' The world will be wonderful, they say. But from whose viewpoint? If one phone call could announce the end of everything? We need to live in a state of suspended animation, like a work of art, in a state of enchantment. We have to succeed in loving so greatly, that we live outside of time, detached . . . detached."

This was a continuing education in Fellini's version of feminine wisdom and masculine uncertainty.

When I Wrote Down My Name

He named me after a Maria Felix movie. *Dona Barbara.* One he screened in Mexico as a much younger man. A movie I somehow missed on the Late Late Show. This man has never called me Mija. But on a night like this, one does not think of killings. Thought turns back and forth and back once more to a stack of movie reels and I remember how this man, he taught me more than he would ever know.

He taught me how to drive in the alleys off of Whittier Boulevard. It was an old '55 or was it a '57 blue and white Chevy? Midnight blue like the Big Dipper skies in third-grade astronomy charts, white coffee-cup-handle steering wheel I pretended to maneuver behind the old Jonson's Market. I don't remember now if the radio ever worked in that old Chevy, but as I sit writing, I can still hear the music.

Maybe it's because I grew up on a strict diet of *musica en Espanol y en Ingles*. Pedro Infante, Sinatra, Los 3 Ases, Nat "King" Cole and Tonia La Negra provided the soundtrack to my East L.A. childhood. It accompanied me alongside the theme music from *The Honeymooners, Perry Mason, The Naked City, Twilight Zone* and *Movies Till Dawn*. I still can hear the music but I . . . I wanted *Movies Till Death Do Us Part*.

I replayed those scenes from the Late Late Show in my dreams and most of the time when I was awake. Early on, I discovered that I could be that very dame draped on the gangster's arm in that Mexican cabaret called *El Cielo* as El Trio Los Panchos sang *"Amor de la Calle"* to receptive audience of the shadiest of characters assembled under the stars. I, the disfigured but still voluptuous woman miraculously transformed and restored to classic black and white Hurrell like beauty by the compassion of one tortured but benevolent composer who just happened to be the best friend *("Casi como hermanos!")* of the most renowned plastic surgeon in all of Tenotchitlan! Or I decked to the nines could stand tall with the rest of the misfits gathered at Rick's Café Americaine, proudly singing "La Marseillaise," tears in my eyes . . . Vive La France! I pledged my allegiance to Humphrey Bogart.

So now, as I sit writing and remembering, is it any wonder that as a child playing alone in my cemetery/backyard I imagined every silver Pan-Am TWA jet that flew over my head was in fact, "just another plane leaving for Lisbon"?

My exit visa was movies.

MY MEDIUM OF CHOICE is prose. I can only write that perhaps it has something to do with my having been born and raised in Los Angeles (a city built around the automobile) and yet never having the desire for a California Driver's License of my own. I choose public transportation as my way of navigating the streets of Los Angeles, notebook in hand with eyes focused through a bus window darkly . . .

VICTOR OLIVARES

Drunk at the Golf Course, Arguing with Li Po

Looking up, I see the red moon tacked to the sky—the old corkboard. I can still recall that the red is caused by remnants of light discarded in the clouds, and that the color of twilight is captured in inkstones …Li Po must have known this. There's no one left at the golf course but me, so I sing to my shadow wrapped around the eucalyptus tree, surrounded by coarse Bermuda grass.

If Li Po could be here now, I'm sure he'd brush something brilliant, onto an old scorecard, about the moon. Or he might say something about how in a ravine, under the subtle interplay of shadow and moonlight, the current gathers with the semblance of dark ink, before cycling its way back to the heavens.

I'm not playing at anything though—I'm dizzy from singing. Sitting on the wet fairway, hunched over, I etch into the sandbar with a split thumbnail: *Even the moon has to bleed in this life, into a dark stone.*

Leaving Santa Ana

Through prostitutes who invest in pimps and bad-mouth the girls who give it up for free; through five men in a back alley huddled around the cigarette they share, blowing the smoke into an empty bottle to make it last; through a river bed of dog piss and newspapers and left shoes, a river bed where salmon once circled confused before dam walls then died; through Nikki Thomson who was even born beautiful but took too much ecstasy, fried her mind and is now lost in a hospital somewhere; through Eddie Vargas who was my friend but just didn't care anymore, shot a boy's face off, and was arrested with the boy's wallet that night at the Pic-N-Save; through these and many more who teach me nothing, or show me nothing of how to live in Santa Ana or anywhere else, through these I see myself, and I realize that I too have had more than enough of it all, seated at a bus stop outside Jack in the Box, seated by a homeless guy listening to headphones with no radio, arguing wildly with the wind.

Metaphysical Relativity in Santa Ana

All first impressions are lies. Nevertheless, I find that pouring out an old can of V-8 into the sink takes me back to junior high, where I was the one called to set the bully straight—I almost killed him. I was only twelve years old, and I'm sure the older girls in the checkered skirts were cheering me on as I smashed his nose back into his face. At the time I was certain and inexperienced, but I've since learned that women confuse me. Today though, staring at the tomato juice rippling in the sink, I realize as I did then, I wasn't ready to see that much blood. And I can't stand to see people cry, something I haven't done since . . . I can't remember. I get along though. I've learned the most from the sure-footed snail who laughs at those of us who think we'll end up with wings.

I believe in God and go to the local Church in Santa Ana. I've seen how Satan and Christ fight over us on the corner of Third and Main, where the bum in the sport jacket just missed the plump prostitute with an empty gin bottle, the glass shattering on the curb like salt from a shaker rolling across the table top, breaking out fast but only lasting a beat. If you've heard the sound of burning coal, or seen how neatly a body can be outlined by chalk in the end, you'd understand.

I've worked in physical therapy. I've helped rehabilitate people of all ages. Those who never fully walk again or lose the use of their right arm, do they still sing the praises of creation or would they make an arrangement with the devil now? How easy it is for the years to gather in one body, to be encased within sweat and dust. Everybody has a story about the value in accumulated years; and as for meaning, I have a hold of the first few straws needed to fill the barn.

Ode to a Lemon Squeezer

On my whitewashed desk lies a lemon squeezer which I named Wilbur. The chrome finish is as smooth as the snail's trail on the windowpane. The snail, gone now, must have winked too many times at those with wings. I wrap my fingers around the handles as though around two legs of a snowflake, or two petal-blades from the snowdrops that bloom in late winter on the slopes of Patterdale, England. My hand, crowned by the chrome plated clamp, is poised to render lemonade, or a nice piccata, or a half of a Tom Collins. Wilbur is a toothless alligator in polished aluminum and I'm bestowed with the means to survive if I were ten, and a visionary—as Neruda put it, "flattered in this way . . ." because I hold the means to squeeze the white blood harnessed through the lemon roots on the hill-sides of Camarillo, or in my back yard, I hold the means to make the juice of Kings, the bitter-sweetness which, in almost all cases, must be what the very essence of life tastes like.

SOMEONE TOLD ME that the images in line poems are comparable to walking down a stairwell, whereas the images in a prose poem are like walking in a field of tall grass and stepping into gopher holes every once in a while. A prose poem is usually absorbed as a whole, though the whole may work on multiple levels. I look at prose poems as giving readers the opportunity to discover the "goods" in a poem (handing the reins over to the reader), whereas a lined poem presents those "goods" more conspicuously. In a way, poems written in prose respect the reader more, because the qualities of the poem are left for the reader to discover according to each reader's capacity, experience or willingness. In other words, the poem isn't holding any hands. Of course, there are exceptions. I don't necessarily think about any of this when I begin to write. Many times, I write a poem in lines and change it into prose to get a better picture of the rhythms and repetitions that may go unnoticed in a lined poem. After further tinkering, I may change a poem that started out with line breaks into a prose poem and then back to a poem with line breaks. If a poem has longer rhythms stretched over several lines, I might change it to a prose poem. If I want to try and add a sense of authority, I might write it as prose. "Drunk at the Golf Course, Arguing with Li Po" is the only one out of the four in this anthology that started out as a prose poem and remained in the form even after several rewrites. I don't feel I have learned all there is to know about prose poems, or any given form poem for that matter. I've read Russell Edson, Morton Marcus, Gary Young, along with other poets who write both prose and lined poems because I enjoy it, and because it helps me better understand the different forms poetry can take or what, at its best, poetry can accomplish.

DAVID OLIVEIRA

Citation

Of course, the injury was in the line of duty—even so, had the officer not been standing at the brothel door where clearly his duty lay, but back, say, at the police station where the fruit seller was reporting the theft of all her night's receipts by a gang of street toughs, or at home roundly snoring beside his wife at 11:30 PM as in the days prior to his friend opening the modest establishment to which the invitation that evening for a late night pick-me-up had obliged him to wait outside (albeit impatiently) to thank his host, he would have missed the bullet entirely from the disgruntled customer with poor aim; but then, of just such luck are heroes made.

Why is there anything?

At the start, you should know I don't have the answer. I don't even know if it's a good question.

For answers, you would have to go see someone who hadn't spent an education using an index finger to track the shadow of the minute hand across the pasture of his watch. For answers, you would have to go see Henry Simas in the days when he rocked on his porch as the seven-thirty light of July or August unfurled to turn Hanford gold for the one minute everyone forgot the wan, humble skin that covered all the other minutes.

The problem with government is, he would tell you, *it attracts politicians.*

As a young man, Henry spent a year at seminary wondering why he wanted to be a priest. After finding the answers he'd been looking for, he ran out so fast the questions got left behind. As a result, Henry always had an answer, but was lost to know what question it was for.

What you have to understand about men and women is it's only one species.

Once, driving the homecoming king and queen in the town's annual parade, he was suddenly struck by the magnitude of fine dental work available in such a small community.

308

If you think about everything long enough, nothing makes any sense.

Another time, at the Kings County Fair, Henry spent forty dollars to win five-dollars of plaster shaped like Our Lady of Fatima.

Whatever God had to do with the world, it was the Devil invented religion.

One year, as *festa* season came around, I asked Henry how he got to be smarter than everybody else.

Hell, I don't know any more than the next guy. I just tell people what they already believe and they think I'm a fucking genius. Truth is the surer people are of something, the surer they're going to be wrong. Nobody knows anything, a fact real smart ones keep locked up.

More than once on those hard Valley nights before people forgot the reason to build porches, Henry looked out and pointed to a star, Polaris, maybe, or Arcturus, and though he couldn't exactly tell you at what, figured he was looking at something—that even if he was the only one doing it, his looking was not nothing.

Why is there anything?

It was the only question he had. Night after night, he sent it to float on the wide evening air, a few words away from the answer.

Festa

1969. Five months since Nixon's inauguration. Weeks before two men arrive at the moon. The war isn't going well and doesn't get better for another forty years. That's me and Bob, my college roommate, standing in the blunt shade of elms on Florinda Street. California elms, so not really elms at all. There is nothing else here to tell this year from the last or from the dozen to come. Even my father's dark hair and handsome smile doesn't tell you, nor does the banner he carries for the Knights of Columbus, and the honor of America, Portugal, and the Holy Ghost. And for his son, going to war in a year—Robert, not me, the other good Bob standing at my side. Behind Dad, the parade of Portuguese queens and their courts, radiant in rhinestone tiaras and weeks of sewing. My young sister is stunning in white satin sheen, her carmine cape trimmed in imitation ermine, 500 seed pearls stitched to the velvet by our mother's hand. From the sidewalk, the two Bobs and I follow the long trains that sweep the street from St. Brigid's to the Fraternal Hall, courtiers for the few blocks allegiance requires. I am born in the hospital just yards from this spot, something I don't mention to the others as I only think of it now.

At the *festa*, the hungry do not wait for the authority of queens. Centuries before this morning's sunrise, Dom Henrique's protégés sail wooden ships laden with sweet tastes from the Malaccas to the Fraternal Hall kitchen. It is the scent of the Azores now—whose sons and daughters, bearing the names of light, come around the world to descend into Hanford, Kings County, California, United States of America, in this year of our Lord. Souza, Costa, Borba, Fagundes, Silva, Bettencourt, Alves, Nunes, Andrade, Gomes, Clemente, Vaz, Cardoza, Pacheco, Brasil, Dias, Coelho, Perry, Azevedo, Gonsalves, Simas. The Latin syllables simmer in huge pots with Asian spices, cabbages and hunks of beef until the aromas swarm the long tables covered in rolls of white butcher paper. Cotta, Machado, Garcia, Avila, Rocha, Barros, Almeida, Fernandes, Pimentel, Carvalho, Neves, Freitas, Madruga, Dutra, Martin, Duarte, Cabral, Lopes, Furtado, Ramos, Ornellas. Generations of impatience crave their *sopas* sipping sodas or beer or cheap wine from Fresno, nibbling lupino beans and linguiça. Mendes, Neto, Gaspar, de Campos, Santos, Faria, Mello, Vigario, Mattos, Braga, Soares, Monteiro, Pinheiro, Cordeiro, Teixeira, Ladeira, Silveira, Vieira, Sequeira, Ferreira, Pereira, Oliveira. The conversation grows louder when large pans of French bread, blessed with sprigs of mint, are brought to the tables—louder still for the pans of opulent soup. I show Bob how to put pieces of bread on his plate and pour the transcendent broth over it. Robert knows how from birth. We are half-finished before the brass band stabs at "The Star-Spangled Banner" and "*A Portuguésa*," as close to grace as anyone here gets.

The leaves at the top of the elms burn in midday fever. The sun gradually turns away from what we're doing, or the earth turns its back on the sun, but the heat gives way to a comfortable evening and we return to eat, drink, dance the *chamarita* as dawn breaks over the Spice Islands and the present warfare. We are survivors. We can all say that after four million years of war. Robert goes to Vietnam and a year later comes back with himself. Bob goes to Ukiah to wait for prison or Canada and disappears. And I—well, it's a long story, but I come here.

310

Laurence Olivier's Hamlet

He is 41, his mother 28. Already blonder than Denmark, there isn't enough dye in the bottle to turn him into a schoolboy. Sweet prince of the theater before the movies, he has a taste for lace cuffs and intricate embroidery, but dons simple tights in every scene—fittingly black for mourning a father.

It's the classic story: The father too preoccupied with work to notice that his bored wife is occupied by his younger brother. Indifferent to the family business, the overprotected son parties away at college perennially shy of graduation credits. When his father dies unexpectedly, the son, victim of chronic vacillation (he has yet to figure out what his major is going to be or not to be), can't decide how best to get home—missing Father's funeral, Mother's wedding, and the coveted crown (he's first runner-up). Not the only son to ever face the ghost of a father, he doesn't handle the situation well—wanting nothing more than to curl up on Mother's busy bed.

Trim enough for the stage, the plot sheds two hours to fit into the movies. Rosencrantz and Guildenstern are gone before they can be killed, something everyone regrets. Olivier and Alan Dent share writing credit—mentioned is the aspiring author of the effusive first draft (unavailable for the rewrite). For Sir Larry, who directs himself, it's all black and white—just the simple "tragedy of a man who couldn't make up his mind."

Snow and the Academy Awards fall on the first day of spring in LA, 1949. Gowns under wraps, actresses and heels slip through Hollywood's icy streets more easily than usual. The great Ethel B., who has been in all the papers for weeks touting brother John's greater Dane, presents the award for Best Picture—the winner's name trippingly on the tongue. The writing, which some find derivative and clichéd, isn't nominated. In London to do a play with wife, Vivien, Olivier celebrates with an extra drink after the show—as do the losers. This night he has a bit of trouble falling asleep, his head reeling in words—sublime, unforgettable words.

I'M A NARRATIVE POET. This is the tradition within which I fell in love with poetry and is the tradition in which I continue to find sustaining comfort, grace and beauty. Of course, art travels in many mysterious directions, and like love, who can say what attracts one to the beloved. Since such attachments are beyond reason, any attempt to impose a rational explanation is certain to fail. This is why we are continually inundated with mostly well-meaning attempts to definitively label the conditions of poetry and are, for the most part, continually disappointed. A poem that wants to tell a story is a prose poem regardless of how the poet lays the line on paper—plain and simple. Those poems of mine that I specifically think of and refer to as prose poems usually started out with typical lines, that is, short lines (or at least, shorter lines) that attempted to stop short of the right margin. Like verse, the language tried to describe the ineffable by dancing around its borders with an inclination toward rhetorical expression and compression. But, like prose, the language progressed to story, becoming generally linear and following, more or less, conventional grammar (as I have come to understand it). Gradually, I allowed the words to line themselves up whatever way they wanted. A poem insists on its form, after all, and who am I to stand in its way?

LE MINH PHAN

Finding a Particular Place for Each Piece of Sky

I spend the summer after college graduation at my cousin's house. Their house has just been renovated, new paint and a new red door on an old address. I stay at home with my nephew, while around us everyone goes to work. My nephew is at an age when handwriting still matters. He is doing a word search and asks me for the meaning of the word *celestial,* but does not put it into context. It has multiple meanings and when I tell him I do not know where to start defining it, he asks me to define his name and asks if he will have the same meaning in every sentence.

After lunch we do a jigsaw puzzle. Blue and white fragments spread all over the kitchen table. I have been holding onto one gray edge of a cloud that seems to fit nowhere. We keep working on a thousand pieces far into the afternoon, sorting and separating the sky parts from ground parts, struggling to fit everything into its proper place. Out the window the clouds have been shifting all day, the sky turning over on itself, as if it were uncertain where to go next.

Impression

My sister's shoes tapped out against the bricks that lined themselves up to the photographer's door. I followed behind, tried to keep up with the bounce in her curled ponytail. The bell above the door rang its stale peal as a tired-looking man stood up from behind the counter. My mother inquired about the prices for passport photos while I silently questioned my choice of outfit—a green turtle neck that hung loosely, khaki pants that were too big around the waist and ended just above my socks. I was at the age were clothes in the right size fit me almost as strangely as pink dresses and patented leather shoes looked. We went into the makeshift studio where a solitary chair stood by itself all day and the off white walls were dingier than the light. I waited my turn while my sister's smile flashed into the camera's light.

Minutes later the photographer squinted at the newly developed photos like a judge examining evidence. He smiled at my sister and said to my mom, "Attractive little girl! She could be in show business!" My sister beamed. I stood next to her, my nose even with the counter, my eyes directed at the photographer. The four o'clock sun made its way in through the blinds, shining its dusty light. "And this one, she could be a doctor!" My eyes remained on him as my mom paid for the photos and I took home the image the photographer had created of me.

Running Errands

We are at the hair salon inside of JCPenney, sitting on the long mauve cushioned bench with the gum stain in the corner. The ladies with rollers in their hair point out how well behaved we are. At the post office we stand along the back wall because there isn't enough room to stand in line with mom. I want to look at the different stamps on the wall but they are too high up for me to see any of the pictures. I can't even see the 25-cent mark on them. Next we go to Litchfield's Toys. It has two floors. Mom says we will get a treat later because we have been good all day. At Albertson's we walk by the cookies and chips to the milk section. Mom picks up a gallon of milk and leads us up the candy aisle, we follow like little yellow chicks through a garden.

We are passing by the barrels that hold chocolates, caramels, white candies with colorful pieces of jelly, and pink and brown coconut pieces. Mom stops. She says we can pick out five each. Any five we want. We seize the slippery plastic bags hanging from a metal hook and look at all the different colors. I put two white candies dotted with jelly pieces in my bag. My sister puts two caramel squares into her bag, then changes her mind. One goes back into the bin. We go from bin to bin weighing out the options. There are too many to choose from. Mom is being patient.

A lady, her white hair done up with a silk scarf the way they do in my third grade reading books walks by us. She glares at my mom then says that we are making too much noise. That she doesn't understand why our mom doesn't know how to teach us. And we should go back where we came from. Later in the car we unwrap our candy in silence. The first sticky piece clings to my teeth, fills my mouth with too much sweetness. After a moment I am ashamed that it starts to taste good.

Monte Vista Elementary School, 1989

Mrs. Kaplan calls us up one by one to go over report cards. I make my way up from my third-row desk. She points to my report card and tells me I'm doing very well for an average student. The yellow grid on the paper holds a row of C's and two B's. I am excelling at being average.

There are seven of them. Their desks are arranged all in a cluster around Mrs. Kaplan's desk. They are all in the top reading and math groups. One of them is Michelle, the only student to get the answer to number 9 across—position relative to that of others: status.

The longest hours of the school day are between recess and lunch. I sit in my third-row desk doing math problems that I don't understand. I pretend it is the year 2003 and I am at work and this is my job, problem after problem to figure out. Then I come across a problem I can do. Finding the mean of two numbers.

$$\frac{114 + 158}{2} = 136$$

We can picture 136 on the number line, and see that it is halfway between 114 and 158. Not deviating towards either extreme.

I USE THE PROSE FORM for poems that have an "everyday" feeling about them, and yet in these everyday settings there is a splash of something that is definitely not everyday. In life, the things that shock us are found in the middle of ordinary days just as the realizations that happen in a prose poem don't look any different on the page, but deliver a strong enough emotional impact to stand on their own without the help of page layouts or line breaks. It is almost as if the ordinary layout on the page matches the simple mysteries of our days.

CHAD PREVOST

After Punishment, Baptism

—for Arthur Smith

What I remember is my father asking to be forgiven for sacrificing so much family time teaching the sinners what they needed saving from. I remember him pounding the pulpit preaching, jaws clenched, brow lifted, stabbing at the air.

I remember Adam and I were killing a Saturday on the marsh banks at low tide, witnessing what the high tide kept hidden—bed frames, beer bottles, coffee cans, shoes stuck in sludge. We hauled a tire up to the small shore, fed an oily rag inside its center. I'd stolen matchbooks from my mother's collection. I lit the rag. Flames leapt like an animal desperate to escape, the head-high wheat by the banks the fuel for its departure. For a moment I stopped pedaling away, and turned to the wind-fed blaze. I'd never seen anything so beautiful and ravenous, eating every hidden thing—rattlesnakes, raccoons, gophers, grackles scattering like thrown pepper. The fire licked at my heels by the highway curb. It was as if I were eye-to-eye with a vision from hell, sirens wailing, heat rising above homes.

What I remember is, still out of breath, lying to the Fire Chief who'd followed us. I blamed it on Adam. My mother discovered the truth. She found missing matchbooks and I confessed first to her, then my father, then the police who showed me snapshots of burned kids. My father dealt seven licks, forbid me to return to the marsh, or to leave home for what seemed at the time as a kind of eternity. Released a few weeks later, I rode to the marsh—black, vast, scarred, there was nothing left.

What I remember is holding my breath, bubbles rising, a glass-fronted tank of greenish water. The good news is I walked up the baptistery steps, a dead rose pinned to my sopping robe that clung to my small body. I was born again. How many times have I been forgiven since I was seven? How many times reborn, returning to that tank, burning, out of breath, burning?

Fever

Am I in the right bed, the one with an imprint of my body shaped like a fossil into the life I bartered for as Professor, Husband, Father, uncapitalized Capitalist, a man with a neatly trimmed yard? Or is my dream whirl pooling away like the tug boats in my son's bath? Am I in my right mind, the one I left at the dinner table? Or am I pushing away from the shore of another life? Am I asking to be excused before I finish my peas? My father has come to take me back. He who immersed me in the Baptistery by the Bay at Tiburon Baptist— El tiburon, the name for shark—has freed me from my recovery. No longer must I wear a gown of shame, or sit in a Time Out cell, or profess in the 12 Steps. The counselors have given me back the items they took from my person—razor blades, acne medication, bracelets, marijuana, pipe, Zippo. Is it true? Have we have sailed around the world from Sausalito to Deltaville, from San Pablo to the Chesapeake? Are we in his Catalina 25? Or are we a vessel from the Old World, armed with a mission, ready to sail off the world's edge to bring Good News? It's early Fall, maybe October. The light is a resinous orange, which could be turning the world to dawn or dusk. In the visible depths, the bay is a universe filled with jellyfish the size of baby fists. We're tacking into the headwind, the choppy spray, the fog, the barely visible world.

Stepping Inside, Mt. Tamalpais

We have learned to step inside ourselves, lay across empty spaces spreading like a blank canvas imprinted by what it touches and going back days or years later and changing the details and the colors, thinning them into tapestries of watercolored worlds, texturizing them into purple-shadowed mountains, blue alcoves with broken windmills spinning one way then the other along thunderous roads without guardrails where lightning splits like a wishbone and the sky lets loose as if saying that all things sad are what we have to live on, food from the sky, the make-up of our bodies and ⅔ of the earth's surface, and here where two moons rise together and rip apart over the jagged mountains which look like a woman on her back, here

317

is where we eat in silence because for now all that needs saying has been said and we watch the moons rise in the mix of stars, here where the light is still good enough to see our shapes in this field of grass and stubbled dirt, a few crooked Joshua trees dotting the surface we float up to the sky as if leaving our bodies behind, dreaming things we mostly forget, the wings inside ourselves extending.

Redeemed

The adults must've thought it was cute, me, the only kid present, waving my hand on a Wednesday night, the Music Minister taking requests, asking for Hymn 444. What can I say? My father was pastor. This was my life. I liked the chorus melody, how safe and sure I felt as we sang, piano hammering the heavy accents, simple lyrics lifting— Redeemed, how I love to proclaim it—from the Baptist Hymnal, carrying out the open side-exit door, where the incandescent glow of headlights and taillights streaming up and down the rocky hillside, were harbingers of God's glory. Redeemed by the blood of the Lamb. When turned heavenward, my father's index finger stood for Sermon Point Number 1. The bare hand slapping the pulpit was God making a point, righteous anger, like flooding the world to save it. Redeemed, how I love to proclaim it. The finger, the open-palm, flesh against flesh, the means to transcending flesh. What does a child know of redemption? These were my most faithful moments— juice was blood. The pulpit, an arc on which I was crossing the bay, which wasn't a bay but a baptistery. Redeemed by the blood of the Lamb. The world's literal imagination lifting itself from the shadows. The spires of the distant bridge were steeples, and boats with sails, dove's wings, and then they become my father's robe, bathed in white, fluttering around me as he lay me back. When I rise he says, "This is my son in whom I am pleased. Come, all who are weary and heavy-laden. Rise and sin no more."

RUBEN QUESADA

Juana, Employee No. 357172

Diamond Creek Vineyards, California

The dishes have been washed and put away. Lupita and Jorge have been put to bed. With dark half-moons under her eyes she lays out her clothes—navy blue work pants, denim blouse, a second-hand bra—all unironed and wrinkled like the corners of her eyes, where a crowd of tears streamed during her lukewarm bath and has now dried. Her brown skin, palms and forearms, stained black and violet from mud and grapes.

Before dawn, she leaves for work on the Eastward Greyhound bus, the same one that returns her each evening with dust in her pockets beneath the purple and blue sky.

Four Rooms

I was four. My two sisters slept on the bed; Mom and I slept on the orange shag carpet. It smelled of dust, of the layers of dead skin from previous tenants, which had come to rest on it having never been vacuumed or swept.

Years later, a check would arrive from the California State Lottery Commission with Mom's name on it for having matched all three of our birth dates in the weekly drawing. We'd move two blocks down the street, to have our own room, and sleep in our own bed. And when I woke up coughing in the middle of the night, I didn't blame the dark corners of the ceiling or the weight of blankets on my chest, but the smell of that dust still in my head.

To William

I'm going to write you a letter to tell you about all the times I saw a pigeon fly off just as I walked by. And with it, it carried a whisper, a word, maybe even an entire sentence I forgot to share with you on the shores of Costa Rica or along Melrose Avenue, sometimes even on my break at work, or just walking through the parking lot

319

at school. They fly away not knowing that they've stolen something meant for you.

I write this letter, thirty-nine thousand feet above the earth—far enough to escape the pigeons and maybe as close to heaven as I'll ever get, so that you might someday know that every word I've ever lost, every sentence, every whisper, will be waiting here for you.

Santa Marta Hospital

East Los Angeles, California

The earth cannot be stopped by the weight of cars to keep me here another day. At 28, I too must be dying. There are no nuns walking past my door, nor the sounds of church bells hammering the afternoon sky—only this white plastic band on my wrist and a paper cup of hot chocolate.

My mother is not at my bedside. Her worn spotted face and creamy smile hovering above me is just an imprint on my X-ray results posted on the wall. There is no flock of aunts and uncles. The children with their bean brown eyes are nowhere to be found. There is no endotracheal tube in my wasted body, in a hospital room overlooking the Los Angeles River, where I see myself sitting on the porch of Tia Leticia's house in Costa Rica, in the chair made of banana leaves and sea grass. Its arms and legs still smell of plantains and sea salt—it once belonged to my grandmother. Its faint salty smell of violets reminds me of her hair, as gray as the smog embracing the buildings reaching to the sky.

THE PROSE POEM is a unique hybridization; it creates a place between the need to utilize a poetic voice and the authoritative credibility of the prose line. Most of my prose poetry deals with my experiences growing up in southeast Los Angeles and they are of a more serious and reflective tone, whereas my line poems are definitely more playful and lighter in subject. I find that the voice of my prose poems creates more empathy for the subject of the poem in the longer line and creates a more inviting space which permits the reader to enter the poem and stay awhile, and through this I am able to connect narrative sequences between the characters of my poetry.

BRADY RHOADES

Los Angeles

Down where the sludge pools between the shit-stained rocks and cats prowl beneath the river bridge, I ponder the buried city, Juaneno, meat feasts. "Existence!" echoes off a crab's back. "You crabs, you bees, you filthy ducks, what do you know, what do you care?" The flotsam of the failed city floats by—a milk carton sucked dry, a Halloween mask. Ju I says to "link with stabilities" and wasn't that the purpose of the bridge?

The trees on San Pedro, condemned against the walls of the Toy District, they should be blindfolded, given cigarettes. The skinny body and beaming corsage of the rain tree translates—if species can be translated from one to another—as a girl stood up on prom night. A parrot squawks for revenge; I flip it thebird. Skid row smells like a zoo. A hooker squats on a woodpile. "The prez'dent's an asshole," says a voice in a cardboard box. "When I thinka the guv'ment, I thinka Saturn eatin' his babies."

Most cities swear they have a soul, too, but Broadway zigzags with hustlers and schizophrenics. The souls of Angelenos, the rumor goes, get sold at Central Market. Look at this —a Rite-Aid across the street from a Rite-Aid, two blocks from a Walgreens. The city is foul, the people are sick. They drop sorties the size of tic-tacs on the Capitol Self. Top story in the *Times*: An oil plant lights up the delta in Eboch, sickens the crops. To blocks away, flies feast on the moist parts of children. We in the Temple of the Holy Pill, in Los Feliz, Boyle Heights and Bel-Air, could commit our lives to putting out the fire. The movement shall be called Enough or Because or Why Not. The purpose: Discomfit the rich, starve flies.

I thumb through Huxley, Carver, Talese, but not Sartre, Shakespeare or James, what do they know of the pale, subtropical mood of Fifth Avenue?

Evening on Bunker Hill. Who but the clock-watching loon calls it a night? Wine, on contact with air, gives up the ghost. I wish to be uncorked so, but no, on bruised legs it arrives, begging for change. Welts the size of every US coin! Uh oh, a violinist, a moneyhat.

"Walk around! You too, walk around!" gadabouts. Go politick, make money, buy gadgets, watch CNN. Toss and turn over credit card rates, buy more insurance. Metaphysically impatient, I'll strip to the core (hair keeps the deer from the roses and shovel the meat to the crows).

To narrow it down: Symbol (there goes the grackle). Who conceived Orion? Some see a badge up there, an earring, a torch, a buckle, a geyser, a blemish, a tooth, a pendant, a seashell, a starfish, a lamp, a tumor, an iris and two bottle caps. I start a story on my wrist: Nat and Tiny give birth to an ovoid ball. Two babies screamwailmoan. An old man belches. This, *this* commands respect. Enough in-between episodes of Mankind, dramatized and repeated on TV, bird anthems and lettuce in the compost concern us now.

On to the pueblo to buy a poncho, a stone bowl to eat from, to put a curse on the rich at *Misión Capilla del Santisimo,* where they shuffle on knees and weep for relief. Sad sad, the lost art of lament, but take heed from the *madres,* who teach us how to care and don't get elected. In the end, stricken with dead legs and cotton-mouth, in a cross-traffic of jabber-gesticulation, wouldn't we meld in their arms for good? Escort them from their pueblos, bungalows, tents and wicky huts, their pied-à-terres, to *Plaza de Los Angeles.* Grab the shy one in the lamplight, grooming her zarape. Bring them en masse, the *madres,* to this city of commerce.

40

Running in the hills of La Habra. On one side, PE students on a field of grass; they look like spastic jelly beans. On the other, a man sweeping a sidewalk. The children and the man exist like memories in a dream.

Turned 40 today, thought of 30. Watched Gilligan's Island and guessed The Professor at 47, the Howells in their 60s. Dylan Thomas, Marilyn Monroe and Roberto Clemente never made it this far. Reagan became president at 70. At 8, I wanted to be 12. That was 1974. I had thought I would arrive by now.

Monday morning, damp, the sound of breath, a breath that is not mine, coming in, going out. Red leaves, yellow leaves, parrots in the yew tree. Hungover cats. Fourteen things to do, large and small. The children see me pass, too far to taunt. The old man looks up from his aura of dust and nods.

Insomnia XXX

That your book? I asked the cabbie, the third time through Hollywood. Oh, that. I been askin' some questions, and you know what? Schopenhauer makes nonsense. He can't say, *you* can't say, no on can. God could if he would but he won't so it don't get said.

Tule, she stayed thin at *fifty.* Do you know she fixed supper if she was sad or glad or sick or whatever, and somethin' else, she wasn't like these whores runnin' around, she was nice, wore dresses to the end, damn pretty *1940s-style,* pretty and not stuck up. Jesus Christ, never let a good woman go, they make life *better.* The food's bad, Christmas stinks, the cat's irate. I got no one, I got nothin'. I don't pray to God no more I pray to Tule but I'm gettin' the feelin' it's too late.

THE POEM "Los Angeles" kept widening, or decentralizing, during the writing process, which, in retrospect, seems fitting. Perhaps it should have been titled "Ode to the Margins." It is one of many formed, at least in my case, from the sprawling inclinations of the hand, and the sentence. What results is impossible to measure or describe, but natural and necessary.

DOREN ROBBINS

"What's Up?"

To walk down a street in that neighborhood and not get hassled, you had to look like you could deal with abuse—you had to be able to look into the lowered car's tinted window when it slowed up to you playing heavy bass you felt inside your buttons until it pulled away because you looked like you knew and were not surprised by what that sound-track to a miserable time on cheap chrome wheels was all about. And you never let up remembering the faces outside wood shop, especially the one you thought was ready to rip your skinny white ass to pieces, and was about to you found out later. And, in fact, you had to know and still better be able to—twenty-five years later in a certain situation—know again how to say in the right kind of tone, "What's up?" And you have to say it with eyes looking straight but maimed and steady with what they know from what they have seen that any harm someone intends for you isn't going to be justified or worth it—and you better say it without anger, and you better say it with your hands outside your pockets, because you have to show in that look that you know the unwanted guest sits on a thorn, so someone wanting to mess with you senses you know it, and knows for sure you deal with it, because you do, and because *that* is going to be your bond.

Just My Luck

I'm reading Bulgakov again. This time: *Heart of Dog.* That's about my speed. But what the hell is Bulgakov saying about the system he lived under? I mean what is he saying about what's left of the under-estimated side of our human nature? In Bulgakov's system the common people are dogs. Eighteen million disappeared into Gulag Pounds—dogs, comrade, dogs. Don't forget—they disappeared for the lowest bark, the least growl of resistance, or lack of obedience, or even suspicion that one might growl, or resist, or wet the floor fearfully, not understanding the command.

Most of my dogs got out—they dug under the fences they couldn't leap. My people got out of Russia. They weren't going to see the revolutionary redistribution of whatever rubled equivalent of nickels and dimes, and now seventy years later a re-confiscation for the worse. My dogs, the men anyway, if they could find them that is, were going to see the front of the front of the front lines, or another Cossack death-squad riding by. They shot from their horses with great accuracy, it is said about the Cossacks; they could *My Lai* a reasonably-sized Jewish village in around an hour or so. For my dogs there has simply been a fifty-five year moratorium on pogroms. Here, anyway. So far, that is. Not everybody's grandparents were smart enough to get the hell out. Not a little thing. I go along with my gratitude for those old-timers that knew how to run, and when to run when they had to run. I bark when I feel like it. So far, no one has called the cops or the Brotherhood of Aryan Shit Lovers.

And for a while I've been unbelievably lucky to keep receiving the uncensored and therefore accurate—if not always kind—facts about myself, so I'm not going to howl at my own reflection like Bulgakov's dogman does. I'm not in a 1937 police state; I'm in a 2002 semi-pseudo-quasi-partial democracy. I'm working it out in one of its global-industrial suburbs. And while I still can, while it is still permitted, I'm goin' t'go sit outside and get me some sun, then I'm goin' back inside and French me some fries, and after that I'm packin' one bag and drivin' down to L.A. to meet my sugar for some tea.

My Defects Call Me Back

Back on the telephone with my defects. They called me again just outside Ventura County where the radiator poured green chemicals on my chest and arms. And it wasn't my need for coolant that brought me back to Los Angeles, I can tell you that. Always some oversight, some lopsided-ness, some offspring of my stunted perceptions leading the way. By Ventura I no longer perceived accidents as accidents, but as the way I arranged every choice around what was least threatening to my weak side. So little agility. My lopsidedness. Some neglect.

My defects called me back to tell me *they* are the real subjects. To them everything else is "conceit, *everything*—just verbal spermicide, topic after topic, right-brain hobbyism, someone working a butcher's scale so it works for him, and how long are you going to look into a tailor's mirror at what is never naked about your self?" Those fucking defects wouldn't get off the phone. And what whining interiors they have, what extremes they think are only tolerable to someone who outlasted the compulsion to live extremely.

Maybe that's all they want me to know. Or is that just another disguise—that identity of extremes, and not needing them? Maybe they're not as deep as they think they are.

There I was, facing the lifted hood again. The real subject was the radiator and the patience that at least got me to Ventura. I had to answer the phone because my defects were calling me back. *I had to answer the phone.* They blamed me for the "stains of coolant," and for the radiator that was "neglected." "Forgetfulness," I said. *"Sabotage,"* they yelled back at me.

The other thing, the weak side, I think it drips here and there so I'll know by the stains not where it is but that I haven't been near it. My defects have trained me. I fixed the leak in the mounted viscera of hoses. The hose root bled because the stalk was over-heated or just worn-out from years of use. But I'm not going to say more than I have to about what happened, and what I think. I really shouldn't be carrying myself anymore like someone who has lost that much.

Night Song

Not all the little birds are sparrows and quiet at three in the morning. I draw the one mocking bird that might never relocate. That mania what it's doing out there it's no longer a type of singing not even mocking bird-like, but tongues of jackals wagging lament alone in the dark in April in the Torrey pine. The long gibing notes build wreckage in my head. What a head. Too much plunges through. As usual. That's my Mocking Bird. That's what it does, that's what the mind and the night want me to know, me, a man diligently plodding to my conclusions, sick of symbolic birds, tallying what I can from my average partial hindsight. And foresight? You can forget about that. I'm looking at *lethargia incurablia* struggling to set in. Still—everything works, the stalk still knows its root, intensity is beauty, one kind of beauty, $^{11}\!/_{16}$ of a truth, I don't mean anything anti-classical, I don't mean anything too Romantical, or even mathematical, and neither do I reject or accept all three. Neither do I know when they'll do something about those hermaphrodite fish living in the rivers of Great Britain that weren't hermaphrodites twenty years ago. I read most of the signs early enough. I don't remember exactly when I stopped drinking out of creeks and streams. On our walks through canyons I never let my daughter or the other kids touch that arsenic juice. And it was hard to stop them. They were small and wild, I was the burro carrying five canteens. Probably too late for me to miss the chemical stew. They're trying to find acceptable levels of poisoned air for the number of cancered people per million. That's what we try for now. Mine are the defenses of a polluted guy obsessed with intensity. Intensity enough is all. I won't stop that. I make a fool of myself thinking I might live any other way. That mocking bird out there in the post-natural wind, the one that either can't locate a mate or attract one or maybe lost one—I hope it gets lucky or chokes on a mosquito's pizzle. Something's got to give.

I DO NOT WORK in formal structures, but I have worked diligently to create "free verse" and prose poem styles that retain the dynamics of what Walt Whitman called "the poetic quality." My current book, *Parking Lot Mood Swing: Autobiographical Monologues and Prose Poetry*, is formulated in prose, but it still retains poetic elements and qualities dynamically concerned with rhythm, repetition, metaphor, dream consciousness, lists, parallelism, diatribe, satire, elegy, comic-hyperbole, dramatic and interior monologue. The subtitle points out distinctions within the genre, that is, imaginative memoir and monologue are a part of my prose poem style in *Parking Lot Mood Swing*. It is well known that Ford and Pound believed poetry should be at least as well written as prose; the opposite is also true, especially in terms of sensitivity to sound, not to mention an active rhythmic phrasing flowing directly or erratically as emotional tone forces arrangements of meaning. Usually let down by what poetry omits, not to mention the glib self-satisfied manner of its implicit sense of such omission, I prefer exploring the works Celine, Miller, Beckett, Marguerite Young, Bellow, Kundera, Vonnegut, the Austrian monologue-novelist Thomas Bernard, Roth, Morrison and Stephen Dixon (in his novel *Gould*). Yes, there are exceptions

327

in poetry, and I am not arguing for the dominance of anything here; writers, once they find themselves, do what they like, that's no secret. We know of Baudelaire's desire to break out of poetry into prose, and within his means he is very successful. Ginsberg makes a strong contribution to the genre in "Supermarket in California," "Howl" and "Kaddish," but little has been said about the disappointing chant form in the concluding parts of each of those poems, and his poetic obligation to add those passages. Shakespeare's incidental prose scattered throughout his plays deliver lively examples of prose poetry: "Bottom's Dream," Iago's monologue of directives to Roderigo to "put money in thy purse," and Falstaff's interior monologues on the battlefield toward the conclusion of *Henry the Fourth* are examples of narrative prose poetry that continue to inform me. And there is room for psychological dimension and rich association concerning the narrator and other characters as Vallejo and Edson show in their prose poems. As a reader and as a writer I have a strong drive for the moment of serious or comic epiphany or non-epiphany that leads to insight. I found many of my "poems" dragging because they sometimes contained subjects demanding greater exposition, something other than lyrical, condensed, image-driven lines. Besides, I became interested in the possibilities of a broader inter-connected narrative within and between separate pieces of prose. That continues to be the basis for my abandonment of any notion of lineation.

VALERIE ROBLES

Belated Birthday

for Scott

The first of April, a decade ago now, but as fresh today as this season's citrus. We were to meet in Mission Grove, and from there, what did we care if the Santa Ana winds pushed us along? There's something simple about not needing to make plans, rising with the desert heat as though the desire to come together was as necessary as breath. We were young and already in love with the weight of ripe oranges, with the way he'd embrace my breast like the Eucharist we are no longer entitled. Oranges were the only fruit then; I'm unlearning love as young as I am. The past will settle into another low inland glow, until the sting of it is gone, but year after year the citrus will continue burning up the trees like ten-thousand tiny suns.

The Huntington Library and Gardens

The sky, low and thick, smoke in a grey afternoon glow. The wet scent of cedar and eucalyptus clung to my skin like linen not quite dry. I was out here admiring these green plums and imaging a place where we might enjoy the stillness of sand. Losing time in a bonsai court with Chinese Elms and California Junipers shaped by wire and light, twisted so tightly together that our minds might go clear as the sky and we might not recall our names, the roads back ...

Fading Empire

I drive the back roads whenever I'm home, no more cities of citrus, only dirt bike trails and sagebrush to absorb the heat, leveling the horizon. Moreno Valley, Riverside, Corona and still the same old sun working its way through the dust like a bruise on my arm. What do I want from this place? I keep coming back, even though I know that tract homes are replacing the groves. Lake Matthews is almost out of water; Perris has receded from drought too. Forget the scent of orange blossoms seeping through the wire window screens, signaling the coming spring. Forget the dock races and jet-ski wars on Lake Elsinore, indulging those insatiable, summer hearts. I'm relying on the dirt to keep my secrets when the rest of the Empire is gone.

A Chance at Letting Go

Sometimes, at night, before the moon could climb over the last stretch of oranges in Woodcrest, I'd sit back in the grass and fondle a patch of poppies recalling the stars I knew as they'd come into focus across the summer sky. I couldn't wait to leave the city. I longed to drive down a street as empty as my pockets, in a town with a pond, to sit under the slack arms of a willow and watch an old woman feed ducks with her bag of bread crumbs, and for once, disregard all the moments a life might add up to . . . Either way, the eucalyptus will shed their skins again. The wind now, stirring the dusty light in a field is little more than a shadow of all I'd ever desired, half glistening in a moment as vague and muffled as the sun. The summer blossoms have withered and blown loose, even the wind is letting go.

I'M A NATIVE Californian, but it wasn't until I moved to the Midwest for a short stint that I realized the power of place. I was obsessed with home, with the Pacific, with the cliffs of whitewashed rock, with the sprigs of seaweed reminding me that everything finds its way back to shore. It's with that sense of home, which, for me, is so firmly rooted in California, that I write prose poems. The prose poem seems the perfect vehicle for my obsession, as it allows for that long cadence of love that doesn't end at the line.

DIXIE SALAZAR

God Speaks to the Death Row Inmate

It is my job to love you like a mother whose child has spit in her face, who has smashed the heirloom grandfather clock, stolen her purse and run. Like a tree loves its fruit, fallen into mushy bilge, like the wind loves the muddy ditch it ruffles, like a fish loves the bait. You with your beard of alibis and drop of stained DNA beneath your nails, with a states evidence smile and rust in your mustache—you who opened up your sister to see how she ticked, who blackmailed the moon, and wept only for yourself when they handed down your sentence. And when they put those photos back in the file, the little girl back in the drawer, I'll still love you because otherwise, my love for her would mean nothing, and because it's my job.

Single File

Waking is always a blow to the kidneys—first sight of sleeping bunkies, steel lockers, hopeless grays and cooped up light. Eight women and two mirrors—somebody's always pissed off. Today I don't forget my ID and napkin. "Wall support, we need wall support, Ladies," Big Cookie screams, as we all hug the walls and "A-hole go to chow" booms over the speaker. "Straight lines, straight lines, keep 'em moving" as we inch forward to the plastic egg and waffle smells at the end of the chow line. Grabbing a light, I pull the first drag off a rollie. We flash IDs—no ID, no food. What do they think? Someone's gonna sneak into prison just to eat the food? We line up again to leave and I get another light from Frosty on B yard coming in, thinking someday these damn things are gonna kill me.

Reflections on "C" Yard

Tuesday, early chow—the yard lieutenant calls herself The Mighty Quinn—one tough bitch. Her mirror glasses reflect the lies I feed her to keep myself fed. But, no lie, she looks like Edwina, my sister who tells her friends I died in a plane crash. Last night I slept in the mouth of a cave, swallowed up in the dripping night. I wanted to keep Edwina safe, but fear dug into my heart, sandbagged my useless feet. She let go of me, and I knew I'd never find a way out. I'd have to make a life in that hole like those prehistoric fish I saw on TV gone blind adjusting to the lack of light. Tonight I roll a cigarette on the yard, walk by the Mexican TV—a blonde woman points a gun at me. I walk by the brother's TV—a baby climbs out of a tire and laughs at me. It looks like somebody spilled mercury all over the yard and the moon is stuck on barbed wire. Big lights fill the sky, blank out the stars like they never were, and I can hear big rigs on the freeway, smashing butterflies home. In my bunk, staring up at water-stains, like maps for lost kids, I hear someone crying into a pee-stained quilt. Tomorrow night I'll go to confession. Tonight, I remember the time I worked the bees from her clotted hair and pulled the stingers from her thumbs, puffed up to the size of cigars. Before I fall asleep, I see Edwina rolling over, confessing all my crimes where I have crept in through the locked back door, a cold draft of air, a tune lodged with the buzzing in her ears like bees behind boarded up windows in a house left empty.

Sister to Brother

No money on my books for shoes, so I had to pay my respects in the finest zories I could borrow. My lawyer begged for this day release, so now there's no mercy on my books either. And they'll transport me back before dark. My first fear is that you won't remember me as you circle heaven. My second fear is that you will. You never forgave me, and now I can't forgive you. But this crush of regret and carnations stops my breath, and my heart is a stone thrown up from a hot core. Last night I dreamed a volcano coming for me, boiling under the full moon between the bars of a steel door. Will my dreams lock you out now that no one can turn you away? The black hearse they slide you into gleams cheerfully. Did you wash it yourself at Red Carpet for a fifty-cent tip? It shines a black mirror that won't reflect me back. I'm just not there—a pool of blankness in the eye of a forgotten storm—a drop of light shrinking in the distance. All that's left to pray to. Whose darkness is greater now, mine or yours? Whose night is heavier?

Contact Visit, County Jail

The big doors will slam behind us like a car crash. Jessee will cover his ears and make that face like a sick dog. When they came and got Mom we had just got Kentucky fried chicken. She wasn't making phone calls but they cuffed her and one of the cops took our chicken. The CPS took me and Jessee to another place where they give us new underwear. There's Tony the driver honking. Mom will hug us together and wet us all up kissing and crying and ask if we've been good. I'm always good—only when Mom tells Jessee Grandpa is at work at the shark farm so he can't visit us and don't cry—she might get out next week ... and then Jessee looks like the Easter bunny just laid an egg in his hand ... then I say Aunt Lily's takin' us to see Superman. When I see Mom's face after that—I'm sorry. Last week we waited downstairs and the other kids were running wild—then they took them up and we had to go back with the driver. He said Mom was sick but I know she was in the hole—wait, that's not Tony—it's the neighbor kids piling into a van with balloons and junk.

Sentencing

I've watched them come back from court, their faces already beginning to set like cool cement, their bodies strung taut as electric wire, zinged with fear, another tattooed teardrop forming, the real ones clotted behind the scabs of their eyes. They look as if the first syllable of a life sentence has just been pronounced. As maybe it has. No one says CYA. No one has to. And the others know too, flashing stony looks of a shared, false courage. And I don't ask them to do another page of math because someone else will count for them now, will count them into lines, count them into tiers, cell blocks and houses. And I won't ask them to write another essay on "My Future" because we all know where they're headed now—on a bus that will pass through waving sprinklers where a sunburnt boy will throw a stick across a carpet of cropped rye for his poodle whose little bell will tinkle softly into twilight as he runs toward the disappearing sun again and again, the stick, the boy and the dog frozen in this endless loop of fetch and return.

T. S. ELIOT PROPOSED that "the supposed freedoms of free verse are only negatives: (1) absence of pattern, (2) absence of rhyme, (3) absence of meter." If this is true, where does that leave the prose poem? Now we are giving up the line in addition, which could lead to the question, what could possibly be gained by using the prose poem form (another contradiction)? Already backed into a corner, the only possible answer that comes to my mind is that one gives in to its oxymoronic, contradictory nature, and lets the poem escape. The nano-narrative emerges, almost a mini-novel, although super-condensed. The rest of the story must be told in individual and personal terms.

These recent poems of mine also were the result of a negative. Let me explain. For about fifteen years I had been teaching visual art and creative writing in the California men's and women's prisons. The poems that resulted from those experiences took mostly a first-person narrator's point of view, an involved viewer/visitor/observer, the outsider looking in. The voice in the poems was a kind of disembodied, floating voyeur. This stance seemed limiting and at times dissatisfying to me.

The discovery of writing in other voices, those of the inmates, was quite liberating, but also challenging. Like attention-starved children, they had pored out their stories, remarkably uncensored. Occasional attempts to color reality seemed almost feebly transparent. The need to be heard and paid attention to, that most basic of human needs, is most effectively denied the incarcerated, and they clamored to be heard.

These voices became the disguise I needed, and with that intact, the need for a vehicle arose (the getaway car, let's say). The prose poem seemed a natural vehicle, with its engine the dominance of narrative. These stories that would be told made their own demands for simplicity and veracity, and the prose poem complied.

It has been a number of years since I have worked in the prisons, but as the voices continue to break out, I am amazed at their strength and the worthy urgency of their demands.

LUIS OMAR SALINAS

Saturday

It's Saturday ... day of apples and turnips on heavy trucks that pass my aunt's house sleeping. My cousin is awake quibbling with his painful back, the corner of the earth surrenders to the anarchy of cows.

We are off to see the movies and the flesh of night is torn into small, little children as angels eat breaded clouds and spiders tell stories to the rabbits of the neighborhood.

A Little Narrative

The day I forgot I was a poet, the heavens were clear—I was lambasting the Mexicans, I was celebrating my birthday. I had my reasons for both. The posters had not arrived announcing me as the Mexican Byron. Neither were there any clouds proclaiming a little shade in the afternoon. I had invited plenty of guests and girlfriends. The topic at hand was poetry, and I felt left out of it. What could I say that would endear me to my audience at this point in the proceedings—before I cut the cake with no candles since I hate fire, and the darkness beyond the fire, equally?

I was beginning to love polemics—villanelles and socialism had been argued both ways. I would even argue with the devil if he were in town. After dinner, we were still in the mood for words. My friends got up and read poems, the syllabics of wind. I sat there shy and quiet for a change, since I had forgotten I was a poet. The evening would not end soon. It lulled on into midnight on the heat's one note. Finally, a cloud crossed the moon like one of Byron's boats on its way to the Italian coast and I poured myself another quiet drink of nostalgia.

Autobiography: The Condensed Version

Out of the hospital and free from cancer, free from social leprosy and the like, I am writing free verse again, still whimsical and poetic with nurses, music and ballet. . . . There's a ham in the house and it's me—my drama goes back to childhood. I was an actor at age six and Don Quixote/Miguel Cervantes was a Spanish friend, and so were my chums at early school. I was in love at an early age with my cousin. My father was a merchant, yet simple and stern. As I grew up we had our battles but somehow the squall reefed and we became great friends before the end. He made money and loved his son. What else? I loved the sea. My mother's mother died young and was beautiful. One of my uncles had three wives and ten children; he was a drinker, but provided and lived a full life. I also drank until the doctors cut that out; I had a few bad patches with the unreal. My friends helped me realize I'm not the only one in the world. I recall Goethe's maxim, Don't overestimate your talent, or underestimate that talent. And I realize seventh heaven comes only while I'm writing or with a good lady friend and love. Yet I owe my life to the devil at times, life that has treated me tenaciously, this miscreant manic-depressive. Nevertheless, I live grandly, if a bit suspicious, and love life with an awkward loneliness.

Love of the Sea

You'll catch him there, walking backwards and forwards before the waves—realistic and unrealistic in whims and subtleties, which, like spindrift, not only reveal his loneliness and love of the sea, but his chivalrous approach to the seagulls whose antecedents go back to the romantics. And that's a long time ago, but to him, it's ever-present. Passing the twentieth or twenty-first century, pathos and sentimentality are all the same. He is turning over shells like bits of clean, clear language, piecing together love from an abstraction and state of mind, the salt of the wind off shore. He's learning his lines and craft. The drama has not begun, nor are the actors prepared as he begins to address the palms. Nevertheless, the ladles are here, Omar's actresses—melancholy lovers, seductive and daring, who are not only talented, beauteous charmers, but sprites turning love into a haunting song, a melody extracted from the sea.

336

Sometimes

Sometimes, and near sometimes, I feel aging, but then again my second youth and romanticism flash through my veins like a silver fish and I'm young again. The girls I've loved, those I haven't, and the women I might love, all make up for my sadness and intoxicating illusions. I have no fear of ending up unknown or unrecognized. The time I dedicate to my work is the time I dedicate to life, its many roads and all its random beauty. If somebody tells me I'm old, I answer, Old for what? Tell me what you know and I'll tell you something you don't. Poetry is not ideas. If I lean on my cane too heavily it's because I won't sit down for anything; I'm a born fighter, a lover of the solid earth.

WITH THE EXCEPTION of "Saturday" from his first book *Crazy Gypsy*, Salinas did not employ the prose poem. A deep imagism, an element of the surreal combined with his ability to target specific emotional states, are the hallmarks of most of Salinas's lined poems. But early on he singles out "Saturday" as a prose poem to convey a simple and quotidian atmosphere of the neighborhood while undercutting that texture with arresting images.

Toward the end of his writing career, Salinas's vision expands and takes in more of the physical and the potentially metaphysical. *Elegy for Desire* contains four prose poems, three of them very near the end of the book. His wit is always in play ("Autobiography: The Condensed Version") but now he wants to take a grander, more weighty view: "I was beginning to love polemics—villanelles and socialism had been argued both ways. I would even argue with the devil if he were in town" ("A Little Narrative"). He wants to collect and offer to the light his major themes and modest conclusions ("Love of The Sea"), and the prose poem form is the one he found that often best accommodated his themes, voice, and view at this point in his life.

—*Christopher Buckley*

ELIOT SCHAIN

Berkeley, Without Mantras

At the beginning of the 1970s I was on the west edge of Berkeley roaming the railroad tracks with somebody else's empty bottle of wine. Not that I was unhappy; in my backpack I had a copy of *Bhagavad-Gita* and a vial of eucalyptus oil, but Berkeley was a strange town back then; everyone knew an era had chewed itself to pieces and all that was left were a few raw chins and slippers panhandling on Telegraph.

I can recall sitting on my friend's window-sill listening to Phil Ochs and realizing he was about to hang himself. It was a beautiful spring day—the cherry blossoms all pink beneath me, the Bay in the distance dotted with white sails. Yet there was a palpable feeling of emptiness, as if a great leader had passed on. The only people with any real zip were the Moonies and the Communists—the hippies were beleaguered and hiring guard dogs to protect their vegetables.

So I retreated into the novels of the Great Depression and began dreaming about the past. I'd be riding my bike down to the Marina— worry beads dangling over the odometer—when suddenly Texas would pop into my head, all gray and flat, a Model T bumping down the long lonely stretch of highway. I'd pull into the Fotomat, and the bang of the screen door would echo like the bang of a screen near Lubbock—its hinges as sturdy as knuckles, its paint peeling away from the hot dry wind.

This was my San Simeon—drab, isolated, one lonely radio cracking in the parlor. How infinitely more peaceful than those peace marches across the Bay! all cluttered with indignation and aphrodisiacs, hundreds of nice people dressed up as a Trident submarine. Whenever Daniel Ellsberg would speak it would rain, so I'd go home disenchanted—cook a burrito, or play backgammon with the astrologer who lived next door. He was a nice guy, and a wizard in the garden—cauliflower, spaghetti squash, Near-Eastern eggplant.

But I wanted something more. I wanted a girl born and bred in a calico dress, who'd never heard of the *Bhagavad-Gita* or the Mothers of Invention. I wanted to stuff Berkeley into a hatbox—things age better that way. Phil Ochs died in March, and the ground crew came to tear up the grass in front of the Library. It didn't matter—no one rallies there anymore; they're all up on Frat Row singing Nazi songs. But I can't say I'm doing much better. In an age lit by false light, we all gather the flotsam of the past and hang on.

Westering Angels

Overlooking the Straits of Carquinez, winter of 1993, the water is the color of pewter, and the hills of Contra Costa rise abruptly from it, their emerald grasses dimming, their canyons like the folds in a brain absorbing our decline. All the rain that falls on the inland valleys— the mountains, the plateaus—all the fears that stall over this state we call California come together here, squeezing through this narrow passage before ballooning into two huge wings and mixing with the ocean, a geographically spiritual moment in a place equipped to understand one.

The oil tankers come here to drink, gliding in under the bridges to Benicia and Martinez—two old towns that straddle this divide, their mystical resource rushing from colored drums on the hillside, down through pipelines and into those massive hulls (so deceptively clam on the water) that drift to the world like milkmen. And huge cooling towers roil the sky with what they say is steam, though on Tule days, those streets smell like a dirty coin, and that steam mixes with the wild ions of the nearby Naval Weapons Station, then settles into the marshes to breed a genetically different age. In the school where I teach, one of my best students had his insides rearranged because of the epidemic asthma. Next time he'll be born that way and we can get rid of the knives.

In 1941 this excess looked like progress—capitalism reborn, jobs for men who'd been wolfing clandestinely in railroad yards and women fresh from euphemistic "trips." We are wedded to this machine, and worse than the rearranged insides is the plague of drunken fathers taking hammers to the stained glass because they haven't worked in years, resent their children's education, their wife's ability to verbalize—who've driven haywire through this culture of abundance, until they've become drug-addicted, food-addicted, TV-addicted, or in the final victory just somebody else, their offspring left to balance on demented vertebrae.

Some manage to live here anyway, amid the rainbow slicks and Coke cans. They climb the hills of the shoreline and gaze west, where the sun is setting into the eyes of the sleeping princess—Mount Tamalpais, beneath which a packed auditorium chants to the beat of a Tibetan monk, or claps, if they're still too Christian, to the news of a resurrected Dodo bird. They heal themselves with the odorous animal inside, and one is reminded of the 1960s, when the people of this city believed if enough of them collectively thought the Bomb away, it would reverse if ever dropped and return through its portal to God. Now the word *reverse* takes on a different meaning, more akin to *desist*, just as *nature savvy* has come to mean *happy* when the wind shifts and the emissions are blowing away from your own child's elementary school.

On clear days this channel is magnificent. Sitting with the Buddha in your lap, you can almost believe survival will surprise us again, that the Turnaround Store in downtown Martinez will grow and feed on the malls—that credit will no longer mean ecstasy, that the peripatetic will stop pumping gas with one hand up the ass of the devil . . . that the drunken remains will pause long enough to insulate their children, in part from those pioneers in Marin whose howling is scaring the coyotes.

Oil will disappear from here eventually, and these towns will gleam again, send paddle-boats into clean water. And these children will no longer have to assume the spanking of abandoned siblings before they've heard of the Constitution, but will grow strong and wily, and pass on man's victory over his own need to be the victor, a memory of when this titanic passage was thick with black lubricant, and the wizardry resorted to made things fast—clean, dark hills beneath starry skies, and water, sweet water (78% of who we are) rushing through this prophecy to inflate the westering angels.

In San Francisco

They all come here—the pansy-assed, tired of television, the poets, determined to get drunk. They come because the enemy is more apparent here. Not the enemy beyond, but the one within, the rift down the center—out one eye the gull sailing over Alcatraz, out the other, the evolution of Descartes—towers beveled into the hillside, the winds from the Pacific fingering them daily.

Because this city is Western Civilization stacked against an apotheosis of natural beauty, there is no better place to contemplate the cruelty of love—the incompatibility of Descartes and the gull, two halves obsessed, unwilling to satisfy. Not mature love, but young, foolish love—two riders on a single horse, one long suspended stride.

Even if you're from Ohio, sell insurance—tolerate a bad marriage, you will still feel it as you look through Chinatown to the moonlit Bay. You will appreciate the scent of new mountains, suffer again the torture of physics.

As the wino with the baked face begins to wail, the hotel lights above will blink off, and you will wish that no one—no city had ever touched you. But your wish will be a mistake, for as you begin to sing with the wino, and billow with crisis, the battery inside will be recharging—the thin peel of your voice a prelude for the synthesis yet to come.

THE PROSE POEM is the logical response to Emerson's call for a new voice capable of expressing our uniquely American experience. When Whitman first answered the call, and extended the poetic line beyond iambic pentameter, he created a style that could incorporate America's diversity and promise through a sound simultaneously pedestrian and sublime. A century later, Ginsberg allowed that voice to give full, untethered expression to anguish over American materialism and the horror of modern warfare. In my own poems, I try to synthesize the two by pivoting—within the extended line—from irony to sentiment, pessimism to hope, the pedestrian to the sublime.

In my experience, the rhythm of such a poem progresses toward climax about three-quarters of the way through, then comes to a resigned acceptance of the paradox of being human. San Francisco is a particularly apt place to write such a poem, because it is here at the end of the American road that we still allow the faith of the pioneer to mix easily with the sorrows of self-destruction. It is here that oceanic emptiness on the horizon can both stimulate our dreams and feed our grief. It is here that we find the natural home for a poetic speech the Transcendentalists hoped would contain everything.

DEBORAH SMITH

Parked Along a Dirt Road Outside Redlands with My Ex-Lover

"She lost the baby," he told me, and began to shiver as his head found the warmth in the arch of my collarbone. His fingers were clenched tightly against his head, digging their pared-moons into the scalp, as if his breath depended on it, as if his body would bleed like a punctured sand bag trailing in circles from its noose. With some coaxing, I pried his hands away, and he kissed me. I pulled away, but saw in his eyes that he needed me. Had he ever needed me that much when we were together? Would there ever be another moment when I could give him "everything" he wanted? The moon was all the light we needed, as my heart strayed further into the dark.

Emergency: Loma Linda Hospital, CA

We are in the emergency room, waiting. My grandmother can barely move after falling against her bedroom dresser. Purple rings swell from her eye to the whole left side of her body, like ripples from a pond where a rock is hurled and forgotten. She hasn't slept in a week, she tells me, because a man in a dark suit stands over her bed. "What does he look like Grandma?" I ask. "He's sorta faceless, like it's been scooped out of a bowl." I think of the dark plums resting at the roots of our plum tree, their inside's gutted out from the crows that peck at the dark, sweet flesh. The same invisible crows that circle her bed at dusk, waiting for her skin to dry, to become a bed in which to nest. Outside, people scramble to haul a gurney out of an ambulance. The patient is rushed to the building like a main course—a swarm of paramedics following the scent of blood. Grandma is still mumbling about demons, she is after all only a crazy eighty-six-year-old woman with a spreading bruise. Her turn is bumped again as if we had all the time in the world . . .

After a Break-Up

I drove the car with two fingers, like a blessing to the steering wheel or a prayer to myself. It was raining, and I was driving through a canyon—a dangerous lick of road that leads out towards the desert, where nothing lives but fifty-year-old cacti, and the fire-brightness of each star. Your memory felt like a spine of fingerprints tapping against my skull. I wanted to feel the night air tighten inside my body, twisting together that hole in my chest where I could feel the tide of the Pacific Ocean tugging me to go west, where the beach once eroded beneath our toes. As I drove, I thought about the time we wrestled, the hot wetness of our hands ingrained in each other's grip, and my black shirt soaked with your dusty scent. I remember how, behind us, the clouds shifted, and we heard the gasp of the ocean prying the shore apart.

Inherited Beauty

My grandmother once said, "A perfect breast is one that can fill a large champagne saucer." As she said this, she took a heavy drag of her cigarette, and looked expectantly down at my own chest. My body sank under her gaze, and my prepubescent breasts seem to tuck into themselves, like snails recoiling from a salty-fingered touch.

Grandma was the town beauty of Versailles, Missouri, courted by men from several different counties. She left her farm at seventeen, and married an Italian who grew the sweetest onions in town. After her husband died of TB, she met my Grandpa, a man who gave her the "best orgasms" in her entire life. They divorced, remarried, and divorced. The next man was a Christian Scientologist who refused to see the doctor even after his testicles swelled to the size of navel oranges. He was the "dumbest of them all" she used to say. And, after that, a man I knew as Grandpa Max, head of the local Mormon Church. He brought breakfast to her in bed every day for fifteen years, never allowed her to drive, and threatened to divorce her when she once wanted to ride a horse. Jim, her last husband, was twenty years her junior, and stole everything of value from her.

344

As I sit beside her hospital bed, she mumbles these stories over and over till her lips dry, and I have to apply ointment on them again. All these different men, different lives, dangle in front of her like a mobile gently driven by the music of wind. I stand up to fix her pillow, and though her eyes are opaque and barely able to open, she says, "You're beautiful." I look back at this woman whose face is hollowed, whose hair is dead weeds, whose breasts have long been chopped from her frail body, and I respond, "It's because I look like you."

WHEN WORKING in prose form, you'll find that you have a harder time lying. You cannot manipulate the look, and there are no clever line breaks to campaign the poem's meaning. There is only your voice, your message, filling the white space to the end of the page. Because I am compelled to write honestly, the integrity of the voice lends itself to the pieces that I create. To write a poem successfully is to be able to have an open conversation with the soul. Prose poetry allows for that kind of truth-seeking.

BARRY SPACKS

Busybodies

My next door neighbor Kathleen complained to the parents of the
cap-gun kids: "Give 'em toy guns, later it's real ones!" Later she told
me: "I shouldn't have said that—they'll torch my house!" Ah no,
Kathleen, too sad. So we trade mock-advice with a laugh: it's best
not to coo at babies, might count as sex-abuse; or go hit your horn
when a kid in a car cuts you off on the freeway?—he may need to
shoot you!

And then, that same day, I'm walking Golita beach where a kid
can't seem to get his kite aloft. "Run at the wind!" people yell, but he
runs in circles—the flimsy thing won't do right so more folks become
a Village to set him straight, the kite starts up, I'm shouting "Let out
more string!" but he runs in more circles—flop; a sad "Aaaah ..." yet
some day, who knows, maybe he'll learn to run at the wind? let out
more string? share the sweet world with my neighbor Kathleen?

Meeting the Mermaid

Man goes to pee at a Hollywood party, finds tiny fishes, fronds,
Neptune-cave in the happy bowl. Can't express himself there, so
he moves along to another bathroom—they have lots—lifts the lid,
looks down at a prancing aquatic unicorn, not the gentle Christ-
kind but a mini-unicorn with a swirling golden horn, a major prick-
penetrater. So our man, in distress now, races toward a far suite—
pink lampshades, closets full of flimsy dresses—and in the bowl, *hola*,
a miniature mermaid. "Oh," she says, "this fable did not bring you
here to *pee*."

Fame

I walked my friend's dog down Panchita Street, flaunting my soft
black Australian hat. I'd been house-sitting, dog-walking, reading
all week Richard Brautigan, who wrote that the beauty is all in the
saying, who would not tie the bird of lunacy by a short string to his

toe, but would rather let her fly in long loopy moves like a book's page-turning, all in the name and the acting-out of freedom—who shot off his head absolutely, done in, they say, by the Bitch Fame-Goddess, broken on her gerbil-treadwheel, depressed, uncheered, remaining a time unidentified so de-headed there and vodka-drowned and *Not,* in Bolinas, California—talk about freedom!

I think he would have liked my hat, and surely my friend's dog Ida, black-and-white border collie with yearning eyes who'd herd anything to safety, sheep or writers, doing her dog-work. "Fame," blind Milton wrote, "is the spur," but he added little of use in Bolinas about "these terrifying honors."

AFTER YEARS OF functioning exclusively as a linear lyricist, I started my first prose poem in an ongoing e-mail exchange with a former student. I do a lot of these, and always with a "rule," in this case an exact requirement of 101 words per ping and its answering pong. I found that the prose poem form engaged me beyond game-playing limitations because it promised ease, especially in terms of structure. I usually work, in linear style, with a magnet leading to a strong finish. For me, prose poetry has its appeal rooted in an invitation to be casual, to elaborate with incidental inventions, to feel less "formal" in the course of composition. But I do see, in reviewing the three poems here, that I still have a tendency, a penchant, for the punchline.

DAVID ST. JOHN

Weather

It might have been the pitch of weather, the hot winds blowing in off
the desert & rattling in the high limbs of the palms. It might have been
the way she posed in the doorway dressed in that old cowgirl outfit,
the long white fringe shaking so erotically—not to mention the two
tiny silver pistols perched on her hips, & that truly ridiculous silver
badge like a forgotten Christmas ornament on her chalk suede vest.

It might even have been the night sirens blazing up the city
streets, their floodlights scouring the alleys & rusting fire escapes
while the dogs next door howled. I don't know what it was, really,
but I know pretty soon we were on the kitchen floor, knocking over
the chairs as we ripped off those lawful clothes, laughing & biting, as
the newscaster joked about the heat of the day to come, tomorrow,
whether we wanted all this weather, or even not.

Simple Blues

Twelve. The Fresno County Public Library, checking out Samuel
Charters's *The Country Blues* & Paul Oliver's *Blues Fell This Morning*.
Blind Lemon Jefferson, Ma Rainey, Robert Johnson. Took that '30s
Hawaiian guitar, with is gorgeous swirled black finish, to play those
bottleneck & slide riffs. Later, put on Mississippi John Hurt to go
sleep at night. Gave my friends the Chess editions of Howlin' Wolf
at Xmas. Twenty-one, living on espresso & mescaline, in the middle
of a breakdown. Walked out at 3 AM to the empty lot next to the small
house, my wife and son asleep, passing out face down in the dew-
drenched furrows, only to awaken to a sound reverberating through
limbs & soul—the flap of an envelope peeled back, lifted open to the
brain. Brutal drum-pulse in the narrow canals. The sorrowing. The
fear.

Passing

Passing, once again someone is passing, & in its simplicity the corporeal dust rises to be dispersed along the winds, the winds passing as the spirit is passing, beyond the margins of the self into its death, the spirit passing, passing, the passing over, the spirit passing, cold in its chill garments, passing all along the evening, & in its simplicity the soul is passing from the body to the realm of the other, of the ether, of the passing of the breath rising in its final celebration, its final elaboration, & who is it we feel this evening passing, passing by, passing beyond, passing from us forever & unto the other side?

Focus

Focus, focus, *focus*. The lens: turning, though the image refuses to come clear. Spring of '68, I lived in a house called "Focus," a perfect metaphor for the time, the age, my own confusion. Its door—the coffin-aperture to this sanctuary—the physical lens through which every friend I'd ever made in this life passed . . . this house, this lens . . . imperfect dilation of our vision, its fierce resolutions. Focus, *focus*, focus. At 18 only certain clarities richochet around one, & the drugs & the friends, & the prayers all passed within that certain shelter. As did the woman I would marry within the year. Gathering constellations of future consolations, those friends, their sweet aspirations—(OK, no more Latinate abstractions of passage).

One day its inhabitants decided the house needed a name, a commemorating appellation, a rare distinction reflecting its service in a sign, a script. Who said it first? Who knows; but in the Super 8 movie Bonnie took just moments later, Steve's lettering in that mock Art Nouveau script—so popular in rock posters of the day— (Along the cream-colored frame above the door, which was open, I remember) the name: FOCUS a fluid, shifting signifier of that wooden lens, that house, the box camera within which we all slept & smoked dope & fucked & played music on fiddles, guitars, electric bass, dulcimers, & mandolins. This single fluid lens clarifying the many paths leading away from this house, & the name above the door signifying to anyone passing through the way we all quite simply came in & out of FOCUS—even then we knew some of us were crystalline, some still blurred, unclear, unwanted—but all of us were there, poised & restless, ready to be delivered into those lives indeterminate & yet already fixed, in & on some new vision, some dark pupil widening with light.

THE FIRST DISTINCTION I try to make with friends and students—both my university and adult students—who ask about the "prose poem" form is to note that, in French, one knows them as *poèmes en prose*. That is, the emphasis is on the piece of writing as a *poem* that happens to be in non-lineated "prose," yet the same requirements of music, phrasing, and the imaginative conjunctions of image and thought we think of as belonging to poems, et cetera, all remain close to those of a "conventional" poem. Of course, all forms (poetic and otherwise) are born to be subverted and exploded. In his superb introduction to *The Prose Poem: An International Anthology*, now thirty years old (still the single most important guide to the prose poem and of course now long out of print), Michael Benedikt outlines in compelling and persuasive detail the many virtues as well as the remarkable flexibility and fluidity of the prose poem. In recent years, we've also seen the emergence of more "prose shorts." The popularity of paragraph-length or slightly longer vignettes in prose (also called "short shorts" by some of my fiction friends) has grown enormously. Jayne Anne Phillips's marvelous collection *Black Tickets*, of course, contained terrific examples of these. Of my generation, Christopher Merrill, Gary Young, and Killarney Clary have all written brilliant prose poems. And though a bit older, Charles Simic is a wonder. I also love the work of David Young—who himself, along with Stuart Friebert, has edited a wonderful anthology of prose poems. I think of my own work in this arena as being both "*poèmes en prose*" and prose shorts as well. Some simply sound more musical to me, more elliptically poetic to my ear; others seem more narrative, even more raw in their progression. But I make no apologies here. I just love writing these; and though, in this work, I might justify the lines, I don't feel the need to justify myself.

JOSEPH STROUD

During the Rains

Driving through the rain to Minden this morning, I saw two men walking in a lake that a week ago was pasture, two men ankle-deep in the shallows, stringing barbed wire and trying to hammer fence posts into water, one holding a stake, the other with ferocity swinging a maul, horses standing around them, miserable, cattle up to their hocks in water, the Carson plain in flood, fields runneled with gills and freshets, culverts washed out, hillsides loosening, slipping, everything disintegrating, coming apart, the dead bear I found yesterday below Loope Canyon, skeleton unlocking, carcass sodden, dissolving in rain, and now this morning those two men near Minden driving stakes into water, stringing wire across a lake, trying to keep it all in, trying to keep it whole, driving these words into the page, as if this could make the bear stay, as if I could lash the body together, not let anything come apart, dissolve, wash away.

Elsewhere

My father picks up my brothers and me at the swimming pool. He is angry and smells of gin. We get in the car. No one speaks. He drives back to the wedding party to get my mother. An aunt takes me aside, puts her hands on my shoulders—"Your father is a good man. Remember this. Sometimes we don't mean to do the things we do." In the car, my mother sits up front. Against her cheek she holds a towel wrapped around ice. We drive across the hot L.A. basin. We are on the freeway, among the other cars with families inside. We are all driving, from somewhere, to somewhere else.

I pick up the phone and it's a woman's voice. She wants to speak with my father. I go back to the dinner table. My brothers drink their milk. My mother looks at her plate. I wait for my father to come back. Our dog is asleep under the table. His name is *Fury*. When my father sits down, he's wearing a face. We go back to eating. Then we're in the den. With our first TV. We all sit before it. No one gets up to change to a new channel. From the night outside, our window glows like a screen. If you were to look in, you would see what appears to be a family.

Over the Edge

When I step to the edge and look down, they're just getting out of the smashed pickup. She appears dazed, stunned, and he's trying to pull something out of the cab, gives up, and looks around. A heavy snow is falling. They begin a slow, awkward climb up the forty foot slope. I start down toward them, kicking footholds in the ice. Halfway, I brace my feet, reach out my hand to his, and pull him up to me. He scrambles past. She's having difficulty. She can't make the few feet between us, so I edge down a little further until our hands can grasp. But then I begin to slip, and for a moment I think we're both going to lose it, we're going to tumble to the bottom. But we don't. We clutch each other, then crab our way sideways to the top. The wind is blazing ice off of the pass. Cars drift past in the blizzard, eerie faces behind glass peering out. I help the man and woman into my car. They don't say much. He has a gash on his forehead. But they're OK she insists. *We're OK.* You're lucky you're not dead, I'm thinking, wondering what they felt when they hit the ice and swerved over the edge. I crank the heater to high. The windows begin to fog. We're all breathing hard. I catch his eyes in the mirror. He looks away, ashamed, I think, the way he hurried up the slope without her. The woman turns in her seat. She's wiping the blood from his face. *We're going to make it,* she tells him. And we drive into the white heart of the storm.

Sky Diving

A morning in autumn, years ago. I was living out back in the shed, the pony barn we called it, a simple white-washed room full of windows, with a bed, woodstove, bookshelves, a desk. I was in bed looking up through the skylight, past the bare branches of the walnut trees, into the sky where a group of seagulls rode a thermal in a huge rotating gyre. I was thinking about the skydiver with a camera strapped to his back, a filmmaker, who the week before leaped after a group of divers who had formed a great circle in the sky—which he plunged into, spinning the camera around. The TV news had shown the footage. I was thinking of this when Sarah called out my name and walked into the shed. I can still see her, standing there, blue jeans and sandals, white T-shirt, her hair damp from a shower, smelling of balsam and resin. She had recently returned from Germany, leaving her husband, beginning the divorce, the ugly struggle. She stood there, hesitant, embarrassed, saying the words she must have rehearsed. I could not cross over. I couldn't even manage the dignity of a *no*. I just let the moment move into the larger day, into the season and the years that have brought me here. I let her stand there to make small talk, to listen as I told her about the news program, how the divers broke off from their circle, doing backflips, tumbles, a crude aerial ballet. And then the part in the film where their chutes unravel and they are suddenly jerked up out of sight while the camera continues to record—the wobbling horizon, ground enlarging from below, the landscape beginning to swing crazily—and you realize something's wrong, the cameraman is out of control. On the morning of the jump, among the crowd and confusion, he hadn't been paying attention, distracted, thinking maybe of his cameras and lenses, and didn't put on his chute, which he realized only when he reached for the cord. And there I was talking away, wondering aloud what his thoughts were those last moments plunging into the uprushing ground—while Sarah stood there, the expression on her face looking at me—our own time and terror crashing down with us as we hurtled to earth.

Taste and See

Walking the trail to the waterfall, I decide to take a new route, and soon I'm in an old conifer forest, when I see them, crowning through duff and needles, a dozen or so mushrooms. I gather them into my pack, and back at the cabin take Arora from the shelf, try to key them: brown cap, white gills, rosy blush to the flesh, partial veil. So. Perhaps they're Blushers (*Amanita rubescens*), edible, if cooked, but poisonous raw. "Not recommended," Arora says. And besides, they're *amanitas*, same family as the Destroying Angel (*Amanita ocreata*). Arora advises, "Better to be safe than sorry." But look at them, spread out on the table, fresh from the earth, delicate gills, stalk turning salmon, an odor of autumn and wood smoke. What might they taste like? What if I sauté a few in butter, with shallots, a dash of *fumé blanc*, some black pepper. Then sit down and wait for the blush. Maybe put on some music, some plainsong. Or something Tibetan, tantric, Gyuto monks chanting the Mahakala sadhana. Lie back. Listen. Wait for the quickening pulse, delirium, visualizing Mahakala, demonic lord of wrath and transcendence, with his six arms, his dagger, his necklace of skulls. I could do this. I could see the worlds within this world. I could invite danger into my life. Look at them, *amanitas*, rubescent blushers, little darlings. I could spin the wheel. Step out on the edge. I could taste and see.

THE TERM "PROSE POEM" has always seemed an oxymoron to me (is the moron pulling the ox, or the other way around?). But I've never come across a better term to use in its place. As a writer, I'm not particularly concerned with theories, or definitions, what a prose poem is, what a prose poem isn't. What concerns me is the writing. When I begin a piece, I don't usually know what kind of shape or form it will take. I am listening to cadence and tone, to rhythm and sound. The *subject* may be given, but the *poem* has to be hunted. Part of the process of writing for me is discovering not only where the poem is going, but how it is getting there. If details (or narration, or scope) begin to overwhelm the line, then more often than not I'll let the page margins determine the shape, and focus my attention elsewhere (plot, texture, scene, etc.). Part of the craft is adjusting to the terrain. You don't want to wear heavy hiking boots on the beach, and flip-flops are not much use in climbing the granite slopes of the Sierra. I'm sure there are greater Theoretical, Aesthetic, and Philosophical issues at stake in all this, but ultimately, I don't care if the poem is a prose poem, or a poem poem, verse or free verse; what I care about are those poems that make a difference in my life. When I find them, I cherish them. And I try my best to write them.

ROBERT SWARD

Dr. Sward's Cure for Melancholia

1. Melancholia

> A grief without a pang...
> —*Coleridge*

Podiatrist Father:

"I'm the dead one, remember? You think maybe now a little peace and quiet I deserve? *Gottenyu!* Thirty years in a casket. Forest Lawn Cemetery. Palm Springs. Well, I can't complain. It's not so bad! But here you are ... again. So, what is it this time? You got a problem maybe with your foot? Your ankle? You're limping. California Foot and Ankle you should see. No? You won't see a podiatrist? Instead you drive ten hours to a graveyard. *Meshuggener.* And look at you, *schlepp, schlepp, schlepp,* poor feet, poor posture, and the eyes—blank. Thirty years I'm dead. But look at me, son. Never better. It's true. That's right. You can die, son, and still—you can enjoy! And you, *oi!* With a face to sadden God. It used to be the living saw the ghosts of the dead. Now it's the dead see the living. So many ghosts! And all the time sad. Once a mind these people had. Once a mind *you* had. A little animal, even, an animal you had inside you. Look at me, son. I gave you breath, remember? A little 'mood disorder' you call it? The 'neurochemistry of emotion'? 'Pharmacotherapy'? What kind of talk is that? Maybe it's not your 'disorder' needs treatment, maybe it's the treatment needs treatment. You think the dead don't read? Melancholia. Black Dog. Depression. Call it what you want. 14 million people a year got what you got. One out of every ten people you see ... and children too, and twice as many women as men. *Oy!* All your life ... look at you, look at you ... and now this. Dogs even got an inner life. I got. Dogs got. You think maybe a little joy you could use? *Oy!* The problem with you is you're not a dog."

2. A Face to Sadden God

"When your father dies, you move to the head of the line. This is a surprise? Truth is, I'm more alive than you think. Ready? So, what is death? You learn to walk without your feet. It's not so bad. Of course you're not your body. You never were. But you're not your mind either. *Oy*, look at you, look at you—With a face to sadden God. You and your 'neurotransmitters.' Mr. 'Mood Disorder.' Some people, when they got no— there's a word. In you it's missing. *Nephesh.* 'Soul' it means! Three years in Hebrew school and what did you learn? No *Nephesh*, no Hebrew, no soul! 'Receptors' you got. 'Serotonin' you got. Zoloft. Paxil. A pill to improve—what? A pill now you need, but not an arch support? Me, I got a reason to look the way I do. I'm dead. But *Nephesh*, at least I got *Nephesh.* Listen . . . There are three parts to the human soul. *Nephesh* is one: Cobra soul. Snake soul. Even to be a reptile you need a soul. It's true. So, where's your *Nephesh?* Second soul is your mind. What wakes when you wake? What thinks when you think? And where has it gone, this mind you have lost? Three: *Eudaimonia*, virtue, conscience. *Eu*, it means 'happy.' *Daimon*, 'spirit.' So, Goddammit, where's your *eudaimonia?* This you need to put your stink in order. Order you need to be happy! Rabbi says, 'The soul needs a soul, the soul needs a soul, the soul IS this and *that* has a soul.' Three souls, one body. But you, where's the *Nephesh?* Where's the mind? Of course I'm dead, but at least there's a ME to be dead."

3. In Heaven, Too, There Are Jews

"Up here they got Soul Retrieval. Lucky for you, son, lucky I'm dead. That's right. I *know* some people. In heaven, too, there are Jews. So, when did you last see—? When did you last have— *Nephesh*, breath, soul? *Nephesh* leaves, but *Nephesh*, it's true, you can bring back. Rabbi says. Meanwhile God says you need to gain a little weight. Thinning hair. Poor posture. Look at you, look at you! Happiness is missing. Confidence is missing. Even what's missing is missing. And that soul of yours? It's splintered, it's in pieces. It's in the Kabbalah. *Ruach, ruah, neshama* . . . all gone. Your soul has left you. So, without the invisible, son, there's no you. What's to be done? A father dies and the son becomes a zombie? Of course you miss me. I'm dead. So what? I'm somewhere else. This is a change? Goddammit, I've always been somewhere else. Where does a father end? Where does a son begin? Pay attention. Time to get the soul back. That's right. But to retrieve a soul you need a soul."

4. The World Is Broken

"What? What do you think I am? I'm alive, I'm dead. Same as everyone else. And you? You got a wife, she wants a divorce. You got another wife. *She* wants a divorce. Now *Eudaimonia* is gone. And you, you want a divorce from—who? Yourself? So. One side of the self is at war with the other? The question is: Which side is which? So divorce yourself and see what happens. How many times do I have to say it? You think the world is broken? Of course it's broken and it's your fault. Enough! Enough! I've said before: Thoughts have souls. Souls have souls. Everything's a covering. And you, with that mug of yours, what are you covering? Tell me, What is a human being? What makes a person a person?

"Yes, you're broken. And yes, you're only visiting your life. So, fine, fine. Why not live then as if you were still among the living? Don't start eternity being depressed."

PHIL TAGGART

9503 Maryknoll

Maryknoll to Allerton, turn right on Tarreyton, left on Mulberry, name changes to Slausen, right on Pioneer and on to the 605, to the Pomona, briefly the 5 spills into the 101, off on Vermont, right on Sunset and into Children's Hospital Los Angeles. Every week.

From junior high into high school my sister and I alternate. She with Dad. Me with Mom. The power divide dark secrets entwined in our family. We are not happy. Janet. Our sister. The youngest is dying. Leukemia.

Somewhere in route. In the car. In my 14-year-old arms. She died. I carried her in as I had time after time before. Instead of sending me to the waiting room with the others. Waiting. I was sequestered. Alone in a room. They didn't think I knew.

I knew. Mom was somewhere signing Janet's body away. An hour alone, I felt relief and in that absolution, I was smothered.

We drove home. No one cried. No one spoke of her. Our house dense with guilt. I was lucky. She died in my arms. I felt her serenity as she left her body. Chemo-ravaged hair gone pincushioned for a maybe cure tomorrow. She was 6 years old. Just out of kindergarten.

Maryknoll to Allerton, turn right on Tarreyton, left on Mulberry, name changes to Slausen, right on Pioneer and on to the 605, to the Pomona, briefly the 5 spills into the 101, off on Vermont, right on Sunset and into Children's Hospital Los Angeles. Every week.

Adjustments

His son a memory, Roberto mows my neighbor's lawn. His adjustment to the fall of the working class. The little money he makes supports three generations living under one roof. They're better off than most. His son tried and caught the last wave of oil as it crashed and the tide receded to another continent. He then contracted a disease that only money could cure, moved his family back home and drank himself to death. Old determined Roberto rarely smiles, puts the mower into an old pick-up truck and drives away.

A Lifetime Ago

I peek out the window into a still Summer night. The heat's demanding. And kids rescued in cars-parked music-pulse release. I remember me, Dean, Critter and Quinn in Whittier on the corner of Maryknoll and Allerton seduced by the night cool relief to an asphalt melting day. An escape delectable. Its joy lost in its sensual iconic continuum. Young boy's *cool* exudes in taunts shared around a **Honda 150 Dream.** We didn't really do. We cruised, talked and told our selves the secret. The heat subsides. Sleep, dream, wake up and walk to school past Lisa's Tacos then Frank's Market where Frank and Sam were shotgunned dead in a robbery a long time ago.

Orange Hair

Mohawked homeless punk screams a mantra on Ventura's beach promenade. **SEXVIOLENCESEXVIOLENCE.** A winter cold, Southern California morning cold, enough to hurt but not kill a young man, a regular on Main Street. **You got money for poor white trash?** A better line than most and he knows to not sidewalk lounge in front of the liquor store. A mantra shift, I pass later on my bike. The cold stinging my hands. He is rapt and screaming. **VIOLENCEVIOLENCEVIOLENCE.**

MANY OF MY POEMS are short-line pieces that have stringent breaks. In using the prose form I can reinterpret and reopen the rhythm possibilities every time I revisit the poem. When reading aloud a prose poem I usually change rhythms from reading to reading and view these poems something akin to the polyrhythm of jazz. Most of my poems start in the prose form, then I find the most pleasing way to cut the poem, but some don't want to be cut.

AMY UYEMATSU

From Tatsuya to Little Willie G.—
An Argument for Dark-Eyed Romeos

1. The Two Georges

Maybe love begins with Greek gods—though at 13 I yawn through
the myths and Mr. Curry's picky distinctions between Ionic, Doric,
and Corinthian. But when Maharis, the first George, rides into my
living room on "Route 66," a new adventure every Friday night in his
shiny corvette, I'm inspired. Maharis is not just gorgeous but a street-
smart brunette—and early on I can measure my growing resistance
to that all-American preference for the blond and boring co-star. As
if on cue, my second George—*née* Chakiris, which almost rhymes—
dances right into that Saturday matinee at the Crown. Three and
a half times, I cry through *West Side Story,* smitten once more by
another pretty Greek—rooting, of course, for his darker crew, the
Puerto Rican Sharks against the Irish Jets, my life already marked
from too many racial scuffles, too many friendships snuffed out at
the schoolyard gate—the Sharks with eyes as dark as my own.

2. Preacher Jackets & Pompadours

In high school only one boy ever asks me out. That is, not counting
popular Douglas Reece, whose folks own the only dime store in
our little town. I hear about it through Karen, who says Doug wants
to invite me to the dance but won't—because I'm Japanese. Andy
Weinberger does. Years later I realize he's Jewish and an outsider
like me. I can't forget that long night when everybody stares—the
message so clear, till I'm mad at sweet Andy for ever asking. My
salvation is our family car and lenient parents who feel sorry for
two *sansei* daughters in a no mixed-dating town. Less than an hour
away are carnivals in Little Tokyo, *obon* festivals in Gardena, dances
in central LA where Buddhahead boys show off in Nehru-collar
preacher jackets and three-inch pompadours, strutting like gangster
peacocks. A few of them really do run in gangs, but mostly it's just the
cool way downtown J-A's walk, talk, dress like their black classmates
(who back then are still called Negro).

3. With Swords & Bedroom Eyes

When Bruce Lee is still a decade away, the big screen only gives us post-war boomers General Tojo look-alikes torturing GI's and kamikaze pilots nose-diving like sea devils on fire. Lucky for me, I discover *chambara* heroes, Japanese warriors at the Kokusai and Toho La Brea. American movies can try to shrink our men to the eunuch-dimensions of Charlie Chan, Hop Sing, *Breakfast at Tiffany's* Mr. Yunioshi, but I have my Toshiro Mifune, direct from Tokyo, who makes John Wayne look sissy, James Dean, unworthy, and even my two Greek Georges lacking in samurai allure. With Mifune as the elder Superman, there's a younger, mysterious Romeo in the wings— Tatsuya Nakadai, stealing every scene with his brooding gaze, he's villain, then hero, but always the seducer. Adult-rated, Tatsuya erases any girlish infatuation.

4. Slow Dancing to Little Willie G.

The fact that he's Latino may have nothing to do with my attraction— though I must admit an irresistible pull toward Carlos Baeza in the eighth grade, and who knows if there's a certain romantic logic connecting Carlos to the Puerto Rican Sharks and now this baby-faced Willie Garcia, lead singer for Thee Midnighters, who can't be much older than me. What tender roll of the random makes way for a lifetime crush like this—the synchronicity of slow dancing with a sansei boy I don't even know, being close enough to touch Little Willie G. as he croons "Sad Girl," and yearning for something I want so much but can't even name. A brief marriage then divorce before I'm falling again—this time it's the grand "El Pachuco," played by Edward James Olmos—my girlfriends wondering how I can adore his pockmarked skin. Eddie turns me into a *Miami Vice* fan, impatient for his brief appearance week after week. And now here I am—a fifteen-year romance with my own dark-eyed man. He's no Willie G. but Chicano to the bone—Santana, César Chávez, and MECHA in his past, an easy *orale* in every step, this lover who slow dances better than anyone I know.

IT'S GOT SOMETHING to do with architecture. A prose poem contains the same basic elements—image, rhythm, music, feeling—but without the line breaks. In fact, its open structure would lose something with those carefully measured line lengths of verse. I've written a dozen or so prose poems and enjoy inhabiting that space. A prose poem can be like a long jazz riff—far-reaching, evocative, unpredictable, in just a few sustained breaths, a slightly different take every time it's read.

JON VEINBERG

Butterflies

I am writing a letter to the President as make-up for an assignment
I flunked in the fourth grade. All immigrants should do so said the
teacher. Even though I got here by ship I don't remember anyone
ever weeping at the sight of the Statue of Liberty. We were cold and
nauseous. But I do remember each of the 23 faces that crammed the
breezeway of the apartment building when the civil defense sirens
went off. It wasn't that the mills of morality stopped grinding or that
I spent too much time eavesdropping on the after-hours anarchists
raging in chirps at the shoe shine parlor, or that each day Susan
Monge dared me to peek up her flower print skirt and caused me
to fail my assignment. I didn't know how to use periods. My rule
was that you used one after each breath, so I had a lot of one-word
sentences, and if there were a lot of breaths with no words the whole
page would quickly fill up with dots. Sometimes when the words out-
sprinted the counting of breaths I would place periods in random
spots hoping God would overrule the rules of punctuation.

I will write a poem for the President that imitates my childhood.
A sonnet on mother earth will do wonders except that we abandoned
her a long time ago. I'll write how I learned baseball in an alley in
Pittsburgh, my cousin whittling a bat out of a 2×4 yanked from
the shed behind the hospital. I've never seen a true cowboy and am
afraid of horses because they hate us. We whip them and have them
stand in stalls for most of the day. So far my lessons in history have
been in remembering wars that my real life is trying to forget. Because
the President is a hard ass who spits on his hands before answering
the phone and I'm out of a job, I'll start the letter in spring and end
it in early winter. I'll drive to the mountains, the coast, trample the
slough weeds of my valley collecting butterflies—monarchs & reds
& lilac-bordered coppers & the erratic hackberry emperor. I'll burn
one wing off each and mail the rest off, tendriled body and all, to the
President. Butterflies are supposed to carry messages from the dead.
Souls are ringing.

Corrosion

The last time I saw you, you were staring me up and down as if wanting to creep inside for some memory of movement, then hobbled off with your sore-hipped gait tilting the earth. Three weeks later we shoveled you out from the crawlspace beneath the house, your body camouflaged by loose wires and rusted pipes, wrapped you up in a plastic grocery bag and buried you in the backyard. Gone are the dead rats at my door and the choke-chained yelps of the neighbor's dog tethered to the patio post and you flaunting your freedom through the chain link fence, barely out of jaw's reach. I liked it that you had no religion or guilt that I knew of and that the world was as two-toned as your fur: things to fear and things to chase, and to pounce on both by moonlight, the stars scattering at the rasp of claws being sharpened in the dark. Do you see me any differently now? Your plot has risen two feet higher from the excessive dirt and bubbled heat; covered with pigweed and morning glory I can no longer control. On a long, Fresno summer evening I shook the chain link fence with all my thunderstorm might to torment the dog next door but he just lied there dreaming with his paws. The moths, thin as shadows, feast at the porch light and tomorrow I will take careful aim at the swelling community of birds that swoop down each year to mate on your grave.

A Dream Manual

Pay close attention to corners and fringes: the impression rain prints out in the ant holes of the earth, or the wind breeding another song, or the colored leaf the sun rises through each day, or the sea roaring its approval the night Taras Bulba and I roasted marshmallows on a beach in Carmel. And how I longed to have zippered a camera inside my dream closet the night I wrestled a goat on the platform of the Paris Metro before he pinned me below an ad heralding cognac and cigarettes. I noticed it wore my eyes. Then, again, there are far too many fires and flights and naked women to ignore.

Always wear a watch on each wrist before going to bed. On one wind it backwards until the stem breaks, then wind it some more until the second hand moves counterclockwise. Sometime in your sleep it will play an event you missed in past dreams as dictated by its importance and the time of its reversal. The other watch will tick forward in the usual way. With practice your dreams will strike a pendulum of balance between past and present. It is snowing and my uncle is standing outside the church door waiting for us to enter. He's bundled up in a black scarf and blue overcoat, tipping his hat to passers-by, his shoes glazed with ice. James Bond is wheeled into the hospital in a straightjacket, cursing the use of mirrors to hunt boar. Buzzards have swarmed my favorite beer garden, bombing the bald and breaking glasses under the slimmest of moons.

Learn to sleep on the side closest to the watch that ticks backwards. Otherwise you will confuse time and invite nightmares. You are a trapeze artist bicycling a wire across the Grand Canyon when the wind knocks you off kilter and you wait to hit the ground with a thud. Windows shatter to sand on a bus you're riding after losing its brakes and sliding and bumping from cliff to cliff. You left your wallet in a taxi. Your dog gets hit by a train. Rats are electrocuting themselves in your cellar. The watch that ticks backwards will have a different and distinct sound—low pitch and high tone—a tone God might use in judging your past, but don't let it frighten you, fear corrodes the senses. Keep an elongated brush at your bedside so the angel of bow ties can comb out the knots, muck and plugged rust of memory.

Dry your bed sheets on a tree branch overnight so you can sleep in the scent of the stars. It will also draw the dead into your dreams and it is good to welcome them. They are calm as fresh bread and never in a hurry, rivulets of smiles creasing their faces. My mother is checking for lice and offering foot rubs for sitting still. She wants to look up her friends for a game of cards; chunks of blood sausage center the table to be used as betting chips. Roberta is feeding popcorn to the ducks at Roeding Park encircled by children waving tiny and colorfully striped flags. Ernesto is measuring a plum tree. Moulton and I are trading jokes. Laughter, he says, is the only thing that can stop time. We smoke cigars, slice apples, and spit. The world harmonizes. My watches are almost in synch.

Lullaby of Leaves

At dusk I lift the blinds and open the window to watch the leaves fall, the clouds swirl in a riot of pink, the sparrows rotate their heads as if fashioning panic, and the barely visible stars toss off the coats that no longer fit. I am three days south of a hundred years old and want to learn to play the piano. I want to hear what the tree hears—leaf tremble and snap, the wind humming through the bared branches, and invent a note for each falling leaf. I have forgotten most of the names of my dead friends but remember how easily music could slide me into a spirit not totally my own. The faster the leaves fall the wilder my fingers burn, colliding as new rhythms, melodies of lost light—joy and regret dropping at the same speed.

A crow fills the empty space of the tree and the leaves fan in through the window skirting my nightstand of photos and false teeth, shivering under lamplight, skimming the table and the leftover game of solitaire until the room is filled with leaves, veined parasols of music rising up to my chin and I ride its current, the bubble between air and earth while the leaves keep falling ever so lightly, as if feathering the scabbed faces of all my dead and not waking them. And the leaves fall into my hands, into my mouth, and I try to recall how to sway into the slow sensation of sleep, into another life as I always remembered dreaming it. From now on my songs will shawl themselves in browns and golds, my head a cushion for death to leave its fingerprints on, my prayer ending in a circle of mist. It will always be autumn.

I ASK MORE of my poems than they ask of me. The first I ask of any poem, while it's still in my head, is for it to identify itself, whether by title, theme, or form. One day when it exclaimed a desire to be a prose poem I thought we would both journey down a doomed path without a hiccup of sense. It kept reminding me of how I could enhance all the elements I once espoused: a storytelling personality and temperament laced with humor, the adventure in using a myriad of themes and as many circular patterns my subconscious could handle, exaggeration to the level of preposterous, unlimited spokes of transition, softer language yet more venom per bite, and best of all, I would exude greater clarity of thought. I don't know if any of these expectations were fulfilled, however, in writing prose poems I always feel as though I'm committing a crime, albeit a misdemeanor akin to stealing hubcaps from the grand limos of novels and/or verse when the rest of the world is asleep. I'm addicted to my crime and my adrenaline is popping.

DIANE WAKOSKI

Describe the Sky on a Postcard

The sky is not like my desk, which makes me nervous. So filled with letters I cannot answer, stacked with books that should be read and then talked about, filled with possibilities of jobs and money, and worst, at the bottom, all the requests for poems that either I am not ready to write or haven't organized myself well enough to type up and send out. No, the sky is empty, even when it is filled with clouds, for no one has to answer a cloud. What is a cloud anyway? Not even as substantial as a poem. How is it we become what we have always made fun of or despised? The clouds in the sky today are like black dahlias. Their edges are smooth and sharp. They contain rain; remind me of my black silk shawl.

V. from Handbook of Marriage and Wealth

There was a beautiful green bird who had everything he ever wanted. A good wife, intelligent healthy children, a secure job as first violinist for the philharmonic orchestra and success as a recording soloist. However, one day he woke up only to find that he had lost all of his feathers. He was a bald naked bird. At first he was very upset; he had been a very very beautiful green bird. Then his good and kind wife reassured him she loved him for himself and not his feathers. His children said, "It's not so bad, Pop; you could have been paralyzed and unable to play the violin." They bought him a suit, something he had never had to wear before. And what with new fashions and all, he looked just as interesting as he had with his beautiful green feathers. When he went into orchestra rehearsal with his new suit, his friends were curious. He told them he had awakened one morning only to find that his feathers had all fallen off. The rehearsal began, and he played just as he always had. Afterwards, one of his friends told him, with concern, that he thought he ought to go to the doctor, just to make sure nothing serious was wrong with him. That started him thinking: was there something wrong with him? It was unusual for all of one's feathers to fall out all at once. Being a sensible green bird, he went right to his doctor's office and showed him what had happened. The doctor was baffled, took a lot of tests, and the upshot was that he could find nothing wrong with the green bird except that he was now bald and there didn't seem to be much chance of growing any more feathers. "You're just fine," said the doctor. "As long as you don't let it worry you that you look different from all other green birds. I'm sure your wife won't leave you, as sometimes happens in these cases and of course you have your work and your children." But it all started him wondering.

Now, there are several ways I could end this story. My favorite way would be to have him go mad and, like a Buñuel character, worrying and wondering about everything until he really lost his wife, his job, his ability to play the violin and his children had to have him committed to a mental institution However, it is a beautiful day, with a bumble bee outside my window, and I cannot get in the mood to end it that way.

I could end it by having him be normal and just wearing lots of interesting clothes and being more and more successful and happy like my friend David Antin who lost all of his hair when he was 19—black and curly it all fell out on his pillow after one night of worry about the draft—a man who turns what the world might see as disadvantages into diamond-mine assets. But while this is best in real life, it doesn't make the kind of melodramatic stories I like.

So I think I will end it this way:

The green bird became a successful schizophrenic, absolutely undetected by society. He becomes obsessed by his nakedness and insists on having a secret life where he always appears naked and shocks everybody he can. He never lets his wife know about this. His symphony orchestra mates never find out. He never confuses the two lives. And everybody wonders why his violin playing improves so much: there seems to be some secret fire, some strange look in his eyes, some magic that conveys another world of fascinations and longing to his audience. The reviewers rave about him. Groupies form at the stage door, a line, but he passes them in his gorgeous fashionable clothing with hardly a glance, going home to his wife on concert nights. Sometimes when he is out in California, being the anonymous naked bird, shocking all his friends and lovers with his

369

nakedness, they put on a record of his violin playing, never knowing that he is that magic, enchanted soloist. He smiles sometimes, and they think it is because of his nakedness.

No one ever knows all that he knows. And that's what's so tantalizing in his music. He is the man who walks in and out, without talking, of the labyrinth.

The Fable of the Lion & the Scorpion

Once upon a time there was a lion from California. A female lion, so she was not grand; did not have the kingly ruff or position of ruler of the jungle. However, she was a lion. Proud. Strong. And quite powerful enough to win the respect of many animals.

One day she was walking in the forest and happened to stop near the edge where she saw something quite strange. A scorpion was sitting there, reading a book of poetry and weeping. Scorpions are sneaky, mean and dreaded creatures, so the Lady Lion suspected that it was probably a trick. But she was kind-hearted and could not bear the thought that some other creature might be in pain and she, just passing unfeelingly by. So, against her better judgment, she went over to the scorpion and said, "Is anything the matter? Can I help?"

The scorpion looked up from the book of poems (written by a California poet named Diane Wakoski) and said that no one could help him—for he was deeply in love with the poet whom he was reading. But he knew she would never have anything to do with him, as he was just a scorpion.

The Lady Lion thought that was probably true, but was too kindhearted to say so. Instead, she said, "How do you know? Have you told her you love her?" The scorpion, who was beginning to notice the Lady Lion's paw and how soft and delicate it was, how eminently suitable for a big vicious sting that would poison the lion for days, said, in his most seductive tone, "Yes, but no one would love a scorpion. Not even a kind and strong lion like yourself could possibly love a wormlike creature like me." As he said this, he began inching his way seductively over to the lion's paw.

Now, this Lady Lion was no fool. She noticed that the scorpion's tears had stopped. That the book of poems was lying abandoned on the sand. And she saw *her* own delicate paw sitting there in front of her and that the scorpion had an odd look in his now dry mean eyes. Quickly, with her beautiful paw, she picked up the book of poems and smashed it down on the scorpion, killing him instantly. She felt badly about killing this creature she had stopped only to console. But she was a beast of the jungle and knew better than to disregard the nature of an animal. That scorpion may truly have loved the poet he was reading, even to tears. But nothing would stop him from the pleasure of using his powerful sting on any unsuspecting creature.

She took the book of poems with her and gave it to her friend the Coyote. When he asked what the stain on the back cover was, the Lady Lion replied that it was the proof that even love and poetry could not transform the nature of a scorpion. The Coyote replied that he felt that should have been obvious to anyone. He did not see why the cover of the book of poems should have been ruined for that. Apparently, this Coyote was something of a book collector, and felt that beautiful books should be preserved. "When I tell you that I had my choice of being stung by the scorpion or using the book to kill him, would you be so fussy?" she asked. But the Coyote was already beginning to read the book and tears were running down his sly narrow cheeks. "Do you like the poems?" asked the Lady Lion.

"I think I am in love with the woman who wrote them," said the Coyote.

"Why are you crying, then?"

"Because she could never love me. I am only a Coyote."

At this point the Lady Lion decided that perhaps she ought to leave. She began to think that she might take up writing poetry, but before she could get far with this project, she met a handsome male lion. After they fell in love and were about to be married, she asked him if he would like her better if she wrote poetry. He let out a terrible roar which could be heard all over the whole jungle. "Absolutely not," he cried. "If you wrote poems, you would have scorpions in love with you, and coyotes. For poetry allows many different forms to come together. But scorpions should not love people or lions. Scorpions

should stick with their own kind. I want a lion for a wife, not a poet."
So, she took his advice and lived happily ever after.

Moral: If you are a lion and want the love of other lions, rather than scorpions or coyotes, don't write poetry. The lady poet, of course, is loved by everyone, but married to none.

Crème Brûlée

Her voice is like good custard, *crème brûlée* perhaps, and she uses one hand always extended as if she's balancing herself. She holds in her other hand, the salamander iron, right out of an old French kitchen that is hot and ready to scald the top of the dessert Julia brought into TV kitchens. I wanted to mention that this woman is probably not a cook, that she was a child math prodigy, that she has eyes like blue equations.

Yet how do we know what we'll be able to contribute to the world—cooks, mathematicians, breeders of whippets? Chef Child brought so much to American kitchens, but she claims that she'll be remembered for only one thing. She believes her contribution to American cooking is the small blowtorch, to take the place of the old wood-fire-heated salamander in our inventory of kitchen appliances.

Last year, Judith Minty asked for a small chainsaw for Christmas. I confirmed recently that I could not be happy without bread, cheese and wine. The math prodigy asked me, opening wide her scallop eyes and speaking like *crème brûlée,* if I could tell her who The King of Spain was. "Yes," I answered, "he comes from fairy tales."

But it seemed more important today, somehow, to figure out why I thought I recognized a name like a constellation? Why it unsettled me so. When did I ever eat *crème brûlée* that was seared the way this woman's voice burned through to my past?

CHARLES HARPER WEBB

Except Ye See Signs and Wonders . . .

We gorged on the clouds' bounty that first day, and blessed our luck: not too much mayo, just chunky enough. Slapped on a slice of TJ's sprouted rye, this manna beat Nate 'n' Al's to a thin slush. "Lawn sandwich!" our three-year-old cried.

When I griped, "It's wrecking my shoes," Kate replied, "People are starving. Or haven't you heard?"

"How can I, with egg salad in my ears?"

As usual, she discounted my hyperbole.

She's not so bloody sanguine now. The stuff's flowed into our crawl-space, and threatens to squeeze up into our living room and spoil two thousand dollars worth of "oak barrel" carpeting.

The hill behind us is heaped high. One little earthquake: home, goodbye.

The news is full of downed trees, fatal wrecks, and power outages. Traffic is mired San Diego to José.

The pump I bought at Home Despot can't keep up with what rains down. As I lug buckets to the street, the landscape looks like yellow tundra with white boulders and a little celery. Drains are backed up; sky, the greenish-yellow of a hard-boiled yolk.

My neighbors yards are worse than mine—all but Reverend Bill's. Barbecue hissing, he keeps lifting charcoaled brisket to the sky. He's dragged out the Christmas creche in mid-July. Speakers blare Handel's Messiah.

The Reverend's property, aside from a few pine-needles, is clear. Even the sky over his head looks almost blue.

"It's so unfair," I say, ready to cry.

"I may rejoin the church," my Kate confides.

Second Son

"Could he ride with you? I'm scared of trains."

—*unknown Asian woman to my wife*

His name is Nathan, but we call him Nate, born as the Enchanted Railroad puffs away from Descanso Gardens station.

Erik, our first-born, yanks bottles of formula from Nate's mouth, bonks him with a Ninja Turtle, knocks him out of his high chair (ten stitches), and brains him with a baseball bat—plastic, thank God. Yet by the time we pass the first crossing—soprano bell pinging, quarter-sized red light flashing as park-goers wave—the boys, in fourth and third grade, stand against the world.

Before we reach the rhododendrons, where a fountain blasts like a sprung water main, Erik has made National Honor Society. Nate has taken up oil painting and shoplifting. Where he got those talents, we don't know.

Erik enters UCLA (English major) as our train chuffs through the woods beside an artificial creek where koi hang, gold fins fluttering. When Nate prefers the army to jail for dealing drugs, the Engineer—80 if he's a hour—toots three times on his Enchanted Railroad horn.

We pass the Wishing Well, where kids drop pennies on a sunken garden gnome as Erik graduates *summa cum,* and starts teaching composition part-time at four colleges.

Cited for bravery in the Middle East, Nate is honorably discharged as orange daisies smile and sway.

Inside the Tunnel of Trees (still hung, in June, with Christmas lights), Erik marries a heart surgeon, and lands a tenure track at Glendale Community College on the same day Nate's one-man show opens at Kreuger Gallery.

As the second crossing-bell frantically pings, its light flashing ambulance-red, Erik's wife runs off with her (female) anesthesiologist, leaving Erik with their daughter, Jacqueline.

Two oak trees later, Nate meets a Hungarian juggler. At the koi pond, they have a baby girl, then give her up for adoption.

Sadly, the boys have grown apart. Nate feels we favor Erik, so we downplay our pride when, as the train slows entering the Walk of

Roses, Erik publishes his first novel—about a single dad whose wife leaves him for another woman.

Refusing help from us, Nate puts himself through night school and, in front of the Frog Fountain, renounces Art to be a CPA. When, three days from his 29th birthday, we reach the station, he jumps off before the train completely stops, scrambles to an Asian lady, and rushes off without saying goodbye.

Martians Land in L.A.

"They'll be on welfare in a week," talk-show hosts say. "What's Martian for *Entitlements*?"

"One more language to print ballots in. And this one uses methane crystals for words," a big-haired newsman quips with a folksy *huh-huh-huh* as Martians fizz through my locked door.

"Look! That's you, conquering L.A.," I say, and point at my TV. I hope that cheerfulness will save my life. But the head Martian—that's all he is: a head on a tripod that leaves snail-streaks—frowns with each one of his hundred eyes.

"Ugh, we're so short and fat," he telepathically groans. "Our antennae look stupid. And our helmets . . . it's like we're wearing *those*." (He points at my fish bowl—empty since little Hohenzollern died).

Despite advanced technology, Martians have never looked closely at themselves. Envy, humiliation, loss?—they've never noticed. Never cared.

"L.A.'s the best place in the world to feel bad about yourself," my friend Damon, a native, used to say.

Now grief, ennui, dissatisfaction, thwarted love laser out of TV screens, the smog-choked air, the heart of every Angeleno still alive.

Tears leak from all the Martians' eyes. Their blue lip-stalks begin to shake. Their putty-cheeks puff in and out as they emit flutey wails and wheezing cries.

"Make us beautiful, please," the Martians moan as their jellyfish-brains float to the ceiling of my condo where they pop, like all *my* prayers: unheard, except by me.

375

No sooner does the ACLU law firm of Agbag, Flopduddle & Schmick order, at $20.95 each, "The Tunisian Feast," than the restaurant door flies open, and Tunisians in turbans and djalabis swarm in, licking their lips.

A huge, fat man with a scimitar and a strong resemblance to a djinn herds the party into a big cage, then uses an enormous winch to hoist them high above the crowd which, with a cheer, begins to feast.

Salad is eaten with the hands, followed by *brika*: sugar-sprinkled puff pastry stuffed with almonds and chicken.

Kous-kous with lamb is next; then, honey-cakes.

Stuffed Tunisians froth into the street.

The HOLLYWOOD sign has been replaced by a video screen where Agbag, Flopduddle, and Schmick can watch their bill climb fast as a gas pump's—six figures, seven, eight, nine, ten.

"What are we," Flopduddle cries, "but ugly Americans faced by the national moral debt?"

As their cage creaks down toward a swimming-pool-sized vat of boiling oil, and the partners fight over whose bright idea brought them here and not McDonald's, a bass voice booms to the Tunisians below, "Who'd like a Coke to go with these large fries?"

JACKSON WHEELER

Oxnard

On a plain drained by Santa Clara River and Calleguas Creek, old
home to Chumash, Sati'quaa and Mu'qu almost unpronounceable.
The city that almost wasn't there, wedged between ranchos and
disputed land claims until five brothers from back east invested in
sweetness. Home of refineries when sugar beets were king, before
the canal was dug, before war in Cuba, the Philippines, Puerto Rico.
All those Moros, dead on Mindanao, and then Filipino stoop labor,
plenty of it. President Grant kidnapped the Queen of Hawaii for
cheap sugar and a place to render whale into oil. Oxnard became the
Lima Bean capitol during the Tong war in 1925. There was murder
in Chinatown up on Seventh Street, newspaper photos of a body
sprawled in the alley—Mr. Soo Hoo's Chinese Imports thirty years
gone from the Boulevard; leaving the Golden Chicken Inn, famous
since 1927. Everything else is Mexican Spanish, the newer immigrants;
ranchos and Alta California, their dream for two hundred years.
Mexicanos just noticed more when Pearl Harbor happened and
the Nishimuris, Tagasakis, and other Japanese families were hauled
away by train to Heart Mountain and Manzanar. More brown stoop
labor and finally an end to the Okie-Arkie migration from the Dust
Bowl. Now soldiers and sailors holed up at Hueneme (why knee
me) not Hueneme (win a me) as pronounced by Hubert Humphrey
losing again and again, tainted by war no matter how much he loved
peace.

The big dream is all about cheap labor, agribusiness, not farms,
the world's seventh-largest economy here, in California, in the city
of Oxnard where everyone dreams, and there is a Wal-Mart and
the dreams themselves are tongues calling their names out to the
blue sky in Spanish, Tagalog, Japanese, Korean, Vietnamese, Thai,
English, but mostly Spanish now. It is all good, *mijo*.

Bowhead

In the spring of 2007, native peoples near the Arctic Circle took
a Bowhead as part of their rationed catch. Buried in two feet of
blubber, uncovered by chainsaw, a lance point from New Bedford,
last manufactured in 1878. This whale lived a long time with its
wound, a century avoiding the ulus of Inuit grandmothers, their
toothless mouths.

Two weeks ago I followed the news of the Humpback cow and
her calf, wending their way up the Sacramento and finally back to
sea.

But the long wounded now dead Bowhead is center page.
Did it complain to its companions underneath the thick ice of an
ache that did not go away, like old Kit Carson, foolish in his youth
to cock his rifle at a pow-wow? He got an arrow in the hip whose
iron tip (hammered from a cooking pot) snagged the bone and
bent, resisting removal til his dying day. Did the Bowhead keen in a
language beyond heard only by kith and kin?

Ars Poetica

Because I was sung to as a child. Because my father shot himself
when I was ten. Because my mother took in ironing and worked
as a janitor. Because, my mother would say, "I could turn on the
radio and you would lie in your crib and listen, quiet as a mouse".
Because there was singing: Kitty Wells, The Louvin Brothers, The
Stanley Brothers, The Carter Family, The Stoneman Family, and
when I was older, Saturday afternoons with my father's mother, her
dark Indian eyes glittering in the twilight of the room—boxing from
Chattanooga, Tennessee, announced by Harry Thornton. Because
I watched my uncles slaughter hogs, because I watched my mother
kill a chicken for dumplings, because I watched the Rescue Squad
drag the Nantahala Lake for drowned vacationers, up from Florida.
Because Southern Appalachia was imagined by someone else—I just
lived there, until I read about it in a book, other than the King James
Bible, which is "all true" my mother said and says, "every jot and St.
Matthew tittle of it." Because God is a burning bush, a pillar of fire,

a night wrestler, a swathe of blood, a small still voice, a whisper in Mary's ear. Because my family is rank with alcoholics, wife beaters, spendthrifts, and big-hearted people, who give the shirts off their backs. Because their stories lie buried in the graveyards, because their stories have been forgotten, because their stories have been misremembered. Because my father's people said they were from Ireland, down Wexford way. Because my father's father baptized people, because my father's mother bore a child out of wedlock and was part Indian. Because my mother's father got his leg crushed at the quarry, because my mother's mother died of brain cancer; My friends think I talk too much, don't talk enough; that I'm too queer for company, that I'm not queer enough. My mother's people were Scots and Welsh, three cheers for the beard of Brady Marr, three cheers for the blood on the shields of the Keiths from Wick, three cheers for immigration, the waves of it and the desperation behind it. Let's hear it for King's Mountain and the Scots' revenge for Culloden. Three cheers for extended family, the nameless cousins, all the petty griefs and regrets, the novels never written, the movies never made, the solace of the bottle, the solace of sex, the solace of loneliness of which there is plenty. All hail the poetic arts, and the art of poetry and the knowledge at the heart of it all: *Words bear witness.*

WHAT MANY REFER TO as a *prose poem*, continues to mystify me. As an adolescent I was swept up by the passages of lyrical prose by certain writers. I will carry, as long as memory allows, the pleasure of James Agee's *Knoxville, 1915,* from *A Death in the Family,* the aspirations of Eugene Gant in Thomas Wolfe's *Look Homeward Angel,* and the achingly beautiful 'Tom Outland's Story," from Willa Cather's *The Professor's House.*

I have discovered as an adult, and one with deep roots in Southern Appalachia, how the prose poem lends itself so well to capturing the anecdote, the oral tradition from which poetry and storytelling evolved. It is with deep appreciation of the work of Jonathan Williams that I have attempted this specific form which defies meter and rhyme and harks back to some older form of utterance.

M. L. WILLIAMS

High Desert

Nothing's been in the rearview mirror so long that I finally adjust it until my eye settles on the glint & wobble of headlamps or stars on the flat desert horizon. It's the same sheen a child focuses on, lying on hot cement in the back yard after running through the sprinkler's wet rainbow over the lawn. Stars of each drop glisten on blond hairs invisible in most light, and each star blurs to arc-lamp snowflakes flaring sun-white over concrete. Get up, leave the wet outline of a body on the ground like the small white tag beside the thorny pyracantha to tell anyone forever how to care for it.

By now it's 105 degrees and these tires bend to it, melt into the road even this late where a giant neon thermometer promises good food and respite from each of these words. The desert never cares. The lime-green antifreeze gives up to the oil-spotted asphalt in the parking lot and the pay phone rings anyway and nobody is there to answer except Nate and Abe, who apologize for being the wrong people and laugh at the adventure of picking up a phone suddenly ringing in the middle of nowhere. Everything evaporates. The wet outline of a child's body. The ringing phone. The oil. The antifreeze. Each memory I have of this coffee steam swirling up into the ceiling fan and the waitress asking how I can drink it in this heat. So I begin to tell her the only thing anyone can tell her when it's this hot and she's been standing there so long and so lovely against the din of the phone and the silence of formica, but it evaporates before her chin turns toward the thick-armed cook, who calls out that all the orders are ready right now, and she serves them. The coins glisten and glisten, but cool nothing on the counter beside the foil-wrapped chrysanthemum.

Stars shimmer and wane in the dead-bug arc the wipers never reach, and for each, here or on a boy's wet, tanned arm, this spectrum's for you: sodium, cobalt, nickel, carbon, helium, hydrogen, argon, manganese, asphalt, soft shoulder, stink thistle, ragweed, 12 gauge, hollowpoint, blown tire, Indio 53 miles, double yellow, slippery when wet, falling rock....

Cartography

Stand at the cliff edge, and, not that you'd jump, but the crust of ground could give way, collapse into the waves and the crushing jagged rocks, that, freed, will wash and wash into pearls of sand.

Pearls of sand, blue starlight, diamonds of bone.

You worry that the ice plant freezes nothing together, that others on sailboats will look vaguely into the sun-hewn depths for the blue pearls of starlight you have become, the blanket of sand washing to, fro among fronds of seaweed and blank desire.

Not that you'd jump. Not that you weren't already there before what's there became cloud, became island of sage and lizards, became any vanishing name.

Your starlight weaves the crest of each wave beneath the frost of foam, and sand collects in cowries of your vision of falling, but you've already walked away, and each time, the ground has given up beneath your leaving. Wind purls bonelight into the starry grass, the visiting weeds.

Subject to Dust
Road sign on Highway 41 between Cholame and Kettleman City

Bone in the dust and tonight's wake this wind draws in sand, and the moon shadow and lizard tracks braid into meaning, if you stand just here, if you stand just out of the way of moonlight's shimmering veil. Otherwise, the bone's dark as a fact, forgotten, like every hagiography on a shelf in a draughty library, like epistles of smoke on the horizon you wonder at till you get to where you can see the burn draw to the water just to see itself in the mirroring lake flicker. So light makes meat shadows on the bone the dark can't consume, muscle under the pressure of wind and sage and the faults twist beneath the road, its own ribbon, taking us on a line across lines until dust settles again and covers up everything the dark refuses. Subject to it, to the dust that takes you, pay it fealty of flesh, of all desire. Leave with your bone memory in its coat of moonlight and your pockets brimming with the earth that wants out of all this, that gives back what grows between anything left behind.

You must change your life

So you do. You head off into the desert where even the land tries to climb out of the heat, succeeds in blue meadows given to cattle and grass and wiry streams pulsing into dark, trout-filled lakes. Cast a line. Pull it and shake the fly. But the fish are tired of all that nylon and the simple jitter of the bug, tired of sitting there turning pale blue and strung out in warm shallow water, tired of catch and release, catch and release. It's still life, a work of art, ice sculpture, dead marble hand, chia head, still life with an open Swiss Army knife and a frayed fly. *Here ya' go little fella.*

Spare change in your pocket fills with light if you hold it up to read the dates in the bright noon sun. This is best if you have nothing to spend it on, if the light matters more than anything, so when the line pulls and the bobber bobbles in the water, you are too distracted to set the hook, and everything goes away, happy, bait-filled, scales shimmering like coins you might have painted as a small detail in the study for the tapestry you will weave sometime, time permitting. Catch and release, and the coins spill into the dust and there are just too many corny songs to listen to, too many memories fading into the asphalt's fading mirage. You drive right through it, every time and without hesitation, because it always disappears, even when what you want most in the world is for the car to splash and sink into the shimmering cool abyss so you can find out what's on the other side. It's still asphalt and the sky dirt and the old silver coins surround the skulls of missing travelers and fish wait to be fished out of the deep, grey sandstone to swim again in displays with carbuncle and pyrite and geodes and quartz crystals and purple amethyst and hematite and steel shoestring nipples and old bottles and railroad spikes. The wind blows box elder leaves into the shape of a rose next to a single blue nickel you leave in the dust, still in this noon sun, to catch you. To release you.

HARD PAN AND TULE FOG on the edge of a small city. Thompson seedless and fig orchards. Not a sea. Train tracks. Ice house. Dust. Hoboes. Dark, pulsing canals and heat-warped asphalt. Lanfranco's farm fed by ditches, filled with frogs and tadpoles and tiny carp and glass shards—first biology class, first conscious crime. Dirt clod fights and hide and seek. Vandenberg's twisted coldwar rainbows across a child's night sky. Dead air-raid sirens. Weeds and flies and Dad's pushbutton Dodge Dart at the curb, trickle of dirty water in the gutter. Summer lightning. Bees on clover flower. Mom worrying. Mountains, white teeth in the distance every spring. My sharecropper grandmother rolling out biscuits. This was the Fresno I grew up in, the Fresno after streetcars vanished and opulent hotels for rich travelers closed, Fresno before sprawl and mall swallowed it and spread itself over the farmland like mayonnaise on Rainbow bread. This is not nostalgia. It's just the Okie Fresno I grew up in, and it's good that some of it has gone by the wayside, become more diverse. But I can't not carry it around. I can't not see that sprinkler I want to run through or a long piece of grass I want to pull out and suck the nectar out of while I lean back and watch the sky frail blue into a white haze. I just can't be from anywhere else I've ever been. Wilson, Cooper Jr. High, Fresno High, Cal (where Tom Gunn taught an Everwine poem called "Desire," first I ever heard of a "Fresno Poet"), back to Fresno to teach and then finally to get a real education from Peter, Phil, Chuck, and Connie, then off to Utah to study with Larry, to Santa Barbara to raise my two kids and teach and write and edit *How Much Earth* with Chris Buckley and David Oliveira, and finally here teaching creative writing at Valdosta State University in a small hot flat city surrounded by farmland on a freeway between two big cities, a lot like Fresno in the fifties except for all the trees.

HALEY WINTER

When I was twelve and had broke my leg

On a Sunday, when it was still dark and lonely in the morning, I sat in my chair by the window. It was then I saw her kneeling and the threads of her bathrobe dangling over the cold concrete. Ms. Healy ripped and sorted through the newspaper, her fingers snatching and pulling at the words. When she found a choice story, or two, she tore them out, stuffed them into her mouth, and began to chew. It was those days that I told my mother I didn't want any breakfast. I didn't think I had the stomach.

The story that somebody once told me, the one I believe, says Ms. Healy used to have a baby. No more than six months they say. Then she woke up one morning to find it had vanished. Some stories say she killed it. But ever since that day, she got the morning's paper and took out articles of crimes, the missing, and the wanted. She pinned some of them to her porch railing. Two days later those snippets had browned and stiffened in the sun. When a small breeze drifted by they rattled like hung toys. The oldest ones made noise for only a month or so before they broke off, drifting and stumbling away in the wind.

Dermatology

I will die from a mole, one that is small and almost overlooked. I do not want a celebration of my life, because I've hardly had one. A high school diploma, twenty birthdays, and then a tumor. These are what I've earned because I am young and I thought it was something good to be pitied. I will want my bed brought to Stinson beach where the rays stream down like fire, so that the light presses into my body and bakes my scarred skin. This will happen because I am young and because I am still stubborn. It will be bright and my parents will ask me to put my shirt on, instead I will swim naked in the ocean. Watch seaweed struggle against the current, hear the roaring waves break over sharp rocks, swallowed in the watery plunge. I will walk out of the ocean dripping beads of my shiny new skin, and in each of my hands I will hold a stone the color of the sun, because I am dying, and it consumes me.

Guilt

My next-door neighbor had a large maple tree, beneath which I usually parked. One day the Santa Anna winds tore a limb the width of my thigh in half, and left it hanging by only a few strands, toothpicks above the place that I always park. For some American reason it annoyed me when I simply moved down the curb. That night I watched the news while the weather wailed outside, and reveled in my decision, knowing that the crushed cars I saw would not be mine. Then a young girl was interviewed while a cut from a branch bled down her temple. And I kept telling myself it had nothing to do with me.

WHEN I USE PROSE POETRY instead of broken lines, it's because what I write has happened. That is to say it has happened to someone, and the prose gives it weight because it reads as an observation, as a record. A clever poet can lead a reader through hoops and bring them to laugher under a dressing of line breaks. With prose poetry the tension is in the content, the context, not the arrangement. It is a challenge to write a good prose poem, but when it is done the writer is left with something pure, naked, raw, and merciless. It takes skill, patience, and a mind willing to stick to the truth, no matter whose truth it is.

DONALD WOLFF

All the World Then

At fourteen, freedom was the ten-speed I rode all over Santa Barbara,
down La Cumbre Road that marked the city limit then, through the
moist sun, over the highway to the beach to see girl skin, or south
over Hope Road and through the oaks to the Queen of the Missions.
I would take the tour again and hear about the adobe walls eight feet
thick, inhale the musty four-hundred-year-old Catholicism, and
wonder at the three skulls embedded in the outside wall over the
northern archway above the thick wooden door. That door led to
the gardens and fresh air where Franciscans still stroll counting their
beads and swinging the white ropes cinched at the waist with their
knots of vows—one each for poverty, chastity, and obedience—that
hurt like hell if you caught one at school across your head as you
tried to remember what you were learning.

From the mission it was a short ride to the Natural History
Museum to examine the stuffed black bears and the condor hung
wide across the low ceiling or the live local tarantulas, like the one
that crawled out the sixth hole when my stepfather bent to retrieve
his golf ball. There were stuffed sea lions to contrast with the seals
and even a mastodon family like the ones that once walked here
before the sun grew warm and the light diffused evenly in from the
sea. In a tableaux was a Chumash family with their children and
artifacts placed carefully about them. I studied the dark aureoles
bearing the raised nipples on the mother's clay breasts. The family
seemed at home while they stared out into the still, dark air, as I stood
wondering where else I could go to see what the world had in store.

What I Can See

At Faria Beach, just north of Ventura, my sister asked me to be sure
to say that when the tide's half way out the sea rocks here seem a
dragon peeking through the surf. Her father-in-law, The General,
said write about the waves that don't just go *womp womp womp* against
the wall. The beach faces south so waves break forever down the

coast. Yes, I have seen patient surfers catch a low wave and ride a hundred yards in the evening, trailing lavender foam on the teal water. Yet, late at night the surf will hit the twelve-foot-thick sea wall with force enough to shake the foundation, the wave but not the water going right through the house beneath my bed toward the road. But usually it's calm enough to watch a pod of dolphins head north or south, five or six breaking the surface, with twice as many unseen below. Once there was a single large gray bringing up the rear his head above the water line, not just his fin but whole back out, one eye toward me, the other looking out to open sea. Sometimes there's a single dark sea lion, his head above the incoming tide, bobbing briefly in the floating kelp, water a second skin like the warm air we wander through. For the time being my eyes are still just sharp enough to pick him out.

Sunset at Gualala, CA

Driving north on Hwy 1, I stop for a peaceful dinner at the Oceanside Café to watch the sun slide into the Pacific, the royal blue water turn to slate, while I dine on Bahamian lobster. My waitress celebrates her fifty-three years with the table behind me—*we're still here*—but the man quietly protests—*barely*—his brain tumor gone four years now, still ready to list the *residual effects* before his order goes in. Angie knows what he means, her cervical cancer cut out back in '78 she says, as I finish my pinot gris. I pay my bill and hit the winding road for another forty miles to Ft. Bragg, the moonlight catching in the restless foam of the waves far below which I glimpse occasionally in the side-view mirror, eyes mainly searching for the way through the sharp dark turns ahead.

FOR ME, THE PROSE POEM permits connections and rhythms I cannot entertain in other forms. Certainly, some poems I know immediately, before I start to write a word, will be (must be) prose poems. In other cases, I must search hard for the right form and will be surprised that a prose poem is best. In a few cases, the poem will work well in short lines as well as in prose; I will write it in both forms. Then I can see more clearly what each wants to say; what can be said. In short line and other free verse forms, I can have a farther range—the poem might go anywhere and back again. In my prose poems, the images and language are more earthbound, the boundaries sharper, everything needs to be tightly connected—more often than not my prose poems are placebound. For that reason, I feel they are directly connected to the California landscape, especially the coast—it perpetually smells like home, both when I return and in memory. The sentences in my prose poems tend toward the Latinate, toward the deeply embedded. I like that because I feel the central trope of such sentences, when they're artful, intimates consciousness—the sentences suggest the way the mind works. And that brings us back to landscape—in such sentences and their poems, the mind, the place, the time, the form, and the language feed one another.

CHARLES WRIGHT
The Poet Grows Older

It seemed, at the time, so indifferent an age that I recall nothing of it except an infinite tedium to be endured. I envied no one, nor dreamed of anything in particular as, unwillingly, I enveloped myself in all of the various disguises of a decent childhood. Nothing now comes to mind of ever embarking upon famous voyages to the usual continents; of making, from the dark rooms and empty houses of my imagination, brilliant escapes from unnatural enemies; or, on rainy winter afternoons in an attic, of inventing one plot or counterplot against a prince or a beast... Instead, it must have been otherwise.

I try to remember, nevertheless, something of all that time and place, sitting alone here in a room in the middle of spring, hearing the sound of a rain which has fallen for most of April, concerned with such different things, things done by others ... I read of the aimless coups in the old dynasties from Africa to Afghanistan, their new republics whose lists of war lords alone are enough to distress the Aryan tongue; of intricate rockets in search of a planet, soon, perhaps to land in a country somewhere outside the pedestrian reach of reason; of the latest, old sailor's account of a water dragon seen bathing off the grizzled coast of Scotland ... It is at times such as this, and without thinking, really, clothed in my goat's-wool robes, that I steal a camel from an outlying Arabian stable, gather together my clansmen, and gallop for days along the miraculous caravan trails to Asia.

Aubade

Over Govino Bay, looking up from the water's edge, the landscape resembles nothing so much as the hills above Genova, valleying into the sea, washing down olive, cypress and excessive arbutus into the slow snapping of the plane trees where I, surrendering to the pulse beat of a silence so faint that it seems to come from another country, watch the sun rise over Albania, waiting—calmly, unquestioning—

389

for Saint Spiridion of Holy Memory to arise, leave his silver casket and emerge, wearing the embroidered slippers, from his grove of miracles above the hill.

The Voyage

At first I was overly cautious, procedure being all-important. I gathered around me those I considered friends, discovering, with a certain shock, a mere handful—nothing else, however, was lacking, as I had for months assembled equipage, and such rudiments as maps of cities, tidal charts, coastal readings, cryptic dictionaries, and guides to unusual monuments. Only, in assuring readiness, I had planned too well . . . As it was, this much should have been warning.

For days on end we waited, close by the north-east docks, admiring the stubborn tugs at work, studying the sea lanes. Such depths of perfect skies over the gaudy ships, outward-bound through the gay whistles of sea birds! . . . And at night the glide and swish of well-oiled engines, the long calls of the horns . . .The weeks lengthened, our patience thickening. Then something altered, if imperceptibly at first: perhaps some quirk of the weather, perhaps of the sea. A little later and it was unmistakable: things tended to incline together, fogging distinctions, ships became less common, and schedules grew erratic; destinations became unsure in my head; the nights were longer, and with them there was the uncontrollable desire for sleep, up till then only vaguely recalled. Eventually, even, some of my friends, sharers of the voyage, vanished . . . .

It is so difficult to come back, perspectives blunted, and to have only the waiting, now in the shuttered light, in the clutter of objects here in this drafty attic, until all is in readiness once more. Soon, perhaps, we shall go back down. But then, what stingy cargo to reload, what slackened baggage, O my stunted puppets!

Nocturne

The weeds have thickened among the orchards and leaves dangle unnoticed under the archways. At nighttime, before, where torchlight once peeled the darkness back from the lawn mosaics, from the formal gardens, where, it has been rumored, the parties attained such a perfection that Bacchus himself, angered at certain contests staged in his name, peered in one twilight, then ordered his image stricken from the household, his paeans discontinued, all is unshingled by the moon. Occasional chords from a ghostly lute, it is true, will sometimes come down the same Alpine wind that continues to herd the small waters into the shore; or a strayed traveller, or sonic misguided pilgrim might, of a summer evening, if he stands quite still and says nothing, imagine he hears the slight off-rhythm of some hexameter line deep in the olive grove, as the slither of night birds moves toward the darker trees. But that is all.

Grotte di Catullo, Sirmione

Storm

And when, that night, the unseasonable rain (the hail a shredding sound in the lemon trees) thudded against the lumbering of the bay, in August, haunting the dark with a querulous whiteness, he retired to the basement room under the house to study the various aspects of water, the ships in sudden counterpoint on the rising scales of the sea, and to wait for the breakthrough, across the barren hills of his brain, of the bronze soldiers, for the swelling flash of their knives.

Positano

ABOUT THE PROSE POEM . . . it does seem to be having a kind of renaissance now, much as it did in the early sixties. Did everyone get tired of thinking about the line? Did everyone get tired of talking about line breaks? I think that sort of happened in the sixties and the whole deal (they thought) was freer (which of course it wasn't, not if you wanted a good prose poem. Good prose is just as hard to write, and to find a rhythm that is prose and lyric at the same time. At least I thought so back then). Maybe people just want to be hip again. The prose poem is always hip, because it's Rimbaud, whom no one has ever been hipper than. I started writing them because they were like pollen in the air and I kept sneezing. As to what I think about the prose poem, I love them and always will. I hope the last five poems I ever write will be prose poems. Of course, I hope that's down the road a piece.

AL YOUNG

Coastal Nights and Inland Afternoons

La múcura está en el suelo, Mamá, no puedo con ella.
Chiquito, si tú no puedes con esa múcura de agua,
Llamaste al buen San Carlos pa' que te ayuda cargarla.
—*traditional Mexican folk song*

The big water jug's on the floor, Mama, I can't deal with it.
The water jug's on the floor, Mama, I can't deal with it.
Well, little one, if you can't handle this big jug of water,
Call on good old Saint Carlos to help you tote it.
—*Al Young's loose translation*

Jesus—or, rather, *Jésus!*—the harvest moon hangs full over Half Moon
Bay this summer-gone night, gone Friday already, gone Saturday,
gone Sunday family-time. You might as well be back in Sinaloa,
Jalisco, Zihuataneco, Chihuahua, Michoacán—this is where you're
coming from. Tomorrow better be better for work. That 700-mile
wall going up around *la frontera,* Gutiérrez, is to keep your colorful
ass out. "When are you Mexicans and Latinos going to do something
for yourselves?" you, a kind-hearted woman who studies evil all the
time, asked. All smiles, the grown man you said flat-out: "When
you are ready to strap on the leaf-blower, and go for yourself." Is
it the undertow, or what, that's got you so quiet tonight? What's
holding you in? Don't go floating no more funny notes in bottles out
across the Pacific. They might explode like some mercury-choked
thermometer. No Waikiki, no Tokyo, no Pyongyang, no Seoul to
reach. Fever—that's what's felling this sweet land you left the sea to
crawl and walk, and now we've got us crawling again. It's all so hard
to throw down, but easy to fix. Mix sexy-night memories of Veracruz
with someone warm to touch and reach for on foggy, dewy nights
on a kidnapped coast. Blanketed, all salt and fetal pull, you warm
your floating bones by fires the two of you alone can kindle, watch
and feel. What about Mazatlán? What about Aztlán, where, when
you messed up, did wrong, got caught or owed too much, you got to
choose: Rot in your Guanajuato cell or get packed off to California—
a distant land named after Califía, queen of a country of Amazons,

black as the sea at night and just as fierce. If you worked hard, if you acted right, you might could pay your debts and even land some land. But, don't you forget, Gutiérrez, you're still property. For now enjoy, *disfruta*. Make sure your tools are sharp, in shape; your body rested. Your mind, at sea right now, adrift, must pull itself ashore to make the journey inland, dreaming of Aztlán all day long. You're one of the lucky ones, you with your seaside room, where, all crash and wash, cold waves of timelessness push back the hours and light the ear. Where do you come from, here do you go? Stuff that time always need to know. You always were, you always are, you'll always be sea-swept and sacred by degrees: 98.6 Fahrenheit, 22.7 Celsius. Jesus, *Jésus!*

The Problem of Identity

Used to identify with my father first making me want to be a gas station attendant simple drink Coca-Cola, listen to the radio, work on people's cars, hold long conversations in the night black that clean gas smell of oil & no-gas, machine coolness, rubber, calendars, metal sky, concrete, the bearing of tools, the wind—true Blue labor Red & White

Identified with Joe Louis: Brown Bomber, you know They'd pass along the mud streets of Laurel Mississippi in loud speaker truck, the white folks, down by where the colored schools was & all of us, out there for Recess or afterschool are beckoned to come get your free picture of Joe Louis, *C'mon & get it kids it's Free, c'mon naow*—What it is is Chesterfield cigarettes in one corner of the beautiful slick photo of Mr. Louis is the blurb, *Joe like to smoke too, see, and he want all yall to follow right long in his footsteps & buy up these here Chesterfields & smoke your little boodies off & youll be able to step up in that ring begloved & punch a sucker out.* It was the glossiness of the photo, I finally figured out years later, that had me going—didn't really matter whose picture was on it altho it was nice to've been Joe's because he was about as great as you could get downsouth, post–World War II as the books say

Identified with Otis (think his name was) worked at grocery store in Ocean Springs, came by, would sit & draw on pieces of brown paper bag, drew in 1940s style of cartoons bordering on

393

"serious" sketching, i.e., in the manner of those sultan cartoons with the harem gals by that black cartoonist E. Simms Campbell you see em all the time in old Esquires & Playboys Well, that's the way Otis could draw & he'd show me in the make-do livingroom seated on do-fold how to do a portrait of a chic perfect anglo-featured woman, say, in profile out of his head built mostly from magazine & picture-show impressions, & he could draw lots of world things, drew me for instance

Later Otis went up to Chicago, sadness, madness, wed, bled, dope, hopeless, catapulted into the twentieth century like the rest of us—rudely, steeped in homemade makeshift chemical bliss of/or flesh, waiting for nothing less than The Real Thing

Sunday Illumination

I've found peace & it's good sleeping late today—head full of eternal ideas, eternal emptiness; Phil Elwood jazz on KPFA, my wife sunny in tattered red skirt & sea blue T-shirt on back yard grass getting her Spanish lesson

"How would I say: Friday I went to a party & heard some good gospel music?"—& I try to explain the preterite & the imperfect perfectly WHEW! but keep interrupting her with poems & to watch a young bee zero in on flaming fuchsia branches, wondering if flower & insect survive ex-lives

Then we go hiking in the Berkeley hills first time all year since Europe, marriage, satori in the slums—New houses have sprung up, split-level clutter; a half finished trap is going up on the spot top of Dwight Way where we'd sit on a pile of lumber for panoramic vista of Berkeley Oakland Alcatraz in the Bay & dazzling San Francisco in the sun—What was it like here before the invasions?

So by now I got to pee & head aches from heat & climb & hot-dogs we bought & ate walking for breakfast, foul fare—no place to sit—Some affluent dogs in heat trail us round a bend—the old motorcycle trail looks dangerously uninteresting, guys go up there scrambling & fall—My shirt's sticking to my sweat & the friends we thought we'd drop in on, what've we to say to them after all?

Descending Arden Steps I make water on a bush, she covering for me—humorous taboo—then comes our pause on the stone bench where we almost ruled out wedlock that torturous fall twilight of long ago Campanile carillon woe

Time to count our blessings as in my heart all pain ceases & for the longest moment all day I see my sad funny self on earth & the gentle terror of her female soul, beautiful, but we're alive NOW accumulating karma, no time to hide in places—no place to hide in time.

Visiting Day

for Conyus

This being a minimum security facility, it feels more like being on a reservation than in a touchable cage

Books are allowed, smiles, eats (you could slip a .38 inside a baked chicken or a file inside a loaf of sourdough french easily enough, but there's really not much to shoot or saw thru)

You sign up, take a seat at one of the open-air picnic tables, & yawn from hours of driving into the beautiful chilled morning

All the black inmates trudging by or hanging out of barracks windows give you the power salute as you consider yourself again strapped down in their skins

You walk, you talk, you toy around with words, you steal guarded looks down into one another

A little food, fruit juice, a lot of gossip, & the sun on the trees under blue sky surrounding us is magnified into one big silly-looking halo

"I'm not into meat all that much anymore, man, & there's a whole lotsa books I wanna talk about &—here, these're some things I wrote last month—thinking about that last letter I wrote you where I said my head was getting peaceful—what's the bloods on the block woofing about these days?"

He looks healthier than he did in the old macrobiotic city yogi wild bustling days when you'd both get zonked on sounds in the middle of the afternoon & reminisce for midnights about stuff that probably never happened

This is what's known as a conservation camp where you cut & prune trees, dig up the earth, seed the ground, weather watch, sweat a lot, do a little basketball, sun on the run, sneak peeks at crotch shots in magazines smuggled in from outside

You think of his woman, you think of his son, you think of them holed up alone in the city, waiting & waiting for him to come home

You think of all the professionals involved: pipe smokers with advanced degrees from state colleges—penologists, criminologists, sociologists who minored in deviate psychology; in clean, classy ghettos where they never take walks, their children snort coke on an allowance

Three tables away from where you sit consoling one another, a slim young man up on a burglary rap is splitting his attention between a 2-year-old daughter & a 22-year-old wife who's shown up thoughtfully in tight-fitted jeans ripped generously enough to allow him to see what she hasn't bothered wearing

Well, it isnt San Quentin, it isnt Attica, & it's no one's official prisoner of war camp, yet you cant help thinking there's a battle going on somewhere out there in the bloodstreams of men

You say good-bye, you shake hands good-bye, you stare good-bye; you wave what you havent said, you grin what you cannot say, you walk away & turn again to wave what neither of you has to say

You gun your engine good-bye & roar off down the California road back out into your own special prison

Weeks later you hear about the steel file some white inmate's driven into the heart of another white inmate found by your friend by some bushes in the rain—dead—because he was your friend's good friend, because he was a nigger lover, a nigger lover

The news chills the tips of your fingers & you sweat

Could it have been the father of the sweet little girl, husband of the gal whose ass was showing?

Could it have been the marijuana dealer who read the *Bhagavad Gita* & meditated nightly?

Could it have been the small-boned cat thief who spoke Spanish with an Italian lilt like an Argentinian?

Could it have been the crinkly eyed loser who made you laugh
& laugh when he talked about his life inside & outside the joint like
a stand-up comic?

You think about the first person you ever screamed at

You think about the first thing you ever stole, or lied about, or
killed

Sarajevo Moonlight

Looking over my shoulder at you this morning, I'm listening to the
tender baritone voice of Radovan Karadzic in the little Church of
St. Michael the Apostle. Radovan is telling us what a sweet, lovable
place this family church of his is, and how the light of history has
shone on it twice. He narrates how St. Michael's was burned to
the ground and how, with the Sultan's permission, it was rebuilt.
The catch was that it couldn't exceed its previous breadth or height.
The heights of nights I measure by your presence are incalculable,
a gift of light so precious that the only way to weigh it would be to
shine on the scales of the fishes in the sea. The deepening blueness
of your eyes in this Islamicized town of such cold weather breathes
a frosty ring around my icy view of you.

Walking along Saraci Street, past the bridge & the great
Yugoslav notion of divided space sliced up in slivers or
crescents or in the polyglot continuum of mountain overseen
by sea or the churning of the unseen side of all space, where
God abides & does the whole show in spare time; the play,
the acting, directing, scenery, costumes, big-Serbo-Croatian-
moon-shining-over-the-whole-stage-showcase-of-everything-
that-was-or-is-or-will-be-including-War-&-Peace-&-Trouble-
at-the-OK-Corral—all said as one word in a single sigh.

GARY YOUNG

When I was five, I knew God had made the world and everything in it. I knew God loved me, and I knew the dead were in heaven with God always. I had a sweater. I draped it on a fence, and when I turned to pick it up a minute later, it was gone. That was the first time I had lost anything I really loved. I walked in circles, too frightened to cry, searching for it until dark. I knew my sweater was not in heaven, but if it could disappear, just vanish without reason, then I could disappear, and God might lose me, no matter how good I was, no matter how much I was loved. The buttons on my sweater were translucent, a shimmering, pale opalescence. It was yellow.

This tumor is smaller than the last one, he said. I'm going to cut it out, and then do my best to stitch you back together. He leaned forward, and pulled a blade across my leg. Smoke rose from the open wound as he cauterized the tiny veins, and while he worked, he spoke to me. Every body is a machine, he said. When they break, I fix them. But there's an art to it, he said. We have to coax some kind of magic or luck out of the body. Some patients die, he said, and others find a way to beat the odds. That's what I expect of you. Do you know what I'm saying, he asked? I nodded while my breath kept pace with the morphine drip. Good, he said, and he put his knee on the table for a better purchase. I watched my leg jump and fall as he jerked on the sutures. That should hold, he said, but you're going to feel it for a while.

I couldn't find the mushrooms under the begonias in the garden, then I remembered I had seen them growing there in a dream. The flowering thistle, dewdrops clinging to the spider's web—it wasn't all a dream. That's coffee I smell, not wood smoke; and here's the glass vial where my wife has saved all our children's teeth.

I discovered a journal in the children's ward, and read, I'm a mother, my little boy has cancer. Further on, a girl has written, this is my nineteenth operation. She says, sometimes it's easier to write than to talk, and I'm so afraid. She's left me a page in the book. My son is sleeping in the room next door. This afternoon, I held my whole weight to his body while a doctor drove needles deep into his leg. My son screamed, Daddy, they're hurting me, don't let them hurt me, make them stop. I want to write, how brave you are, but I need a little courage of my own, so I write, forgive me, I know I let them hurt you, please don't worry. If I have to, I can do it again.

He wheeled a corpse into the narrow furnace, and said, there's something I want to show you. He lit the gas, and the head rose from the table, the arms flew open and the body sat there for a moment in the fire. The flesh peeled away from the bones, and the bones snapped and burned with a fierce blue flame. When the oven had cooled and the door was opened, the ashes and bits of bone threw off a pale, opalescent light. That light, he said, is what I wanted you to see.

Acrobats vanished behind a veil of thick, blue smoke. Jugglers tossed hatchets and knives, but it was hot, my son was restless, and we wandered out to the deserted midway. My son ran between the empty amusements while a loudspeaker blared, come see the world's smallest horse. I could hear the animal whinny from its stall while the disembodied voice called, come on over, come on in, this is something that you'll never see again. My son pushed his way through a padlocked gate and was too excited to answer when I called him back, or perhaps he couldn't hear me over the tape's continuous loop crying, he's alive, he's alive, he's alive.

Last night I dreamed about a bobcat, and this morning I found one sleeping beneath the persimmon tree. I was almost close enough to touch him when he woke, fixed me with his eyes and disappeared into a thicket. The air was damp with last night's rain. The matted leaves cushioned my steps, and persimmons blazed in the branches of the tree like a hundred suns. I don't know if the cat appeared because I dreamed of him, or if I dreamed of him because he was so near.

⟶

Near midnight, walking uphill by starlight, the ground still wet, the air brisk and moist after the storm, I was startled by a pocket of warm air. A breath from the mountain, the redwoods, the stream? I turned to look. No, the moon.

⟶

In western Massachusetts, a man wandered into the woods to live alone. He tried hunting, but the only animals that stood their ground, the only animals he could catch were skunks. The man was sprayed, or course, but he caught them, ate them, and dressed in a cloak of rancid pelts. When he was found, the scent was on his breath, his skin, and when I heard his story, I thought, comrade.

BIOGRAPHIES

Tony Barnstone is a professor of English at Whittier College, and has published his poetry, fiction, essays and translations in dozens of major American journals. His books of poems include *Sad Jazz: Sonnets* (Sheep Meadow Press, 2005) and *Impure: Poems by Tony Barnstone* (University Press of Florida, 1998) in addition to the chapbook *Naked Magic*. His other books include *The Anchor Book of Chinese Poetry; Out of the Howling Storm: The New Chinese Poetry; Laughing Lost in the Mountains: Poems of Wang Wei; The Art of Writing: Teachings of the Chinese Masters;* and the textbooks *Literatures of Asia, Africa and Latin America, Literatures of Asia,* and *Literatures of the Middle East.* His forthcoming book is *Chinese Erotic Poetry* (Everyman Books). He has received fellowships from the National Endowment for the Arts and the California Arts Council and is the recipient of the Pushcart Prize in Poetry, among other national awards.

Polly Bee: Former newspaper reporter, feature writer, columnist, editor. poet and freelance writer. Author of novel, *The Silent Voice of Bosie Bosell— The Lesbian Who Played It Straight.* Hangs hat in Ojai, California. Shares bed with Jack Russell.

Robert Bly is one of our most important and senior poets. As publisher, poet, translator, and essayist, he is responsible for many of the changes and expansions in American poetry over the past four decades. With regard to the prose poem, he has been the most important figure in its writing, definition, and promotion since the early 1970s. He has published more than forty collections of poetry, edited many others, and published translations of poetry and prose from such languages as Swedish, Norwegian, German, Spanish, Persian and Urdu. Among his many awards for poetry is the National Book Award. *Eating The Honey of Words, New and Selected Poems* was published in 1999 by HarperCollins.

Laurel Ann Bogen was born at California Hospital in downtown Los Angeles in 1950. She has lived the majority of her life within the palm tree- and neon-lined borders of the city, where she teaches poetry for the Writers' Program at UCLA Extension, and is a member of the critically acclaimed poetry performance ensemble Nearly Fatal Women. Her most recent collection of poems is *Washing a Language,* published by Red Hen Books.

Nadya Brown is a visual artist and writer who lives in Lompoc, California. Her paintings have been in many group and individual shows, and she has published poems in literary journals. She teaches at Allan Hancock College in Santa Maria, California.

Christopher Buckley's fifteenth book of poetry, *Modern History: Prose Poems 1987–2007*, will be published by Tupelo Press in 2008. *Rolling the Bones* will appear from Eastern Washington University Press later in 2008. With Gary Young, Buckley is the editor of *The Geography of Home: California's Poetry of Place* (Heyday Books, 1999), and has recently edited the poetry anthology *Homage To Vallejo* (Greenhouse Review Press, 2006) and, with Alexander Long, *A Condition of the Spirit: The Life and Work of Larry Levis* (Eastern Washington University Press, 2004). He is a Guggenheim Fellow in Poetry for 2007–2008. He teaches in the creative writing program at the University of California Riverside.

Elena Karina Byrne is a visual artist, teacher, editor, Poetry Consultant and Moderator for The Los Angeles Times Festival of Books, and former twelve-year Regional Director of the Poetry Society of America. Her most recent publications include *The Yale Review, Paris Review, American Poetry Review, Poetry, Volt, Denver Quarterly, Colorado Review, Ploughshares, Verse, TriQuarterly*, and *Best American Poetry 2005*. Books include *The Flammable Bird* (Zoo Press/Tupelo), now available through Tupelo Press and Consortium; *MASQUE* is forthcoming from Tupelo Press.

Maxine Chernoff is a professor and chair of the creative writing program at San Francisco State University. With Paul Hoover, she edits the long-running literary journal *New American Writing*. She is the author of six books of fiction and eight books of poetry, most recently *Among the Names* (Apogee Press, 2005). With Paul Hoover, she has translated *The Selected Poems of Friedrich Hölderlin*, which will be published by Omnidawn Press in 2007. She has read her poetry in Liège, Belgium; Cambridge, England; Sydney, Australia; Berlin, Germany; São Paolo, Brazil; Glasgow, Scotland; Yunnan Province, China; and St. Petersburg, Russia.

Marilyn Chin's books of poems include *Dwarf Bamboo, The Phoenix gone, The Terrace Empty* and *Rhapsody in Plain Yellow*. She was born in Hong Kong and raised in Portland, Oregon. She has won numerous awards for her poetry, including the Radcliffe Institute Fellowship at Harvard, the Rockefeller Foundation Fellowship at Bellagio, Italy, a Lannan Fellowship, two NEA grants, the Stegner Fellowship, the PEN/Josephine Miles Award, four Pushcart Prizes and a Fulbright Fellowship to Taiwan. She teaches in the MFA program at San Diego State University. These prose poems are from a collection called *Revenge of the Mooncake Vixen*, soon to be published by Norton.

Killarney Clary was born and raised in Pasadena, California and lives in Los Angeles. Her most recent collection of poems, *Potential Stranger*, was published by the University of Chicago Press. She is the recipient of a Lannan Foundation Fellowship.

Wanda Coleman has appeared in Norton's *Postmodern Anthology of American Poetry, The Outlaw Bible of American Poetry,* Paul Beatty's **Hokum** and Camille Paglia's *Break, Blow, Burn.* Her books include *Mercurochrome* (poems), nominated for the 2001 National Book Awards, *The Riot Inside Me: More Trials & Tremor* (Black Sparrow Books/David R. Godine), *Wanda Coleman's Greatest Hits 1966–2003* (Pudding House) and *Ostinato Vamps* (Pitt Poetry Series). Her latest book is *Wanda Coleman: Poems Seismic in Scene.*

Scott Creley lives and writes in Claremont, California with the patient support of his girlfriend, Carly. California is the heart and soul of his writing.

Brad Crenshaw is a graduate of the MFA program at the University of California Irvine, where he studied with particular intensity with James McMichael and Charles Wright. He is currently teaching at the University of Massacusetts in Amherst, and is practicing neuropsychology in his private practice when he isn't fighting fires around his home in Fallbrook, Calfiornia—a seasonal occupation. He is the author of *Limits of Resurrection* (Greenhouse Review Press).

Dominican-American **Alba Cruz-Hacker** teaches creative writing and is also the Director of Special Projects for the General Consulate of the Dominican Republic in California and the US Western Region. Her poetic and scholarly works have appeared in *The Caribbean Writer, Canadian Woman Studies, Miller's Pond, DMQ Review, Spillway Review,* and in the Hispanic volume of the *American Encyclopedia of Ethnic Literature,* among others.

Marsha de la O's first book of poetry, *Black Hope,* won the New Issues Press Poetry Prize and a Small Press Editor's Choice Award. She is the winner of the dA Poetry Award and the Ventura Poetry Festival Contest. She has published in journals such as *Barrow Street, Passages North, Solo,* and *Third Coast.* She was raised in the Los Angeles area and now lives in Ventura, California, where she is co-editor for the literary journal *Askew.*

Ana Delgadillo's poetry can be found in *SENTENCE, Border Senses, Freshwater Review, Homage to César Vallejo,* and in the Firewheel Editions anthology *An Introduction to the Prose Poem* and its companion anthology *100 Contemporary Prose Poems,* published by Shanghai Educational Press. Her chapbooks include *Things Surrounding Me* and *Wild Blooms and a Gentle Wind.*

Juan Delgado is the author of *El Campo* (Capra Press), *Green Web* (University of Georgia Press) and most recently *A Rush of Hands* (University of Arizona Press). He is currently a professor of English at California State University, San Bernardino.

David Dominguez's first book of poems, *Work Done Right*, was published by the University of Arizona Press. *Marcoli Sausage* was published as part of the Chicano Chapbook Series. His work is featured in the anthologies *The Wind Shifts: New Latino Poetry* and *How Much Earth: the Fresno Poets*. He teaches composition, Chicano/Latino literature, and poetry writing at Reedley College.

Terry Ehret is a fourth-generation Californian. She has published three collections of poetry: *Suspensions, Lost Body,* and *Translations from the Human Language.* Literary awards include the National Poetry Series, California Book Award, and the Pablo Neruda Poetry Prize. From 2004 until 2006 she served as Poet Laureate of Sonoma County, where she teaches writing and lives with her husband and daughters. *Lucky Break,* a new collection of lyric and prose poems, is scheduled for publication in 2008.

John Olivares Espinoza was raised in the chaparral of Indio, California, where he and his brothers worked as gardeners with their father. Author of *The Date Fruit Elegies* (2008) and two chapbooks: *Aluminum Times* (2002) and *Gardeners of Eden* (2000), he has been awarded a 2001 writing grant from the Elizabeth George Foundation, the 2001 El Andar Prize for Literary Excellence in Poetry and a 2002 Paul and Daisy Soros Fellowship for New Americans. His recent work appears in *Homage to César Vallejo* (2006) and *The Wind Shifts: New Latino Poetry* (2007). Espinoza teaches writing and literature at The National Hispanic University in San José, California.

Peter Everwine's most recent collection of poems is *From the Meadow: Selected and New Poems* (University of Pittsburgh). Previous collections include *Collecting the Animals* (Atheneum), which was a Lamont Selection and a nominee for the National Book Award, and *Keeping the Night* (Atheneum). He has received fellowships from the National Endowment for the Arts and the John Simon Guggenheim Foundation.

Ann Fisher-Wirth is the author of two books of poems: *Blue Window* (Archer Books, 2003) and *Five Terraces* (Wind Publications, 2005). She has also published two chapbooks: *The Trinket Poems* (Wind Publications, 2003) and *Walking Wu Wei's Scroll* (online, Drunken Boat, 2005). Her poems have appeared in *The Georgia Review, The Kenyon Review, The Connecticut Review, ISLE, Solo, Feminist Studies, Runes,* and many other journals and anthologies. She teaches at the University of Mississippi.

404

Diane Frank is author of five books of poems, including *Entering the Word Temple* and *The Winter Life of Shooting Stars*. She lives in San Francisco, where she dances, plays cello, teaches writing workshops, and creates her life as an art form. *Blackberries in the Dream House*, her first novel, was nominated for the Pulitzer Prize.

Julie Gamberg and has been living in the San Francisco Bay Area for the past ten years. She has taught poetry writing to homeless five-year-olds, teenagers in Juvenile Hall, and older adults. Julie won the 2005 Blue Lynx Poetry Prize for her debut poetry collection *The Museum of Natural History*.

Richard Garcia's recent books are *The Persistence of Objects* from BOA Editions and *Chickenhead*, a chapbook of prose poems from Foothills Publishing. His poems have recently appeared in *The Georgia Review, The Notre Dame Review, Crazyhorse* and *Ploughshares*.

Amy Gerstler's most recent books of poetry include *Ghost Girl, Medicine*, and *Crown of Weeds*. She does various kinds of journalism, including art criticism, and teaches in the Bennington Writing Seminars Program in Bennington, Vermont and at Art Center College of Design in Pasadena, California.

Janice Gould is of Konkow descent. She grew up in Berkeley, California and attended the University of California Berkeley, where she earned her BA in linguistics and her MA in English. She received her PhD in English from the University of New Mexico. Janice has published two books of poetry, plus a poetry artbook/chapbook, and has also published scholarly work on American Indian poetry. She has been awarded grants for writing from the National Endowment for the Arts and from the Astraea Foundation.

C. G. Hanzlicek was born in Owatonna, Minnesota, in 1942. He is the author of eight books of poetry: *Living in It, Stars* (winner of the 1977 Devins Award for Poetry), *Calling the Dead, A Dozen for Leah, When There Are No Secrets, Mahler: Poems and Etchings, Against Dreaming*, and, most recently, *The Cave: Selected and New Poems*, which appeared in 2001 from University of Pittsburgh Press. He has translated Native American Songs, *A Bird's Companion*, and poems from the Czech, *Mirroring: Selected Poems of Vladimir Holan*, which won the Robert Payne Award from the Columbia University Translation Center in 1985.

James Harms was born and raised in Pasadena, California. He has published five books of poetry, most recently *After West* and *Freeways and*

Aqueducts from Carnegie Mellon University Press. He has received an NEA Fellowship, two Pushcart Prizes, and the PEN/Revson Fellowship, among other distinctions. He lives with his son and daughter in Morgantown, West Virginia, where he teaches in the MFA program at West Virginia University.

Lola Haskins grew up in Mill Valley, California and graduated from Stanford. She has published eight poetry collections, most recently *Desire Lines, New and Selected Poems* (BOA, 2004). Her prose books, both 2007, are *Not Feathers Yet: A Beginner's Guide to the Poetic Life* (Backwaters Press) and *Solutions Beginning with A,* an illustrated collection of original fables about women whose names begin with A (MB Editions).

Robert Hass is the author of five books of poems, most recently *Time and Materials, Poems 1997–2005* (2007). He has co-translated several volumes of poetry by Czesław Miłosz. His book of essays, *Twentieth-Century Pleasures,* received the National Book Critics Circle Award for Criticism. His many honors include a John D. and Catherine T. MacArthur Fellowship. In 1995 he was selected to serve as Poet Laureate of the United States. He teaches at University of California Berkeley.

Eloise Klein Healy is the author of six books of poetry, the most recent being *The Islands Project: Poems For Sappho* (Red Hen Press). Her work has been anthologized in *The World in Us: Lesbian and Gay Poetry of the Next Wave; The Geography of Home: California's Poetry of Place; Another City: Writing from Los Angeles;* and *California Poetry: From the Gold Rush to the Present.* Co-founder of Eco-Arts, she is the originator of the Red Hen Press imprint at Arktoi Books. Healy has lived in Los Angeles since 1954.

Juan Felipe Herrera is a poet, photographer and performance poet. Currently, as Tomás Rivera Endowed Chair in Creative Writing, he teaches at University of California Riverside. His recent work includes *Cinnamon Girl: Letters Found Inside a Cereal Box* (Harper Collins) and *Downtown Boy* (Scholastic Press). He lives in Redlands, California with poet Margarita Robles.

Jane Hirshfield's six collections of poetry include *After* (HarperCollins, 2006) a finalist for England's T. S. Eliot Poetry Prize, and *Given Sugar, Given Salt* (HarperCollins, 2001), a finalist for the National Book Critics Circle Award and winner of the Northern California Poetry Award. She also is the author of a collection of essays, *Nine Gates: Entering The Mind Of Poetry.* Other honors include the Commonwealth Club of California's Poetry Award (twice), the Poetry Center Book Award, and fellowships from the

Guggenheim and Rockefeller foundations, the NEA, and the Academy of American Poets.

Sandra Hoben: I inherited my wanderlust from my great-grandmother, Mary Murphy, who had traveled from Dublin to New England. It must have been close to her hundredth year when she gave me her last bit of advice: *If I had all those stuffed animals,* she told me, *I'd sell them and buy a bus ticket to California.* So I took a Greyhound to San Diego; hitchhiked to San Francisco; lived with artists and musicians in Berkeley; took poetry classes with Edith Jenkins at Grove Street Community College in Oakland; and finally drove to Fresno, in the scorching heat, to study with Philip Levine and Peter Everwine, and unbeknownst to me, to befriend, among others, Roberta Spear. I live now just north of the Golden Gate, with its glorious fog and redwoods, but I left my heart in Fresno.

Garrett Hongo was born in Volcano, Hawai'i and grew up on the North Shore of O'ahu and in Los Angeles. His work includes two books of poetry, three anthologies, *Volcano: A Memoir of Hawaii,* and *Coral Road,* a forthcoming volume of poems. Among his honors are the Guggenheim Fellowship, two NEA grants, and the Lamont Poetry Prize from the Academy of American Poets. He teaches at the University of Oregon, where he is Distinguished Professor of Arts and Sciences.

Alta Ifland was born in Eastern Europe, studied literature and philosophy in France and currently lives in Northern California. She has a collection of prose poems, *Voice of Ice* (Les Figues Press, Los Angeles, 2007).

Mark Jarman is the author of *Body and Soul: Essays on Poetry* from the University of Michigan Press; *To the Green Man,* a collection of poetry, from Sarabande Books; and *Epistles,* a collection of his prose poems, published by Sarabande Books in 2007. He teaches at Vanderbilt University.

Janine Joseph was born in the Philippines, and now lives in both California and New York, where she is completing an MFA in creative writing at New York University. Her work has appeared in *Fugue, Askew,* and *Oberon.*

Richard Katrovas lived and taught karate on Coronado Island through the seventies, and graduated from San Diego State University. His newest book, his eleventh, *The Years of Smashing Bricks,* is an anecdotal memoir about sex, drugs and karate in early-seventies southern California. He taught for twenty years at the University of New Orleans, and now teaches at Western Michigan University. The father of three Czech-American daughters, he is the founding director of the Prague Summer Program.

407

Claudia Keelan is the author of five books of poetry, including *Utopic,* which won the Beatrice Hawley Award from Alice James Books in 2001. She is a professor of English and creative writing at the University of Nevada, Las Vegas, where she also edits *Interim* (www.interimmag.org).

Born in Los Angeles in 1947, **Stephen Kessler** received a BA from Bard College in 1968 and an MA in literature from the University of California Santa Cruz in 1969. He has published seven books and chapbooks of poetry (most recently *Tell It to the Rabbis*) and more than a dozen books of literary translation (most recently *Written in Water: The Prose Poems of Luis Cernuda,* winner of a Lambda Literary Award). *Moving Targets,* essays on poets and poetry, and *Eyeseas,* poems by Raymond Queneau (co-translated with Daniela Hurezanu) are due for publication in 2008. More about his works can be found at stephenkessler.com.

Christine Kitano is a native of Southern California, having lived in and around West Hollywood, Los Angeles, Santa Monica, and Riverside. She works as a copywriter and plays cello with the Inland String Quartet. Her most recent poetry appears in *Snake Nation Review.*

Ron Koertge taught at the city college in Pasadena for thirty-five years. Now he writes and bets on horses. His latest book of poems is *Fever* from Red Hen Press. His latest young adult novel is *Strays* from Candlewick.

Steve Kowit: I moved to the Bay Area during the heyday of the counterculture revolution, did an MA at San Francisco State, and refused to serve in Vietnam. I was in the US Army Reserves. I told them I would never put their fucking uniform back on, and went AWOL. . . . Years later I became an Animal Rights organizer here in San Diego, where I've lived for the past three decades.

Judy Kronenfeld is the author of two books and two chapbooks of poetry, the most recent being *Light Lowering in Diminished Sevenths,* which won the Litchfield Review Prize, and *Ghost Nurseries* (Finishing Line, 2005), as well as a book on Shakespeare, *King Lear and the Naked Truth* (Duke, 1998). She was the co-winner of the first annual poetry contest sponsored by the dA Center for the Arts, Pomona, California. She has taught in the creative writing department at University of California Riverside since 1984.

A finalist for the National Book Critics Circle Award, **Dorianne Laux's** fourth book of poems, *Facts about the Moon* (W. W. Norton), is the recipient of the Stafford/Hall Award for Poetry. She is also author of three collections of poetry from BOA Editions, *Awake* (1990) introduced by Philip Levine, reprinted by Eastern Washington University Press (2007), *What*

We Carry (1994) and *Smoke* (2000). Red Dragonfly Press will release *Superman: The Chapbook,* later this year. In 1994 she moved to Eugene, where she's now a professor of creative writing at the University of Oregon. She lives with her husband, the poet Joseph Millar.

Philip Levine is the author of sixteen books of poems and three collections of prose. For his poetry he has received two National Book Awards and the Pulitzer prize. For many years he taught at California State University Fresno. He and his wife, Franny, divide their time between Brooklyn and their home in Fresno.

Larry Levis is a native of Selma, California, and he attended Fresno State College in the sixties, where he worked with Philip Levine. He received an MA from Syracuse University and a PhD from the University of Iowa. At the time of his death in 1996, he was professor of creative writing at Virginia Commonwealth University. *Wrecking Crew,* his first book, won the United States Award of the International Poetry Forum and was published in the Pitt Poetry Series in 1972. *The Afterlife* won the Lamont Award, and in 1981 *The Dollmaker's Ghost* was a winner of the Open Competition of the National Poetry Series. He received three NEA grants in poetry, a Fulbright Fellowship, and a Guggenheim Fellowship. His last book, *Elegy,* was edited by Philip Levine and published posthumously in the Pitt Poetry series in 1997. *The Selected Levis* (2000) was edited by David St. John.

Gerald Locklin came to California from graduate school in Tucson for his first teaching job at California State College, Los Angeles in September 1964, and moved a year later to Long Beach State, where he has been teaching ever since, and where he will in fall of 2007 presumably complete his final year of teaching. For the past twenty years he has lived in the Los Altos area of Long Beach, north of the university campus. Early books include *The Toad Poems, Poop, Son of Poop,* and *The Case of the Missing Blue Volkswagen.* Among recent titles are *Charles Bukowski: A Sure Bet; Go West, Young Toad; The Life Force Poems; The Firebird Poems; Candy Bars: Selected Stories; The Pocket Book: A Novella and Nineteen Short Fictions,* and *New Orleans, Chicago, and Points Elsewhere.* An annual series of *dos-à-dos* jazz poem chapbooks with Mark Weber is published by Zerx Press.

Perie Longo has published three books of poetry: *Milking The Earth, The Privacy of Wind,* and most recently, *With Nothing Behind but Sky: a journey through grief* (Artamo Press, 2006). In 2007, she was selected as Poet Laureate of Santa Barbara, California. She teaches the poetry workshop for the annual Santa Barbara Writers Conference and her own three-day summer workshop.

Glenna Luschei is the founder and publisher of the poetry journals *Café Solo* and *Solo* (1969–2007). She was named Poet Laureate of San Luis Obispo for the year 2000. Luschei has also published an artist book of her translation of Sor Juana Inés de la Cruz's *Enigmas*, Solo Press, 2006. *Libido Dreams* is scheduled for release in May 2007 by Artamo Press.

Morton Marcus was the 1999 Santa Cruz County Artist of the Year. He has published ten volumes of poetry and one novel, including *The Santa Cruz Mountain Poems, Pages From A Scrapbook of Immigrants,* and most recently *Moments Without Names: New & Selected Prose Poems* and *Shouting Down The Silence: Verse Poems 1988–2001.* In 2007 a new volume of prose poems, *Pursuing The Dream Bone* was published. *In a Dybbuk's Raincoat: The Collected Poems of Bert Meyers,* co-edited with Meyers's son, was published in 2007. In 2008, his literary memoirs, *Striking Through The Masks,* will be published. His poems have appeared in over eighty-eight anthologies, and he has read his work and taught creative writing workshops throughout the nation and Europe. He cohosts *The Poetry Show,* the longest-running and oldest poetry radio program in the country. A film historian and critic, his reviews appear regularly in West Coast newspapers, and for the past seven years has been the cohost of a TV film review show, *Cinema Scene,* which broadcasts in the San Francisco Bay Area. His website is www.mortonmarcus.com.

Stefanie Marlis's most recent book is *cloudlife*, published by Apogee Press in 2005. She has three previous collections of poetry: *Slow Joy,* (University of Wisconsin); *rife* (Sarabande Press); and *fine*—also published by Apogee Press and nominated for a Bay Area Book Reviewers Award. A selection of her poems will appear in a Norton anthology, *American Hybrid.* The recipient of numerous awards, including an NEA Fellowship, the Brittingham Prize, and the Joseph Henry Jackson Award, she has just finished a novel titled *Love (K)not.* She currently lives in Santa Fe, and works as a freelance copywriter.

Francis Ruhlen McConnel has published two books: *Gathering Light* and *One Step Close,* an anthology of West Coast women poets, from Pygmalion Press; and two chapbooks: *A Selection of Haiku* and *white birches, black water,* both from Bucket of Type Printery Press. A new book of poems, *The Direction of Longing,* will be published later this year by Seattle's Bellowing Ark Press. She spent twenty years teaching in the creative writing department at the University of California Riverside.

Derek McKown is a graduate of the MFA creative writing program at Syracuse University, and has been teaching creative writing at the

University of California Riverside for the past ten years. His book of poetry, *Arrows in Hand*, is published by Fountain Mountain Press.

Czesław Miłosz was born in Lithuania and worked with the Polish resistance in World War II. In 1960 he took a position at University of California Berkeley, and he lived in Berkeley most of the rest of his life. One of the greatest poets of the twentieth century, he was a member of the American Academy and Institute of Arts and Letters, and received the Nobel Prize for literature in 1980.

Bill Mohr moved to Los Angeles in 1968, and was the editor and publisher of Momentum Press from 1974 to 1988. He worked for many years as a blueprint machine operator and as a typesetter. He attended the University of California San Diego, and received a PhD in 2004. He is currently an assistant professor in the English department at California State University, Long Beach. His most recent collection of poetry is *Bittersweet Kaleidoscope* (If Publications, 2006).

Fred Moramarco is the founding editor of *Poetry International*, published at San Diego State University, where he has taught American literature and creative writing for many years. His chapbooks, *Last Minute Adjustments, Act Three and Other Poems, Love and Other Dark Matters*, and *One Hundred and Eighty Degrees* are published by Laterthanever Press. His books (co-authored and co-edited) include *Modern American Poetry, Containing Multitudes: Poetry in the US since 1950, Men of Our Time*, and *The Poetry of Men's Lives*.

Melissa Mutrux is a southern California native currently living and working in Upland, California. She writes both lined and prose poems, as well as fiction. Her most recent work appears in *Mosaic Magazine*.

Marisela Norte is an East Los Angeles–based writer. Norte's work has appeared in *Rolling Stone, Interview, Elle, Option, Venice, Los Angeles Weekly, Buzz, Chicana Art, WEST, Ciudad, BOMB* and the upcoming issues of *Propagandist*. She co-authored the play *Black Butterfly*, honored at the Kennedy Center and later nominated for an Ovation award. She is the 2007 recipient of the Ben Reitman award from City Works Press for *Peeping Tom Tom Girl*, which will be published in fall 2008.

Victor Olivares was born in California of Cuban parents. He has worked at a cement manufacturing plant, as a physical rehabilitation therapist, and as a quality control technician at a radio station. He works and writes in Syracuse, New York, where he lives with his wife and two sons.

David Oliveira is a native of the San Joaquin Valley. He attended California State University, Fresno, where he studied poetry with Philip Levine. He was publisher and editor of Mille Grazie Press, and in 2000 was chosen Santa Barbara's Poet Laureate. He has published one chapbook, *In the Presence of Snakes,* and his first book, *A Little Travel Story,* will be published by Harbor Mountain Press in 2008. He currently lives in Phnom Penh, where he is professor of English at Paññasastra University of Cambodia.

Leminh Phan grew up in La Crescenta, California. Her latest work appears in *White Pelican Review.* Glendale, California is where she currently works, writes and lives.

Chad Prevost was born in Fairfax. He lived in Corte Madera during his elementary school years. On his way to school each day he could see San Quentin across the bay. He currently teaches creative writing and rhetoric at Lee University. His *Snapshots of the Perishing World* is available from Word Tech Press's Cherry Grove Imprint (2006). A chapbook, *Chasing the Gods,* is forthcoming from Puddinghouse Press.

Ruben Quesada is a native of Los Angeles. His early work was first collected in 2005 as *Mornings in Cudahy* in a chapbook from El Molino Press. His poems and translations have appeared in *Rattle, Third Coast, Luna, Toledo Review,* and *OCHO.* A forthcoming chapbook of poetry translations of Luis Cernuda entitled *Exiled from the Throne of Night* will be issued by Aureole Press at the University of Toledo, Ohio.

Brady Rhoades's poetry has appeared in *ARC, Antioch Review, Blue Mesa, California Quarterly, Slipstream* and other publications.

Doren Robbins's poetry, prose poetry, autobiographical monologues, and short fiction have appeared in over seventy literary journals. His most recent collection of poems, *Driving Face Down,* won The Blue Lynx Prize (Lynx House/Eastern Washington University Press, 2001). In 2004, Cedar Hill Publications published *Parking Lot Mood Swing: Autobiographical Monologues and Prose Poetry.* Eastern Washington University Press will publish a new book of poems, *My Piece of the Puzzle,* in spring 2008. He currently teaches creative writing and literature at Foothill College, where he is coordinator for The Foothill College Writers' Conference.

Valerie Robles is the Marketing and Events Director at *Riviera Magazine,* a Modern Luxury Media publication in Orange County. Valerie's poems have previously appeared in such literary magazines as *White Pelican Review, Many Mountains Moving* and *Montserrat Review.* She is currently living in Newport Beach.

Dixie Salazar has published three books of poetry: *Hotel Fresno* (Blue Moon Press, 1988), *Reincarnation of the Commonplace* (National Poetry Award winner, Salmon Run Press, 1999), and *Blood Mysteries* (University of Arizona, 2003). *Limbo,* her novel, was published by White Pine Press in 1995. She currently teaches writing and literature at California State University, Fresno, and shows oil paintings and collage work at the Silva/Salazar studios in Fresno, California. She has taught extensively in the California prisons and the Fresno County jail.

Luis Omar Salinas's first book, *Crazy Gypsy* (1970), is now a classic of Chicano poetry. With Lillian Faderman, he co-edited in 1973 *From The Barrio: A Chicano Anthology.* His second book, *Afternoon of the Unreal,* was published in 1980. A sense of melancholy, a romantic longing and wildness balanced by wit and irony, surfaced in his following books— *Prelude To Darkness* (1981) and *Darkness Under The Trees / Walking Behind the Spanish* (Chicano Library Press, University of California Berkeley, 1982). In 1984 he received a rare General Electric Foundation Award to support his writing, and in 1985 he read at the Library of Congress with Sandra Cisneros. *The Sadness of Days, Selected and New Poems* appeared in 1987, and his most recent book is *Elegy for Desire* (University of Arizona Press, 2005). He has been a prominent voice in contemporary poetry for over thirty years. He lives in Sanger, California.

Eliot Schain first came to San Francisco as a child in 1964, and spent his adolescence in Los Angeles. He moved to Berkeley in 1974. His most recent book of poetry, *Westering Angels,* is available from Zeitgeist Press. He has served as program director for the Poetry Society of America, as well as Arts Benicia in Benicia, California. He was poetry editor for *Columbia: A Magazine of Poetry and Prose.* He currently teaches in Martinez, along the Carquinez Strait, the confluence of the Sacramento and San Joaquin Rivers.

Deborah Smith is a freelance writer who grew up in Moreno Valley and in Taipei. She obtained her MFA from University of California, Riverside, and is planning on teaching in China.

Barry Spacks, Poet Laureate of Santa Barbara, California, has published novels, short stories, nine collections of poems, and three CDs of his poetry. He has been teaching literature and writing for years, mainly at MIT and University of California Santa Barbara.

David St. John has been honored with fellowships from the National Endowment for the Arts and the John Simon Guggenheim Memorial

Foundation, both the Rome Fellowship and an Award in Literature from the American Academy and Institute of Arts and Letters, the O. B. Hardison Prize from the Folger Shakespeare Library, and a grant from the Ingram Merrill Foundation. He is the author of nine collections of poetry, most recently *The Face: A Novella in Verse*, as well as a volume of essays, interviews and reviews entitled *Where the Angels Come Toward Us*. He is presently completing a new volume of poems entitled *The Auroras*.

Joseph Stroud is the author of four books of poetry: *In the Sleep of Rivers* (Capra Press, 1974), *Signatures* (BOA Editions, 1982), *Below Cold Mountain* (Copper Canyon Press, 1998), and *Country of Light* (Copper Canyon Press, 2004), as well as three chapbooks/limited editions: *Unzen* (Tangram Press, 2001), *Burning the Years* (Tangram, 2002), *Three Odes of Pablo Neruda* (Tangram, 2005). His work earned a Pushcart Prize in 2000 and has been featured on Garrison Keillor's *Writer's Almanac*. In 2006 he was selected by the Poet Laureate of the United States for a Witter Bynner Fellowship in poetry from the Library of Congress. He divides his time between his home in Santa Cruz on the California coast and a cabin in the Sierra Nevada.

Robert Sward has taught at Cornell University, the Iowa Writers' Work-shop, and University of California Santa Cruz. A Fulbright Scholar and Guggenheim Fellow, he also received a Villa Montalvo Literary Arts Award. His twenty books include *Four Incarnations* (Coffee House Press), *The Collected Poems*, and *God is in the Cracks* (Black Moss Press). Born and raised in Chicago, he later worked for CBC Radio, and as reviewer and feature writer for *The Toronto Star and Globe and Mail*. He returned to the US in 1985 and now lives in Santa Cruz.

Phil Taggart was born and bred in the San Gabriel Valley, and now lives in Ventura. He's co-editor, with Marsha de la O, of the poetry journal *Askew*. He is also producing and compiling poets on video through the *Askew* video/poetry project. His book of poetry, *Opium Wars*, was published by Mille Grazie Press.

Amy Uyematsu is a third-generation Angelino of Japanese ancestry. She has published three poetry collections: *Stone Bow Prayer* (Copper Canyon Press, 2005), *Nights of Fire, Nights of Rain* (Story Line Press, 1998) and *30 Miles from J-Town* (Story Line Press, 1992). *30 Miles from J-Town* received the 1992 Nicholas Roerich Poetry Prize. She was poetry editor for *Greenmakers: Japanese American Gardeners in Southern California* and a co-editor for *Roots: An Asian American Reader* (UCLA Asian American Studies Publications). She has worked as a high-school mathematics teacher for over twenty-five years, and is currently an instructor at Venice High School.

414

Jon Veinberg lives and works in Fresno, California. His books include *An Owl's Landscape, Stickball Till Dawn,* and *Oarless Boats, Vacant Lots.* He is a two-time recipient of National Endowment for the Arts Fellowships.

Diane Wakoski, who was born in southern California and educated at University of California Berkeley, lived and began her poetry career in New York City from 1960 until 1973. Since 1975, she has been Poet In Residence at Michigan State University, where she continues to teach as a University Distinguished Professor. Her poetry has been published in more than twenty collections and many slim volumes; *Emerald Ice* won the William Carlos Williams prize from the Poetry Society of America in 1989; *The Butcher's Apron* (2000) is her most recent book. Currently she is working on a big project, annotated poems as autobiography, of which the first volume *Blue Noir 1956–68* is complete. She is also looking for a publisher for a collection of her new poems, *The Diamond Dog.*

Charles Harper Webb's book *Amplified Dog* won the Saltman Prize for Poetry and was published in 2006 by Red Hen Press. His book of prose poems, *Hot Popsicles,* was published in 2005 by the University of Wisconsin Press. Recipient of grants from the Whiting and Guggenheim Foundations, he directs creative writing at California State University, Long Beach.

Jackson Wheeler was born and raised in Andrews, in the mountains of western North Carolina. He attended graduate school in California, where he has lived since 1975, working with people with disabilities. He is the author of two collections: *Swimming Past Iceland* (Mille Grazie Press, 1993) and *A Near Country: Poems of Loss* (Solo Press, 1999) with Glenna Luschei and David Oliveira. He co-edited *SOLO: A Journal of Poetry for ten years.* Since 1990 he has hosted a reading series at the Carnegie Art Museum.

M. L. Williams is a native of Fresno. He coedited *How Much Earth: The Fresno Poets* with Christopher Buckley and David Oliveira. His work has also appeared in *The Measured Word: On Poetry and Science, Isotope, The Alehouse Review, TheScreamOnline.com, The Best of the Prose Poem, Verse and Universe, The Geography of Home, Rattapallax, Quarterly West* and elsewhere. He is an associate professor of English, teaching creative writing and contemporary literature at Valdosta State University in Georgia.

Haley Winter was born in San Francisco and raised in Oakland. He still lives in Oakland, dividing his time between writing and playing minor-league baseball for a single-A farm team.

Born in Los Angeles, **Donald Wolff** moved to Santa Barbara when he was ten; later he graduated from the University of San Francisco. He now lives in eastern Oregon with his wife and two teenage children. His chapbook, *Some Days,* appeared in 2004, while a book of poems, *Soon Enough,* will be published by Wordcraft in 2007.

Charles Wright, winner of the Pulitzer Prize, the National Book Critics Circle Award, and the National Book Award, teaches at the University of Virginia in Charlottesville. Among his many books of poetry the most recent are *Scar Tissue* and *Littlefoot.*

Al Young is the author of more than twenty books They include *Heaven (Collected Poems, 1956–1990), The Sound of Dreams Remembered (Poems 1990–2000), Coastal Nights and Inland Afternoons (Poems 2001–2006),* and most recently, *Something About the Blues: An Unlikely Collection of Poetry.* His novels are *Snakes, Who Is Angelina?, Sitting Pretty, Ask Me Now,* and *Seduction By Light.* His musical memoirs: *Bodies & Soul, Kinds of Blue, Things Ain't What They Used to Be, Drowning in the Sea of Love* and *Mingus Mingus: Two Memoirs* (with Janet Coleman). He edited the classic *African American Literature: A Brief Introduction and Anthology.* Young is the recipient of NEA, Guggenheim and Fulbright Fellowships, and most recently received the Stephen Henderson Award for Outstanding Achievement in Poetry, Pacifica Radio's KPFA 2006 Peace Award, the 2007 Richard Wright Award for Literary Excellence, and Santa Barbara Book and Author Festival's 2007 Glenna Luschei Distinguished Poet Fellowship. In 2005 he was appointed Poet Laureate of California. When he isn't traveling worldwide or performing his work to music, he lives in Berkeley.

Gary Young is a poet and artist whose honors include grants from the National Endowment for the Humanities, the Vogelstein Foundation, and the California Arts Council. He has received two fellowship grants from the National Endowment for the Arts, a Pushcart Prize, and his book of poems, *The Dream of a Moral Life,* won the James D. Phelan Award. He is the author of several other collections of poetry including *Hands, Days, Braver Deeds* (which won the Peregrine Smith Poetry Prize), and *No Other Life,* winner of the William Carlos Williams Award. With Christopher Buckley he edited *The Geography of Home: California's Poetry of Place.* His most recent book is *Pleasure.* Since 1975 he has designed, illustrated, and printed limited edition books and broadsides at his Greenhouse Review Press. His print work is represented in numerous collections, including the Museum of Modern Art, the Victoria and Albert Museum, The Getty Center for the Arts, and special collection libraries throughout the country. He teaches at the University of California Santa Cruz.

ACKNOWLEDGEMENTS

All poems, prose complements, and essays in this anthology are used by permission of the individual authors to whom the editors are profoundly grateful.

Special thanks to Robert Bly for permission to reprint his essay, "The Prose Poem as an Evolving Form," and to the College of Humanities and Social Sciences at University of California Riverside for an Academic Senate Grant, which partially supported production of this anthology.

Tony Barnstone's prose poems are from *The Golem of Los Angeles*, Red Hen Press, 2008.

Christopher Buckley: "Eternity" first appeared in *Sentence;* "The Sea Again" in *Hotel America;* "Dispatch from Santa Barbara" in *Rivendell;* and "Paris Dispatch" in *5 AM*. These poems are included in *Modern History: Prose Poems 1987–2000*, Tupelo Press, 2008.

Elena Byrne: "Place Fable" first appeared in the literary web magazine, Speechless, and is forthcoming in Byrne's new book This Fable Language, Tupelo Press.

Maxine Chernoff: "Form and Function" first appeared in *Caesura.*

Killarney Clary: "Clouds of birds," "Near four o'clock" and "White sand, tall grass" appeared in *Who Whispered Near Me*, Farrar Straus Giroux, 1989. "She lied" and "Through a panel" appeared in *Poetry Northwest.*

Wanda Coleman: "Union Station" is from *Mercurochrome*, Black Sparrow, 2001. "Crossing Campus" appears courtesy of *88: A Journal of Contemporary American Poetry*, 2005, and "Going to Blazes" appears courtesy BrickBat Revue, 2006.

Ana Delgadillo: "Surrounding My Birth in Veracruz" first appeared in *Sentence.*

Terry Ehret: "Dark Birds" and "World in Need of Braiding" appeared in Translations from the Human Language, Sixteen Rivers Press, 2001. "Sea Change on the Embarcadero" appeared Lucky Break, Sixteen Rivers Press, 2008.

John Olivares Espinoza's poems are from his book, *The Date Fruit Elegies*, forthcoming from Bilingual Review Press. "No Weeds, No Work" first appeared in *The Wind Shifts: New Latino Poetry*, ed. Francisco Aragón. University of Arizona Press, 2007. "Mrs. Flores's Oranges" appeared in *Aluminum Times*, Swan Scythe Press, 2002.

Peter Everwine: "A Short Novel" and "A Story" are found in *From The Meadow: Selected and New Poems,* University of Pittsburgh Press, 2004.

Ann Fisher-Wirth: "Five Terraces," "Kisses" and "Reading Dinner" were first published in *Five Terraces,* Wind Publications, 2005.

Richard Garcia: "Ponce de Leon and the Ten Milkshakes" appeared in *The Persistence of Objects,* BOA Editions, 2006. "A Hero in the War" appeared in *The Flying Garcias,* University of Pittsburgh Press, 1993.

C. G. Hanzlicek: "Prague, Late November, 1989" is from *Against Dreaming,* University of Missouri Press, 1994.

James Harms: " 'Goodtime Jesus' and Other Sort-of Prose Poems" first appeared in *West Branch.* "Gridlock" appeared in *Quarters,* Carnegie Mellon University Press, 2001. "Union Station Los Angeles . . ." appeared in *Freeways and Aqueducts,* Carnegie Mellon University Press, 2004.

Lola Haskins: "In Tide Pools" first appeared in *The Hudson Review.*

Robert Hass: from "The Beginning of September," from *Praise,* copyright © by Robert Hass 1979, reprinted by permission of HarperCollins Publishers. "A Story About the Body," "Conversion," and "The Harbor at Seattle" from *Human Wishes,* © Robert Hass 1989, reprinted by permission of HarperCollins Publishers.

Eloise Klein Healy: "Asking About You," and "In the interests of examining the connection" are from *Passing,* Red Hen Press, 2002. "Oh, Dr. Surgeon" first appeared in *So Luminous the Wildflowers: An Anthology of California Poets,* Tebot Bach, 2003.

Jane Hirshfield: *"Tears: An Assay"* and *" 'Ah!': An Assay"* first appeared in *The Georgia Review.* "Ryoanji: An Assay" appeared in *The Atlanta Review.* "Between the Material World and the World of Feeling" appeared in *The American Poetry Review.* *"Of": An Assay* appeared in The American Scholar. "Sentence" appeared in *The Kenyon Review.*

Sandra Hoben: "Parallel Lines" first appeared in *St. John's Review.* "Gopher" first appeared in *The Marin Review.*

Garrett Hongo: "Cruising in the Greater Vehicle/A Jam Session" and "Body & Fender/Body & Soul" are sections of "Cruising 99" from *Yellow Light,* Wesleyan University Press. Those poems and "Bugle Boys" are used by permission of the author.

Alta Ifland: All poems are from *Voice of Ice,* Les Figues Press, 2007.

Mark Jarman: "In the Clouds," "For the Birds," "To the Trees" and "Through the Waves" are from *Epistles,* Sarabande Books, 2007. "A Fall Evening in Berkeley, 1970" was published in *New Letters.*

Janine Joseph: "The Undocumented Immigrant Poem #79" was published in *Oberon.*

Claudia Keelan: "Everybody's Autobiography" first appeared in *American Poetry Review.*

Stephen Kessler: "Autumn Rhythm" and "Final Exam" appeared in *Tell It to the Rabbis,* Creative Arts, 2001. "Long Story Short" first appeared in the *Santa Cruz Express.*

Dorianne Laux: "The Line" was previously published in *Smoke,* BOA Editions, 2000.

Philip Levine: "Old World" and "Not Worth the Wait" first appeared in *Five Points.* "News of the World," was first published in *Threepenny Review.* "Fixing the Foot," appeared in *Ohio Review.*

Larry Levis: the section from "Linnets" appeared in *The Selected Levis,* University of Pittsburgh Press, 2000. "A Brief History of California," "Schoolhouse," "The Plains," and "In a Country" by permission of the estate of Larry Levis, Sheila Brady, Executor.

Gerald Locklin: Acknowledgment is made to the *Wormwood Review* and Water Row Books—*Go West, Young Toad* and *Charles Bukowski: A Sure Bet*—for previous publications of these poems.

Morton Marcus: "Incident from the Day of the Dead," "I Find the Letter," "Into the New Millennium" and "The Letter" appeared in *Moments Without Names: New and Selected Prose Poems,* 2002, White Pine Press. "A Little Night Music" appeared in *Pursuing the Dream Bone,* Quale Press, 2007. "The Fu: China and the Origins of the Prose Poem" first appeared in *The Prose Poem: An International Journal.* "Riding the New-Backed Beast" appeared in *Striking Through the Masks: a Literary Memoir,* Capitola Book Company, 2008.

Stefanie Marlis: "rife" appeared in *rife,* Sarabande Books. "shape" and "creek" appeared in *fine,* Apogee Press. "wooded or windswept" and "being neither" appeared in *cloudlife,* Apogee Press.

Frances Ruhlen McConnel: "On Highway 15 to Las Vegas" first appeared in *The Direction of Longing,* Bellowing Ark Press, 2007.

Derek McKown's poems are from his new book, *Arrows In Hand,* Fountain Mountain Press, 2008.

Czesław Miłosz: "Kazia" and "To Find My Home in One Sentence" from *New and Collected Poems: 1931–2001,* © 1988, 1991, 1995, 2001 by Czeslaw Milosz Royalties, Inc. Reprinted by permission of HarperCollins Publishers. Alexandria," "Autumn," "Pity," "A Polish Poet," "Watering Can" and "Where Does It Come From?" from *Road Side Dog* by Czeslaw Milosz, © 1998 by Czeslaw Milosz. Reprinted by permission of Farrar, Straus and Giroux, LLC.

Bill Mohr: "Milk" and "Why the Heart Never Develops Cancer" are from *Bittersweet Kaleidoscope,* if Publications, 2006. "Milk" first appeared in *Momentum,* "Why the Heart Never Develops Cancer" first appeared in *Grand Passion: The Poets of Los Angeles and Beyond.* "Alarm" first appeared in *Beyond Baroque NEW,* and was reprinted in *The Streets Inside: Ten Los Angeles Poets* in 1978.

Fred Moramarco: section 2 of "Six Traumatic Scenes from Childhood" first appeared in *In the Palm of Your Hand* by Steve Kowit, Tilbury House, 1995.

Marisela Norte's poems will appear in her book *Peeping Tom Tom Girl,* which won the Ben Reitman award from City Works Press.

Victor Olivares: All poems from his manuscript *Drive-Thru Experience.*

David Oliveira: "Citation" was first published in *Askew.* "Laurence Olivier's Hamlet" was first published in *In a Fine Frenzy: Poets Respond to Shakespeare.* "Why is there anything?" is from *A Little Travel Story,* Harbor Mountain Press, 2008.

Ruben Quesada's poems are from his manuscript, *Nowhere To Be Found.*

Doren Robbins: "Just My Luck" first appeared in Patterson Literary Review.

Luis Omar Salinas: "Saturday" is from *Crazy Gypsy,* 1969. "A Little Narrative," "Autobiography: The Condensed Version," "Love of the Sea" and "Sometimes" are from *Elegy for Desire,* 2005. Used by permission of the author.

Eliot Schain: "Berkeley Without Mantras" was first published in *American Poetry Review,* "In San Francisco" was published in *Sculpture Gardens Review.*

Joseph Stroud: "During the Rains," "Elsewhere" and "Over the Edge" appeared in *Country of Light,* Copper Canyon Press. "Sky Diving" appeared in *Below Cold Mountain,* Copper Canyon Press. "Taste and See" will appear in *New and Selected,* forthcoming from Copper Canyon Press.

Robert Sward: "Dr. Sward's Cure for Melancholia" appeared in *Ambit 190.*

Jon Veinberg: All of these poems are found in Jon Veinberg's new manuscript, *The Speed Limit of Clouds*.

Diane Wakoski: "Describe the Sky on a Postcard" is from *Waiting for the King of Spain*, 1976. Section V. of "Handbook of Marriage & Wealth" from *Smudging*, 1972, both from Black Sparrow Press. "The Fable Of The Lion & The Scorpion" is from a limited edition chapbook by Pentagram Press, 1975. "Crème Brûlée" is from *The Butcher's Apron: New & Selected Poems*, Black Sparrow Press. 2000.

Charles Harper Webb: "Martians Land in LA," © 2005 by The Board of Regents of the University of Wisconsin System, used by permission of the author and University of Wisconsin Press.

Jackson Wheeler: "Ars Poetica" first appeared in *Askew*.

Donald Wolff: Donald Wolff's poems are from *Soon Enough*, Wordcraft, 2007.

Charles Wright's prose poems are from *Country Music: Selected Early Poems*, Wesleyan University Press, 1982.

Al Young: "Coastal Nights and Inland Afternoons" appeared in *Heaven: Collected Poems 1956–1990*, 2006. "The Problem of Identity" appeared in *Heaven: Collected Poems 1956–1990*, 1975 and 2006. "Sunday Illumination" and "Visiting Day" appeared in *Heaven: Collected Poems 1956–1990*, 1976 and 2006. "Sarajevo Moonlight" appeared in *Heaven: Collected Poems 1956–1990*, 1996 and 2006.

Gary Young: "When I was five," "I discovered a journal" and "He wheeled a corpse" first appeared in *No Other Life*, Heyday Books, 2005. "Acrobats vanished" and "I couldn't find the mushrooms" first appeared in *Pleasure*, Heyday Books, 2006. "This tumor is smaller" first appeared in *Quick Fiction*. "Last night I dreamed about a bobcat" first appeared in *Askew*.